W9-ANX-860

POPE JOHN AND THE
ECUMENICAL COUNCIL

Carlo Falconi

POPE JOHN AND THE ECUMENICAL COUNCIL

A Diary of the Second Vatican Council, September - December 1962

Translated from the Italian by Muriel Grindrod

THE WORLD PUBLISHING COMPANY
CLEVELAND AND NEW YORK

Published by The World Publishing Company
2231 West 110th Street, Cleveland 2, Ohio

Library of Congress Catalog Card Number: 64-12054

FIRST EDITION

GBWP

Printed in Great Britain.

Contents

Foreword 9

Introduction: Pope John XXIII 13

Part I: The Build-up 35

Part II: The Council 143

Part III: The Aftermath 335

Appendices

I The Roman Curia 361

II The Preparatory Organs of the Council 362

III Organs of the Council during the First Session 363

IV The Popes, Vatican I to Vatican II 364

Index 365

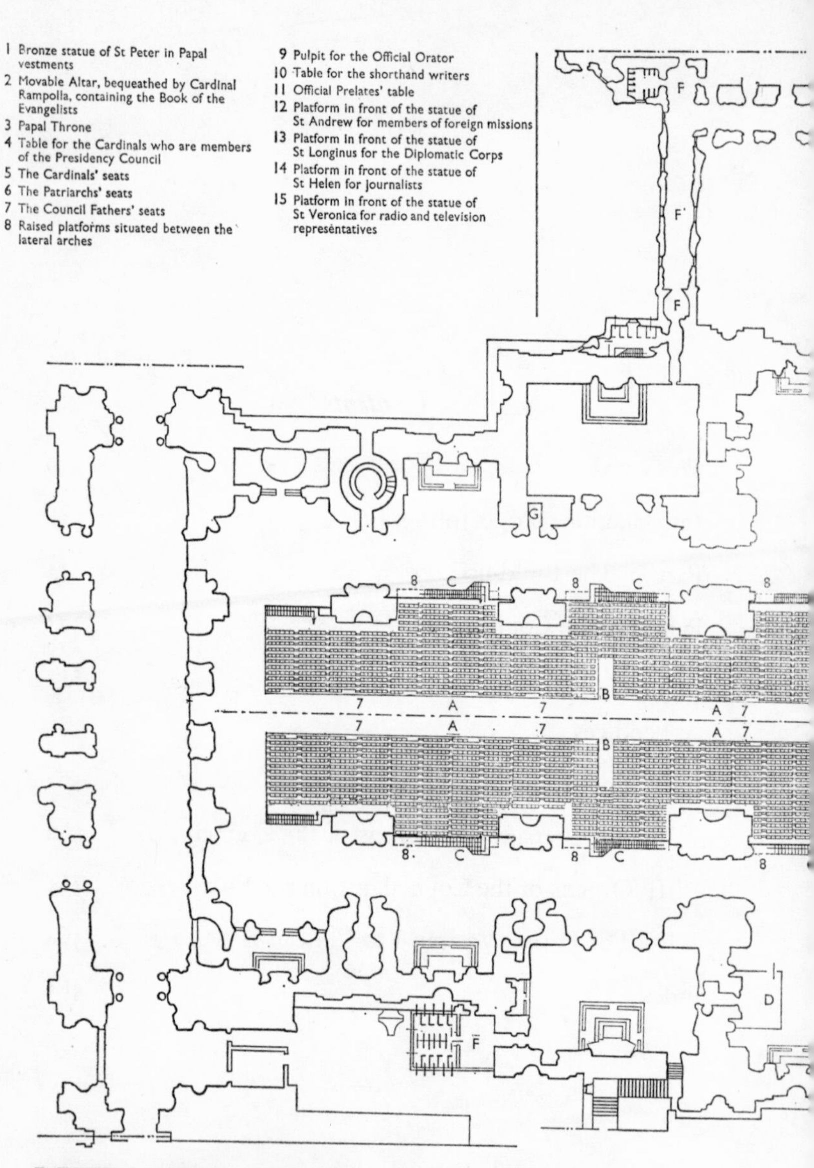
1 Bronze statue of St Peter in Papal vestments
2 Movable Altar, bequeathed by Cardinal Rampolla, containing the Book of the Evangelists
3 Papal Throne
4 Table for the Cardinals who are members of the Presidency Council
5 The Cardinals' seats
6 The Patriarchs' seats
7 The Council Fathers' seats
8 Raised platforms situated between the lateral arches
9 Pulpit for the Official Orator
10 Table for the shorthand writers
11 Official Prelates' table
12 Platform in front of the statue of St Andrew for members of foreign missions
13 Platform in front of the statue of St Longinus for the Diplomatic Corps
14 Platform in front of the statue of St Helen for journalists
15 Platform in front of the statue of St Veronica for radio and television representatives
F
F
F
G
8
C
8
C
8
7
A
7
B
A
7
D

KEY TO THE PLAN OF ST PETER'S DURING THE COUNCIL

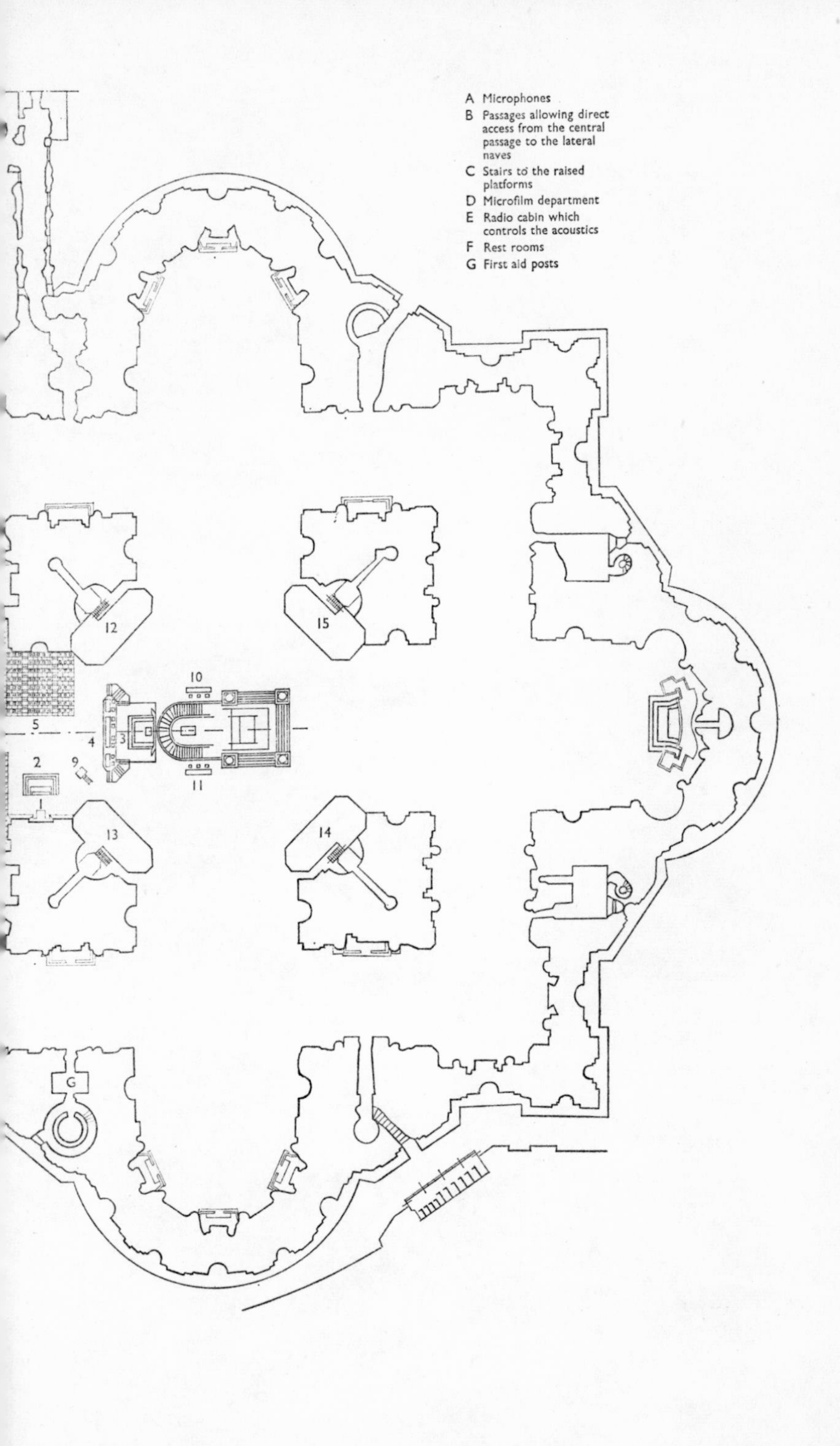

A Microphones
B Passages allowing direct access from the central passage to the lateral naves
C Stairs to the raised platforms
D Microfilm department
E Radio cabin which controls the acoustics
F Rest rooms
G First aid posts
12
15
10
5
4
3
2
9
11
13
14
G

Foreword

ALTHOUGH THIS DIARY did not exist in its present form when the question of publication arose, it is in no sense a diary made up after the event. About two-thirds of it are, in fact, copied directly from my own personal diary for the period from September to December 1962. Naturally, since this is to be a diary of the Council I have omitted all extraneous matter. On the other hand I have expanded or inserted background explanations or comments illustrating facts or episodes the significance of which it would otherwise be difficult for the reader to understand. In such cases the material used has been taken from earlier notebooks or from articles which I wrote for various papers. Any other alterations to the original text are negligible.

The fact that the diary was reconstructed around events that are now in the past might have enabled me to correct mistakes of fact or estimate or, more particularly, to lay claim to prophetic gifts to which I have no pretensions. Instead I have preferred to keep the text just as it was, and to confine myself to correcting factual errors where necessary. In this way the reader can follow the course of events day by day, sharing the same expectations or doubts that I myself felt when writing.

For obvious reasons, several of the people quoted in these pages are indicated only by pseudonyms. In some instances I have even altered the physical or other details describing them. But this does not mean that they are imaginary persons. None of the testimonies specifically attributed to other people in this diary is the outcome of pure imagination or bias.

The reader may wonder how I come to be so familiar with the Vatican world. The answer is simple: up to 1950 I was an official and active member of the Catholic Church, and indeed from 1939 onwards I was a priest in it. I left the Church in 1950 as the result of an intellectual and spiritual crisis which began in 1945 and which had various causes – partly the impact of existentialist philosophy, partly the effect of my more concentrated theological studies, and partly a re-valuation of the Church's recent history. But in doing so I felt no rancour either towards the Church itself or towards its members.

My family came from the region of Bergamo, but I myself was born in Cremona and as a child lived in several of the big towns of Lombardy until my parents eventually settled in Milan. When, at the age of eleven, I entered the seminary there it seemed a perfectly natural and normal consequence of the deeply religious atmosphere in which I had been brought up; and until I left it, and indeed through the war period which, including as it did my service as an army chaplain, left me little time for detached reflection, I lived my life of faith with enthusiasm and devotion. When that faith left me – or, to be more precise, when it became reduced to a mere belief in the unfathomable mystery of God – I could not in honesty remain at my post. But there was no break in my friendly and often close relations with my former friends, which still continue unchanged. (To mention only a few, these have included Monsignor A. Dell'Acqua, Deputy in the Secretariat of State, a friend of my family; Monsignor E. Camagni, Secretary of Briefs; Monsignor Giovanni Colombo, now Archbishop of Milan, and various bishops; Padre S. Tromp, Secretary of the Theological Commission of the Council, my tutor at the Gregorian University.)

Friendship naturally did not prevent me from expressing, in my new guise of a lay student of present-day Catholicism, some pretty drastic opinions on the situation of the Catholic Church. This occurred chiefly, however – for obvious and quite objective reasons – during the period of Pius XII. Under the Pontificate of John XXIII, though my views on the Church itself did not alter, I found myself more in sympathy with the revolutionary changes that Pope Roncalli was gradually introducing. Christian ecumenicalism, the meeting together of all faiths on a common natural basis of religious feeling, the progressive de-temporalization of the Catholic Church, especially at its centre of power – these are ideals which I share and which I eagerly watched coming nearer to fulfilment through the courageous advances instituted under the new Pope.

To return to this diary: it only remains for me to disclaim any intention of making scandalous 'revelations'. Certain leaders of the Church would undoubtedly welcome a reversal to the more relaxed conditions of the last decade of Pius XII's Pontificate and are far from inactive in that direction; but the atmosphere which Pope John XXIII was at pains to generate has compelled them to adopt a tone which, while it may be more insidious, is certainly more cautious and in most ways less provocative than in those days. Moreover the Vatican Council itself is too serious a matter, both for the Catholic Church and for all religions in general as well as for the secular world, to permit of any tampering with its record: the story is absorbing enough in itself without dragging in non-existent intrigues or palace conspiracies.

[illegible] spread through the community [illegible] [illegible] Europe.

[illegible] to be the delicate [illegible] reconciliations [illegible] . Gerald Larger of [illegible] and [illegible] of [illegible] equal [illegible] [illegible] communicate and [illegible] certainly where [illegible] it was [illegible] [illegible] institutions as [illegible] [illegible] that [illegible] Council [illegible] [illegible] that it [illegible] for the [illegible] that [illegible] world [illegible] [illegible] in their [illegible] [illegible] [illegible]

Introduction

POPE JOHN XXIII

THIS DIARY OPENS at the point when John XXIII goes into retreat early in September 1962. Nine months later when it was just about to be sent to the publishers, John XXIII had once more gone into isolation for quiet and meditation, but this time he did so at an unusual time of year when the Holy See's activities do not normally allow of interruption. The reason was that the state of the Pope's health had deteriorated so seriously as to compel him to obey his doctors and stop work. He therefore decided to abandon his normal routine and make the customary annual pause for meditation and communion with God then, at the end of May, rather than later in the year. The Church calendar, moreover, offered a suitable occasion in the nine-day period between Ascension Day and Whitsun.

Ever since his earlier attack in November 1962 those around him had had a presentiment that worse was to come. Their fears were to be realized. This was to be John XXIII's last retreat, from which he never emerged. The retreat should have ended on 1 June, the Saturday before Whit Sunday, but on 31 May a fresh crisis developed which was at once seen to be so serious that hope was abandoned and the Pope received the Last Sacrament and supreme unction. His death agony lasted with lucid intervals for four days until on the evening of 3 June at 7.49 pm he died.

What happened in Rome and throughout the world during those days before and after his death was something quite extraordinary. It seemed as if the whole world was sharing in that last prolonged spiritual retreat of John XXIII's around his sick-bed, which the ailing Pope himself had called his altar, so transforming the drama of his death into an immense act of worship, unforeseen and knowing no rules, solemn like everything that is spontaneous and natural, and farflung to the five continents.

As I write, his body has just been buried in the crypt of the Vatican Basilica, yet this impressive retreat of all humanity still goes on, uniting in the same emotion believers and unbelievers, like a true Pentecost at once tumultuously silent and stimulating whose influence reaches to the furthest points of the globe, returning ever and again to draw fresh impetus from this single centre: the marble tomb of a man who has not yet ceased to offer to his fellow men in all benign humility the gift of a limitless love.

A manifestation of this kind is, on such a scale at least, something absolutely new, without precedent even among those periods in the history of Christianity before and after the schisms of the twelfth century, when the Western Church was, geographically speaking, an appendix of the European continent, threatened from south and east by the grip of Islam. Subsequently, with the Reformation, the North European countries – Britain, Germany, and Scandinavia – broke away from what they regarded as the aberration of Popery. And if it happened that the death of a Pope aroused emotion even in countries and peoples detached from his faith and outside his authority, this invariably arose from some particular tragic circumstance – as with the death in exile of Pius XI, sent by Napoleon as a prisoner to Valence – or from admiration for an individual Pope, as in the case of Leo XIII dying at the climax of a wise and politically successful reign. But no Pope ever stirred to religious feeling people of all faiths, ideologies, and social strata as did John XXIII. For not only did he sincerely proclaim peace and concord but he also offered an example of peace and concord in himself, in his own person and actions, thus becoming in some sense a living symbol of the unity and solidarity of the human family.

Even his advent, on 28 October 1958, upon the throne of Peter had something unusual and disconcerting about it. From the disclosures of his secretary, rather inopportunely published while John XXIII was still alive, it is known that the then Patriarch of Venice spent the night before the election, the last night of the Conclave, weeping in his cell. Yet twenty-four hours later when he appeared on the balcony of St Peter's for the first benediction 'Urbi et Orbi' the world saw only the serenest of smiles upon the face of the newly-elected Pope. Shortly before, in the Sistine Chapel, he had shown an unexpected resolution in placing his Cardinal's *zucchetto* on the head of the secretary of the Conclave, a custom fallen into disuse since the days of Pope Leo XIII. The very next day the stories of his *bons mots* and his unconventional actions began to circulate – the beginning of that series of typical sayings and acts that were soon to become known in Franciscan fashion as the 'Fioretti' of Papa Giovanni.

But if in those first weeks John XXIII appealed instinctively and therefore immediately to the masses, he left the more highly qualified circles, the politicians and intellectuals, in a state of bewilderment. They imagined they had to do with an old parish priest who was, indeed, still witty and lively, but over-ingenuous, and who risked seriously compromising the prestige of an office till lately held by that inimitable aristocrat in intellect and bearing, Pius XII. True, the latter's Pontificate had crumbled and dissolved almost immediately upon his death, but many still believed that in homage to his exceptional personality a distinction should be made between the man and his reign.

To such people the Conclave's choice seemed wellnigh incredible. Indeed they could hardly bring themselves to believe that the newly elected Pope could have had in the past a diplomatic career culminating in eight years of office in Paris. If only some illuminating revelations had been vouchsafed from France . . . but instead all they got from that source was the story of how he recalled the Biblical apple when sitting next to a very décolletée lady at dinner, or the other story of how he recommended a book on good manners to the brother of de Gaulle, the Premier who did not regard the new Nuncio as being on a level with his own 'grandeur'. (Roncalli began his term of office in Paris by supplanting the Russian Ambassador, Bogomolov, in the duty of making the annual speech of good wishes from the diplomatic corps. Bogomolov had prepared his speech thinking it unlikely that the representative of the Holy See would arrive in time. Roncalli took over the speech and read it just as it stood except for introducing, with the agreement of Bogomolov who was delighted at his new colleague's courtesy, a reference to Providence.)

Bit by bit, however, among the sensational occurrences which followed in quick succession the new Pope's election, certain constant factors began to emerge which reduced to their true proportions his seeming whims and improvisations and suggested ever more clearly not only that there was something completely original about this Pontificate but also that the innovations were controlled and conscious. Thus it was soon apparent that the new Pope wished and intended to be the Bishop of his city of Rome, a thing which no Pope since Pius IX had troubled to be, and that he was going to peer into every corner of it so as to become thoroughly at home there. It was equally apparent that if he admitted any predilections they were for the lowliest and most neglected, beginning with the humblest of his court. From the carpenters, gardeners and radio technicians of Vatican City, with whom he made jokes about the 'fat men's party', the only party to which he had ever belonged, and to whom he sent bottles of *Spumante* before raising their wages, he went on to interest himself in the conditions of Rome's inhabitants, especially of its poorest quarters.

But at the same time this interest in simple ordinary people in no wise clashed with his other intention of establishing familiar rather than condescending relations with his colleagues of every rank in the Curia. Pius XII, especially in his last years, was in close relation with no one except his Secretary of State and even neglected to make the customary regular visits to the heads of the Church's departments in Rome. John XXIII re-established these important meetings and among his promotions to the Cardinalate and other vacant posts even included notoriously Pacellian officials, besides going himself in person to visit the various Congregations, a custom neglected for more than a century.

The final awakening, which convinced everyone that the idea of a transitional Pope noted mainly for his charmingly unexpected gestures and witticisms must be abandoned, came on 25 January 1959, only three months after his election. John XXIII then announced simultaneously the three special aims of his Pontificate: to revive the diocesan Synod in Rome, to hold an Ecumenical Council, and to bring up to date the Code of Canon Law. These were obviously not just gestures made for popular appeal; many people had so regarded his visits at Christmas to two hospitals and the Regina Coeli prison in Rome, but these new projects were undertakings of a kind to frighten even a young Pope at the height of his powers. Moreover, the particular long-term objective which had caused John XXIII to summon the Ecumenical Council was obviously concerned with inter-Church union, yet so far nothing had been done in the Catholic Church to prepare for such a move.

The Cardinals were alarmed at this threefold announcement and their attitude stiffened immediately: clearly the Pope's objectives were not to be easily realized. But, as we now know, it was not the concealed but skilful resistance of the Cardinals that won in the long run, but the smiling confidence, covering a patient tenacity, of the 'buon nonno' John XXIII. At the time when the Cardinals of the Curia assembled in the chapter-house of St Paul's heard this unexpected programme for the new Pontificate, they were already aware of another utopian scheme of the Pope's – the attempt to establish new relations with the Governments of the countries under Communist régime. For this reason alone he had in fact caused the Primate of Poland, Cardinal Wyszynski, to prolong his stay in Rome for some two months after the Conclave. But it was thought that the reactions aroused in all parts of the world at the bare idea of any such attempt would soon cause the Pope's optimism to wane.

A year after his coronation, indeed, no one could have foretold the developments that were silently but surely maturing. For example, the Holy Office had despite the Pope's known views actually renewed and amplified, on the occasion of two Italian regional elections, the celebrated anti-Communist decree of 1 July 1949[1]; and the Congregation of Seminaries, impinging on the province of the Congregation of the Council, had put an end once for all to the experiment of the worker-priests, delighted thus to humiliate the Archbishop of Paris who had come to Rome confident that he would be able to settle the question satisfactorily now that he could, as he thought, count on the unconditional support of the 'Pope of the French'.

By the second anniversary of his coronation the state of siege surrounding the ageing Pope seemed even more invincible. John XXIII could of course indulge whenever he wished his whim of making picturesque sorties from the Vatican; but his major long-term plans for innovation seemed destined to be blocked

[1] This decree provided for the excommunication of anyone supporting or furthering the Marxist doctrine.

one after the other, as had already happened with his idea of reviving the Roman Synod. The decisive encounter between the Pope and the adversaries of his policy, however, inevitably came about over the Ecumenical Council. In the latters' view the Council was to be the exclusive concern of the Church of Rome, at no point touching on the treacherous ground of relations with the separated confessions; indeed, as a purely internal affair of the Roman Church it should culminate in a manifestation of immutability and triumphant traditionalism in the face of a world increasingly ready to become involved in a vain search for sensational novelties.

And the first round certainly did not go to John XXIII. All the Preparatory Commissions of the Council fell into the hands of the Curia leaders, while he got his way only in relation to the Secretariat for Christian Union, a modest organization in which the interest of the Protestants and Orthodox was at that stage far from certain. Nevertheless, only a few weeks after the establishment of that Secretariat's headquarters, on 2 December 1960, the Primate of the Anglican Church came to Rome on a courtesy visit to John XXIII. This was a quite exceptional event, seeming as it did to put in parentheses and almost to wipe out four centuries of hostile and difficult relations and marking the beginning of a new era in relationships between the Christian Churches. From then onwards Rome became the scene of a whole series of encounters at high level which attracted the attention of the world: their results were seen at the opening of Vatican II, when fifty observer-delegates were present as representatives of fifteen different Churches or organizations.

But the salvaging of Vatican II's aim regarding inter-Church union did not necessarily mean the salvage of John XXIII's ideals for the Council as a whole. During the preparatory stages the Curia had continued to pick and choose as it pleased, selecting at will from among the Bishops' suggestions for discussion topics sent in response to Cardinal Tardini's circular questionnaire; and the subject material they chose was exclusively ecclesiastical and traditional, strictly linked with the theoretical and practical problems which constitute the regular administrative work of the Roman Congregations. The net result of their labours was 69 drafts of decrees and constitutions[1] representing, indeed, an

[1] See note, p. 45.

encyclopaedic synthesis of all the main theological doctrines – but primarily of the canonical doctrines of the Roman Church. Not one of these drafts, or at most only one or two and that only in part, touched on the major problems of the modern world in its present difficult transitional phase. Moreover this compendium of theological theses lacked any guiding theme or inspiration which might have welded them into an organic and more malleable whole. In addition – and this was even more displeasing to John XXIII – the drafts worked out by some of the Commissions adopted repressive and violent standpoints radically in contrast with his conception of the Church and its relations with the world.

He had expressed his ideas on the subject in a number of speeches. On 20 June 1961, for example, he said: 'The Council is not an assembly for speculation but a living, vibrant organism which surveys and embraces the whole world; a house adorned for a festival and resplendent in its springtime decoration; it is the Church that calls all men to itself.' But he had already said, on 10 February 1959: 'God has called us to clarify men's consciences, not to confuse or compel them . . . He has called us to restore health to our brethren, not to terrorize them.' And on 4 November of that year: 'Christianity is not that combination of compulsions of which men lightly speak who have not the faith; it is peace, joy, love, life constantly renewed, like the secret sap at work in early spring.'

With his natural tact, John XXIII had refrained from interfering personally in any way during the preparatory stages; but at the point, at the Council's opening, when he handed over to the Bishops themselves he hesitated no longer and, while avoiding any intimidating display of his own authority, he set forth his view of the spirit that should govern the Council's labours and the line they should take – a line centring round the need to open a courageous if prudent debate between the Roman Church, the numerous Christian denominations, the other religions, and the whole world. Readers of this diary will be able to judge for themselves how great was John XXIII's achievement in guiding the work of the Council, intervening only when it seemed absolutely necessary. Suffice it to say here that during the sixty days of that first session not only was there no repetition of those regrettable scenes between Pope and Bishops which more than once arose under Pius IX during Vatican I but, instead, relations between the Pope and the episcopate strengthened so much that, as one bishop said: 'Today I have grasped the need for a head of the Church.'

If John XXIII was successful in the ecumenical sphere and in that of the Council, he was no less so in gradually and serenely imposing his new line of policy in international affairs. This line could be described in negative terms as one of non-interference in the internal concerns and situations of the various States, and on the positive side as an effort to guarantee co-existence and international peace both through the abandonment of any equivocal crusading spirit and through practical measures faithfully pursued towards effecting a *modus vivendi*.

John XXIII has himself left behind a striking expression of his ideas on his programme for an anti-temporalist policy in the notes he made during a spiritual retreat at Castel Gandolfo from 10 to 15 August 1961, extracts from which have just been published in the few days since his death. On 13 August he wrote: 'The sublime, sacred, and divine task for the Pope within the Church, and for the Bishops within their individual dioceses, is to preach the Gospel, to lead men towards eternal salvation, and in going about it they must take care that no other terrestrial concern should impede or hinder or disturb this prime duty. Hindrance may arise especially from human opinions in political matters, which produce divisions and contradictions in thought and feeling. But the Gospel rises above all the opinions and parties which disturb and trouble society and all humanity. The Pope reads it and together with the bishops comments on it, neither he nor they as participants in the worldly interests of anyone, but as dwellers in that untroubled and serene city of peace from which descends the divine rule which is well able to direct the terrestrial city and the whole world. That, indeed, is what wise men expect from the Church, and nothing else.

'I can be satisfied in having a good conscience as to my conduct as a new Pope during these three years . . . It is very important to emphasize that all the bishops should do the same: and the Pope's example must be a pattern and encouragement to all. To each and all equally and in general terms one must preach justice, charity, humility, meekness, gentleness, and all the other virtues of the Gospel, defending with a good grace the rights of the Church whenever they are violated or compromised.'

The most delicate point in this last connection undoubtedly arose over those régimes whose ideologies had been condemned by the Church because their basic philosophical tenets were subversive of religious truths. But John XXIII had made no mystery of his own intentions: in private he would go so far as to say, 'We must not talk about crusades: we must honour the cross of Christ but not embark on crusades' and 'Communism is the enemy of the Church, but the Church has no enemies', while in public he declared: 'The Pope wishes truly to go out beyond the walls to meet his children' (20 March 1960) and 'We prefer always to stress what unites men and to go with them as far along the road as possible without prejudicing the demands of justice and the rights of truth' (26 June 1961).

Thus when, as the result of a highly delicate and cautious diplomatic operation, the possibility seemed to be guaranteed of a fruitful and unequivocal *rapprochement* with the Soviet bloc, and then the supreme authorities of that world gave concrete proof of their readiness to bring about a more acceptable co-existence over and above ideological disagreements – by setting free imprisoned bishops and priests, allowing episcopal delegations to take part in the Council, and supporting the participation of observer-delegates from the Moscow Patriarchate – John XXIII even dared to make such co-existence a principle of political conduct. Indeed he went so far as to include in an encyclical the affirmation that no ideology, however erroneous in its origins, can be considered so totally false and harmful in its practical applications that honest and acceptable elements should be excluded by sincere believers; and that precisely those positive elements can constitute a basis for human relationships susceptible of development – apart, naturally, from any connivance in error – in the fundamental higher aspiration of thus guaranteeing a more human co-existence and eliminating the useless dangers of war.

The encyclical *Pacem in terris*, the document in which John XXIII incorporated this principle of combined civil and religious tolerance, undoubtedly constituted the culmination of his Pontificate. But this 'priest of the world' has not bequeathed to history that encyclical alone, for at least two others are of equal importance if of different scope. The one most unjustly neglected, even by Catholics, is the missionary encyclical *Princeps Pastorum*

(28 November 1959), which contains the most explicit professions of anti-colonialism ever pronounced by the Holy See in the past century, and in which, besides expressing for the first time his anxiety for the under-developed countries, John XXIII envisages the bold experiment of making use of the secular Catholic *élite* in missionary countries in order to accelerate their economic, social, cultural, and political advance.

The way was thus open for *Pacem in terris,* for propounding a solution in international political relations within the framework of a super-community of all States. This he succeeded in doing only a few weeks before his death, but in time to be aware of the tremendous response aroused by that great encyclical.

A careful examination of these encyclicals of John XXIII and their steadily broadening scope shows how his most profound originality lies in reaching out to the world horizon of contemporary problems and indicating a solution for those problems not each in isolation but treated as a global and harmonic whole. And a revolutionary part of these schemes was the place which he as Pope gave to the Church. For he refused to regard the world and the Church from an angle of precedence for either: in his consideration of these problems he avoided putting the Church first and the world second, thus implying that the world should adapt itself to the Church; instead, he set out from the premise of the Church's presence in the world to affirm their reciprocal complementary character, insisting especially on the 'service', as he strikingly expressed it, which the Church is pledged to fulfil in relation to the world.

In contrast with the dominating and imperialist (if imperialist *sui generis*) conception of the Church typical of Pius XI and Pius XII, John XXIII's vision of the Church was purely evangelical, indeed an almost homely and peasant conception. As he said on 13 November 1960 (but the recent publication of his diaries proves that he had made use of this particular image for at least thirty years), the Church is 'the old village fountain whose waters gush forth for the generations of today just as they have done without interruption for generations in the past'. And this was not just simple if edifying literary rhetoric, for from this conception of the Church as servant and instrument rather than as ruler and conqueror he did not hesitate to draw sensational conclusions, especially with regard to relations between Church and State and the method of presenting the Church not as a power ('It is time to shake off the imperial dust which has accumulated upon the throne of Peter from Constantine onwards') but as 'the Church of the poor' – not to mention the completely new way of regarding his own person and office.

But the most daring conception, even if studiously in conformity with Catholic orthodoxy, is undoubtedly that of the new relationships indicated by John XXIII between the Catholic Church, the other Christian confessions, and all the other world religions, or the 'ecumenism of the three stages' (unity among Catholics, among Christians, and among all religious spirits). In his view, the unification of the world and its pacification, the most vital problems of contemporary humanity, need for their speedy solution to have the support and immediate stimulus of a single common denominator – reason combined with natural religion. Hence the real revolution, apparent even in their language, introduced by him in the technique of the encyclicals and in the method of conducting the dialogue between the Church and the world.

Before John XXIII, the documents of pontifical instruction were not only drawn up in an inaccessible form of language but were also governed by a wellnigh impenetrable 'scholastic' mentality even when, as happened only rarely, they touched on technical economic or political questions, with the result that they were virtually accessible only to the clergy and a few lay experts. The team chosen by John XXIII to compose *Mater et Magistra* and *Pacem in terris,* however, was expressly asked to adopt ordinary language, a simple and clear vocabulary, a lucid method of setting out problems, and a logical way of solving them as befitted the times. The social encyclical, *Mater et Magistra,* seemed when it appeared to be a model example of successful communication between the Church and the contemporary world; but *Pacem in terris* surpassed it not only on the technical plane of economy and sociology but also on that of philosophy and law.

But the adoption of a new form of language is a relatively secondary factor by comparison with the new type of argument introduced by John XXIII in the official documents of the Church, setting out as it did not from premises of a dogmatic nature but from ordinary reasonable principles. In fact his last two encyclicals which we have just cited expressly and deliberately avoid setting out from doctrinal pre-suppositions to arrive at their conclusions. Their point of departure is one of pure reason and scientific experience, and their point of arrival is the result of natural logic and the parallel affirmation of revelation, presented as converging if not actually identical.

The first encyclical of his Pontificate, *Ad Petri cathedram* (of 29 June 1959), might be reckoned among the initial disappointments provided by Pope John. And indeed, objectively speaking, it would be difficult to deny some reason for dissatisfaction. It was certainly a very modest document. But, seen in retrospect, rarely can an encyclical issued at the beginning of a Pontificate have shown such consistency in relation to the programme to come. Its three key words, truth, unity, and peace, seemed typical of that banality which so often attacks and humiliates the sublime: there is nothing more obvious and predictable, more verbose and meaninglessly magniloquent, than certain commonplaces of ecclesiastical language in general and pontifical language in particular. John XXIII, moreover, lacked the philosophical and theological gifts to construct on so vague a basis of abstract if noble terms a profound and convincing dissertation. Conscious of his own limitations, he could easily have had recourse to trusted collaborators. Instead, and this is highly symptomatic, he preferred to draw up his first encyclical himself, exactly as he used to do as Patriarch of Venice when writing a pastoral letter. The importance of that trio of words was in fact to be revealed not so much in the objective and theoretical development of a philosophical thesis but rather in the subjective meaning, the personal significance, and above all the practical application with which he was preparing to endow them through action.

But if disinclined to speculation John XXIII possessed instead a really remarkable and almost mediumistic intuition about men's fundamental needs and hopes. His own need of contact and converse with individuals and with the masses was a natural result of this for one who lived as he did in a constantly vibrant state of expectation and receptiveness towards the messages emanating from his fellow-men: such contacts served both to confirm his views and to provide a guarantee against misunderstandings and hallucinations. He did not go among men, in fact, from curiosity, desire for distraction, or vanity, but in order to be able to do good even if only by bearing witness to goodness among them. He wanted to help them 'to make their sojourn on earth less sad' (30 May 1962), because he was convinced that 'everything can serve to bring a little sweetness into life' (10 January 1959). And in order to do good to men he strove to approach them 'in humility and gentleness' (14 November 1960).

Especially in the early days of his Pontificate, his anxiety to go outside the Vatican confines if only for a few hours was completely understood and was attributed to a generic horror of being shut in or even to a human and comprehensible need to escape. But it was really just the same need for human relationships that had accompanied him throughout his life. As apostolic delegate in Bulgaria, Greece, and Turkey he was never easily to be found at his headquarters; and yet, except in cases of necessity, he never undertook inquisitorial journeys. He simply went wherever he thought he could learn something new about men and the surroundings in which they lived. Even in Paris not a day passed without some new encounter, 'from the *clochards* of the Seine to the little seminarists of Cannes, from the fishermen of the Sables d'Olonne to the vine-growers of Beaune, from the parochial liturgies of Saint Séverin to the patriotic celebrations of 14 July'. In 1950 he undertook a 38-day journey by car of over 6,000 miles across the whole of North Africa. Even in these last weeks when he was fully aware of the inexorable advance of his disease he would go out every Sunday to discover some new quarter on the outskirts of Rome beyond the gates or as far afield as Monte Sacro.

It is a fact that during his Pontificate the expressions most frequently heard and most typical were precisely those which under his predecessor were the most strongly disapproved: 'dialogo' and 'apertura' – 'dialogue' and 'opening'. But his dialogue with the world was never abstract and theoretical like those classic dialogues with cultural pretensions which, pronounced in a void, never succeed in establishing communication. Jean Guitton has recorded a magnificent simile used by John XXIII one evening at Castel Gandolfo when, pointing to the cupola of the Observatory of the papal villa standing out against the sky, he said: 'You see, these learned astronomers make use of the most complicated apparatus to guide men. I know nothing about such things. Like Abraham, I content myself with advancing through my night step by step by the light of the stars.'

Unlike his predecessors, in fact, he did not look at the world from afar through the customary theological spectacles which make it appear an absurd and distorted abstraction; but he went down and moved about among men seeking to know their needs, anxieties, and aspirations. A journalist at Lourdes seeking to unearth some recollections of the recent Popes lit on the following story about Pius XII, then still merely Cardinal Secretary of State, who went there as pontifical legate in 1934. 'One afternoon' – so he was told – 'he expressed a wish to visit the valley of the Bigorre towards Saint-Savin with its monumental fortress-church. A carriage and pair was brought round and a priest from the sanctuary got in beside the Cardinal to act as guide. But to the priest's surprise, as soon as they left the town Cardinal Pacelli took no notice of the view but began to read his breviary. He prayed for an hour and then said, "It is time to go back, monsignore". The carriage turned round and Cardinal Pacelli closed his eyes and became immersed in meditation. At the end of the journey he got out of the carriage outside his apartment, turned to the priest with an "Excuse me", and went into the house.'

Cardinal Roncalli also went to Lourdes as pontifical legate in March 1958. In addition to the disconcerting preface to his official speech ('Beloved brethren, now I have to read you the official speech. It is rather long, but be patient. I will read and you will listen. Thus we shall do honour to the Madonna who loves us. If at a certain point you grow too weary, make a sign to me and I will stop and you can read the speech tomorrow in the newspaper . . .') they tell the following episode about him there. 'One day he was going by slowly in his car when he saw among the crowd a little boy crying. He looked at him, stopped the car and got out, and going up to the child caressed him. The little boy's mother said, "Your Eminence, he's crying because they keep on pushing him about". The Cardinal at once secured a special place for the mother and child, and turning to his companion remarked: "I hope that little boy will be happy now. I'm so sorry I haven't even a medal to give him".'

For anyone who has not seen Pope Roncalli during one of his encounters with the townsfolk of Rome or the people of Latium, Umbria, and the Marche (during his pilgrimage to Loreto and Assisi) it is difficult to imagine the genius he had for making contact with them. An Italian politician, the Socialist leader Pietro Nenni, comparing him with his predecessor wrote: 'In place of the hieratical figure of the Pope who intimidates there came the pastor who touches the heart.' Others have recalled how, unlike Pius XII who never smiled and above all never made jokes, John XXIII's great charm lay in his smiling good-nature with its constant fund of stories and witticisms. His confessor, Monsignor Alfredo Cavagna, has revealed in an article of 9 June 1963 that while in the first years of his Pontificate John XXIII made efforts to learn English, in his last days he was frequently to be found studying a Russian grammar because, as he said, knowing a little of Slavonic languages 'it would be easy for him to learn at least a few words and so to show how much he loved that great people.'

From these direct contacts with men Pope John derived those sudden perceptions which, in his own priestly parlance, he used to call 'inspirations'. And there is something symptomatic about the insistence, the half-excited trepidation, with which he spoke of them, especially when we remember how much he used to be irritated by devotional sentimentalities or claims of supernatural phenomena such as visions or apparitions. He had only quite recently been elected Pope when someone tried to attribute to him a vision of Pius X, his predecessor alike in the patriarchal chair of Venice and the chair of St Peter in Rome, and he at once issued a brusque denial. A few years later he actually allowed a devoted prelate to express himself very caustically in the *Osservatore Romano* against certain phenomena indulged in under the preceding Pontificate and even by his predecessor himself.

His own eager and unquestioning belief in ultra-rational messages was one of the most characteristic aspects of his simplicity – a simplicity whose remarkable quality only came to be understood by most people in his latter days. There is, indeed, nothing more complex than true simplicity or more various than the different complementary and even contradictory elements which real simplicity must assimilate in order to produce the synthesised whole that is characteristic of it. Simplicity is a combination of candour, spontaneous enthusiasm, and faith; but a candour accompanied by the knowledge of evil and the ability to surmount it, else it will fall into mere ingenuousness, a ready enthusiasm that can also discern and avoid the dangers of credulity, and a faith that is not foolish and that can keep out of the hands of the cunning and the intriguers.

In Pope John, the qualities that germinated and drew their vital sap from his simplicity were above all transparency, optimism, and open-mindedness. In Paris the *mot* going round about the new nuncio some weeks after his arrival was that he was 'the least diplomatic of the diplomatists'. It was the highest praise that could have been given to his diplomacy, which for that very reason was bound to embarrass and disconcert the professionals in astuteness occupied in vying to outdo each other in subtlety and reticence. (But in Paris Roncalli showed himself an unsurpassed diplomatist not only in relation to the representatives of the worldly Powers but also *vis-à-vis* his superiors in Rome who imagined they could act as they pleased simply because they held the central levers of power in their hands. For eight years, in fact, he continued to hold in check the cleverest and most reactionary men in the Curia, who were thoroughly shocked at the enterprise shown by the Church in France in every sphere of activity. So successful was he, indeed, that they only realized much later that their efforts had foundered entirely because of him, the one sure shield of that unquiet episcopate.)

On his deathbed a few days ago John XXIII admitted – with that childlike quality that was so captivating because it was so authentic, a form at once of original innocence and of an innocence conquered and defended – that he had kept faith with the promise he made as a child to his mother, that he would never allow himself to tell a single lie. He was, indeed, as spontaneous as he was sincere, with a spontaneity that sometimes verged on the impulsive. It was impossible to come upon anything faked or artificial in his words and gestures. Indeed his great charm came from that same spontaneous genuineness which delighted and set at their ease all who came near him.

But transparency can be a container without content, just as glass proves to be a jewel only if it contains a sparkle of light. And the richness of Pope John lay above all in his optimism, from which derived his faith in finding a way to all men's hearts. In this particular characteristic his peasant origins undoubtedly came out: in that trusting and almost supernatural acceptance of the natural that is so typical of the countryman and so remote from the bitter, disillusioned, critical and even desolate and despairing acceptance typical of the intellectual; yet not a feeble acceptance but rather the fruit of strength and courage, even though it may appear to be born of insensitivity and fatalism.

John XXIII in fact accepted everything and had faith in everything. It was one of his maxims that 'The habit of thinking ill of everything and everyone is depressing for oneself and for the surroundings in which one lives . . . one must have compassion for the evil of others and turn it as far as possible to good' (14 November 1960). Thus he reached the point of never remotely believing he could have enemies, or at any rate have them for long. Those around him came to despair of the possibility that he might, however courteously and generously, get rid of people who barred his way or beset it with pitfalls. He would reply that they too were necessary and had their uses like so many unavoidable facts of life such as illness, death or natural disasters, and that victories are born of dispute as joy is born of grief or life of death.

Yet his faith in men was not founded on any illusion about their natural goodness, but on the inability to believe in the immutability of any man, especially as to his bad side: he knew that the tendency for good, even if it does not conquer, will survive in spite of acquiescence in evil, in short that the good is the element destined sooner or later to triumph. 'The Lord holds in His all-powerful hands the threads of human history and directs it towards His own ends of goodness and grace.' As for men, they 'are all on the road that leads to Christ' (5 January 1962).

For this reason, to bear misfortune without inveighing against the wrongdoers was one of the most notable lessons he taught, as it was also one of his most invincible weapons in diplomacy and as Pope. All his predecessors, for example, threatened the persecutors of the Church with the penalties provided under Catholic law; but he, instead, regularly ignored them, among other things avoiding the recall of his nuncio from Cuba and refraining from showing any special coldness to Castro's ambassador in Rome, bringing no pressure to bear on the Government of Guinea, and accepting without difficulty a reconciliation with Perón. Perhaps the only stern words that he allowed himself in public as Pope – spoken at a time when he could no longer delay assuming his own responsibilities, at the opening of the Council – were directed against certain men within the Church, because of their intolerant intransigence. Yet afterwards he showed no lessening of his usual warmth and generosity towards any of them. Indeed when on the point of death one of his most cordial last meetings was reserved for the Secretary of the Holy Office, Cardinal Ottaviani, with whom he had in the past had frequent and profound if not openly expressed disagreements. He asked that he should be called to him and saying exultantly: 'See, we are about to enter the tabernacle of the Lord' he embraced him.

About Pope John's goodness so much has been written, especially in these last days, and much of it in so superficial and even insidious a strain (as if to screen off others of his qualities to be kept in the background), that the result has been to make it appear a gift of nature, whereas it was the fruit in him of a long and hardwon struggle. Even from a cursory perusal of his spiritual diaries the reader will perceive that one particular word recurs often: the word 'effort' – 'the effort to find some good side', 'the effort to keep silent without bitterness', and so on.

His goodness, in fact, like every real virtue, was anything but a facile goodness made up of compliance and weakness rather than control and vigilance. Spontaneity and conscious will could be said to vie within him in his effort for ascetic virtue. This is shown in the following extracts from his diaries, which in their acuteness and lucidity of analysis could bear comparison with the writings of some great psychologist and observer of human nature:

'The *simple* man is one who is not ashamed to acknowledge the Gospel even before men who do not esteem it as other than weakness and childishness to do so, and who acknowledges it in all its parts, on all occasions, and in the presence of all; he does not let himself be deceived or prejudiced by his neighbour, nor lose his serenity of mind for any behaviour of others towards him.

'The *prudent* man is one who knows how to keep back a part of the truth which it would be inopportune to proclaim and which when unspoken does not harm or falsify the part of the truth that is told. Such a man is one who knows how to arrive at the good ends he has in view by choosing the most effective means of will and action; who is able in every case to foresee and calculate the difficulties to be met and overcome and to choose the middle way of lesser difficulty and danger; who, having placed before himself a good and noble and great end, never loses sight of it but surmounts all obstacles and brings it to fulfilment; who distinguishes the essential in every matter and does not let himself be hampered by accidents but keeps his forces compact and directs them towards the desired end; who in all this at bottom hopes to achieve a good result through God alone, in Whom he trusts, and who even if he should fail in whole or in part knows that he has done well in relating everything to the will and the greater glory of God.

'Simplicity in no way detracts from prudence or *vice versa*. Simplicity is love, prudence is thought. Love prays, intelligence is watchful . . . Love is like the cooing of a dove: operative intelligence is like the serpent that never falls to the ground or strikes against anything because it seeks out with its head all the rough places along the road.'

These extracts give an implicit answer to a view fairly widely held, at least until the eve of his amazing death-agony, that Pope Roncalli's spiritual gifts were of a rather mediocre kind. In fact the exact opposite is true. The richness of John XXIII's humanity had no other source but in his deep religious life, in that particular brand of spirituality which lies in the total abandonment of self to God. He himself, indeed, has given wonderful expression of this in his preaching as Pope ('We must let ourselves be borne by God . . .'), especially on such occasions as his Wednesday general audiences and his other meetings with the masses. But before preaching it from his exalted office he, who wrote of himself 'I have never made any choice', 'God knows I am there, and that suffices for me', practised it in secret and in bitterness. His desolate and lonely mission as pontifical representative in the Balkans lasted, as we know, for almost twenty years. This is what he wrote in his diary after the first eight years, on 25 November 1933: 'Still at Sofia keeping my birthday *in solitudine et spe* . . . According to the insinuations of so-called human reason I might be tempted to think that this *incolatus* in Bulgaria *nimis prolongatus est*. But that does not depreciate my ministry, my service; it makes it more precious and meritorious before the Lord. My wish is to continue to study always to remain serene and imperturbable at my post. I am not worthy, I say this and I write it, that the Holy Father should concern himself with me. I am here and here I wish to stay, cost what it may. That other I who is always within me though enchained would sometimes try to make me sorry for myself and rattle its fetters and murmur and cry out. Let it stay there in its prison *usque ad mortem et ultra*. I bear my banner ever high and unabased with its motto: "*Oboedientia et Pax*". Nevertheless in this study to achieve more perfect abandonment to the Lord's holy will

I feel the need of His grace. I find in this abandonment so much sweetness and so much strength.'

John XXIII, in short, was no less highly privileged in his natural gifts than in the greatness of his own personal ascetic co-operation. Hence the exceptional character of his Pontificate.

The commentator who declared that the chief characteristic of his reign lay in the fact that he definitely closed a phase in the Church's history of the last few centuries, the phase of 'flight from the world', was stating an incontestable truth. And if this is a miracle, John XXIII did indeed perform it. But a miracle of the same kind could have been possible long before – and this is something to be emphasized and remembered – at any time during the Church's darkest hours from the French Revolution to the Combe[1] laws and the Hitlerian and Communist persecutions. What was always lacking was the magic touch to operate the miracle – a Pope who, like John XXIII, could forget to be a theocratic sovereign called to reign over the whole world and instead remember only to be 'the servant of the servants of God'.

Nor were the times ripe, as is sometimes said, when John XXIII came to the papal throne. Within the Church, lively hopes and desires for reform did indeed exist, but only or at least mainly in a few large European communities; and they were certainly counterbalanced by the reactionary conservatism of many others. In relations with the separated Churches nothing, or hardly anything, in the situation had changed for a century or more. Even in certain Central European countries where the war had brought together Christians of both persuasions, fresh rifts were now beginning to open and new antagonisms to arise. In the sphere of international politics the trend seemed to be moving away from the left and détente and reverting towards the right with the consolidation of de Gaulle's position in France, the Fanfani Government's difficulties in Italy, and so on. The very weight of the inheritance of Pius XII invited his successor to accept the existing situation as being the most obvious and convenient.

But in spite of this, in spite of his advanced age, and in spite of promptings to accept his position as a transitional Pope, John

[1] The laws passed by the French Government under Emile Combe's premiership (1902-5) which led to the rupture of diplomatic relations between France and the Holy See (30 July 1904) and to the triumph of secular legislation in France.

XXIII decided for revolution. With the summoning of the Church to the Ecumenical Council, with the holding out of a hand alike towards the separated brethren and their persecutors, in the name of the Gospel alone, the rights of man, and the fundamental needs of justice and universal aspiration for peace, he wrenched the world out of its lethargy and compelled it to hear once more the echo of a word long forgotten: the word of faith in goodness and brotherly love, in God the Father of all.

Because of this it is no exaggeration to say that the death of John XXIII signified the death not of *a* Pope but of *the* Pope: of the Pope who made every effort to put away from himself all equivocal signs of a disputed and disputable authority, and if in some instances he yielded and adopted them he was nevertheless strong enough for them to be regarded as negligible; of a Pope who presented himself not as the head of a presumptuous and absolutist Church but as the meeting-point of all faiths and all human values, as the symbol of religion reconciled with progress and of justice linked arm-in-arm with peace.

Never since St Francis of Assisi had the world experienced so sensational and compelling an encounter with a follower of Christ. For this reason it gave him immediate recognition and will not cease to remember and love him.

Rome, 10 June 1963

PART I
THE BUILD-UP

Rome, Saturday, 1 September 1962

This evening, precisely at 6.25 pm, the big black Mercedes of John XXIII passed through the Arco delle Campane, bringing the Pope back to the Vatican. He had been away from it for six weeks for the customary summer 'change of air' at his villa at Castel Gandolfo and was now returning earlier than usual because of the approaching Vatican Council. But today's *Osservatore Romano* says that from the 10th to the 17th John XXIII will go into isolation again, and this time into complete isolation, for a week's spiritual retreat.

Usually, the so-called spiritual exercises in the Vatican, in which the Pope also takes part, fall in the first week of December, bringing to a halt all the activities of the Curia and the Court. This year, those who generally attend them have been asked to make their own arrangements, since the Council is to last until 8 December and immediately after there are to be some canonizations.

John XXIII will not, in any case, make his retreat in his own private apartments. He will only go back there to sleep each night. He will spend the days from dawn onwards alone in the Tower of St John in the Vatican walls, near Porta Pertusa. Until last year the Tower was overshadowed by an enormous iron lattice-work supporting the antennae of the Vatican Radio: that has now been removed and transferred to the Radio Centre of Santa Maria in Galeria, 20 kilometres outside the city.[1] In addition the Tower has been restored and raised to a height of seven storeys, including the service floors. Some parts of it have been converted for residential purposes, and it is there, away from the world, that the Pope has decided to spend the next few days.

[1] The Centre belongs to the Holy See and therefore counts as extra-territorial.

Through the walls of Nicholas v, also restored last month, a covered way leads from the Tower of St John to the so-called Torrino, near the Grotto of Lourdes. Thus John xxiii can easily visit the statue of the Madonna of Massabielle of which he is known to be a devotee.

According to one of my main informants, Antimori (son of a noble Roman family and a Chamberlain *di spada e cappa*, thoroughly inside the Vatican world), only two people can have access to the Pope during these days (unless, naturally, some unexpected situation should make it necessary for some important person from the State Secretariat to consult with him): these are his secretary, Monsignor Loris Capovilla, who is constantly at his side, and Monsignor Alfredo Cavagna, a bishop elect, his confessor.[1]

Rome, Sunday, 2 September

Visiting Sonnino this evening we talked about the Council. Sonnino clearly has no belief whatever in the revolutionary possibilities which many people attribute to it. John xxiii, on the other hand, has a strange capacity for making him uneasy, though normally he never seems to be other than at ease: in fact, he doesn't yet venture to define him. He was always irreverently cruel about Pius xii. That 'over-stylized speech' (this is the mildest of the things he says about him, most of them couched in Old Testament terms) made no impression on his theories about religion. Roncalli's peasant background, on the other hand, worries him: 'Those old roots,' he mutters, 'just when they seem rotten they begin putting out unexpected and powerful shoots.' But the Council is another matter. If he plagues me with questions about it, it is because he wants confirmation of its failure which he is constantly prophesying.

Once again this evening, after having provoked me into talking, he listened for a long time and then propounded again Monsignor Roberts' theory of survival which he first mentioned to me a year ago. Monsignor Roberts is a Jesuit whom Sonnino is almost prepreared to tolerate for various reasons, one of which undoubtedly is that he resigned from the important diocese of Bombay, of

[1] A Dominican theologian, Padre Ciappi, Master of the Sacred Palaces, also visited him daily to keep up his practice in speaking Latin with him.

which he was Archbishop, to make way for an Indian. No one knows whether Monsignor Roberts was particularly anxious to resign, still less whether he asked to do so for so noble a reason. But Sonnino has been struck by the fact that Monsignor Valeriano Gracias, the present Cardinal, was an assistant of Roberts in 1950, at the time when Roberts resigned, and for some reason he has got it into his head that the Holy See would never have given him the affront of removing him to make his immediate subordinate his successor.

Monsignor Roberts, however, feels strongly about the problems of peace. According to him, humanity is threatened on the one hand by Communist slavery, on the other by the atomic weapons of the West, in short by 'a new Belsen and a new Hiroshima', and such slogans as these please Sonnino, who is a believer in non-violence.

Added to this, the ex-Archbishop of Bombay is a man of sparkling paradoxes, and Sonnino feels himself rejuvenated when he meets someone who has a real English sense of humour. He heard him speak by chance in New York, if I am not mistaken, at a lecture he gave there some weeks after the Council was first announced, in March 1959. Among other things this very English definition of the supreme Vatican assembly aroused his enthusiasm: 'An Ecumenical Council, for us Catholics, is a football match in which all the players are bishops.' The thing that particularly struck him, though, was Monsignor Roberts' idea of a 'Council of Survival' as an interim prelude to the Ecumenical Council proper which, in his view, would demand years of preparation. Rome, Canterbury, Istanbul, and all the Christian churches of the world realized the immediate urgency of surviving the physical threat of an atomic era. Hence the need for a pre-Council Commission which could confront the traditional doctrines of Christian morality with the researches of experts in science, strategy, medicine, and above all international law.

In Sonnino's view, men like Roberts might succeed in postponing the end of the traditional religions and even in putting off a third world war. But what can these rare Cassandras do in face of the presumptuous bureaucracies of the various religions, and in particular of the absurdly euphoric and optimistic bureaucracy of the Vatican? Monsignor Roberts did not even receive an acknowledgement of his proposal from the Vatican. 'He is as congenial as a person out of Chesterton', Monsignor Z of the Consistorial Congregation said of him one day to Sonnino, 'what a pity he doesn't devote himself to literature . . . and to nothing else.' 'Ah, the Gandhi bug! . . . ,' was the comment of a Nuncio attached to the Secretariat of State, who then went on to expound for the hundredth time his theory of the 'rotation of offices' in order to effect the necessary 'change of mental atmosphere'.

Rome, Monday, 3 September

Looking up a quotation in *L'église a-t-elle encore sa chance?*, published by the Editions du Cerf, my eye fell on some pages by Karl Rahner, the theologian who in the last ten years has dominated Catholic theological thought in Germany. Speaking to his brother priests and interpreting their state of mind, Rahner said: 'We feel like strangers in the world and undertake our apostolic labours with a strong sense of discomfort. We are inhibited men . . . we proclaim the word of God, but in fear and trembling . . . We have only a qualified belief in victory . . . We are no longer certain of saying something really worth while . . . Much of what we say sounds strange to us, the stuff of yesterday or the day before. We are not afraid to confess it . . .: we are often discouraged, sad at heart, almost soured, or at best glad if the world shows signs of still putting up with us.'

Rahner wrote thus in 1953, if not earlier (the book was published in 1953), at the height of Pacelli's reign. But his words, read now on the eve of the Council, seem to have an even more dramatic topicality. He goes on to say that there is no lack of 'good reasons to feel so depressed', 'objective' reasons, of course, 'which justify so secret and destructive a defeatism'. A few quotations will suffice to show what he has in mind.

'Beyond the Iron Curtain, Christianity is persecuted. It is being slowly but definitely stifled by all the means at the disposal of a police state . . . In ten years' time . . . Christians, and especially Catholics, will be sociologically on a par with the Hussites, the Waldensians, and the Dutch Jansenists of the seventeenth-eighteenth century . . . Humanly and morally speaking, these Christians have no future.'

'In Western countries . . . the world of the ready-made is

replacing that of organic development, the world of the factory that of human relationships.' It is a world 'profane and profaned', where God is put 'on official leave' and 'Christians seem to survive only because time is needed to liquidate the worn-out remnants'. Catholics live purely on the defensive: 'Any effort to take the offensive is immediately nipped in the bud. We continue to defend the historical façades, the rights and customs of a public life, a State and a civilization that are Christian, but we defend them with the unacknowledged feeling that we no longer have the right to do so, because the surface is more Christian than the reality it covers . . .' 'The springtimes of the Church that followed the First and Second World Wars have had no summer . . . In this old Europe of ours even the Church seems worn out . . . We have given a legal status to paganism . . . Our theology is weak . . . and what has become of holiness?' And with regard to the world as a whole ('for the first time in history . . . this world is one world') the question is 'whether Christianity can still act as a force in the life of these peoples and in the history of this now unified world'.

Karl Rahner was not called on to give an explicit answer to this question and obviously he did not do so. At this point I recalled the tables given some months ago in the *United Nations Year Book 1961* (New York 1962) and the little work, also published by the UN, on *The Future Growth of World Population* (1958). The 2,500 million of 1950 had already increased to 2,995 million by 1960, thus exceeding the estimates by some 85 million; and by 1980, 1990, and 2000 they were expected to reach respectively 4,220, 5,140, and 6,280 million.

The most worrying problem, however, is not that of survival but of predominance. For within the total population of 6,300 million envisaged for the year 2000, 60 per cent will be Asiatics (principally Indians and Chinese), not including the trans-Ural Russians. The Europeans, excluding the Russians, will be barely a tenth of the world population, and barely a sixth counting in the European and Asiatic Russians. The rate of increase (over 2 per 1000 in Asia and Africa, as against 0·8 in Europe) makes inevitable the removal of humanity's centre of gravity from the West to the East, in other words from the traditionally Christian continent to the regions of Hinduism and Buddhism (and now to considerable extent of Marxist atheism). True, the West, and in particular Catholicism, can count on the immense reserves of Latin America, but who knows what political and ideological developments will have occurred in that continent by AD 2000?

In any case, the terrifying and inexorable problem confronting the Church of Rome lies, quite simply, in the statistics which forecast that Catholics, today representing 20 per cent of the world's population, 5 per cent of whom are practising, will by AD 2000 be reduced to 9 per cent, 1.8 per cent of them practising.

Statistics, unlike Rahner's affirmations, cannot be accused of rhetoric. In any case, taken in combination with a revealing analysis like that of the Innsbruck theologian they constitute perhaps the only convincing reason for Rome's decision to hold the Council, and for the insistence of Catholic theologians and sociologists in recent years on the urgent need to put the whole Church on a missionary footing.

Quantity – sheer weight of numbers – is never in the long term more powerful than quality, but if the quality itself deteriorates the greater is bound to submerge the less. In other words, the Church's struggle – Sonnino and his Monsignor Roberts are right here – is a struggle for survival, and not only of the Roman Church but of all Christian churches. The significance of the ecumenical movement is, in fact, no different from that of the Council: both are born of the same urgent need to seek safety. For this reason they have come together, and the Christian world now strives to present a united front against what has been defined in religio-racial terms as the new barbarian invasion.

Rome, Tuesday, 4 September

Re-reading what I have written, I am more convinced than ever that it was a situation brooking of no delay that impelled John XXIII to summon the Council.

The Council, indeed, is plainly not to be thought of as just another of the many imaginative gestures of the present Pope – on the contrary, its summoning reveals a different side of that serene and radiant old man, the inward-looking side conscious of a secret anxiety caused by the shadow of death advancing not so much towards himself as towards his whole Church. But in that case what is the answer to those who assert that the Council comes either too late or too soon?

To deny outright either of these contentions at the present stage is obviously risky, and I shall not do so. Clearly, if the Council had been held fifty or thirty years ago, it would have been a very different affair, adapted to the particular needs of those times. But a Council held under the Pontificate of Pius X or Pius XI would never have been concerned with the world and with other faiths (including the different Christian confessions): it would have been an exclusively internal affair of the Church, dominated by the strictest anti-modernist reaction under Sarto, characterized by an abstract and anachronistic theocratism, on a line with that of the dictatorships, under Ratti. Moreover provision for the modernisation of the Church was already being made (under Sarto) or had been made (under Ratti) by means of the Code of Canon Law which Benedict XV inherited in an advanced stage from his predecessor and published in 1917.

As for holding a Council in the post-war period of Pacelli's Pontificate – on the supposition, of course, that Pius XII would ever have countenanced a project so repugnant to his authoritarian and totalitarian mentality and that, had he done so, he would have refrained from converting it into just another monologue or spectacle – that period within the world of Catholicism was still seething with too nebulous and violent aspirations and desires; while beyond it the clouds and dust of the Second World War had not yet dispersed sufficiently for the future to be seen in perspective.

On more concrete and specific grounds, a Council would not have had much to offer before the advent of Communist expansion in the world, which took place only after the political and economic isolation of Russia came to an end with the Second World War. The reason is twofold: first, because the Church generally waits until its security is threatened before initiating reforms – and Communism is the only real 'error' and danger on a world scale to confront it so near home in modern times; and secondly because Communism, in conjunction with other post-war phenomena such as the end of colonialism and the nationalistic upsurge of the coloured peoples, has created a crisis in the efficiency of the Church's central administration, among other things raising the need for greater autonomy among the national and continental episcopates (including political autonomy, for instance, in view of the relations of the Churches beyond the Iron Curtain with the Governments of the People's Republics).

Moreover, in addition to the Communist threat, the central organization in Rome has been thrown into confusion during the past fifteen years both by the striking developments in the political and economic relations between the peoples of the various continents and by the increase in scale of Catholic ecclesiastical structures and organizations in the various countries (multiplication of dioceses and parishes, constitution of an independent church hierarchy in territories hitherto run by missions, etc). Official statistical data, given in the *Annuario Pontificio,* for 31 December 1949 and 31 December 1961 provide a striking comparison: metropolitan residential sees have risen from 257 to 345; the archiepiscopal sees from 41 to 46 and the episcopal from 1,062 to 1,370; while titular sees (those assigned to assistant or suffragan bishops) jump from 799 to 1,722, plus a further 972 reserved for nuncios, internuncios, apostolic delegates etc.; lastly, the numbers of prelatures and abbeys without see have gone up from 56 to 98. Only the numbers of Apostolic Vicars (251-139), Apostolic Prefects (132-107), and missions and districts '*sui juris*' (11-6) have fallen, since they are now promoted to the status of ordinary jurisdictions.

The ecclesiastical hierarchies have also been faced since the war with a serious and hitherto unthought of internal problem about the Church's lay arm, Catholic Action. So little, indeed, was any such problem envisaged in the past that under the Pontificate of Pius XI (1922-39) Catholic Action reached its highest point. But after the war the militant lay forces which had defended the Church against the assaults of secularism in the second half of the nineteenth century and the first decades of the twentieth suddenly became conscious of their power and refused to be regarded merely as a subsidiary organization for the Church's manoeuvres *vis-à-vis* the lay world. Instead, they wanted wider recognition with an autonomous status and duties of their own; and until this could be achieved they cut down their organizations' activities as far as possible.

Finally, we must not forget the other ecumenical movement, of Protestant origin later reinforced by the Orthodox Church.

Throughout the Pontificate of Pius XI this movement seemed to be well-intentioned and it merely aroused his disparaging irony. But after the first assembly of the World Council of Churches in Amsterdam in 1948 it quickly became so powerful as to threaten to isolate the Roman Church unless the latter hastened to establish relations with it. Bureaucrats and theologians, priests and jurists, strove to come to terms with such problems in all their real significance; but there is much that they have failed to grasp, and even the most far-sighted of them are a long way from finding the necessary answers.

But if the Vatican Council were to do no more than awaken a collective consciousness of the present problems and affirm its leaders' decision to hasten their solution, even the most sceptical would have to admit that it had fulfilled a historical function. The first condition for making history is to enter into it; and the first way to do that is to open the mind to an understanding of the times. The rest follows of itself.

Rome, Wednesday, 5 September

I find in the *Osservatore Romano* a full résumé of the Pontifical *motu proprio* which accompanies and promulgates the Rules of Procedure for the Second Vatican Council. The document is aridly official, but the optimism of its early passages concerning the preparatory stage concluded last June seems to me inopportune.

It is one thing to listen to the placatory speeches of the Pope, and of a Pope like John XXIII for whom all are ready to make the greatest allowances; but an official document, which can never depart from a strict and detached objectivity, is quite another matter. Moreover only the superficial can confound Pope John's intentional optimism with an optimism based on judgment. He, if I mistake not, uses optimism as would a teacher, as a pastoral method to invite the faithful to see, in things as they are, as far as possible things as they ought to be. When, at a public audience on 8 May 1962, he told the story of how he announced the Council to the College of Cardinals on 25 January 1959, he said (I give his own words):

'Humanly speaking, it might have been expected that after

hearing the Allocution the Cardinals would have crowded around Us to express their approval and good wishes. Instead, there was a devout and impressive silence. The reason was explained only in the following days when the Cardinals attending in audience one by one came to Us and said: "We were so deeply moved, and our happiness was so great at this precious and unlooked for gift extended to the Church by Our Lord through the medium of the new Pope, that we could find no words to show our rejoicing and our limitless obedience. We are ready for the work".'

It is by now no secret that the shock felt by the Cardinals was of a quite different or at any rate much more complex kind. Just think of the state of mind of many of them at that moment. For three months the new Pope had given them a series of unexpected surprises; but up till then these had amounted only to splashes of colour, sometimes disconcerting but for the most part the fruit of felicitous improvisation: 'fioretti', trifles, as someone put it, which would never have been expected from a Pope. Now, however, John XXIII in the most natural way in the world suddenly and simultaneously announced three sensational events: the Synod of the diocese of Rome (which had not been convoked for at least five hundred years); the bringing up to date of the Code of Canon Law (when the drafting of the law for the Eastern Church was still at sixes and sevens); and, last but not least, the Ecumenical Council.

Seeing that such important matters were at stake, the least to be expected by the members of the Sacred College – who, whether or not of Pacellian allegiance, believed that a new leaf had been turned over in the matter of absolutism – was that the new Pope would invite them to express their views on the subject and not confront them with a *fait accompli*. As far as the Council, in particular, was concerned, from the way in which he had spoken there could be no doubt that it was to be largely concerned with union among the churches. Now, such a Council had no justification, either historical or psychological, in the recent evolution of the Christian churches, let alone in that of the Church of Rome; its failure, about which there could be no doubt, would risk dealing a mortal blow to the Church's prestige.

The rigid silence of the Cardinals did not, in fact, arise from a paralysing emotion of a supernatural kind but from well-founded and serious perplexities, quickly translated soon after the Pope's speech into an explicit request to the Secretary of State, Tardini, that publication of the full text of the speech should be held up. A résumé of it had in fact been given in the *Osservatore Romano* following requests for a different version from that provided by the press agencies. But now postponement of publication of the full text was urged, at least until the Cardinals had been able to suggest to the Pope that while there might be good reasons for an internal Council, a Council directed towards union was a very different matter.

It would be easy to compose a complete anthology of the Pope's encomiums concerning the preparatory work for the Council. On 23 January 1962, for example, at the end of the third session of the central Preparatory Commission, he addressed its members in the famous words of St John Chrysostom: 'You have sanctified the very air.' And on 20 June, at the final conclusion of that Commission's labours, referring to the various stages of the preparations for the Council he defined them as 'three years of magnificent, edifying, devoted and ardent activity'. Such praise was clearly disproportionate since, whatever conclusions they may reach, the labours of the 'filter-committee', as the central Preparatory Commission might be described, have in themselves nothing whatever to do with the Council's decisions, which indeed, as the history of the First Vatican Council shows, may well turn out to be quite different.

But was all this praise only a matter of form or propaganda, or did it correspond to objective fact as regards the results achieved?

From the point of view of quantity, the Preparatory Commission's labours certainly amounted to an impressive total: 69 drafts[1] (54 of decrees and 15 of constitutions), contained in 121 booklets amounting altogether to 2,100 printed pages. Running through the titles, one wonders whether any single branch of the disciplines, structures, organizations, and activities of the Church can have been forgotten. Even if all the doctrinal themes have not been delved into, the disciplinary and pastoral material has been, one might almost say, exhausted if not exaggerated. This was in

[1] 'Draft' is used throughout here to translate *schema,* the word actually used in this connection. The decrees are concerned with practical matters, the constitutions with doctrinal matters. (*Translator's Note*)

fact to be anticipated, given the large number of Commissions set up not only parallel with the departments of the Curia but also above them. But was not all this perhaps a work of supererogation which could only end by paralysing the Fathers of the Council?

It is difficult to reply in the negative, although there was relatively little criticism even in the foreign Catholic press about this huge number of drafts. I made a note at the time of a few malicious remarks, such as that of Father X, member of one of the Preparatory Commissions, who suggested that the key to the number of drafts lay in the Curia's own secret vendettas: 'The Fathers will not know what to choose from among so much material; and when they decide on some particular topic, they will always have to take a "curial" text at least as a point of departure.' But perhaps that was just being malicious.

The mountain of drafts was not all. Worse still was the lack of co-ordination between them. As far as one can tell, the work of the ten Commissions and the two Secretariats which drew up the 69 drafts was in fact conducted on independent parallel lines, except for some partial records prepared by sub-committees. It was not unlike a work of excavation carried out in isolation in a dark tunnel. It should have been followed up by a second stage co-ordinating the various different analyses. But such a work of simplification and synthesis could have been carried out only in the light of a few definite guiding principles so as to reduce and adapt the raw material; this was what was lacking.

It should undoubtedly have been the task of the central Preparatory Commission to produce such a synthesis. Instead, it proved to be an organ merely for verification, not for construction: a means of overall control rather than of production. And it seems fairly obvious that even the control was directed towards form rather than substance, towards indicating an absence of organic defects in the pre-fabricated pieces rather than deciding on their co-ordination, functional purpose, or interdependence. The very speed with which this control was carried out appears significant. The total number of sessions devoted by the central Commission to examining the 69 drafts occupied 44 days, including the time taken up by the Pope's opening and closing speeches and various other ceremonies: in other words, on an average two drafts, each of about 30 pages, were discussed each day.

In conclusion, one cannot but ask oneself how the Fathers will manage when confronted with this gigantic puzzle where they are given all the pieces but not a single plan to show them how to use them. Will they, too, exhaust their efforts in a mere hasty checking of the quality of the individual pieces without bothering about the whole? Or will they have the intuition and imagination to create from them an original and modern construction? And even if they do so, will they not have doubts about rejecting useless material or demanding, if need be, something different? All this we shall know in a few weeks. Only then will it be possible to judge the real value of the three-years' work of preparation for the Council.

Rome, Thursday, 6 September

The *Rules of Procedure for the Council* (which I have obtained in the official edition issued by the Poliglotta Vaticana) have been drawn up by the Procedure sub-committee, under the chairmanship of Cardinal Francesco Roberti, an authentic pillar of the Roman Curia.

When John XXIII made him a Cardinal (which was at his first consistory, on 15 December 1958) the then 69-year-old Bishop of Pergola, in the Marche, probably held the record among holders of office in the Holy See. The Roman Curia consists of eleven Sacred Congregations (or departments), three Tribunals, and a similar number of Offices, together with 15 permanent commissions which are often of considerable importance (e.g. the Pontifical Biblical Commission). Monsignor Roberti, as he then was, with the title of Excellency though without episcopal qualification, had at least one seat reserved for him in each of these branches of the Vatican administration.

In the Congregations, he was actually Secretary of the Congregation of the Council (an office equivalent to that of under-secretary in a civil ministry) and was advisor in three others, the Oriental, the Sacraments, and the Seminaries and Universities; in the Tribunals he was referendary prelate of the Apostolic Signature; in the Offices, he was even legal advisor of the Secretary of State (a new office invented by the former pro-Secretary, Montini); and lastly, in the Commissions, he was a member of the presiding council of the pontifical commission for cinema, radio, and TV, member of the commission for ecclesiastical archives in Italy, and advisor of the pontifical commission for the authentic interpretation of the Code of Canon Law. These were naturally only the major offices, for in the Congregation of the Sacraments alone he was Deputy Commissioner for dealing with cases relating to ordinations and member of the commission for the vigilance of ecclesiastical tribunals concerned with matrimonial suits.

It is difficult to imagine how he managed to keep up with so many jobs at the same time. But presumably he did so successfully, for it is unlikely that it was he who asked to be thus inundated with them. And, by long-standing tradition practically amounting to a right, the Secretariat of the Council alone would be enough to ensure him the Cardinal's hat.

Be that as it may, the Procedure sub-commission assigned him four eminent members of the Sacred College as auxiliaries: Cardinal Jaime de Barros Camara, André Jullien, Arcadio Larraona, and Theodore William Heard – four foreigners, only one of them living away from Rome, whose appointment was therefore largely nominal: a Brazilian (the Archbishop of Rio de Janeiro), a Frenchman, a Spaniard, and an Englishman. Despite their different nationalities, however, with the exception of the first-named all of them had belonged to the Curia for many years, Jullien and Heard being Auditors at the Holy Roman Rota for more than thirty years and Larraona first under-secretary and later secretary of the Sacred Congregation of the Religious.

It is therefore not to be wondered at if the 70 articles and more than 130 paragraphs of the Council's Rules of Procedure, concise, concrete, and welded into an organic whole, constitute a little masterpiece, at any rate for a layman like myself. The document is divided into three parts, dealing respectively with persons participating in the Ecumenical Assembly as members of the various branches forming it (9 chapters, 18 articles); rules to be observed during the Council (12 chapters, 25 articles); and the conduct of the work itself (3 chapters, 27 articles).

A glance at the text shows that the Commissions of the Council have been reduced to ten (there were 11 preparatory ones) through the suppression of the one dealing with Ceremonial, while the Secretariat for press, cinema, and TV has been absorbed into the Commission for Lay Apostolate; neither of these changes is important. What is important, however, is that the ex-chairmen of the Preparatory Commissions remain the same despite the different composition of the corresponding Council Commissions, two-thirds of whose members will be nominated by the Council and one-third by the Pope (16 and 8 respectively). The rôle of the Council Commissions is in fact quite different from that of the Preparatory Commissions, indeed in some ways it may prove the exact opposite: for example, if a draft worked out at the preparatory stage is rejected by the Fathers of the Council and the relevant Commission is charged to replace it by a new or amended one. Obviously in such cases the presence of a chairman associated with the earlier draft is not likely to facilitate the task of redrafting.

But the most serious matter is that the confirmation in office of the ex-chairmen reaffirms the pre-eminence of the Curia's influence on the Council's labours: and that, while barely permissible at the preparatory stage (when, clearly, John XXIII gave in about it *pro bono pacis*), is something quite unacceptable during the Council itself. Such men as Ottaviani and Pizzardo, to mention only two, with their well-known conservative principles will inevitably make more difficult the introduction of any new proposal, however sound. But also the Curia Cardinals as a whole, quite apart from any personal tendencies, are bound to stick together in firm opposition or resistance whenever the powers of the Church's central administration are discussed or threatened by suggestions of cautious decentralization; or whenever the question arises of affirming the powers of the episcopate, either within the framework of the already existing episcopal conferences[1] (which, however, lacking legal recognition have little effective influence) or within the general framework of the Church by means of some sort of collective direction.

Clearly, John XXIII has had to put up once again with the presence of these men of the Curia at the head of the Council Commissions, consoling himself at least with the fact that during the Council such Commissions are largely executive, since every proposal of theirs has to be submitted to the approval of the ecumenical assembly of the Fathers. But has he at least retained some counter-advantages? At any rate two, if I am not mistaken. The first lies in the creation, new in the history of the Councils, of a Secretariat for Extraordinary Questions, whose task is 'to examine the particular new questions proposed by the Fathers

[1] An episcopate signifies collectively all bishops, whether of a country (e.g. 'the Italian episcopate') or of the world. An episcopal conference denotes the official organ of a country's episcopate.

and, if necessary, to submit them to the Pope'. The intention is plainly to circumvent by means of this Secretariat possible 'die-hard' opponents within the individual Preparatory Commissions or obstruction by the General Secretariat. Thus no subject can be excluded at Commission level or in any other way without the possibility of appeal. The Secretariat for Extraordinary Questions will act as a tribunal of appeal, studying and evaluating each question from a disinterested standpoint in order to bring it, if need be, before the Pope himself so that he may allow it to be discussed in the Council.

The second advantage, in part accepted as a matter of course but none the less important for that, is the retention of the Secretariat for Christian Union. It will, however, not only continue to watch over relations with the 'separated brethren' (both with those whose presence at the assembly is already assured and with those who are still uncertain or who for various reasons have decided not to come) but will also keep an eye on all the Council's labours in order to ensure that their conclusions are always set forth in such a way as to further ecumenical understanding, avoiding especially anything that might make it more difficult or even compromise it.

The Rules of Procedure are bound to disappoint those who hoped that they would solve *de facto*, almost tacitly, and before the Council could do so *de iure*, one of the chief obstacles to agreement between the Roman Church and the Eastern Churches (not excluding, in this case, the Uniate Churches): namely the question of precedence as between Cardinals and Patriarchs. Paragraph 1 of Article 24, in Part II, lays down that the first to speak or vote, according to the importance of their offices, shall always be the Cardinals (ranged in their turn in the three orders of bishops, priests, and deacons), followed by the patriarchs, primates, archbishops, etc. Even the punctuation used seems to emphasize the difference in kind between the Cardinals and the other Fathers of the Council. Though it must be admitted that it would have been arbitrary of the Rules of Procedure to anticipate a hypothetical decision which only the Council can take, if it thinks fit.

Yesterday's issue of the Vatican daily also made known the nominations to the various organs of the Council.

The ten Cardinals in the *Presiding Council* are all, with the exception of Tisserant and Ruffini, chairmen of national episcopal conferences. But since Tisserant is Bishop of Ostia, and thus of the principal 'suburbicarian' diocese, even he is no exception to the rule; and Ruffini was co-opted to replace Siri, who is chairman of the Italian episcopal conference but who has been transferred, possibly more suitably, to the Secretariat for Extraordinary Questions.

Among the episcopates, and hence the countries behind the members of the Presiding Council, five are European, those of Italy, Spain, France, Holland, and Germany; two American (one US, one Argentine); one Australian; and one from the Middle East. Strangely enough, there are no representatives of Afro-Asian countries, nor are they represented in the Secretariat for Extraordinary Questions. The Church plainly continues to keep jealous guard over precedence by seniority as regards both individuals and nations.

In addition, the Cardinals of the Presiding Council are, except for Alfrink and Gilroy (who are, respectively, 62 and 66), among the oldest members of the Sacred College. Apart from this relatively unimportant characteristic, they seem to have only one other, and that applying to only half of them: competence in the field of liturgical studies. Side by side with the brilliant organizer and politician Spellman, the philosopher Pla y Daniel, and three exponents of pastoral activity, Tappouni, Gilroy, and Caggiano, there are, in fact, five biblical scholars, three of whom – Tisserant (recently received among the immortals in the French Academy), Liénart, and Alfrink – are still actively engaged on their work. It would be interesting to know if this particular qualification of theirs was taken into account in choosing them or if, instead, it is quite fortuitous. Certainly among the observer delegates, particularly from the Protestant world, it helps to increase their personal prestige and, by reflection, that of the assembly. But at barely twenty years' distance from the encyclical *Afflante Spiritu*, might it not be excessive to interpret it as a foretaste of the biblical orientation destined to prevail in the coming Council?

The most marked characteristic among the members of the *Secretariat for Extraordinary Questions*, on the other hand, is the comparative youth of six of them: Siri, Montini, Confalonieri, Doepfner, Suenens, and Meyer. Doepfner, Archbishop of

Munich, is actually under fifty, three are under sixty (Siri 56, Suenens 58, Meyer 59), Montini is 65, and Confalonieri 69. This time it seems that coincidence can certainly be excluded. Here John XXIII must have decided to show no preference towards seniority but instead to aim expressly at entrusting to men nearer to the present generation the weighing-up of the exceptional problems, '*extra ordinem*', which might and certainly will be laid before the Council. For this reason, rather than choosing learned men or experts in some particular field, those selected are in their different degrees and ways – sometimes so different as to seem opposites – all of them men who are sensitive to the voice and needs of their times. If there is anything surprising and without apparent justification, it is the prevalence of the Italians.

One last observation: the chairmanship of this Secretariat, entrusted to the 79-year-old Cardinal Cicognani, seems to me highly significant. In this post, more than in any other, the presence of the Secretary of State – and thus, in a certain sense, of the Pope's deputy – clearly reveals the Pope's wish to act with more immediacy, without the inhibiting intervention of a strong personality.

Spoleto, Friday, 7 September

I came to Spoleto this morning to attend the Conference of historical studies on 'Benedict XV, the Catholics, and the First World War.'

This is the second conference (the first was at Bologna, in December 1960, on 'Aspects of Catholic culture during the Pontificate of Leo XIII') organized by a group of *avant-garde* Italian Catholic periodicals. The first conference, the records of which I read some weeks ago, showed, despite some setbacks, a maturity in evaluation (if not in research) and critical autonomy which rightly impressed the laymen present. Someone, under the shock of this discovery, even spoke of the 'debunking' of Leo XIII's Pontificate; which is not only exaggerated but also inaccurate (one needs only to read Marrou's report, which made the greatest impression at the time, to perceive that after an over-confident start he declined into an ignominious repudiation of his earlier claims). Nevertheless there was some effort, if at times over-polemical in tone, towards a new perspective, enough at least to justify surprise at this ingenuous and almost pathetic manifestation of non-conformity directed with pointless masochism against one of the greatest Pontificates in the whole history of the Papacy – and all, moreover, under the auspices of 'culture'.

This was, in any case, not the ideal terrain on which to prove the courage of the Italian Catholic intellectuals (who, moreover, have been more than equalled in this respect by some of their French colleagues). Everyone knows that even official authority is prepared to allow considerable licence in criticism when directed towards a sufficiently remote period. The extent of any real 'swing' towards greater open-mindedness on the part of Italian Catholic culture, following the French initiative, could be estimated only after a conference dealing with situations and problems more directly connected with the present day. But it would be naïve to expect that the next conference might dare to tackle the Pontificate of Pius x. A revised judgment on the anti-modernist repression is still for various reasons, whether sound or otherwise, taboo. Moreover, the aura surrounding Papa Sarto is still too recent to permit of distinguishing between the man himself (the only Pope to be canonised and worthy to be declared a saint) and the Pope.

So the chosen field was the Pontificate of Benedict xv. But there are different ways of going about such an undertaking, and the one chosen by the organizers of the present conference seems rather strange. It is obvious, as can be seen from the list of papers to be given at it, that some of the speakers will confine themselves to discussing Giacomo Della Chiesa's diplomatic activity in relation to the First World War, while others will deal exclusively with the conduct of Catholics in various countries during the war. The first group will inevitably be reduced to making a gratuitous apologia, since no adequate sources are available either to prove or disprove the Pope's pacifism; while the second will only be able to advance purely subjective and arbitrary moral judgments on the conduct of their co-religionists at that time. The two themes, in fact, will inevitably risk running on parallel lines taking no account of each other.

Perhaps the organizers' secret hope is that speakers, perceiving the restrictions of the debate and its insuperable duality, will converge on the only common ground that could give the discussions some unity and liveliness, even though this would not be a historical ground but merely the premise for historical evaluations. I mean the subject of the Catholic doctrine concerning war and, in particular, the responsibilities of Popes in relation to armed conflicts, not so much as diplomatic mediators but rather as spiritual guides of their own followers divided among the opposing sides.

In the particular case in question Benedict XV certainly took action on the diplomatic plane, though it is not yet possible to form a judgment about the way in which he acted – which, in any case, was probably a good deal more complex and subtle than is generally believed. What is however certain, so certain indeed as to constitute the only firm ground in the conference, is that he abstained from publicly expressing any judgment on the permissibility or otherwise of recourse to arms in 1914; and by his silence he fostered the belief that neither side was in the wrong and that it was therefore permissible, or even a duty, for his followers to fight and kill each other.

History has neglected to make mention (though perhaps some reports at this conference will do so) of the fantastic and deplorable confusion produced by so equivocal a line of conduct. It caused an ideological Babel, some extolling war for wrong or positively sacrilegious reasons while others opposed it even to the extent of practising a masochistic pacifism; but it had even more drastic effects on men's consciences, torn by doubts and inhibited, both individually and collectively, from taking possibly vital resolutions by the Pope's 'neutrality' and the contradictory attitudes adopted by the intermediary hierarchy.

A discussion of this kind can be conducted fruitfully only among theologians, moralists, lawyers and sociologists – historians can at best merely provide the material for comparisons with earlier or later similar situations (Pius XI's conduct in relation to the Spanish civil war, that of Pius XII in 1939, etc.); with the obvious result that the only thing left for the conference is to declare itself incompetent to deal with the subject. But in doing so it would at least testify for sound reasons to the need for a religious rather than a diplomatic line of conduct on the part of the head of the Catholic Church, which would also be of effect as a deterrent against war. At the same time it would bear witness to the urgent need for an organic Catholic doctrine on war, on its permissibility or otherwise, on the right or duty to rebel against a clearly unjustifiable declaration of armed intervention, on conscientious objection, etc. In other words, it would constitute a lively and pertinent introduction to the themes of the Council, a sort of secular pre-Council debate.

Fr. B., who is here as reporter for his paper, tells me that this is just what the organizers of the conference are hoping for but I can't help feeling sceptical about it.

Spoleto, Saturday, 8 September

My prophecy was only too right. The keynote for the pontifical apologia was given by Maurice Vaussard in the introductory speech, followed by Monsignor Leflon, who went even further. The best papers, those of Scoppola and Prandi, were on the conference's subsidiary theme, that of the attitude of Catholic trends in the various individual countries.

I was unable to hear Prandi's contribution, which I am told was very good, but I think neither he nor Scoppola succeeded in overcoming the fundamental ambiguity of a view of history which claims to go beyond Crocean historicism merely because, instead of taking nature as the absolute norm, it makes history depend on and culminate in Divine Providence. These two scholars, who belong to the progressive wing of the Catholic intelligentsia, must be given credit for their scientific integrity and for the fact that, while refraining from useless or provocative polemics, they are not afraid to take up a definite stand. But, like all Catholics who think as they do, they unfortunately fail to convince either the laity or their own leaders – a thankless and unhappy position with which one cannot but sympathize. At Spoleto, however, since the progressives were the promoters of the Conference they were not in any sense *sub judice*. Moreover the few integralists present did not dare to provoke them to battle since, largely for the reasons I mentioned yesterday, the whole thing ended up as a sort of dialogue between the deaf. Perhaps the conservatives avoided measuring themselves against their opponents mainly in order to avoid displaying their internal disagreements under the eyes of the liberal and Communist historians; or perhaps they were simply not sufficiently prepared on the subject of debate.

There was thus good reason for them to keep silent and avoid making unsuitable or absurd interventions. One of them, however, was not wise enough to refrain – Monsignor Alberto Giovinetti, attached to the first branch of the Secretariat of State, compiler of a collection of the public documents of Pius XII on the Churches of Silence and of a volume on the same Pope and the war. Small, stout, and rubicund, with curt manners made the more clumsy by self-confidence, and with face and hands scrubbed until they shone, as the etiquette of his world demands, this Vatican diplomat suddenly began to impart a pedantic lesson on the methods of work of his office, at the same time making statements so naïve as to provoke general laughter and amused comment.

There was also a rather pathetic speech from Count Dalla Torre, who until early in 1960 was for forty years editor of the *Osservatore Romano*. Of all the things he had meant to say he remembered only one, of which he was reminded at the last moment by his ex-deputy Alessandrini[1]: this was that Benedict XV's famous expression, 'the useless slaughter' (used in a Note of his of 1 August 1917 to heads of belligerent States), was indeed the Pope's own, which he defended against all suggestions that it should be omitted. If the conference had been about Pius XI he would have risen to speak with the same proud conviction of his own consistency to defend the Pope's crusading determination. In fact, the consistency of official apologists, of whatever faith, embraces all the inconsistencies of their creed and its representatives.

Alessandrini, on the other hand, very wisely did not speak; he was representing the press, not historical studies (here, at any rate – for in the Vatican editorial office they work as a team and share out all the jobs). But at the conference he behaved with the stern seriousness befitting his august duties. One felt that he did not move alone but carried the atmosphere of an invisible halo with him. Every time I happened to run into him I found myself wondering how many years it must be since he laughed or even smiled and whether he could still do so if he tried. That dark and hirsute face, as of a watchdog of Mother Church, with great pockets under the glassy eyes and with a purplish double or treble chin, seemed to have nothing human about it: it was the swollen yet rigid mask of an anonymous office.

[1] Federico Alessandrini is the present assistant editor of the *Osservatore Romano* together with Cesare Lolli; the editor is Raimondo Manzini.

This evening I watched him accompany the Count to the official black car that he has as a Knight of the Sovereign Military Order of Malta. The ritual was carried out in the almost deserted piazza before the theatre where the conference was being held, at the foot of Rocca's statue on its green pedestal. The driver of the car had just shut the door. Alessandrini, massive and self-contained as usual, wearing his customary dark grey suit, began to move away at a regular pace when he suddenly stiffened with the typical jerk of a soldier who forgets he is in mufti. The driver took some time to start, and he never moved an inch, his arms straight by his sides. When the car seemed about to go, his head and the upper half of his body slowly inclined forwards in a bow. Then, seeing that the car wasn't going yet, he returned to an erect position. This happened two or three times until at last the car moved silently forward. Even then he waited until it had disappeared from the side-street before straightening himself. Perhaps during this manoeuvre the ghost of an official smile flickered over the rigid mask of his countenance: but when he turned back towards the theatre the mask was stern and withdrawn as ever.

Rome, Monday, 10 September

Back in Rome, I have been running through the newspapers, reading among other things the accounts of the first television feature on the Council – '1962, the Council Year' – shown on the 7th, on which the Catholic dailies carry long reports, giving the full text of the main speeches.

I have heard some very favourable comments about this first broadcast, but I have the impression that it concentrated especially on the cliché of the Council as a Council of unity, and this should be avoided at all costs. Apart from the historical introduction, giving a retrospect of the first twenty Ecumenical Councils, and the theological conclusion, given by Monsignor Carlo Colombo, there appeared on the screen Cardinal Bea, chairman of the Secretariat for Christian Union, Athenagoras, the Orthodox Patriarch of Constantinople, Dr Visser 't Hooft, secretary-general of the World Council of Churches in Geneva and himself a Calvinist, and Dr D. H. Asmussen of Heidelberg representing the Lutheran Church.

But the Council is not going to be a round table of representatives of the main Christian Churches or federations. The world aspects of the Second Vatican Council are not concerned with union but with the problems of the Catholic Church at its centre and in relation to the various national and continental communities. Later broadcasts will possibly deal with this side too, but to subordinate it in this way gives a false impression of its real significance. For the majority of television viewers, the thing that counts is what they see rather than what they hear, and for that reason equivocal propaganda of this kind can be harmful to the cause of the Council.

This method of presentation must clearly have been prompted by the desire to react against the apathy of the general public, who may be interested, as Patriarch Athenagoras said, in the formation of 'a single front among the various Churches', but who have shown quite clearly that they are not prepared to take much interest in the internal problems of the Catholic Church. Italians, in particular, are generally sceptical about the internal reforms of their Church. And in any case they are ready to bet that if the Council changes anything it certainly won't be in Italy, where, as they say, priests will always go on wearing cassocks, bishops directing politics, and the Pope moving above all in the gestatorial chair.

Moreover, what happened in Rome over the diocesan Synod – the first of the three great objectives announced by John XXIII on 25 January 1959 – proves them right. And since the Pope himself has more than once stated that the Synod should be regarded as a sort of dress rehearsal for the Council, the Italians, and particularly the Romans, have drawn the logical conclusions. The Pope has also several times expressed his hope that the Second Vatican Council will occupy only a couple of months. How can one escape the deduction that the two to three thousand bishops taking part in it are coming to Rome merely to appear in a solemn spectacle and listen in reverent and admiring silence to the voluminous outpourings generated within the Preparatory Commissions and Secretariats?

The Synod, which took place from 25 to 27 January 1960, produced a by no means negligible code of more than 700 articles (the Code of Canon Law for the Church as a whole, completed under Benedict xv and still in force today, has 2,414 canons). The Fathers present – in this case the officials of the Vicariate, parish priests, representatives of the basilical chapters, superiors of religious orders, rectors of Roman seminaries, 40 assistant parish priests, ten teachers of religion in State schools, ten hospital chaplains, etc. – also numbered some 700. They met in the Hall of Benediction in the Vatican. There were only three sessions, none lasting more than three hours. The first three-quarters of an hour were occupied in celebrating Mass in the Sistine Chapel and in the subsequent procession to the Hall; another half-hour was devoted to an ascetic sermon from the Pope, which however had no direct connection with the Synod's statutes; and the rest of the time was spent in simply reading through the canons – 87 on the first day, 195 on the second, and bits of the rest (186 in all) on the third. Since the reading was from the original text, drawn up in a polished Latin, and since it involved highly condensed and carefully weighed legal formulae, one can imagine that the subject matter was not easily understood, let alone evaluated. In any case, the Fathers present were absolved from any discussion and even from having to indicate their agreement. At the end of the sessions, the singing of the *Te Deum* expressed their implicit and inevitable approval.

True, the drawing up of the canons was effected by an imposing preparatory commission (meeting 41 times for a total of 115 hours) which worked on the drafts prepared by eight subcommissions (meeting 124 times for 400 hours in all). But the Code of Canon Law formally requires (Can.360 para.2) that the Fathers of the Synod shall receive in advance the drafts of the decrees, and, in particular (Can.361), that all the subjects dealt with ('praepositae questiones omnes') shall be freely debated by the members of the assembly ('liberae adstantium disceptationi . . . subiiciantur'): and this did not happen at the Roman Synod, despite the appointments made with due pomp at the first session (25 January) to the sterilely honorific office of Examiners and Judges of the Synod.

A Diocesan Synod is, of course, in no sense a legislative assembly, since those present have a purely consultative vote, the only legislator being the bishop; but even so, why take from it, and in Rome of all places, even the bare appearance of democracy provided by free debate? Rome had not had a synod since 1461, although the Council of Trent prescribed that they should be held regularly in every diocese. It could and should have been the ideal occasion to demonstrate the new spirit animating the Pontificate of John XXIII. But the opportunity was lost.

'There were no wigs to abolish', was the sadly ironical comment of an archivist who some time ago dug out the plan of the Roman Provincial Council held under Benedict XIII in St John Lateran from 25 April to 29 May 1725 (more than a month!), alluding to the law to that effect which was passed then. But the bitter side of the joke is that, just as two-and-a-half centuries ago wigs continued undeterred to cover the clergy's heads, so too Rome after the diocesan Synod of 1960 has remained exactly the same. A few parochial routines have become more complicated, but for the rest the city's religious life has experienced neither shocks nor stimulus.

Rome, Tuesday, 11 September

Pellicani was more excited than usual this evening. He is always tired, always tense, but despite this always full of passionate enthusiasm and ready to inspire it in others.

This evening, the subject of his discourse was, once again, John XXIII. The Pope had just been speaking on TV an hour before Pellicani came to my house, but neither he nor I had managed to hear the broadcast. However in the afternoon Pellicani had had one of his usual meetings with the *bussolante*, or papal attendant (behind this picturesque term he conceals a pretty influential person in the papal court whose identity he will not, for obvious reasons, reveal). The latter told him that since yesterday morning the Pope has been living completely isolated from the court and the Curia in the uppermost rooms of the Tower of St John for an eight-day spiritual retreat. 'What other Pope in our times ever had such a splendid idea?', cries Pellicani, who, though he has an audience of only half a dozen, shouts and gesticulates as if he was haranguing a crowd. 'And that's not all. At least two or three times yesterday the guards on duty in the gardens saw him standing at the battlements of the tower holding a pair of large field-glasses and looking round over the panorama of the city from all sides. According to reports from his secretary, Monsignor Capovilla, John XXIII amuses himself by recognizing, among all the towers, steeples, and other buildings, the hundreds of Rome's churches, and in particular those recently built in the remoter suburbs.

'That may be. But I believe that, especially when he takes the glasses from his eyes, Pope John sees much further: he sees, because he imagines them and evokes their semblance by the thousand in his mind's eye, all the churches and chapels of the five continents, from the Cathedrals of Notre Dame, St Edwiga in Berlin, and St Paul to the famous sanctuaries of Lourdes, Compostella, and Guadeloupe, down to the lowliest missionary's hut... The Pope with his binoculars on the Tower of St John! That's how I'd start a broadcast on the Council. . . . I told my *bussolante* so: I very nearly lifted him off his feet and shook him: I wanted to persuade him to let me secretly into the Vatican gardens or palaces so that I could make a real first-hand picture of it all. . . . There isn't time, with the Council in the offing, to ask for a permit and fulfil all the regulations and then persuade the Pope to go back to his retreat in the Tower. And anyway someone else would steal my idea. . . . I can't tell you what fantastic things I promised the *bussolante,* but nothing would make him yield an inch. But just think: the Pope on the top of the tower with his binoculars like an admiral on the bridge of his ship at sea, or a general on the summit of a hill before giving the order for battle. . . .

'And the wretched man [for obviously the *bussolante* refused to give in] added other details to annoy me: for example, that John XXIII has had brought out for the occasion a field-altar given him by the Chinese when he first became Pope and celebrates Mass each morning at this altar rather than in his private chapel; and that it was from his tower-top hermitage that he read his broadcast message to the world this evening. . . . In short, I was so exasperated that I left the man without even saying goodbye.'

I had also invited the Hudsons, who wanted to meet Pellicani. And, as I'd told them to expect, he reiterated his theory – not a very original one, really – about outstanding men being actors. By outstanding men he means public figures bearing national or international responsibilities. Naturally, though today a convinced republican, his preference in this connection is for the descendants of the great ruling dynasties: they alone, in fact, have in their veins the vocation for the theatrical aspects of royalty (a very different thing, of course, from the capacity for true kingship). Modern democracies, in his view, have not yet solved the problem of translating the sacred sense of authority into some medium with a general appeal. Dictators, on the other hand, instinctively know what to do: they have no inhibitions about improvising and achieving cheap but telling effects in tune with the precarious nature of their own ventures.

But the most effective and subtle theatrical producers and actors ever since the beginning of time have been the priests, of whatever faith. At this point P.'s expositions usually vary unpredictably. Since he has lately devoted himself to producing a whole series of documentaries on the rites and liturgies practised by various peoples in a vast variety of periods and countries, he has only to choose one to suit his argument. This evening he confined himself to some examples from the rites of Egypt and some African tribes. Then, finally, he came to the Catholic Church and wound up with his *pièce de résistance* on the Popes as great actors.

Pellicani knew only the last three Popes: Pius XI, a son of the Lombard *petite bourgeoisie*, Pius XII, the prototype of the lesser 'black' aristocracy, and now John XXIII, a born peasant. Of the three, the only real 'king', according to him, was the first. He recalls him at the height of his glory in 1929, on the morrow of the Lateran Agreements between Church and State. The cry of 'Viva el papa rey!' remained impressed on his memory after an audience at that time when he found himself among a party of Spanish pilgrims. Such a cry had not been heard for decades and later would not have been allowed; but it applied to Pius XI as to no other Pope. Of medium height but well proportioned, he had a magnificent head, both powerful and authoritive. His manner of speaking was quiet, like a true king who has no need to raise his voice or gesticulate to command attention. He had only to show himself on foot, moving with his sure gait, to make his presence felt. Anyone meeting him by chance alone in a corridor would have halted awestruck before him.

It was only in his last years that Pius XI's supernatural qualities became striking. Behind the often half-closed eyes and the face marked by suffering he already seemed far away, enveloped in an atmosphere of eternity. In the first ten years of his Pontificate, on the other hand, he was only a sovereign – a particular kind of sovereign, obviously, but nevertheless always and pre-eminently sovereign: a great patron and lover of the arts and sciences, architect of ecclesiastical buildings and seminaries, promoter of missionary conquests in far-off lands, and so forth. Significantly, he was the particular Pope who propounded the doctrine of Christ as King. The papal mitre did not crush him: nevertheless it was not he who adapted it to himself but rather the mitre that brought the man to conform.

The hieratic quality, on the other hand, was the typical characteristic of Pius XII. Without his concentration in prayer and his liturgical gestures Papa Pacelli would have seemed just an ordinary man. His histrionicism (in the original meaning of the term) corresponded exactly, indeed exclusively, to that of the high priest. Thus he exercised minute and punctilious care over the staging of his non-ritual appearances, even to the point of sometimes accepting compromises with *mises-en-scène* of totalitarian origin.

A comparison between the two Piuses from the angle of stage personality would undoubtedly go, according to P., in favour of Pius XI, an actor so authentic, impressive, and confident as to have no need of a stage on which to perform. By comparison Pacelli was an apprentice, an artificial product, the result of hard work and attention to detail, who, lacking genuine inspiration and authentic originality, had no choice but to trust to technique.

Not greater than the other two, perhaps, but certainly richer and more striking in his sureness of touch and the naturalness of his bearing is John XXIII. Neither kingly nor priestly, he is the complete, original, and perpetually unpredictable incarnation of humanity and genuineness, in an office where such characteristics are usually overwhelmed by the anonymity of ritual and protocol. P. had an endless fund of stories about him, his original actions and his *bons mots*, especially in the first months of his Pontificate – a whole series of them which, he said, simply couldn't last, and which in fact slowed down, though not of calculated purpose but rather out of a natural wisdom and sense of moderation. But the surprises and unusual or revolutionary gestures were only the more appreciated as they became more infrequent.

As to the stage-management of the Council, to which the Hudsons took exception, Pellicani defends it on the ground of its irreplaceably symbolical function. He has no fear of its running into bad taste. Rather, he is curious to see how the spirit of John XXIII will stand up to this taxing encounter with the tremendous might of the great Vatican assembly.

Rome, Wednesday, 12 September

Contrary to what the *bussolante* told P., John XXIII did not speak yesterday evening from the Tower of St John but from his private library, to which he returned specially for that purpose.

The *Osservatore Romano* particularly says so, and even without that the photographs would have revealed it, showing the Pope reading his broadcast message with behind him the precious tapestry showing the promise of the Church's establishment and to the right of his desk 'the cross and the globe of the world'. 'Though speaking with his accustomed paternal kindliness,' says Lolli in his usual tiresome style, 'his voice showed a special ardour of soul, a profound aspiration of the heart. These were moments of comfort, of inspiring faith and magic.' One detail that must have roused Pellicani's enthusiasm: 'At the end, for the short but stupendous final prayer, the Holy Father rose to his feet.' The inevitable Lolli spoils everything by the piously banal addition: 'His countenance bore witness to his emotion and faith.'

Apart from the sickly-sweet comments of the Vatican reporter, the broadcast message is a document destined to arouse echoes more especially in the secular world. If I had to define it I would describe it – paradoxically in words but not in meaning – as 'an appeal to the Gentiles'. Indeed it was the Pope himself who developed in it the theme of 'Ecclesia Christi lumen gentium' ('The Church of Christ is the light of the peoples'). John XXIII, who has been an ardent and imaginative promoter of the Council for the past three years, launches with this broadcast message what one might call its secular manifesto, with the obvious intention of demonstrating that the Council is an event which concerns the lay world as well as the religious.

After summing up in a few lines the Church's 'internal (*ad intra*) vitality' – a vitality deriving from its 'titles of service and honour': to vivify, to teach, and to pray – he concentrates almost exclusively on its 'external (*ad extra*) vitality' in relation, as he says, 'to the demands and needs of the peoples'. 'The Church has constantly at heart,' he goes on, 'the acutely serious problems of the modern world. It has therefore made them the subject of attentive study and the Ecumenical Council will be able to offer in clear language solutions which are postulated by the dignity of man and of his Christian vocation.'

The past is clearly not so simple; but now, and this is what counts, John XXIII gives public and solemn guarantees that the Council is deeply pledged to tackling even the most burning questions of social international law, family morality, and the relations between State and Church. The list of subjects provided in the speech might be more logical and better arranged, but the important thing is its substance.

The first subjects to be mentioned are: 'the fundamental equality of all peoples in the exercise of rights and duties vis-à-vis the whole family of the nations; the strenuous defence of the sacred nature of marriage, which calls for wise and generous love from the partners; and, arising out of this, the procreation of children, considered in its religious and moral aspects, within the framework of the wider responsibilities of a social nature today and for eternity.' Further on he says that 'in relation to the underdeveloped countries the Church presents itself as it is and wishes to be, as the Church of all, and particularly the Church of the peoples. Every offence and violation against the fifth and sixth commandments of the holy decalogue: neglect of the obligations laid down in the seventh commandment: the miseries of social life which cry out for vengeance in the sight of God: all these things must be clearly acknowledged and deplored. It is the duty of every man, and the compelling duty of a Christian, to regard what is superabundant in the light of the needs of others, and to take due care that the administration and distribution of the good things created may be effected to the advantage of all.'

But the most felicitous passage in the message is undoubtedly that on peace: 'The Ecumenical Council is about to meet, seventeen years after the end of the Second World War. For the first time in history the Fathers of the Council will truly belong to all peoples and nations, and each one will make his contribution of intelligence and experience to heal and make sound the scars of the two conflicts which have profoundly changed the face of all countries. – Mothers and fathers of families detest war: the

Church, the mother of each and all, will once again raise the cry which originates from earliest centuries, from Bethlehem and Calvary, to pour itself out in supplication for peace: peace which shall ward off armed conflicts: peace which must have its roots and guarantee in the heart of every man. – It is natural that the Council, through its doctrinal structure and the pastoral action it promotes, should wish to express the longing of all peoples to pursue the road indicated to each one by Providence, to co-operate in the triumph of peace so as to render existence on earth more noble, just, and meritorious for all.

'The bishops, pastors of the flock of Christ *ex omni natione quae sub coelo est* ('out of every nation under heaven' – cf. *Acts* 2,5), will recall the concept of peace not only in its negative expression, which is detestation of armed conflicts, but even more in its positive demands, which require of every man the knowledge and constant practice of his own duties: leadership, harmonization and service of the spiritual values open to all, the possession and use of the forces of nature and technical knowledge exercised with the exclusive aim of raising the spiritual and economic standard of living of the peoples. Co-existence, co-ordination, and integration are most noble aims which echo throughout international assemblies, arousing hope and inspiring courage. The Council will strive to exalt in the most sacred and solemn terms the deepest applications of fraternity and love, which are natural needs of man, imposed upon the Christian as rules for the relationship between man and man, between nation and nation.'

At a certain point, John XXIII inadvertently mixed up public and private law, questions of charity and justice, and sociological and moral needs: confusions which his lucid and logical predecessor would never have made. Moreover, even the finest words about peace are bound to carry little conviction in a world full of pacifist slogans launched simultaneously with atomic bombs. Only when compared with the concrete results of the Council (a formulation of the doctrine of war more in conformity with the Gospels, the acceptance of non-violence and conscientious objection, etc.) will it be possible to estimate their real effect.

There was a reference to 'relations between the Church and civil Society' which seemed to me unfortunate, couched as it was in terms of rights, not duties, as regards the Church and completely ignoring the fact that the Roman Church is not the only institution in the world to make exclusive claim to religious truth. Yet it seemed as if the initial statement would lead the Pope much further afield. 'We are living,' he had said, 'face to face with a new political world. One of the fundamental rights which the Church cannot renounce is that of religious freedom, which is not only freedom in all respects but a specific freedom that the Church claims and teaches, and for which it continues to suffer pain and grief in many countries. The Church cannot renounce this freedom, because it is bound up with the service that the Church is committed to fulfilling. This service is not to be regarded as a corrective or complement of what other institutions are intended to do or have undertaken, but is an essential and irreplaceable element of the design of Providence to set man on the road towards truth; truth and freedom are the stones of the edifice on which human civilization is raised up.'

The new political world to which the Pope referred is thus first and foremost of the Soviet variety, not the secular world which succeeded the Christian eras and the *ancien régime,* the world of freedom of thought and conscience, in short the world of ideological and pragmatical pluralism. But despite these limitations the message is substantially an announcement of good will. Indeed more than an announcement, a programme which the Council cannot repudiate without irrevocably humiliating the Church.

Rome, Friday, 14 September

Is my description of John XXIII's broadcast message as an 'appeal to the Gentiles' really correct? If so, it would, among other things, emphasize the favourable contrast between the coming Council and Vatican I.

At the root of this message, in fact, there lingers a vision of reality which is tinged with hankerings after both supremacy and dichotomy–in short, a Manichean vision. Even supremacy in service is supremacy implying a distinction between superior and inferior, between patron and beneficiary. An emotive terminology based on evocation of the 'Father' and 'Mother' concepts ('Holy Mother Church') cannot go on bemusing people indefinitely. And then, why 'Mother Church' when it is a child of its own children, both generating and generated? Not to mention that few loves can be so egoistically possessive as the maternal. In any case, this 'Mother Church' which knows no limits in maintaining the myth of the eternal feminine in Mary nevertheless completely excludes women from its own hierarchy, entrenching itself in a rigid male oligarchy employed in teaching, legislating, and governing by every means, including (certainly in the past so why not in the future?) the most cynical and violent.

Recoaro, Friday, 21 September

(At a conference on the theme 'A Crisis in Religion?' organized by the periodical *Sacra Doctrina* issued by the Dominican Fathers in Bologna.)

Yesterday Cardinal Giovanni Urbani, Patriarch of Venice, made the opening speech. The conference is organised in three parts: the crisis of religion in culture, in industrial society, and in the family, and so I had imagined that the Patriarch would provide a definition of 'religion' after first discussing the historiographical and psycho-sociological aspects of the religious phenomenon. But instead he at once announced an unexpected subject: 'The sovereign presence of God in our consciences.'

He read his speech with true Venetian grace. But that stereotyped smile which never left his face for an instant, that unctuous voice which he tried to make persuasive but which was merely irritating, were in fact less annoying than the superficiality of what he said, lacking as it was in vigour of style or presentation.

At a certain point he had the bad taste to reproach the cosmonaut for his unfortunate witticism about not having met God in space; but even then he never allowed his voice to change or his smile to vanish. He even went on smiling when he recited, in tones reminiscent of amateur parish theatricals, the whole of the famous passage in Manzoni's *I Promessi Sposi* about the Innominato's nights of remorse. This was tedious for an educated audience, but he didn't stop there; instead he went on to read most of the description of the meeting with Cardinal Federico.

At the end of the speech the applause was chillier than I had expected. His exit was even more embarrassing. The Cardinal Patriarch continued to smile and give greetings with outstretched arms all the way from the platform and down the central gangway of the hall; but the two hundred people who had been listening to him were only concerned to get away as quickly as possible.

Urbani is not to be the only Cardinal at the conference, for on Sunday Efrem Forni, a former diplomat now attached to the Curia in some capacity, is to be there at the closing session. There will also be three bishops: the diocesan bishop, Zinato; Poma, of Mantua; and Bartoletti, auxiliary bishop of Lucca. For a three-day conference this is a real turn-out of Cardinals' hats and scarlet skull-caps. The organizers in conversation with me justified it on the ground of the delicate theme chosen: they could never have held a conference of this kind without at least a flash of purple and some violet cassocks, especially as they were also asking such well-known figures as Bo, Fabbri, and Acquiviva to speak. But it remains to be seen whether equivocal or evasive contributions such as that of Urbani will not end by sinking the affair in a different way.

I have come across the name of the Patriarch of Venice in connection with the opening of other conferences during the past few weeks. This may be another reason for his unfortunate appearance today. But I fail to understand how it is that the generally recognized standard of mediocrity of these episcopal appearances at conferences does not persuade the organizers to give up competing for the presence of eminences and excellencies. Conferences like that at Spoleto, where there was not a single high church dignitary on the platform, are a rare exception in Italy today.

In any case, nothing can justify the time spent by bishops in attending these more or less sterile academic affairs, which are held by the dozen all over the country between July and September, at a time like this when they are about to embark on a vast and complex mass of work at the Council in Rome. Certainly their light-heartedness in this respect does not arouse exaggerated illusions about the background preparation they will bring to it. For what will be expected from them there is not only up-to-dateness in their studies and reading but also the capacity to grasp problems, to see them in broad perspective beyond the usual narrow diocesan or national confines, to transcend analysis in synthesis, and so on: all of which demands both precise knowledge of the subjects and, more important, thought and meditation, and hence withdrawal and quiet.

Urbani's irritating speech makes me wonder, in particular, what contribution the College of Cardinals is likely to make to the Council. A mere generic and superficial comparison with the College that took part in the First Vatican Council, in 1869-70, leaves no doubt that the situation is much better today, especially in the more even distribution of qualifications.

At Pius IX's Council there were, as today, most of the Curial Cardinals; a fairly representative number of resident bishops; and some ex-nuncios, mostly from the European capitals, since Latin America, the only other continent to have them, had at that time abolished diplomatic representation with the Holy See. Today, the ex-nuncios number ten and thus come near to balancing the Curial Cardinals (15 or thereabouts) though the resident bishops outnumber both. And since the more stringent criticisms are generally directed towards the Curialists, the fact that they are in a definite minority is reassuring.

Strictly speaking, the ex-nuncios also belong to a branch of the Curia, that of diplomacy; but it is obvious that the greater activity of their lives, subject to constant moves from one country or even continent to another, helps to rid them of preconceived ideas and to form a spirit of adaptability ready to grasp the most unexpected situations. The generally accepted idea of the real Curialists, on the other hand, refers exclusively to those who have spent their whole career in the Roman departments waiting for the inevitable evolutions which will bring them ever nearer to the goal of the Cardinal's purple. These men, it is said, and not without justification though sometimes with exaggeration, far from adapting their own decisions to the needs of different and distant surroundings, are exclusively concerned to impose them, constraining the most intractable facts within the stereotyped formulae of their bureaucratic practice.

Today, however, the Curia has, if nothing else, lost that promiscuous and equivocal character which it had in the days of the temporal power; in those days the laymen in it were almost as numerous as the ecclesiastics, and from one day to the next the most promising (or the most protected) among them could be seen to move over into the clerical sector, quickly achieving the highest offices by the simple application of the tonsure and donning of clerical garb. As a result of this mixture, there was often no distinction in ways of behaviour between the ex-layman, a simple cleric with the Cardinal's hat, and a Cardinal who had gone through the whole gamut of the ecclesiastical career. Some years before the Council, in the Curia of Pope Pius IX, there were several 'worldly' Cardinals whose escapades were the talk of everyone. By 1869 Cardinal Antonio Matteucci, famous for his relations with the 'bella Nina', was dead; so too was Ludovico Altieri, notorious not only for a pomp reminiscent of the Renaissance but also for his association with 'la comarella', and Ugolini who daily paid a ritual visit to the beautiful Polish countess Natalia Spada de' Medici (whose husband was an ex-Monsignore and who counted among her other assiduous admirers Cardinal Gaude and Monsignor Fiorani). But their colleagues Grassellini and Pietro de' Silvestri were still there to carry on the tradition, not to mention the Secretary of State, Antonelli, whose antechamber was always more crowded with lovely ladies than with ambassadors.

Many prelates obtained a Cardinal's hat less by their own merits than through family influence and quarterings, with the natural consequence that their knowledge of religious matters was often practically non-existent and they often lacked even a modest smattering of secular culture. In 1869 the Italian Cardinals (representing four-fifths of the Sacred College) included only five with any cultural prestige: Cardinals Bilio, Caterini, Morichini, Trevisanato, and Vannicelli Casoni. Bilio, whom Pius IX wanted as chairman of the theological and dogma commission, had the dubious renown of being the man chiefly concerned in drawing up that chaotic document the *Sillabo*[1], and Vannicelli, archbishop of Ferrara, had brought out a nine-volume work on methods of agrarian reckoning in the Papal State in relation to the metrical system. Of the others, Caterini was justly famed for his share in framing the Bull *Quod Divina sapientia* on the reform of studies of Leo XII, and for the *Collectio legum et ordinationum de recta studiorum ratione*; Morichini had written two historico-statistical volumes on public charity institutions and primary education; and Trevisanato, Patriarch of Venice, was a well-known orientalist.

Today the Italian Cardinals are very different in both habits and

[1] A collection of errors to be condemned, compiled by Pius IX and published on 8 December 1864.

culture, though especially the former. In any case the influence of the Italian Cardinals is much less strong in the present College, where they now represent only a third of the whole, numbering 28 as against 57 of other nationalities. It is true that almost all the non-Italian Cardinals are resident bishops (there are at present only five of them in the Curia) who are compelled by their diocesan duties to remain in their own sees and concern themselves with the Church in their own countries. But they have widely varying backgrounds, some spent mainly in pastoral activities, some in administration and more frequently in teaching; and at the Council all the different backgrounds can intermingle. This could happen only to a very limited extent a century ago, when a mere ten out of fifty Cardinals were non-Italians, and even they were all from Europe.

The only remaining objection, therefore, is that of age, an inevitable feature in a 'senate' like that of the Vatican. With rare exceptions, even Cardinals do not escape the rule that mental rigidity occurs in direct proportion to sclerosis of the arteries. But not all the pillars of the Sacred College are enfeebled by age: true, sixteen of the Cardinals are over 81 (only one is 90) and 32 are between 71 and 80, but almost as many (25) are between 60 and 70, while eight are under sixty and three actually under fifty.

As for Urbani, at sixty-two he is certainly one of the younger ones. Though his immediate background is the care of souls, exercised exclusively in the Veneto, he has the advantage of having moved about a great deal through repeated transfers from one part of the country to another during the ten years when he was assistant-general of Catholic Action in Italy. Until he took on that office he had had a modest career, spent entirely in the circles of the patriarchal Curia of his native town of Venice, where he was known as a fine-looking man, a polished speaker able to please rather than fascinate, and an inimitable diplomat. As teacher of religion in the State high schools he was sought after by the Venetian upper bourgeoisie and aristocracy; but the thing that really brought him into public view was his conversion of the famous barrister Francesco Carnelutti.

An outsider might have thought such a career only moderately promising, but he himself had very optimistic ideas about it and made no secret of his high hopes of preferment. In the spring of 1940, Ferdinando T. happened to be a guest at the convent of

German nuns in Venice (in Campo Santo Stefano near the Fine Arts Academy) where Urbani was either living or going in for meals. One day at dinner the canon and monsignore, as he then was, confided to him in that typical way of ecclesiastics who want to show off but with due modesty, of course, and to the glory of God: 'Yes, I must confess I feel myself destined to rise.'

And he was right. He received the impetus from Cardinal Piazza, a rugged Carmelite from Belluno whom Pius XI had sent to Venice as Patriarch in 1935 and who was appointed by Pius XII in January 1946 as chairman of the Episcopal Commission to study the new statutes of Catholic Action in Italy. Piazza proposed Urbani as secretary of the Commission and in the following October got him a bishopric. During the previous years, under Piazza's influence and the pressure of events, Urbani had gradually veered away from sympathy for the Fascist régime and towards anti-Fascism. Consequently when he found himself faced inside Catholic Action, and at its very head, with a powerful duplicate, if Salazarian, version of the Duce in the person of Professor Luigi Gedda, its president, he had no hesitation about going into opposition – an opposition to his credit since it had little hope of success, and in which he was helped by that instinctive flexibility which had always distinguished him. This happened, significantly, simultaneously with Monsignor Montini's own change of view in the same direction at the turn of the Holy Year, 1950.

But the decisive gesture came in the spring of 1952, when Gedda embarked on his notorious piece of political speculation, making use as a figurehead of the veteran founder of Christian Democracy in pre-Fascist days, Don Luigi Sturzo[1]. From that moment relations between the president-*duce* and the assistant-bishop were confined to formal cordialities. In 1954 a crisis in the youth branch of Catholic Action, led by Mario Rossi, found a sympathizer in Urbani. Gedda wanted no better excuse and demanded Urbani's head. But first, at the end of 1954, Montini's head had to fall and he was transferred to the Archbishopric of Milan. Some months later Urbani knew his hour had come: the Consistorial Council informed him that the Pope had appointed him – *promoveatur ut amoveatur* – Archbishop of Verona.

It was there, in the beautiful bishop's palace behind the Cathe-

[1] This was opposed by both Urbani and Montini.

dral, that a year later he was visited by Carlo Carretto, former president of Catholic Action Youth and Rossi's predecessor in disgrace, who had found forgetfulness in becoming a follower of Père de Foucauld in the Sahara. When he left the 'little brother of Christ' told his friends: 'He is unrecognizable. The Urbani who almost managed to forget his episcopal dignity when he was among us young people has vanished for ever.'

Carretto, however, had judged only by appearances, and intentional appearances at that. The reserve and evasiveness that shocked him were only in part an adaptation to the prefectorial-episcopal convention typical of Venetian tradition. They were at least as much a tactical necessity in those last years of Papa Pacelli's Pontificate, and disappeared completely when Urbani found himself in private conversation with bishops under a cloud like himself, such as Montini in Milan and, even more, Roncalli in Venice.

In any case, it is certain that Roncalli's esteem for Urbani, then his suffragan bishop, was born in the course of the meetings and confidences they exchanged between 1955 and 1958. Thus when, only a fortnight after he became Pope, Roncalli appointed Urbani as his successor in Venice, the promotion of this former assistant-general of Catholic Action bore the same significance of reparation for past injustice that applied also to Montini's appointment as Cardinal in a special position above all the other new members of the Sacred College.

Whether, and to what extent, Urbani is really a progressive is difficult to say. He has always avoided the nervous oscillations of Montini, carefully maintaining in his own bishopric a regular and tranquil form of administration free of disturbances or problems. Above all he has avoided making any striking personal pronouncements, cleverly exploiting his exceptional position as successor of the Pope and eclipsing his own dominant figure behind this rôle.

But since John XXIII is in the habit of associating him publicly with his predilection for Venice, the newspapers feel obliged every so often to make mention of Urbani's appointment to some new office (such as that of chairman of the episcopal commission for the higher direction of Catholic Action in place of the intransigent Cardinal Siri) and they sometimes even indicate him as the heir-presumptive of John XXIII. This last is without foundation, quite apart from the fact that a Pope can only very rarely do anything to influence the succession to himself. Besides, a new Pope is always a surprise phenomenon, an unknown quantity made up of any number of different factors. The reaction between his own personal qualities and background and the exceptional situation in which he suddenly finds himself (something utterly novel which has no connection with the earlier vicissitudes of his career) is completely unpredictable; and no less unpredictable are the effects of his impact on the Court and the Curia, and, most of all, the psychological effects of finding himself at the apex of a kingdom which virtually knows no confines.

Bologna, Sunday, 23 September

An unexpected programme today. On my way back from Recoaro I gave a lift in my car to a deacon from Bologna – a pleasant, intelligent young man who apparently is going to carry on his studies at the Biblicum – and in return he took me to see the Documentation Centre in Bologna and then to Monteveglio, some twelve miles out of the town, to visit Don Giuseppe Dossetti. Dossetti is the former leader of the Christian Democrat party's left wing, a brilliant opponent of De Gasperi within the party fifteen years ago, and now a hermit priest in some original religious community founded by himself.

Dossetti is undoubtedly one of the strangest people in Italy today, especially in the politico-cum-religious sphere. Anyone who neglects him, even out of respect for Dossetti's own wish for self-obliteration, deprives himself of one of the most exceptional, paradoxical and stimulating experiences of his life. For that reason I gladly agreed to meet him.

He first revealed his quality in the Constituent Assembly of 1946-7, especially in the debates on the inclusion of the Lateran Pacts in the State's new Constitution. In the history of Church-State relations, the success of the 'professorino', as Dossetti was called, is undoubtedly an obscure chapter: but that does not diminish the fact of the tremendous personal impression he made. Dossetti had accepted his entry into political life as a task imposed on him (it was his friend Don Pignedoli, Montini's future assistant, who inflicted it on him: he went to visit Dossetti in hospital after a car accident which had happened while he was on the way to Rome for the express purpose of convincing his friends in the Resistance that politics was not his job). But if political activity had been confined to the legislative sphere Dossetti could have borne it. Instead, he found his idealism and moral consistency put to too hard a test by the need for compromise; and he also discovered that every party success inevitably coincided with a further postponement of the programmes which he had at heart.

He had come to Rome in September 1945 with three friends and colleagues, Lazzati, Fanfani, and La Pira, all of them university lecturers like himself. They all found shelter in a particular sort of hermitage after the style of St Philip Neri in the heart of the oldest part of Rome near the Chiesa Nuova where they started what became known as the 'comunità del porcellino' (literally, the piglet community[1]). In 1947 the community became transformed from a simple refuge for prayer and study into a hive of intellectual and social activity. The group connected with the periodical *Cronache Sociali*, besides being much larger, had its headquarters elsewhere, but its brain and heart remained beside the Chiesa Nuova where it had first been planned.

The majority within the Christian Democrat party was gradually moving further towards the right, forgetful of the social aspects which it should have been striving to promote, while Dossetti and the other 'professorini' were fighting for a programme which would be more intransigent as to principles and more progressive in the way of reforms. They were opposed to any sharp division between the political blocs, whether in foreign or internal policy, and disliked purely sterile and demagogic manifestations of anti-Communism. Instead, they continued to maintain the usefulness of a coalition government with the Communists and Socialists even after the three-party coalition between those parties and the Christian Democrats had come to an end; they fought unremittingly for unity in the trade-union field; and, most important of all, they upheld the need for structural reforms aimed at replacing the old liberal form of State by a new structure in consonance with the present day. Staunch in their Catholic faith, they were, or at any rate wanted to be, unprejudicedly free and dynamic in every other sphere.

[1] From an emblem on the house.

Their mistake lay in being in advance of their times and refusing to adapt themselves. The overwhelming victory of the Christian Democrats in the general election of 18 April 1948 had the swift effect of driving the party in on itself. For a short time in 1949 it seemed as if the Dossettian Left might be able to stem this tendency and bring the Christian Democrats back to the line of their original ideals; but this proved yet another illusion. *Cronache Sociali*, after a period of silence in 1950, withdrew from the struggle in 1951. Dossetti resigned from his membership of the party secretariat and from Parliament in 1952.

One day when travelling by train from Rome to Bologna he had started to read a book which someone had recommended to him: *Il mistero dell'anno liturgico* (*The Mystery of the Liturgical Year*). He was much struck by it. He at once wrote to the author, Don Divo Barsotti, a Pisan priest in the diocese of San Miniato, who through La Pira's intervention had become confessor of a convent in Florence but had soon withdrawn to a sort of hermitage near San Gimignano. The two eventually met at Dossena just at the time when Dossetti was deciding to abandon political life. Dossetti had already started in Bologna both the Documentation Centre, which was extremely up to date especially as regards theological periodicals, and also two lay religious groups. The aims of these groups were still undefined, but the general intention was to prepare themselves for the re-evangelization of the world after the deluge which they believed was bound to assail it soon. They were, in fact, like two pre-catacomb communities dedicated exclusively to spiritual activities: mystical practice, theological re-elaboration in a 'kerygmatic[1]' sense, community in prayer and church services, and so on.

To La Pira, this living in catacombs before one need was not convincing. But Dossetti, and Lazzati with him (Fanfani had by this time thrown himself completely into politics and was in a certain sense La Pira's right-hand man there), no longer had any doubts about the inevitable decline of Western society. According to them, the Communist steamroller would soon pass over Europe and probably America too, and the task of conquering the conqueror would fall on the Church – a Church renewed, emerging from the catacombs of silence, prayer, and sacrifice. Better, therefore, to withdraw from a world irrevocably con-

[1] The theology of preaching.

demned and let its end come rather than prolong the agony with inadequate doses of oxygen.

In order to dedicate himself exclusively to this vocation of precursor of the future, Dossetti gave up teaching canon law at Modena University and also refused a chair at Bologna, where he now lived permanently. He was left undisturbed in his retirement for some years, until one morning in the winter of 1956 Cardinal Lercaro asked him to come to the bishop's palace. The Cardinal told him that in the following May municipal elections would be taking place; it was essential to win over from the Communists their important stronghold of Bologna, and in order to do this Dossetti must return to political life and head the local Christian Democrat list of candidates. Lercaro was more than Dossetti's bishop, he was his spiritual father, the man of God who had approved his community experiment; so Dossetti yielded to what he could not but regard as a manifestation of God's will.

The result was a resounding defeat, for several thousand votes from the bourgeoisie, terrified by Dossetti's Savonarola-like propensities, went to his adversary. Dossetti himself welcomed it with relief as a proof that politics were not for him. As soon as he could get permission from the Cardinal he resigned from the borough council and declared his intention of entering the priesthood. This was the final eclipse of Dossetti as a politician. The newspapers only mentioned him again on the day when he took the tonsure and later, at Epiphany in 1959, when Lercaro ordained him a priest in his private chapel. Immediately afterwards the new priest disappeared from view. He was said to be living as a monk with some other priests in the monastery of the Madonna of St Luke, the famous sanctuary on a hill outside Bologna. Finally, about a year ago, it was rumoured that he had definitely moved to Monteveglio, taking over an abandoned monastery in a beautiful situation on a hilltop rising up above the vast pre-Appennine plain.

Everyone but the people of Bologna might have supposed that he had abandoned every kind of activity and buried himself completely. But the fact that he remained virtually invisible even to them did not mean that he was doing nothing: the reorganization of the diocese, now being carried on in accordance with a coherent and original programme, pointed to the presence of a secret but vigilant intelligence at work behind the scenes. Moreover, it was always his name that was whispered when some particular innovation was made. My guide told me this, citing a whole series of ventures inspired and watched over by Dossetti.

But now our car was negotiating the hairpin bends leading up to the monastery-castle, and the road and the view took up all our attention.

I can still see Dossetti in the bare parlour into which he took me after himself opening the monastery gate to us. He sat facing me in the middle of the room beside a table covered with an ugly green cloth; and he sat so erect that it seemed as if in penitential spirit he was trying not to lean against the back of his chair. He said nothing, and his eyes seemed deliberately to avoid mine, but I don't know if they rested on anything else; perhaps they didn't want to see anything, although the concentration of the pupils suggested a perpetual search for something.

I felt embarrassed at turning up unexpectedly like this, suddenly forcing upon him by my visit the emotional reaction of an experience so different from his own. Beyond his courteous manner I noticed some quality of stiffness in him, a certain dubiousness, I imagine, as to the reasons that brought me to violate his peace, reasons of personal curiosity perhaps, or, worse still, professional reasons. He quite understandably suspected, I expect, that my only aim was to collect some foolish gossip about him to be poured out later in the kind of magazine that has no mercy for anyone, least of all for men of the Church.

We began to talk in snatches. I had the almost physical feeling that every word I spoke was dragging him away from something essential, interrupting what for him was the only thing that mattered, meditation or converse with God. And yet, I thought, he was not really a hermit, and talking with men should seem to him like another way of continuing that converse with God. But probably – although he denied this and seemed to have no recollection of it – he reproached himself for having evaded several years ago, soon after I publicly left the Church, a meeting with me which he had himself suggested, and which I had welcomed with interest mingled with curiosity.

But even were that so, he still remained impenetrable. I could only go by his face with its annoying little fixed half-smile as if veiled in a thin mask of wax. He has a very fine face, almost suggesting a sort of transfiguration: regular and heart-shaped, with thin lips pressed together as if they had just closed on a consecrated wafer, and with great black eyes, the luminous, burning eyes of a contemplative. Every time I looked at them they seemed in their fixity to accumulate more light. The eyebrows above never stirred, the pupils remained steady as crystals. But I would not say they were peaceful eyes: at bottom, they concealed a half-appeased but still untamed restlessness.

Tall and thin to the point of emaciation, he seemed to find a sitting posture uncomfortable. He had on a rather worn cassock with a dark grey pullover over it, but without any of the slightly Bohemian air of a worker-priest.

We continued our efforts to make our tête-à-tête natural and normal. It was nearly always I who took the initiative, choosing my words carefully so as to avoid making it seem like an interview. He for his part replied politely but evasively, often leaving his answers half-finished as if he felt himself called back to something more essential that could not wait. I found the pauses rather embarrassing and, as they went on, provoking. I thought he was longing to become absorbed in prayer – a prayer to touch the heart of the rebel before him – or that he was searching for something to say that would stick in my mind like a goad to bring me grace.

Suddenly this situation of mutual embarrassment reminded me of another similar occasion: of my encounter with Monsignor Montini on Christmas Eve 1950 when he, not I, was the visitor. A few minutes before I had been miles from expecting anything of the kind. When he spoke on the telephone I thought at first that it must be his brother the MP, now Senator, rather than the Assistant Secretary of State himself. But ten minutes later he was knocking at my door. I had never seen him before, and now this well-nigh mythical *éminence grise* of the Vatican was sitting stiff and embarrassed before me on the little gilded fake Louis XVI divan.

Perhaps my room contributed to his embarrassment. It was in one of the old streets of Rome between the Corso and Piazza di Spagna: a pied-à-terre with a divan-bed covered in a dark damask which unmistakably proclaimed its function. I had found the room at a reasonable price and was using it for the time being as a place to live and work in. Just then I was working on my second book in the 'Clandestine' series, *La Chiesa al bivio* (*The Church at the Cross-roads*), writing at an inconvenient little table without reference books or notes of any kind. If he had looked he would have seen the last pages lying there.

But Montini was finding it difficult to collect himself from the shock of finding me in these surroundings. He managed, however, to say that he had come to see me knowing that I was alone on Christmas Eve when solitude is particularly hard to bear. As to the step I had taken in leaving the Church, he passed no judgment on me, and in any case, he added, we could have a talk later on if I wished. Now, unfortunately, he must go away again at once: at a time like that I could easily imagine how much was going on at the Vatican: it was by mere chance that he had a free quarter of an hour and seized the chance to come.

I never saw him again, I don't know why. Perhaps he thought it was useless to attempt to bring me back. And ever since I have continued to be half-moved, half-irritated at my recollection of those few minutes: moved because of the gesture, prompted as it was by no thought of publicity, and irritated because of the pretences and contradictions in which at a certain point Montini had become involved.

What suddenly reminded me of that episode as I sat in the parlour at Monteveglio was a reference of Don Dossetti's to my books: 'I am always seeing new books of yours in the shop-windows,' he said. 'I haven't read them, of course: I have no time for any sort of books nowadays.' But in fact I know from a reliable source that the exact opposite is true – not about my own books, of course (though I have seen copies of them at the Documentation Centre), but about books in general and books on religious subjects in particular. And I just can't find a justification in my mind for that puerile reticence, that wanting to seem more remote from the world than is in fact the case. It doesn't surprise me, for I know only too well that 'need of the world' that one finds in the restless correspondence of other hermits-from-protest like him, from Brother Carlo Carretto, former head of Catholic Action Youth in Italy, to the Trappist monk Guala, ex-director-general of Italian television. I am not surprised, but that does not mean that I don't feel disappointed.

Dossetti, moreover, did eventually shed some of his reticence. At a certain point, perhaps in reaction to a slightly malicious remark of mine, he put up quite a lively defence of the consistent course his life had followed, beginning in action and broadening out into contemplation, unlike my own (his eyes – but only his eyes – implied) that began in the established faith and ended up in religious open-mindedness.

In any case the hermit of Monteveglio did not disappoint me afresh, or at least only temporarily, when, in an attempt to fathom something of the nature of his theology of the catacombs and the future, I asked him what credible reasons he would put forward for an acceptance of the Church in general and of certain dogmas in particular. 'But,' he answered, and repeated the words when he saw my surprise, 'when one has accepted Christ as God, all the rest follows of itself.' At first I thought he meant that if once one admits that rationally most unsurmountable mystery, the mystery of God made flesh, all the rest is easy to believe; I only realized later that his avowal could also include the idea of sacrificing any further theological speculation beyond the personal mystery of God.

While I thought this over we had already reached the outskirts of Bologna and plunged into the evening traffic. But can it be, I asked myself, that this monk, still so clearly thirsting for peace and mortification, can have come so near to freeing himself from the yoke of theology?

Rome, Monday, 24 September

On Saturday night, but for a chance, St Peter's would have been blazing against the Roman sky. It seems that from the latter part of the morning onwards the bomb was there wrapped up in a sack on the ground in a corner of the Council hall ready to burst into flames once it was set off. But about 3.30 pm a workman went to move the sack. He noticed a strange object sticking out of it (this later proved to be the detonator), put his hand in, and to his surprise drew out a bottle. It never entered his head that it might contain anything dangerous; he merely thought it must have been hidden there by one of his mates meaning to pick it up at the end of the day. However he began to be alarmed when he saw some sparks coming out of the neck of the bottle just near where the connecting wire of the detonator emerged. After a moment's hesitation he instinctively threw the bottle away from himself and towards the middle of the nave. The bottle broke, but the detonator did not function, and the whole thing finished in a slight flare-up and a cloud of black smoke.

The bottle was found to be full of muriatic acid; it would have exploded when the acid had completely corroded the sheet of aluminium at its base. Work in St Peter's was stopped at once and a careful search was made throughout the building, the only result of which was the discovery, beside the statue of St Andrew near the entrance to the crypts, of another harmless detonator which the incendiarist had probably left behind as useless.

The position of the bomb left no doubts as to its object. Moreover on 14 July there had been another similar attempt using even more rudimentary methods. Consequently the affair has made a tremendous impression, especially in the Vatican. Everyone shudders at the thought that the fate of the Council depends on the whim of some obscure fanatics or maniacs who, as far as one can tell, will not give up until they achieve their end. But who can they be, and how to discover them? Friends whom I have telephoned tell me that army weapons experts are to examine the remains of the bomb, but there seems little prospect of finding out much. The mystery will probably remain unsolved, the worst of that being that if the incendiarist is an isolated madman he will probably try again.

So the question once more arises, who would do an irresponsible thing like this? Gossip in Vatican circles advances three theories: it might be activists from some extreme right-wing movement, angered at the support given by the Vatican hierarchy to the Government's Centre-Left policy; or some Protestant fanatic hostile to the reconciliation of the evangelical Churches with Rome; or some ex-priest or priest, victim of canonical censure and jealous of the fresh affirmation of the Church's power at the Council.

If I had to choose, I would have no hesitation in picking the first theory, for the other two seem quite absurd. Moreover, there are some precedents to support it such as, for instance, the bomb which exploded some years ago in front of the bishop's palace in Milan. Religious fanaticism exists, and it would be prejudice to deny it; but in the hundred years and more since 'sects' set out to conquer the country, no elements among those whom the 'servant of God', Cardinal Ildefonso Schuster, described in a pastoral letter of 1952 as the 'fifth column' operating for the dissolution of the country have ever dared to attempt anything of the kind. They did not attempt it when it would have been both easier and almost splendid to do so, namely between 1870 and 1915, in the years when even baptized Catholics or patriots were so imbued with anti-clerical rancour that they tried to throw Pius IX's coffin into the Tiber and shouted 'Down with the Pope' in Piazza San Pietro. Nor did they attempt it when there was more reason, as after the war, especially in 1945-55, when the police made use of unconstitutional Fascist public security laws in order to stifle evangelistic movements, particularly in the South.

The only recorded episode of Protestant fanaticism goes back to 1949, but it seems to have had no foundation beyond the statement of a visionary. On the evening of 9 December in that year, according to subsequent newspaper reports, Pius XII recited the Rosary in his private chapel in the presence of some Roman transport workers and Vatican workmen. Afterwards the Jesuit Father Rotondi, right hand of Father Lombardi, the now disavowed 'mouthpiece of God', presented the members of the congregation to the Pope, among them Giuseppe Cornacchiola, well known in Rome and Latium for his claim to have seen an apparition of the Virgin near the Tre Fontane, at the gates of the city. Cornacchiola wished to make a revelation to the Pope and offer him two gifts. The revelation was that when he had been a member of a Protestant sect his fanaticism had reached such a pitch that he resolved to kill the Pope. After his conversion to Catholicism he had kept 'the Bible he had used to harm the Church' and the dagger he had bought, waiting for a suitable occasion to lay them at the feet of the Vicar of Christ with a renewed request for pardon.

The story, which would certainly have moved to tears the readers of Fr Bresciani's *feuilletons,* smacked too much of invention and was too oozing with edification to be credible. If only there had been an actual attempted papicide with witnesses! But no, the only evidence of the sacrilegious design was the dagger, which could perfectly well have been bought the evening before in any second-hand shop. Even the papers in their brief reports of the episode seemed half-ashamed of recounting it to their readers. But what might appear edifying under the miracle-inclined Pontificate of Pius XII is today quite forgotten. In the new ecumenical climate one hesitates even to suggest the hypothesis of fanaticism on the part of a non-Catholic sect.

The *Osservatore Romano,* indeed, took good care not to venture on any such theory, or on the last theory either, the one suggesting as the guilty person an ex-priest or a priest who had been severely censured. In Italy, in consequence of Article 5 of the 1929 Concordat, canonised together with all the Lateran Pacts in the Constitution of 1948, these two categories of civil pariahs, as Antonio Gramsci called them, cannot exercise any State office which brings them into contact with the public – which in practice means that they cannot hold public office or teach in schools. For many of them with no psychological preparation for other activities, this means being condemned to starvation or to manual activities which they find humiliating or degrading. They might therefore have good reason to feel desperate; but even so, in the thirty years and more since the Concordat has been in force there has not been a single case of violent action by them against the hierarchy.

At one time, the first suspicion concerning an attempt of this kind would inevitably have fallen on the anarchists. They have by no means ceased to exist, though their activity now mainly consists of polemical outbursts in the local press. But obviously anarchists have ceased to be news.

And with the decline of the cult for heroes, it seems, we have lost the fount of that strange race of topsy-turvy people, the 'black heroes'. Our times are not made for producing other Erostrates. The monsignori across the Tiber can rest tranquil. Today the Churches are not destined for pyres but for the void left by the faithful, little heroes through indifference.

Rome, Tuesday, 25 September

Nothing new, of course, about the mysterious perpetrator of the outrage in St Peter's. Instead, a great reckoning-up of what the damage would have been had the attempt succeeded. Apart from possible danger to the monuments in the Basilica and the fabric itself, which cannot be calculated, destruction of the Council hall alone would have meant the loss of an enormous amount of material: miles of metal tubes (the hall measures 280 x 70 feet), tens of thousands of joints, hundreds of yards of planks, over 3,000 yards of damask and 2,000 of velvet, hundreds of yards of fringe and gilded fittings, and a score of tapestries serving as acoustic screens as well as adornment for the hall; getting on for 200 miles of electric, radio, telephone, and television cables, 40 large projectors for lighting (independent of that normally used in the Basilica), a multiple recording apparatus with its temporary studio and four large stereophonic recording machines, an internal telephone plant with 40 telephones and its own switchboard, 30 loudspeakers and 40 microphones with temporary studios, a computer for voting with perforated slips, and so on.

All this makes one think of what it must have cost already to set up the various services for the Council, from the pre-preparatory Commission, established on 10 May 1959 and housed in No. 10, Via Serristori, to the erection of the hall in St Peter's. The administrative Secretariat presided over by Cardinal Di Jorio (the secretary of the Conclave in 1958, who received the Cardinal's red skull-cap from the new Pope in the Sistine Chapel, on the occasion when all the canopies over the electors' thrones fell down except the one above his own seat) was not created till more than a year later, on 5 June 1960, but before that its chairman must have had to concern himself with the income and expenses accounts of the pre-preparatory Commission in his quality of pro-Chairman of the Pontifical Commission of the Vatican State and Chairman of the Institute for the Works of Religion (a pious nomenclature which in fact signifies the Bank of the Holy See). Apart from the technical apparatus of cataloguing, forms, and co-ordinating the replies to the Tardini questionnaire sent out to all bishops, the most expensive item was probably the printing of the 16 volumes of the *Acta et Documenta Concilio Oecumenico Vaticano II apparanda*. This produced a deficit because except for the first volume it was printed only in small quantity and not put on public sale.

Naturally, outside the Vatican precincts no one will admit that the Council preparations alone must have cost milliards (of Vatican or Italian lire – it's all the same, given the financial agreement annexed to the Concordat of 1929 which equalizes the two currencies). But there can be no doubt that this is so. The planning and execution of the Council hall alone cannot have cost less than a milliard – not only because of the enormous amount of material used, as I mentioned just now, but also because of the difficulties involved in setting up all the complicated apparatus. The necessary cables, for example, had to be laid underground beneath the floor of the Basilica and carried through the interior of the structure of the stands carrying the Council Fathers' seats. Bars and cloakrooms had to be installed and special tribunes for the diplomatic corps, for foreign missions, radio reporters, journalists, and so on.

And the hall was not the only thing that had to be tackled in St Peter's. The portico was completely restored and cleaned. Other restorations were carried out at various points in the ceiling and the floor (inserting, incidentally, the coat-of-arms of John XXIII, re-designed by Manzù); the Michelangelo Pietà was lowered and brought forward, correcting the angle to make it easier to see; Filarete's bronze central doors were thoroughly cleaned by electrolysis (by means of cloths steeped in the liquid, since given their size it would have been impossible just to wash them). The lighting arrangements in the Basilica, in the hands of Phillips, are not yet completed but promise to be remarkable. The aim is to achieve an artistic lighting effect at night and also, by means of special projectors, to bring out particular architectural and decorative features in daytime.

As well as the work on the Basilica, much is also being done on the Vatican buildings. During 1961 it was decided, as I mentioned on 1 September, to raise the Tower of St John and also to restore the Porta Pertusa and Porta della Torrina and make the necessary alterations in the area near the Vatican gardens. Other restoration work was done on the ancient walls of Nicholas V, the *casino* of Pius IX (seat of the Pontifical Academy of Sciences), the fountain of the Sacrament, and the great Hall of Congregations of the Cardinals on the third floor of the Loggie (which had to be adapted for the plenary meetings of the central Preparatory Commission of the Council). Some of the other work carried out in the same year in the Vatican palaces had nothing to do with the Council; but another innovation connected with it was the re-opening of the famous passage-way – 'Er Corridore dei Borghi' – which joins the Apostolic Palaces with the Palazzi dei Propilei (where most of the Congregations are housed) in Piazza Pio XII, before arriving at Castel S. Angelo.

This last restoration was finished only a few weeks ago except for a lift. But it would be tedious to give a complete list of all the works going on in the past nine months. Suffice it to say that they include the courtyards of San Damaso, the Pappagallo, and the Triangolo. More immediately connected with the Council are the alterations in Via delle Fondamenta, renovations to the lift connecting the Basilica of St Peter's with the Pauline Chapel, and extensions to the radio studios near the Museo Petriano.

In short, it is no exaggeration to say that the Vatican City has become a vast workshop in the past two years. Clearly, the cost of all this cannot be said to count under normal administrative expenditure. Moreover the budget also has to include travel and housing expenses in Rome for the non-resident members and advisors of the Preparatory Commissions, numbering some 300, or about a third of the total (875). Though some of them have made their own arrangements, a good many had to be subsidized.

Thus many of the administrative Secretariat's meetings must certainly have been spent on the problem of finding the necessary funds as well as on approving the plans for the Council. Pius IX with his customary wit once remarked à propos of the expenses of the first Vatican Council, 'I don't know whether I shall emerge from the Council fallible or infallible but I shall certainly come out of it failed' (i.e. bankrupt – the play on words in Italian between *fallabile* and *fallito* is less telling in English). This was a forecast that in no way compromised the Holy Spirit, for he had virtually 'failed' already, as contemporary budgets of the former Papal States bear witness. And if the Holy Spirit did not warn him about what was to happen on 20 September 1870, when Italian troops entered Rome at Porta Pia, that was to avoid discouraging him still further.

His more fortunate successor is spared such anxieties. At the present moment there is no undertaking or venture that could cause the Head of the Catholic Church any fears on account of its financial repercussions. From Cardinal Cremonesi to Cardinal Canali and Di Jorio, not to go outside the ecclesiastical circle, the Holy See could not have hoped for wiser administrators. But it would be unfair to the laymen to neglect mention of such men as Nogara, Spada, Sacchetti, Oddasso, Galeazzi, and others.

Moreover the financial drain on the Holy See has been reduced to a minimum by the way in which the various episcopates have competed to tax themselves to help the poorer among them. The list is headed by the American episcopate, followed, according to my friend Monsignor Martinez (Canon of an arch-basilica and adviser to two Sacred Congregations), by Canada, Germany, Holland, France, and Belgium. Even Peter's Pence, the international contribution used since 1870 to help towards the upkeep of the Vatican, has been diverted only in part to paying for the Council, for the income from it went up so much in view of Vatican II that it was able to serve for both purposes.

Rome, Wednesday, 26 September

Today's papers report the first death of a Council Father: the English Franciscan Monsignor John Foster Hogan, Bishop of Bellary, in India. He died yesterday of a heart attack, soon after landing in Naples. Born in Liverpool, he was 67 years old and had been a bishop since 1949.

The news took me by surprise. For some reason I was certain that the Fathers would not begin arriving till early October. But the advance guard has already taken possession of Rome. Quite a number of bishops from overseas, mostly travelling in groups, must already have arrived in Italy. Rome, of course, is so used to the constant coming and going of tourists and priests that it has not yet noticed anything, but still pursues its accustomed vague and indifferent way through these late-summer days.

I think of the journeys all these Bishop-Fathers are making to come here from every part of the world. For all of them, but especially for the more distant ones, it must be a solemn and significant event. In Italy itself, few bishops will need to think in terms of aeroplanes; many of them will even come by car as if for a tourist trip or a business journey. Most of them will probably be accompanied to their local station by a procession.

Some time ago I read and copied down an account of the arrangements made early in the summer by the bishop of a small Calabrian diocese, Oppido Mamertina. Quite apart from the style, it is not without its picturesque qualities. There is a Spanish or even Spanish-colonial flavour about its attitude towards the local inhabitants which would delight a sociologist. This little proclamation of a bishop *in partibus* is practically a Government programme. He may be destined to be snubbed by the other priests, whether for his laziness and indifference or for his intelligence and innate wisdom; but his programme corresponds to a baroque idea of his mission that is at once childish and presumptuous, strident and charismatic. Here it is:-

a) Meeting of the faithful for the departure of Monsignore the Bishop for Rome;
b) the crosses on the bell-towers shall be illuminated;
c) display a large pontifical coat-of-arms on the façade of the church; also a picture of the Pope, if possible seated on a throne 'in cornu evangelii' (i.e. on the Gospel side of the choir);
d) festive ringing of the bells at the evening *Ave Maria*, to be prolonged as an exceptional measure each day for fifteen minutes; daily call to prayer;
e) daily High Mass in the Cathedral and in parishes which are seats of the Vicariate;
f) High Mass in other parishes in turn;
g) childrens' prayers in afternoon;
h) in the evening, prayers for the Council at which the Blessed Sacrament shall be solemnly exposed;
i) the exercise of sacrifice, charity to the poor, sick and needy, and daily participation in Holy Mass are strongly advised;
l) various communications to the people in order to interest them in the work of the Council, to be taken only from the Vatican official bulletins and the Catholic press, shall be made known, if possible, in every parish by means of a daily notice put up on the walls; this method can also be used when the Council is over to announce diocesan and parish activities;
m) towards the synodal law: preparatory study is urged for the diocesan Synod to be held after the Ecumenical Council. The Venerable Vicars are therefore asked to undertake preliminary study.

Rome, Thursday, 27 September

With a little patience and a lot of telephoning I have ascertained both the state of nerves prevailing at all levels of the Council preparations and the large number of Fathers and their accompanying assistants who have already arrived in Rome.

A usually well-informed Catholic daily some weeks ago forecast the arrival of 'secretaries, theologians, and canonists to the tune of some 3,500'; hence, including the Fathers themselves, 'at least 6,000 in all'. These predictions probably err on the side of excess since not all the bishops, especially the missionary bishops or those coming from distant or underdeveloped countries, can allow themselves the luxury of bringing one or more adviser-secretaries with them. But if these figures are correct about a tenth of the expected number has already arrived, and within a week half of them should be here.

Up to now the arrivals are mostly groups of bishops who have come by sea from the Far East and Latin America, or Fathers travelling separately who want to secure reasonably comfortable accommodation. At Rome's main station, Fiumicino airport, and the port of Naples an Italian Government committee headed by an ambassador, Guidetti, has arranged for special waiting-rooms to be reserved for the Fathers, for their speedy passage through customs and passport control, and for cars or buses to take them to their lodgings. Up to now there have not been many arrivals by air, but soon Fiumicino will be as busy as Rome station and Naples.

The rush has already begun at the offices of the Technical and Organizing Committee presided over by Cardinal Gustavo Testa, a former diplomat from Bergamo, with as his secretary the secretary-general of the Council itself, Monsignor Felici, and his under-secretaries. In general, the Fathers have either already applied to the Committee before leaving home or else they turn up at its office on arrival, especially if their search for a lodging has proved fruitless. During the past months the Committee has sent out thousands of circulars by post as well as replying to individual requests. One circular, for example, exhorted the Fathers to select their lodging and inform the Committee of their choice on a form enclosed. In addition to ecclesiastical colleges, monasteries and convents, hostels, etc., the Committee has arranged to take over whole hotels, mostly of the medium category. Another circular advised the Bishops, for understandable reasons, not to take rooms with families or private persons as 'paying guests'. Yet another one courteously recommended the choice of colleges or hotels in the Borgo Pio area, as being both quieter and easier of access to St Peter's, since even with the car services available rapid transport to other parts could not be guaranteed.

The Committee has been faced with quite a number of special problems: for instance, it has had to order De Gaulle-sized beds for Cardinals Ricketts E. Landazuri, Archbishop of Lima (over 6 foot), Valeriano Gracias, Archbishop of Bombay, and Rugambwa, Bishop of Bukoba in Tanganyika (both around 6ft. 4).

I have also been told that one of the headaches of the Committee – on which, in addition to Cardinal Testa, there are eight other Cardinals including Spellman, Montini, Doepfner, and Traglia, the pro-Vicar of Rome – is that a number of the Fathers, and indeed whole episcopates, were going to hotels in the fashionable parts of Rome, the Via Veneto and Parioli, where the night-clubs are and which are frequented by cinema actors and actresses. Consequently it was a great relief when Cardinal Spellman announced that he had taken over a hotel specially for the US episcopate – the Hotel Michelangelo, near the station for St Peter's and thus only a step or two from the Vatican.

The Michelangelo is, of course, a modern hotel of the first order which can stand comparison with many of those in the fashionable quarter and can ensure that each bishop has at least a room with bath, telephone, and air-conditioning as well as an altar. The management has laid on – at an additional cost of 30,000 lire per guest – a stock of altars with tubular black steel legs specially made to fit in with the style of the rooms (teak and washable plastic chintz). Spellman suppressed only one detail: that the local orchestra will continue to play in the hotel in the evenings. But even if he had mentioned that fact, the hotel's vicinity to the Vatican would have set at rest any anxiety about its suitability.

Rome, Friday, 28 September

Among the post that piled up during my absence, I find a copy of *Adesso* of 15 September. Recently I have only occasionally read Don Mazzolari's fortnightly and with no particular enthusiasm. Even before its founder died, in the spring of 1959, it had become a good deal more colourless; since then it has merely shown a rather pathetic will to survive. (Probably the thousands of subscribers who have remained faithful to it don't think so. But some loyalties are always stronger than the pretexts advanced in their support.)

At Recoaro, Walter Peruzzi talked to me quite a lot about it. According to him, 'disciplinary difficulties' had recently become so acute as to force the editors to take a definite decision. 'But just before the Council,' I said in genuine surprise, 'in the midst of this climate of debate between laymen and the hierarchy?' He shrugged his shoulders.

Had it not been for my recollection of that conversation I might not have looked at this copy. But there I find on the first page in heavy type just beside the editorial the announcement, '*Adesso* chooses silence.' The notice reads as follows:

'With this issue we suspend publication of our review. The difficulties that *Adesso* has experienced in the past 14 years are well known. The fact that they have recurred grieves rather than surprises us. We do not, however, wish to raise any sort of scandal, and we prefer to keep silent rather than produce an *Adesso* which does not correspond to our convictions. Perhaps a different sort of layman is preferred in Italy, either more amenable or more pronouncedly in opposition? Certainly a critical discussion of problems is not much sought after or even, in many cases, expected. – Among so many different voices our own silence will be noticed by few, but we hope that what we have written during these years will not be entirely useless. For ourselves it has stood for the affirmation of some Christian values and of a liberty to which we shall remain faithful.'

This is both laconic and dignified, but I wonder whether silence will not swell suspicions and provoke more serious reactions than might have been caused by a moderate and dispassionate account of what really happened. For the present, at any rate, it seems that we must content ourselves with the accusatory moral contained in the editorial, significantly entitled 'The Middle Way in Thought and Opinion'. The article, after summarizing the disputes in the Catholic daily press which since the beginning of the year has been divided about the Centre-Left Government, makes an appeal for the defence of democracy and recognition of a 'healthy secularization of the State' advocated in his day by Pius XII, and concludes as follows:

'This healthy secularization of the State can exist only if the political relationship is carried on in reciprocal tolerance, both internal and external. And it is one of the laws of tolerance, and hence of co-existence, that the "middle way" in thought and opinion should be recognized not only in theory but also in practice. Instead, it has often happened that an atmosphere of fear and intimidation has been created such as to reduce the "middle way" to the point where it receives only theoretical recognition. It is perhaps logical and necessary that the "middle way" in thought should have to be fought for, and be achieved only with difficulty, and this is true in relation to any power that tends to exceed its place and become absolute, seeking to exact obedience even when it has no right to it.

'The individual aspects of the question are clear: that this conquest of the "middle way" in thought carries with it difficulties and misunderstandings; that it shows up where divergences lie (generally, as to the idea of power); that it demands constant and courageous re-thinking lest the claim and right to free opinion may lead to a use of it in practice which falls below the necessary moral and intellectual standard. The famous pastoral letter of the Italian episcopate on secularism was, in our view, right when it affirmed that there is a secular vice in Italian society but a vice of exaggerated authoritarianism too. Both vices have the same psychological root which leads to regarding tolerance as a weakness. We hark back to certainties – which may be the Goddess of Reason or the Faith – in order *not* to have to encounter a discussion or an awkward situation. With the result that the favoured ones are the amenable, not the argumentative.'

All this is well and vigorously said, but will the implications of the formula 'not the argumentative but the amenable' be furthered by choosing silence? Moreover, the suspicion is bound to arise that to agree to disappear is to choose the easy way and avoid being forced to do so. The defunct periodical bore as its motto the words of Christ: 'But now, let him who has no sword sell his cloak and buy one.' Did the editors remember this?

It is superfluous to add that the end of *Adesso* is the more surprising and distressing because it took place in Milan, under pressure from Cardinal Montini. Thus the enigma of this man, who at one time, and not for negligible reasons, was considered an exponent of progressive Catholicism and became the notorious victim of his own daring, recurs yet again, and in a perhaps more disturbing way than ever before. What, in fact can be the meaning of an act of force which has induced *Adesso* to silence itself on the very eve of the Council? Can it be that Montini wanted before leaving for Rome to get rid of a paper in his own diocese that was critical of him, if only indirectly, or was he afraid of what it might do in his absence?

Only last August, Antimori assured me on unimpeachable authority that the Archbishop of Milan's recent journey to Africa was undertaken with the consent of John XXIII and against the view of the Propaganda Fide, which had rejected the proposals of various African episcopates for a pre-Council meeting in their country, or even in Rome, on the eve of Vatican II. Thus Montini must have decided on a pre-Council journey to orientate the African bishops and missionaries and their people with regard to the coming great event in Rome.

Now, how are we to reconcile this progressiveness outside his see with the conformity displayed at home? It would be naïve to retort that Montini did not ruin his chances of becoming Pope by his journey to Africa whereas he might ruin them if he allowed a periodical like *Adesso* to survive in his diocese. If his present programme is to conserve himself for his future supreme destiny, why the mission to Africa? This, incidentally, was not a sudden recent idea but had its forerunner some time ago when he sent his auxiliary, Monsignor Pignedoli, as apostolic delegate to Lagos. And if not, why the surrender over *Adesso*?

In the last few days I have been writing an article for *Il Mondo* about this Hamlet-like figure of the Sacred College. An objective study of Montini's whole career, including his eight-year-long exile in Milan, has led me to a disappointing if not unexpected conclusion: namely, that the constant struggle between the opposite sides of his character has prevented his realising his full potentialities as he would have wished. An important factor in this duality undoubtedly lies in his bourgeois origins – his father was a successful banker who also achieved a political career as one of the few early Catholic members of Parliament, as well as being interested in cultural matters and something of a journalist – and his education, which included such different experiences as the

Jesuit *liceo* and the much freer atmosphere of the San Filippo Neri college. But another probable reason is his ideal of asceticism, sincerely believed in by him though hardly borne out by his own philosophical and theological ideas, which under an appearance of sacrifice and renunciation has had the effect of furthering his career. (Though I have studied and thought about him for years I would not classify him among the 'atheistic cardinals', of whom even today there may be some in the Sacred College.)

Montini was assistant of the FUCI (the Italian Catholic Students' Federation), first in Rome and then in the whole country, at two critical periods, in 1924 and 1931, when as a consequence of Ratti's policy of neutrality it had to give in unwillingly and under protest to Fascism: on both occasions Montini dissociated himself from the students, and the Pope, who is said never to have forgiven him for this lapse, made him pay for it.

And what of the disappointment in Milan, and indeed throughout Italy, where such high hopes were entertained of the self-styled 'Archbishop of the Workers'? Only a year after his appointment, and while he was still awaiting the Cardinal's hat, that description was completed by everyone with 'and Cardinal of the Industrialists'. His restless journeys all over the place by car, his ubiquitous presence at insignificant inauguration ceremonies, were unimportant details; but far from unimportant were his ambiguous attitude in relation to the Catholic trade union and political organizations which supported the 'Opening to the Left'[1], the documents sent to the clergy, supposed to be secret but regularly revealed, and the continual reticences in his speeches and writings. During Pius XII's lifetime such strange behaviour could be explained by the caution necessary for a man in disgrace, but when Roncalli became Pope and Montini immediately received advancement there was no change, even down to his tergiversations in regard to the Centre-Left Government at the beginning of 1962. The coldness of the Milanese, so unlike their normal character, was the fruit of their instinctive mistrust of all this.

Deep human relationships cannot be established without clarity of speech, a frank regard, and a genuine warmth of handshake. People cannot be governed, even the faithful (believers, not subjects), merely by solemn official gestures and rites. Above all, a

[1] i.e. collaboration between the Government and the Nenni Socialists.

man cannot be their guide who speaks to them in enigmas and treats them with diplomatic caution.

But supposing the diocese of Milan were one day to expand to the whole world and Montini were to be announced from the balcony of Piazza San Pietro as the new Pope? Perhaps then his Hamlet complex might dissolve, putting an end to the conflict between liberty and authority, between discipline and autonomy, which has torn him till now. Perhaps then the one-time pro-Secretary of State from Brescia would succeed at last in being himself. But what if yet other complexes were to emerge, and his acquired second nature were to continue to suffocate and hold prisoner his original character?

I see I am wandering: in Rome in a fortnight Montini is awaited not by the Conclave but the Council, and the end of *Adesso* is not a gesture of decision and courage on his part but of resignation and capitulation. Or shall I be proved wrong?

Rome, Saturday, 29 September

This evening's *Osservatore Romano* gives the list of the 'experts' to the Council nominated by the Pope. There are 201 of them, experts in theology, law, sociology, missionary work, Latin, Church history, etc., and they have the right to participate in the General Congregations[1]. But according to the regulations they cannot speak unless invited to do so. In addition, they are to collaborate in drawing up texts and reports if the various chairmen of the individual Commissions of the Council so desire.

Once again the Italians preponderate (75 out of 201) but, whether among Italians or others, the proportion from the Curia is much higher: they number 105 in all.

The members of the secular clergy are only slightly more numerous than those from religious orders – 105 as against 93. Those from the religious orders come from 29 different Orders or Congregations: 24 Jesuits, 17 Dominicans, 10 Franciscans, 6 Benedictines, 4 Conventuals, 3 each from the Order of Clare and the Oblate Missionaries of the Immaculate, two each from the discalsed Carmelites, the Redemptorists, and the Salesians, while eighteen other religious orders have one representative each.

[1] i.e. Plenary Sessions.

Only a fifth of the experts – 39 to be precise, 27 of them Italians – are newly appointed, and among them the Curialists, numbering 26, are strikingly predominant. This is another reason for regarding the new appointments as insignificant. There are some exceptions, however. Three of them – Monsignor Arthur Schwarz-Eggenhofer, Monsignor Pal Brezonoczy, and the Premonstratensian Fr Sandor Klempa – are apostolic administrators of three Hungarian dioceses, those of Esztergom (Cardinal Mindszenty's diocese), Eger, and Weszprém. This means that the Holy See has been counting on their arrival at the Council for quite some time (possibly since the beginning of August, as Monsignor Martinez told me on the 20th of that month). The same is true of Canon Josef Stankevicius, administrator of the diocese of Kaunas in Lithuania.

But I think the importance of these arrivals will escape the press. On the other hand the belated but triumphant appearance of Père Jean Daniélou, at the firm insistence of the French episcopate, should arouse a certain interest. In Italy the name of this French Jesuit, Dean of the faculty of theology and professor of Christian origins and patristic theology at the Catholic Institute in Paris, is known because of La Pira, who often brought him to the fore in Florence. This does not, of course, mean that much is known here about his thought or writings, only a few of which, including the more popular articles, have been translated into Italian. But the general public is bound to have thought that a Jesuit hand-in-glove with La Pira cannot but be an *avant-garde* Jesuit of the left, in short a Jesuit *sui generis* whom Rome can handle only with caution. Which, in a certain sense, is undoubtedly true. A fact unknown to most people here, however, is that after World War II Père Daniélou relaunched the 'new theology' with an article in *Études* (the French Jesuits' review, comparable in importance, though not in trend, to the Roman *Civiltà Cattolica*) which roused a hornets' nest first in his own country, then in the Roman universities, and finally in the Vatican, the consequences of which matured only in 1950, with Pius XII's encyclical *Humani Generis*.

The fact that Père Daniélou was not accepted by Cardinal Ottaviani on the theological Preparatory Commission therefore surprised no one. Ottaviani had already swallowed some other bitter pills (to mention only two, the appointments of Père Congar and

Père De Lubac): more could not be expected. This time he would not have withdrawn his resignation, and John XXIII above all needed peace if he was to realize fruitful labours. Caught between the hammer of the Secretary of the Inquisition and the anvil of the French cardinals, Papa Roncalli evolved a reasonable compromise: he agreed to Père Daniélou's exclusion during the preparatory period but insisted on his acceptance for the period of the Council proper.

After the list of 200 experts the *Osservatore Romano* also publishes the following official announcement: 'His Holiness has graciously deigned to appoint as Custodians of the Second Vatican Ecumenical Council Don Aspreno Colonna, Prince Assistant at the Pontifical Throne, and Don Alessandro Torlonia, on whom he has also conferred the title of Prince Assistant at the Pontifical Throne *ad personam* and for the duration of the Ecumenical Council.'

This office of Custodian is one that nobody had thought of apart from scholars of pontifical diplomacy and heraldry and the few interested members of the black aristocracy. The *Annuario Pontificio* makes no mention of it, a fact to be explained by its rare occurrence. Indeed the *Annuario,* whether intentionally or not, does not even suggest the existence of a Custodian of the Conclave; though since the time of Pius XI it has firmly insisted on recording among the members of the Pontifical Chapel the 'Custodian of the Sacred Triple Crown', an office which has since then regularly remained vacant.

However, Pius IX established the office of Custodian of the Council at the time of Vatican I. It is therefore strange that no mention of it appears in the 103 volumes of the *Dizionario di erudizione storicoecclesiastica,* where 26 different kinds of Custodian are listed for the Pontifical Court and for Roman duties alone (excluding, therefore, those relating to the Papal States). The author of this work was Gustavo Moroni, formerly barber to the future Gregory XVI (1831-1846) and later first chamberlain to him and to Pius IX, a most zealous man, self-taught, who owed his initiation into learned research to the job of transcribing the entire catalogue of the documents of the Propaganda Fide, as well as managing thanks to his razor to enter the Conclave on two occasions. He must have forgotten to mention the office in the monumental, prolix but extremely valuable Dictionary to which he devoted half a century.

But if no one thought about the office of Custodian presumably no one felt the need of it. Hence yet another reason for surprise that Papa Roncalli decided to revive it. But John XXIII, despite his smiling diatribes against etiquette and ceremonial, the use of the gestatorial chair and the processional fans, the ceremonial escorts and the Swiss Guards' halberds, has left everything of that sort unchanged (influenced, possibly, by the natural feelings of a man of humble origins who has reached the very highest office). Moreover, one must not forget his hobby for what might be termed the archaeology of history, for minute and remote erudition, the cult, in a word, for old things sanctified by tradition which Monsignor Giuseppe de Luca, overcoming the colder instincts of scientific research, has promoted to the honour of a historian's vocation on the part of his august protector.

The whole Pontificate of John XXIII, from his first speech in the Consistory on the Cardinal's biretta down to this appointment, is punctuated by these touching escapes into the world of sacred antiquity, and certainly no one would reproach him for it. Between the minatory and Savonarola-like type of priest who would hurl all vain things on to a pyre and this simple, kindly Pope who stands in childlike wonder before the curiosities of the past, the choice is instinctive and immediate. But the appointment of two Custodians of the Council, which is really just a verbal title and an honorific extension of the office of Assistant at the Throne, shows something else as well – the courage of John XXIII in stirring up the turbid waters of certain scandals.

It must, in fact, be confessed that the public first became aware of the office of 'Prince Assistant at the Throne' through the notorious affair of Filippo Orsini. It happened in 1958 in the last year of the Pontificate of Pius XII, a year so unfortunately if also providentially full of Vatican scandals. On 9 January 1958 Filippo Orsini, Prince of Solofra and Duke of Gravina, ascended the papal throne in his ceremonial dress (a Spanish costume of black velvet with white lace collar and sword) for the last time. He had done this for thirteen years, ever since that honour was handed down to him by his grandfather Don Domenico; and that was not on account of the death of his father, Don Virgilio, but because his father had renounced the title after his divorce from his first wife, an Italian, and his remarriage to an American.

In 1946 Filippo was about twenty-six and had just married or was about to marry the Ferrarese Countess Franca Bonaccossi. This fact, in combination with the opportunities of the post-war years, caused his friends to entertain high hopes of him. Those who knew him best had no doubts as to where his secret ambition lay: he aspired to bring back the Orsinis to the great palace beside the ruins of the Teatro Marcello, near Palazzo Venezia, where his ancestors had dwelt for centuries.

In their view it would not have taken him long to succeed. Energetic and full of initiative, he seemed to regard his noble title as an additional incentive to action. In 1948, for example, he started a press agency in support of the Christian Democrat electoral campaign. His party's political success assured him the gratitude of government circles, while his reputation for seriousness and hard work opened up promising prospects in business.

But as the times degenerated and irregularities and excesses multiplied both without and within the Vatican walls, the energetic Prince's virtues began to be undermined. Inherited tendencies could not be indefinitely suppressed. Filippo was not a slavish imitator of his father but, substantially conformist as he was, he accepted the fashion of the day. His cousin Raimondo had had some sort of an affair with Linda Christian. Filippo too began to pay court to a cinema actress, Maria Felix. That, at least, was the first episode of its kind that the popular journals attributed to him.

The subsequent affair with Belinda Lee at first aroused less comment. It was Belinda herself with her uninhibited English ingenuousness that occupied the attention of the gossip-columnists. She had come to Italy to make the film *La Venere di Cheronea* and within a few weeks became friendly first with Massimo Girotti and then with Jacques Sernas and Orsini, who, however, seemed likely to make only a temporary appearance among her admirers. In any case, Belinda left for South Africa where the caste for *Nor the Moon by Night* was awaiting her. The Prince showed no signs of being disturbed by this separation: he was soon found regularly visiting the Pipistrella in the company of an Egyptian girl, Signora Irene Guinle.

But suddenly Belinda flew back to Rome, took refuge in a friend's flat, and tried unsuccessfully to get into touch with the Prince. When at last she did so she probably got a dusty answer, for the next thing was her anything but symbolic attempt at suicide – she had to be put in an iron lung for several hours and only after two days could be transferred from hospital to the 'Castello della Quiete' nursing home. But no sooner was the drama of Belinda over than the drama of Orsini broke out. The Red Cross got a telephone call saying that a man at 52 Via Panama had cut his wrists with a razor-blade. The man was Prince Filippo; but when the ambulance men came to fetch him, he already had both his doctor and his lawyer with him.

Why had he done it? Given the whole background, it seemed unlikely that he had tried to commit suicide for love of Belinda: for if so, as the press pointed out, why now and not earlier? Was it nearer the mark to suggest, as one of the evening papers did, that 'the fear of scandal following Belinda Lee's attempted suicide, rather than his own desperate and impossible love for her, prompted the Prince to try to end his days'? Or, more bluntly still, 'what seemed like a sad and romantic affair after the fashion of Carolina Invernizio is instead just the drama of a man who lacks the courage to take the moral responsibility for the consequences of his flirtation' – consequences, the paper hastened to add, connected not so much with his family as with the circles of the 'black' aristocracy and the Vatican, which would inevitably ostracize him.

Subsequent events were to prove such judgments too facile. Nearer to the truth probably is that Filippo Orsini acted as he did both to prove his love for Belinda and to overcome once and for all the fear of the consequences of his act. His obviously calculated attempt at suicide was in fact meant to be, on the one hand, the answer to the woman who had risked death for him and, on the other, a public demonstration of his decision not to let any other considerations come between them. After that the two had no more doubts or hesitations, and the papers were able to report to their heart's content their various indiscretions.

The same papers naturally did not fail to give considerable publicity to Vatican reactions to this latest scandal. Publicly acknowledged to be guilty of two of the worst sins, adultery and attempted suicide, Filippo Orsini – so the usual unnamed informers in the Pontifical Court averred – had by his own act forfeited his right to the high office that set him beside the Pope at the most solemn moments of his duties as Vicar of God on earth, and the *Annuario Pontificio* would certainly cease to harbour his name. But it was also quickly realized that fear of adding to the scandal would prevent any official pronouncement being issued. In fact, neither then nor after did the Vatican make any declaration on the subject.

Nor did the black aristocracy. Its displeasure was shown only in its behaviour towards the culprit: it just ignored him. (Much the same thing, R. told me yesterday, happened about Sofia Loren and Carlo Ponti. The 'Società romana per la caccia alla volpe' (Rome Foxhunting Association), a club notoriously confined to the nobility, recently refused to invite them to some affair at which Don Aspreno Colonna, Assistant at the Throne, was expected to be present as the encounter would have been embarrassing for him.)

Orsini and Belinda, for their part, did their best to ignore the prophylactic isolation imposed on them and took themselves off to the Riviera. But the matter did not end there. Last July, an urgent petition came up before the Rome Tribunal for a declaration of bankruptcy in relation to the SIAC (Italian Building and Contracting Company), of which Orsini was chairman. According to reports, this petition was a result of the unexpected suspension of credits to the Company guaranteed by the state-controlled housing organization, Italcase. The SIAC found itself in deep waters and went into liquidation. Orsini also lost his chairmanships of Arpa-Cit and the Industrial Insurance Company. 'I challenged society and I've been made to pay for it,' he confessed lately to a journalist. He has indeed: in addition to his financial losses and his removal from the Vatican he is ostracized by the aristocracy, legally separated from his wife, and has lost his inherited birthright.

Now Filippo Orsini lives in a flat off Corso Francia (where among the photographs on his desk Mussolini's picture looms large) and is writing his memoirs 'in order to live'. Not surprisingly, they are destined for a non-Italian publisher, and it seems they will include some outspoken comments on Alessandro Torlonia, whom John XXIII has put in Orsini's place at the Vatican. He had tried to form a film company to make a film about the Italian Navy but was prevented from doing so: so, since he can't do anything else, he has decided to become a writer, and doubtless these first memoirs will be followed by others. But the thing he cares about most, and has cared about for the last ten years, is to preserve the title of Assistant at the Throne for his son Domenico when he comes of age. Hostile to him in everything else, his wife and he are at one in this.

Rome, Sunday, 30 September

I have in front of me two plans: one of the United Nations building, reproduced from the *New York Times* of about a year ago, and the other of the Council Hall for Vatican II, included in the plan of St Peter's published by the *Osservatore Romano* of 28 June. These are the seats of the two most unusual and individual parliaments in the world, the second of which has met on an average only once in a century. Its history therefore goes back nearly two thousand years, whereas the Parliament of the United Nations has had less than two decades of existence in the UN, or less than fifty years if we include its predecessor, the League of Nations.

Observing the two plans in detail, in addition to the difference in the aims and functions of the two assemblies (the religious character of the second, for example, is evident from the arrangements made for kneeling) two other main differences strike the eye: the method of seating, according to nationality in the first, and the presence of the throne beyond the chairman's table in the second. The UN parliamentarians are divided into delegations, one for each State Member, sitting side by side with the other delegations but each of them distinct from the others. The union and the political separation of the world could hardly be more visibly expressed. In the assembly of the Roman Church, on the other hand, the geographical and ethnical backgrounds of the individual members are as if obliterated; Fathers from the most distant continents and of the most widely differing speech and colour are all mixed up together, lined up side by side in their stalls as far as the eye can see.

Distinction of rank, which at the United Nations are indicated within the individual delegations (Heads of State, Prime Ministers, Ministers, delegate representatives, ambassadors, etc.), are shown in the Council Hall by the grouping of seats. The Cardinals, for instance, have combined book-rests and kneeling-stools, covered in red material, and arm-chairs; the same for the patriarchs, but with ordinary stalls covered in green, instead of arm-chairs; and the arrangements for the archbishops and bishops are similar but in a less exalted position. Cardinals, patriarchs, archbishops, and bishops all occupy numbered seats in their respective sections according to their seniority of appointment. The numbers are practically invisible. In the hall of Vatican I, however, they were so big that, as a chronicler of the time put it, the Fathers ended by looking like a crowd of numbers.

The chairman's table in the UN Assembly Hall, where the Secretary General, the Chairman, and the Deputy Secretary sit side by side, demonstrates at once the democratic character of that assembly. In the Hall in St Peter's, on the other hand, the presence of the throne behind and above the chairman's table, dominating it from a height of fourteen steps (eleven for the pedestal, three for the throne itself), indicates that the assembly is sovereign but subordinate to the approval of the monarch. True, the pedestal together with the throne is mounted on wheels and can be moved away when necessary, but that arises from the fact that the throne has the confessional altar behind it. The pontifical throne is therefore moved whenever a solemn occasion demands the use of the papal altar, and in that case the normal throne is used, situated in the apsidal nave of the Church.

The seating capacity of the two halls, leaving aside tribunes for the press and public, differs considerably. The UN Hall can house at most 1,090, whereas the Council Hall has, in addition to 85 Cardinals' stalls and six for Patriarchs, 2,265 seats on stands for the archbishops and bishops. From the point of view of representation, however, the situation is reversed. The UN delegations represent 99 countries (at the date in question Sierra Leone had not yet become a member) with a total of 2,152 million inhabitants, distributed over 48,765,396 square miles. Whereas the Fathers of the Council, besides coming from fewer countries, represent only about a quarter of the number represented at the United Nations.

Leaving aside these comparisons between the two halls and concentrating solely on the plan of the Council Hall, one is at once struck by the organizers' insistent care in distinguishing, and even separating, the Fathers from each other according to the criteria of rank established by the notoriously punctilious protocol of the Roman Church's legal and caste system. This is shown, in particular, by the excessive importance given to the position of the Cardinals as compared with the Patriarchs.

The title and office of Cardinal are not only exclusively Western and Roman in origin but also of relatively late date. Before the twelfth century, indeed, the title of Cardinal was given to the deacons of the city of Rome who exercised administrative and supervisory functions in its various districts comparable to those of the present-day 'vicari foranei' and who, while constituting the 'presbytery' or senate of the Bishop of Rome, had no powers to operate outside the city. The first embryo of a Curia emerged only in that century; and it was only from then onwards that the rôle of the cardinals became gradually more complex and influential, partly as a result of the fact that the election of the Pope eventually became confined to the members of their College.

Of a very different order were the prestige and historical importance attaching to the Patriarchs in the East from the end of the fifth century onwards – a prestige similar, in a certain sense, to that enjoyed by the Pope in the West, but in more propitious circumstances and substantiated by a more direct exercise of power. The Pope was, in fact, the equivalent of a Western patriarch with the additional point in his favour that whereas in the East the first patriarchs (of Antioch and Alexandria) were soon joined by others (of Constantinople and Jerusalem), to be followed eventually by the 'Catholicates' or quasi-patriarchates, in the West there were no political or religious seats to compete with Rome, and the Bishop of Rome therefore remained the sole patriarch or primate of the West. (Hence the development of the idea of 'primacy', which was also furthered by the universal supremacy of the distinction enjoyed by Rome as an episcopal see founded, according to tradition, by Peter and Paul, 'the chief among the apostles'.)

Yet another great difference exists between Cardinals and Patriarchs. The dignity of the Patriarch's office has always been linked with its episcopal character and with the government of a historic see pre-eminent beyond other suffragan sees and indeed having jurisdiction over whole ecclesiastical provinces. The title and functions of a Cardinal, on the other hand, were associated exclusively with Court offices, and did not therefore involve sacramental power; still less, especially in the early stages, were they linked with the episcopate – indeed up to a few decades ago some Cardinals had only the tonsure and the right to fulfil the duties of the minor orders.[1]

The anomaly arising from the establishment of the new Roman institution soon became apparent. For not only did it lead to the creation of two quite different hierarchies, the one of sacramental order, based on the Sacrament and established by Christ, and the other of purely canonical jurisdiction and hence of exclusively human origin; but also the first hierarchy, that of 'order', ended by being overpowered by the second, with the result that a Cardinal who had only just received the tonsure and entered the ranks of the clergy could enjoy greater rights than all the bishops and priests in the world, even including the ancient 'Popes' of the East. Historical circumstances favoured the caste of the cardinalate, for eventually all the Patriarchs of the Eastern Church separated from Rome, and it was only much later that their 'doubles' the Uniate Patriarchs came on the scene, deriving from the schismatic minorities which reverted to the Catholic Church. Thus the Cardinalate was able to gain the upper hand which it still retains today.

It is true that the Catholic Patriarchs of the East, the Uniates, have jurisdictional powers of an indisputably exceptional character when compared with those of metropolitans or primates in the Western Catholic Church. According to the new code of Eastern canon law (Can. 216-314) they have powers of ordinary and personal jurisdiction over metropolitans, bishops, clergy, and the faithful of their own rite. With the approval of their Synod (another original institution which has no counterpart in the West) they can establish ecclesiastical provinces or dioceses and can unite, circumscribe, divide, dismember, or suppress them without requiring confirmation from the Holy See. They can also elect bishops according to a particular procedure, confirmation from

[1] The tonsure is a sign of consecration to ecclesiastical life and signifies a candidate's official introduction into the ranks of the clergy without yet involving his participation in the sacrament of the order of priesthood. The latter takes place in seven stages, the first four being the minor orders, and the last three the major (sub-deacon, deacon, priest).

the Pope being merely nominal; and they have the right to transfer metropolitan bishops, whether residential or titular, to accept their resignation, and to appoint auxiliaries.

But although these powers give the Eastern Patriarchs a much stronger position than any Western archbishops or metropolitan bishops enjoy, they do nothing to modify their status vis-à-vis the Cardinalate. Since 5 April 1962, as a result of the *motu proprio Cum gravissima,* all Cardinals who are not yet bishops at the time of their appointment must at once receive episcopal consecration. This disposition complicates things even more, however, because its result is to consolidate still further the College of Cardinals, whereas both the Eastern separatists and the Uniates hope for its suppression. One of the conditions laid down by the Orthodox Church for its eventual reconciliation with the Church of Rome is recognition of the Patriarchs as being at the highest level in the hierarchy, and the Bishop of Rome should be only *primus inter pares* in relation to them. The Uniates, of course, are more inclined to preserve the primacy of the Pope, but they too favour precedence of the Patriarchs over the Cardinals.

A reconciliation between these two opposing theses of the primacy of the Cardinals or the Patriarchs might, and probably will, come about through an equalization of the two institutions and a combination of the two titles. If, as seems likely, the Council is to tackle the reform of the Church's structure in a radical way, this problem, associated as it is with the whole question of unity, cannot be evaded.

For the time being one can only register the fact (as I did some days ago) that the Rules of Procedure of the Council avoid reference to innovations and stick closely to the existing situation. This is further confirmed by a significant detail in the organization of the Council Hall, namely that the Cardinals have been given a special entrance and exit, while the Patriarchs, archbishops, and bishops all use the same ones. The only sign of any sensitiveness about this matter, which is not just a question of precedence under protocol, has been shown by those in charge of organization for the opening ceremony: for it appears that on the morning of 11 October the Patriarchs are to enter St Peter's immediately after the Pope, thus preceding the Cardinals. But, all the same, when they leave it is the other way round and the Cardinals go out before the Patriarchs.

Rome, Monday, 1 October

My usual monthly meeting with Monsignor Bontempi. (Monsignor Alfredo Bontempi, titular bishop of Palmyra, who died in February 1963, was Rector of the Pontifical College of St Nepomuk, which houses ecclesiastics from Czechoslovakia while they are studying in Rome.) This evening we met outside Santa Maria Maggiore. He confirmed that a delegation of bishops is expected from Czechoslovakia but, perhaps to prevent my questioning him further about this matter, which concerns him closely, he quickly moved off to another topic. His other and much more intriguing piece of information was that the Pontifical Secretariat has up its sleeve two encyclicals, both in an advanced state of preparation, one on international order and the other commemorating the eleventh centenary of ss Cyril and Methodius.

According to Bontempi, the more important of the two is the first, so much so, indeed, as to bear comparison with the Council itself as far as the future of John XXIII's Pontificate is concerned. Papa Roncalli has always, in fact, had two main aims: to break the ice with Christians of the other confessions, thus opening up the way to religious co-existence of all the faiths; and to establish a bridge between the West and the East on a basis of a co-existence which would eliminate for ever the slow suicide of the cold war and the danger of a fresh world conflict. In the first case, he had no doubts that after some initial difficulties Catholicism would end by imposing itself on the other Christian confessions; in the second, besides securing a political détente in the world, he was certain that he would be able to ensure the revival of the Churches of Silence in the East and to open up the whole Communist world to religious propaganda.

But, contrary to his expectations, the major obstacles came from certain trends within the Catholic world, and especially from the Roman Curia. The Pacelli group, in particular, fought every inch of the way for three years; among other things they tried to alter the original objective of the Council, that of church union, and having succeeded in that they tried to get the whole organization of Vatican II into their own hands. The same circles showed even stronger opposition, if that were possible, to John XXIII's attempts to make a gradual change in his predecessor's policy with regard to the Communist world. From the boycott of the plan prepared with Cardinal Wyszynski in the first months of his Pontificate down to the resistance still being offered today, they did everything to prevent him from realizing his plan for détente.

Papa Roncalli's original idea was to announce the new trend which he planned to impart to Church policy by means of a document on the proposed programme for a new departure in relations between civil and religious society within an international framework. But such a document might well have taken by surprise not only the simple-minded but also many thoughtful people who had grown up in an atmosphere sometimes verging on that of a fanatical anti-Communist crusade. Therefore in order to avoid spreading confusion among large sections of Catholic public opinion he decided first to issue another document of a social character dealing with the most burning present-day problems, thus demonstrating how the Church could without prejudice itself adopt the most daring solutions advanced for them by the lay world and even by the Communists. In this way, according to Bontempi, the encyclical *Mater et Magistra* was born, as an essentially interim measure.

The success of that encyclical throughout the world convinced John XXIII that a great step forward had been achieved towards carrying out his plans. It also confirmed him in the belief that he had gathered round him a first-class staff of collaborators who would be invaluable in helping to draft the decisive document. These were Monsignor Pietro Pavan, lecturer in social economy at the Pontifical University of the Lateran; Monsignor Agostino Ferrari Toniolo, professor of comparative labour law in the same university; Monsignor Sante Quadri, central assistant at the ACLI (the Catholic Workers' Organization); and his own confessor, Monsignor Luigi Civardi, one of the most senior assistants-general of Catholic Action.

Pavan and Ferrari Toniolo had already been appointed by him as members of the theological Preparatory Commission for the Council to deal with questions in their special spheres, and all four were members of the Preparatory Commission for Lay Apostolate. Nevertheless towards the end of 1962 Papa Roncalli also entrusted to them the preparation of the second and more significant encyclical, that on international order, which was supposed to be ready before the opening of the Council.

He could then decide himself when it should be published.

The staff got to work and finished in time. But judging from what Bontempi was told at the Secretariat of State, John XXIII became convinced that it would be inadvisable to publish the document on the eve of the Council or while it was in progress, for the attention of the world would then be focused on the Council and this might prevent realization of the encyclical's full significance. Moreover the international situation had altered and it seemed better to postpone it.

Bontempi could tell me nothing about the contents of this 'fundamental' encyclical, as he kept on calling it, but he assured me that the highest Vatican circles regarded it as 'revolutionary' both on the ideological and even more on the practical plane. On the other hand he appeared to know all about the second encyclical, the one concerning SS Cyril and Methodius. 'It was practically born in my house,' he averred. This had come about six or seven months ago, when some of the Czechoslovak priests staying at the St Nepomuk College showed him the text of a memorandum destined for the Holy Father which had originally been drawn up by some of their fellow-priests and co-nationals under the direction of Monsignor Grutka, Bishop of Gary, Indiana, in 1956. The memorandum contained a petition to John XXIII asking that religious celebrations might be promoted in honour of the two great missionary apostles of Moravia and the adjacent Slav regions on the occasion of the eleventh centenary of their mission, especially in view of the fact that the Communist authorities in Prague planned to hold purely civil commemorations of what they described as the 'Byzantine mission' of the two apostles. In short, it was proposed to supplement the celebration of the two saints' cultural and economic work by a celebration of what was more truly their own specific activity, that of evangelization.

Bontempi could only agree with his priests and he supported their initiative when the petition set out on its way through the Secretariat of State. An encyclical of this kind presented no particular difficulties of drafting. He soon heard that the Pope gladly agreed to the proposal and had given orders for the most suitable form of presentation to be worked out. The document is believed to be practically ready now, but it seems that John XXIII is waiting for some 'special event' to promulgate it.

Rome, Tuesday, 2 October

In the early afternoon the special editions of the newspapers announced that on 4 October, the liturgical festival of St Francis of Assisi, the Pope is going first to Loreto and then on to Assisi itself.

All the press, radio, and television world is now seething with rumours. The news had been allowed to leak out in order to permit the necessary arrangements to be made with the least possible chaos. But chaos, or at least the feeling of it, there already is and it will get worse.

So John XXIII has reserved his great gesture for the last few days before the Council opens. A wizard of publicity and stage-management could not have done better. The *Osservatore Romano*'s devotional communiqué speaks piously of a 'pilgrimage', of 'fervid invocation of celestial aid' etc. But for that there was obviously no need for the Pope to go by train across the entire peninsula from the Tyrrhenian to the Adriatic.

Tomorrow the Council will win its most clamorous plebiscite.

Rome, Thursday, 4 October

As I write – it is about 9 am – the special train reserved for the Italian President, placed for the occasion at the service of Pope John XXIII, has already left Rome some hours ago. I listened to the broadcast account of the departure from the Vatican station, the first stop in Italian territory at Trastevere, a few minutes away, and the stops at Orte, Terni, and Spoleto in the early stages of the journey. From the reports coming in from press agencies at various points along the route and from places in Umbria and the Marche it is already obvious that Papa Giovanni's great publicity discovery has had a huge success.

In the last few days those in control of Vatican protocol have been hard put to it to keep abreast of the amount of work that overwhelms them. On 1 October the new Ambassador from Nicaragua presented his credentials, on the 2nd the Japanese Foreign Minister paid a private visit to the Pope, and yesterday it was the turn of the new Spanish Ambassador. And now, as a sort of curtain-raiser for the Council, we have this journey to Loreto and Assisi – the first real journey outside Rome to be undertaken by a Pope since Pius IX's in 1857, but with very different aims.

The press, absorbed in this exceptional event, has relegated everything else to the background, including an audience which had particularly significant connections with the coming Council. The audience given to Cardinal Lercaro on 1 October was not, in fact, one of the customary concessions made by the Pope to the Archbishop of Bologna. The Cardinal was not alone as he waited in the pontifical antechamber, and when Monsignor Capovilla came to fetch him Lercaro was followed by a tall thin priest with dark hair barely tinged with grey and cut *en brosse*. Behind him was a little group of priests and laymen. Some minutes later a radiant John XXIII in his private library was holding in his hands a volume bound in white damask silk while he listened with evident enthusiasm to what the tall thin priest was saying to him.

The volume that the Pope admired was called *Conciliorum Oecumenicorum Decreta* and in 792 pages it assembled for the first time in history all the decisions of the Councils, from the Council of Nicaea to Vatican I. The priests and laymen admitted to John XXIII's presence were the collaborators in this work, which had been undertaken by the Documentation Centre in Bologna and published by Herder of Fribourg-in-Breisgau. The priest presenting it was Don Giuseppe Dossetti.

The work, conceived and planned in 1959, contains all the texts in the original Greek or Latin (in the first case with a Latin translation facing), as well as a parallel text in Armenian or Arabic for the famous decrees of union with the Armenian and Coptic Churches, which go back to the Council of Florence. The importance of the collection is further enhanced by the names of those concerned with its production, from Hubert Jedin to Giuseppe Alberigo, Perikles Joannou, Claudio Leonardi, and Paolo Prodi.

I think again of that meeting I had with Dossetti last month, on 23 September, on the hill of Monteveglio, and I ask myself why it was that he never made the slightest reference to this volume that his Centre was preparing – was it ascetic detachment, or reaction against the spirit of vanity, or what? But above all I reflect on its significance. A book of this kind, worthy of the noblest monastic intellectual tradition, is not only a work of valuable research into the past but has also a modern topicality and betrays its planners' preoccupation with the present. Can Dossetti be returning by the route most natural to him to the contemporary world from which he so publicly detached himself? And if so, will his collaboration with the Council end there, or is this just the beginning?

10 pm

As I take up my pen again, the President of Senegal, Léopold Senghor, is at this moment sending out a pre-Council message from the Palazzo Vecchio in Florence to Africa, Europe, and the whole world. I was reminded of this by happening to come upon the text of the letter which Giorgio La Pira, Mayor of Florence, sent to Heads of State and of Governments throughout the world, mayors of African capitals, and the Fathers of the Council, telling them of Florence's spiritual participation in the Council. With these letters, which were sent out early in September, La Pira enclosed a fine reproduction of the Bull of Union between the Greek Church and the Latin Church, concluded at the Council of Florence in 1439.

This is a strange form of civic participation in the coming Council, and one, I believe, without precedent. But I do not find the text of the message to the Fathers particularly felicitous; indeed it seems to me both verbose and vague. Certainly a good many people will find the whole thing pretty superfluous. But La Pira's gesture in sending a copy of the five-centuries-old Bull of reconciliation, on the other hand, besides showing a kindly courtesy gave symbolical expression to an incontrovertible fact which has hitherto been kept secret: namely, the efforts of La Pira himself and his collaborators, and hence symbolically of Florence, to bring about a rapprochement between the West and the European and Asiatic East above and beyond the present ideological rivalry.

La Pira has been working for this for ten years, ever since he initiated his Congresses for Peace and Christian Civilization in 1952, a year before Stalin's death and thus at the height of the cold-war period. These Congresses did not involve a new departure for La Pira, for what they really did was to transfer to the plane of a high-level debate the discussion of the ideas which for years he and the other 'professorini' had been putting forward in the pages of *Cronache Sociali*. Such discussion could be the freer because the Congresses were to have no direct political implications.

The Vatican was nevertheless well aware that despite the Sicilian-Florentine[1] legend of the 'Saint-Mayor' the Florence Congresses would not be content to remain on a purely academic level. In 1955, the first year of *détente,* a few months after the fourth Congress yet another one was held, this time of mayors from capitals all over the world. Thirty-six of them attended, including the Mayors of Moscow, Warsaw, and other capitals behind the Iron Curtain. Such an event was too eloquent to be ignored or underestimated; but most people just shook their heads or appeared shocked by it.

I myself was more surprised than convinced at the time. Although I believed in La Pira's honesty and sincerity I felt, instinctively rather than rationally, doubts about the mixture of the sacred and the fantastic which had always characterized his manifestations. And I must say that even now, though I appreciate many of his enterprises and in particular that one, I still cannot bring myself to sympathize with the man. Such men as La Pira can be accepted as imaginary personages in a novel but there is something about them that repels one in real life. Their nonconformity is so complete and so personal as to be unpleasant and irritating not only to conformists but also to those semi-nonconformists so frequently to be found among people professing nonconformity. In addition to this he is eminently a Southerner, with that Southern mixture of gifts which are part attractive, part repellent, ranging from genuine inspiration and poetic quality in certain of his intuitions and ideas to something histrionic about the too-frequent smiles and gesticulations. Above all, there is that impenetrable mystery arising from his combination of apparent frankness and highly subtle astuteness.

I have known La Pira for more than twenty years and my attitude towards him has remained practically unchanged. In the early days we were both on the same side, yet I used to avoid even the most spontaneous contacts with him. When I first knew him in Milan in 1936-7, when he was about 32 or 33 and was already a university lecturer, he wore shabby short coats that made him

[1] La Pira is a Sicilian by birth.

even thinner and smiled and gesticulated as he does today with that look midway between delight and surprise that also has a glimpse of subtle irony in the eyes. And even then, when not among his students he was with the poor, and the only way to be sure of finding him was in church. People used to say he prayed so much that he forgot his university lectures.

At that time I was positively besieged by plain-clothes saints. But not all of them stayed in their niches. Raimondo Manzini, for example, who was the most idolized of them all and who never seemed so deeply inspired as when he spoke of virginity, ended by marrying; he was regarded as a man in the clouds unable to touch solid ground with his feet, but he turned out to be a most astute politician. The most consistent of them all was La Pira. But even he eventually went into Parliament and became, I believe, Under-Secretary in the Ministry of Labour after the war – he had opposed Fascism, publishing a review called *Principi* which was suppressed. If he hasn't changed, that is because he was authentic in the first place.

His poverty, for instance, has always been perfectly genuine. Another 'plain-clothes saint' who went into Parliament like La Pira told me that, on his periodical journeys from Rome to his home town, he used to put his good felt hat and overcoat in his suitcase as he neared home and do a quick change into the shabbiest old clothes. La Pira, on the other hand, has always lived as far as possible in conventual surroundings (in Florence he lived for years in a cell at San Marco's like any monk in a monastery) and given away his university or parliamentary salary in charity.

I have always recognized and appreciated all this, but it has never succeeded in altering my attitude towards him.

I was there in Florence at that congress of Mayors in October 1955, and I well remember La Pira in the rooms and on the terraces of the Uffizi at the official reception, trotting along like a ragamuffin between the Mayor of Moscow and the Russian Ambassador, Bogomolov. Between smiles and gesticulations he ventured on scraps of phrases in a French that would have disgraced an emigrant labourer; he seemed like a gnome, a court dwarf jesting to entertain his guests, but at the same time between explanations in the style of Baedeker he interspersed verses from the Bible, quotations from the Fathers or St Thomas, and invocations to the Madonna. He even succeeded in getting the atheist Mayors to attend Mass and arranged for them to meet Cardinal

Dalla Costa. Half-dazed, half-amused, but also rather fascinated, they all took part in the game.

Pius XII, who had not much sense of humour, felt little affection for this utopian and spoil-sport Mayor. Indeed, if La Pira had not had the protection of both the Quirinal and Cardinal Piazza in Florence, he would probably not have stayed long in the Palazzo della Signoria – especially as every so often letters in the style of St Catherine would arrive from him on the Pope's desk, and Papa Pacelli could not bear the thought that messages of the same kind were also going off from Florence to Khrushchev, Eisenhower, De Gaulle, and Franco.

In addition to Pius XII's tacit but resolute hostility, the events of October 1956 in Hungary and Poland had the effect of putting La Pira's plans in quarantine for a year or two. But once Papa Roncalli was elected Pope and a new *détente* began to dawn, La Pira turned up in Moscow. It was on 15 August 1959, and the 'Saint-Mayor' told the journalists who came buzzing round him that he had come 'to set up a bridge of prayer between East and West'. Such a bridge could equally well have been raised from Santa Maria del Fiore or San Giovanni in Florence, but the fact was that he had in mind other bridges as well; and for those he needed to visit not the ancient Orthodox Sanctuaries but Khrushchev and his colleagues. One of those bridges established by La Pira served to bring to Moscow in February 1960 Giovanni Gronchi, President of the Italian Republic and also, to use Dante's periphrasis, 'cittadina di quella Roma onde Cristo è romano' (a citizen of that Rome whence Christ is a Roman).

For various reasons that journey was not a great success, but it marked a historic turning-point: the beginning of new relations between Rome and Moscow, and not so much Capitoline Rome as the Rome of the Vatican. Now, across the bridges built at least in part by La Pira, co-existence between the Church and the Communist world is beginning to move. During the past year, and especially of recent months, the mediation of the Mayor of Florence, whether directly or indirectly, has been decisive.

'Don't fix your eyes too much on Istanbul,' Antimori said to me yesterday. 'It is Moscow that will move first and decide everything. Perhaps,' he added, 'if the world is still capable of amazement, it will soon have something remarkable to be amazed about.' As usual, he refused to be more explicit; it was only after

I had pressed him insistently that he relented a little and added in that emphatic way of his: 'It is a fact that for some time now journeyings between the Vatican and the Kremlin have become much less rare. If I am correctly informed, even a Cardinal went behind the Iron Curtain not long ago, under the guise of a harmless and impeccable scholar, the guest of a Moscow Academy.'

All in all, it is no bad thing if a little saint in plain-clothes plays the jester and poet and forgets his university lectures to recite the Rosary before the tabernacle if his dreams and inspiration lead to such results.

Rome, Friday, 5 October

I have just finished looking at the newspapers. Nearly all of them, secular, Communist, and agnostic included, devote their front pages, and often other pages too, to reports of the Pope's journey given under large headlines. Most of them have an editorial about it: a form of implicit and unasked-for justification which can be regarded as a point in favour of that residue of conscience and dignity which the press has evidently managed to salvage from its long servitude to the 'demands of information'.

Antimori tells me that this morning in the Vatican the aftermath of yesterday's triumph was slightly marred by a communiqué of the Belgian press agency CIP, known to be influenced by that country's episcopate, on the imminent departure of the Belgian bishops for Rome which stated:

'The time when the initiative came from the Pope and the Secretariat of the Council is now past. From now on it is the bishops who take affairs into their hands. This seems to be indicated by the reserve surrounding the Holy Father and his Secretariat now that the great event is imminent. The Pope is extremely discreet and, contrary to what some expected, has established no agenda for the Council. He has confined himself to making known through his collaborators the line he would like to see followed. But the bishops remain free to follow it or not.'

This plain speaking has rejoiced the progressives as much as it has irritated the conservative elements. The fact is that this indirect declaration of the Belgian bishops has been an effective lash of the whip for everybody, and a summons not to let themselves be lulled by the rosy publicity of yesterday.

The Council's Press Office

Rome, Saturday, 6 October

Since mid-day yesterday the Press Office of the Council no longer occupies its modest quarters in Via Serristori. Instead it is installed in two big rooms with a large entrance-hall and half-landing on the first floor of the palazzo at the corner of Via della Conciliazione and Via Rusticucci. The new equipment is on a par with the size of the apartment. There are 60 tables in the larger room with several dozen brand-new typewriters, 10 tele-typers of Radiostampa, two of Italcable, 30 telephones in booths connected with all the international lines (TETI, the central telephone company, has told off ten of its best switchboard operators to man them), and, lastly, a dozen television apparatuses to enable the ceremony to be viewed by those journalists who cannot get into St Peter's because of the limited capacity (400) of the press tribune.

The Cardinal Secretary of State himself, Cardinal Cicognani, came to inaugurate the Office, accompanied by two important officials of the Secretariat of His Holiness, the deputy-secretary Dell' Acqua and the under-secretary Casaroli, by the Secretary-General of the Council, the director of the Press Office itself, Monsignor Fausto Vallainc, and various other prelates and lay personalities of the Vatican. Nothing could show more clearly the anxiety and trepidation felt by the Church in relation to the press and its representatives. Everything would have passed off all right if Cardinal Cicognani had confined himself in his speech to expressing his satisfaction at finding himself among the journalists, referring to the importance of information about religious matters today, and concluding with good wishes for their work. But this was only the preamble of his speech, which went on to illustrate the dignity and responsibility of the journalistic profession and applied this in concrete to the way in which the Council should be followed, inviting those present to serve the truth by their accurate reporting and to 'treat with the greatest respect news which touches so nearly the very life of the Church'.

Seeing who the speaker was, this was an extraordinarily impolitic speech which, coming from anyone else, would have been described as – to say the least – surprisingly ingenuous and provocative. For the Cardinal had to remember that among all the journalists he was addressing a mere minority, or at most a bare majority, were Catholics, whereas hundreds of others were agnostics or belonging to other confessions, some of them Christian but also Jews, Muslims, and so on, and even militant atheists like all the correspondents of the Communist papers of the West and East. But clearly the habit of preaching sermons plays these tricks on even the most capable ecclesiastics.

It would have been a good thing if, rather than bothering so much about providing first-class technical services, the Secretariat-General of the Council had initiated a radical change in the methods of functioning of the Press Office. Its operation during the preparatory phase was in fact most inauspicious. From its establishment on 18 April 1961 to today, it gave out altogether only just over a hundred communiqués or bulletins, some of them explaining the various organs of the Council and their aims and constitution, but most of them giving an account of the work of the Central Preparatory Commission's sessions. As these were official communiqués, criticism of their style and language, however justifiable, is a secondary matter, but the value of their contents is of the greatest importance. Viewed from this angle, even more than from that of form, the emanations of the Council's Press Office seemed to be not so much classics of reticence as rambling texts where the real news was so deeply embedded in comment as to make it impossible to decide where the one began and the other ended.

The particulars given were so vague that it was impossible to discover the exact title or number of the drafts examined, let alone get an idea of the subjects dealt with and the trend of the discussions. Moreover the comments were like little tracts so out of focus or ill-related to the general argument of the drafts that it would have been a good deal more useful to quote the relevant 'common doctrine' from one of the more popular theological manuals. Moreover their method of treatment was such as to arouse the suspicion that they reflected not the traditional points of view but the attitude of the Commission that presented the draft and the Central Commission that examined it.

The patience of the Catholic journalists was so sorely tried that some of them rebelled and demanded the abolition of this 'Chinese Wall' or 'smokescreen' set up around the Council's labours – these were the expressions used, for example, by the Dutch *De Linie* and some Western European weeklies. Some gaffes occurred, as for instance when Bulletin No 96 affirmed that in the search for union 'great care is needed not to fall into mistaken forms of religious indifference or of interconfessionalism or compromise', a statement which produced a sharp reaction from the World Council of Churches; but even then the desired changes were not made.

To all intents and purposes the Council's Press Office at that time meant its director, Monsignor Vallainc. The Curia had wanted an Italian as head of the Office, and that being so it was almost inevitable that the choice should fall on him, not because there were no other journalist priests in the country but because he was the only one with some experience in organizing a press agency. Since 1949 he had directed the SIS (Press Information Service), in other words the agency under Catholic Action, which deals with the 120-130 diocesan weeklies in the country.

Some years before, when an ecclesiastic adviser was to be appointed to the Catholic Press Centre and also to the Catholic Press Union, there was not much doubt as to who it should be: Vallainc was the only possible man in Rome, and he was given both offices. Moreover, when the restless Monsignore Strazzacappa, owner of the weekly *Settimana del Clero*, moved its headquarters to Rome and had to find a new editor for it, it was Vallainc who was chosen. Vallainc is obviously one of those unique and irreplaceable people who, perhaps in virtue of the Gospel saying 'To him who hath more shall be given', seem to be the predestined collectors of offices and honours, irrespective of whether they deserve them or not.

In his case, anyone who is familiar with the desolation of the Italian diocesan Catholic press, or who compares the Padua *Settimana del Clero* with the Roman edition, cannot but wonder how he can have been kept on to run either of them. This vigorous priest from the Val d'Aosta, now about fifty years of age, is certainly pleasant, courteous and friendly, but there can be no doubt that it is his personal fortune, in combination with the friendships and protection that he has managed to secure, which has made people ready to forgive his limitations on the technical side. Small wonder, then, that in October 1960 while still retaining all his old jobs he was also appointed to the staff of the *Osservatore Romano,* with the duty of arranging for the press service of the Council, under the Secretary-General, and adviser to the Council Secretariat for Press and Entertainment. Thus the way to the headship of the Council Press Office was opened up, and his appointment was announced in the following April.

But in spite of what I have said, I don't feel like making Vallainc the scapegoat for the Office's blatant disservices. Even under a better head than he, or someone less occupied with other things, the results of the Council Press Office would be much the same. So there is little ground for optimism in the news that from now onwards, owing to the need to issue communiqués in several languages and make contact with hundreds of journalists from every country, he is to be assisted by a little court of colleagues, priests and journalists like himself. Everything of course depends on how far they can be independent and how much freedom they have, as well as on the kind of news available to them. So far it is not yet known whether they will be able to accompany Monsignor Vallainc to the General Congregations and so prepare their reports on a basis of first-hand knowledge. Monsignor Vallainc has the right to sit in the Council Hall in his capacity of 'expert'. Will an exception be made for them? But anyone present at a General Congregation is pledged to secrecy: he thus becomes a mute witness. The problem therefore is to see how far the gag may be relaxed for him and his colleagues.

Rome, Sunday, 7 October

I read in the latest numbers of *Civiltà Cattolica* and the Catholic weekly *Orizzonti* of two occasions on which Cardinal Siri has adopted a definitely controversial attitude about the Council.

The Jesuits' fortnightly review, *Civiltà Cattolica,* summarizes a letter of 29 August from Siri, as Archbishop of Genoa, to the clergy and people of his diocese. The most important statements in it, according to the summary, are the following (taken from the original text):

'The Council is not just a spectacle or a novelty: it is a fact which can decide – as future generations will realize – about the whole direction of our era at one of the most interesting and complicated junctures in history . . . Do not believe, my children, that the Council will be able to tell you that something less will be needed in order to come with serenity before the judgment of God. It is very probable that the Council will ask something more from priests and laymen in order to hasten the coming of the Kingdom of God and of equitable human co-existence. None of us can dilute the Gospel; instead, it may be that the sternest injunctions that Christ laid upon his followers may stand forth as urgent imperatives.'

These are affirmations of a disciplinary integrity that needs no comment. But here is another statement, more pungent in its brevity, which makes the eminently pastoral character of Vatican II a merely secondary affair: the Council, Siri says, 'is directed above all towards divine truth, which is to be handed on perpetually in a pure and useful way'.

The interview with Siri published by the Pauline weekly, *Orizzonti,* in commenting on these two points emphasizes them still further. Here are the Cardinal's own words:

'The Council will certainly have to deal with extremely important doctrinal matters. In my modest opinion these are, as was the case in almost all the Councils, its major function. It must not be forgotten that the first great task entrusted by Our Lord to His Church is the teaching of truth . . . That the Council has to carry out a great pastoral work no one can doubt, precisely because it is confronted with a particular historical situation and because it has to see to the care of souls, the Church's true task. In the way in which the question was put to me . . . I hear the echoes of misleading things that are sometimes said on this subject. Pastoral work does not consist of distributing caresses, smiles, and acts of condescension at whatever cost. Pastoral work lies in carrying out in relation to the faithful what Our Lord Himself did, and wanted us to do in the same way (according to circumstances) in which He Himself acted. In all this the first pastoral task is to present all the truth revealed by Him . . . It is absolutely wrong to think that the pastoral duty can characterize a Council, as if the other Councils had not also had the same most sacred duty. Above all, it is I will not say misleading but wrong to believe that the time has come to set aside sacred doctrine as if it had become less necessary or inconvenient, in order to do things which are purely and simply pastoral. That would make no sense.'

About the 'errors of our times' Siri was a good deal more cautious. After referring to the communiqués of the Press Office concerning the preparatory work for the Council he said: 'More I am not in a position to say. But the outside observer knows very well that the Church is confronted with pernicious doctrines and serious errors.' But he was extremely stern about the claims of the lay world: 'As to the powers of laymen, they must continue substantially to be those traditionally accepted and defined by Our Saviour when He established the sacred hierarchy. Here it is not a question of discussing powers, but the duties of apostolate.' Lastly, he was almost equally unbending about the so-called de-Westernization of the Church: 'the West has not to be repudiated in any way; but the West must adapt itself better to the needs of all the others.'

Never till now have the integralists dared to take up so definite a stand: it might indeed be said that hitherto they have preferred the carrot to the stick, even if their aim in holding out the carrot was to be able to wield the stick more easily. Typical of this attitude for example, was the personal and public avowal of adherence to the Council made by their leader, Cardinal Pizzardo, in the course of an official series of lectures under the auspices of the Lateran University in the autumn of 1960. The manner of it was, indeed, so fantastic as to seem an intentional caricature, but the style of the Prefect of the Congregation of Seminaries is too well known to justify so malicious an interpretation. Pizzardo, then, compared the city of Satan of the modern world (which, according to him, had its prototype in Communism) with the city of God (symbolized by the small silent city of the Vatican). The first of these, he said, 'the new city of Babel, rises on a basis of crude materialism and blind determinism, built by the unconscious toil of the conquered and bathed in their tears and blood, like the old pagan Colosseum: a ruin washed over by the Christian centuries. It rises up monstrous, holding out before the eyes of the deluded hordes of slaves – bringing bricks and pitch for its making – a vain mirage of perfect prosperity and terrestrial felicity . . . But at the same time on the glacis of the new Babel there arise the launching ramps for missiles, and in its storehouses the ogival nuclear weapons pile up for the universal and total destruction to come'. The city of God, on the other hand, had 'on its glacis and in its storehouses. . . ., instead of missile ramps and nuclear ogives only the "Transfiguration", the "Dispute of the Sacrament", and the "Last Judgement" of Michelangelo'.

When he came to draw the implications from his comparison, however, the Cardinal abandoned his romantic symbolism to affirm suddenly how, 'animated by an unconquerable hope which is divine certainty, John XXIII invites his children from the four winds to a free, peaceful, and universal assembly of prayer and study, from which fruits of extraordinary efficacy are hoped and expected at a time which he foresees and describes as one of renewal.'

Pizzardo was not a man from whom an open and explicit standpoint was to be expected. Trained by a long diplomatic apprenticeship in the Secretariat of State (he was the Holy See's representative at the Rapallo Conference in 1922, when he met Chicherin), he has always been the cautious, silent, invisibly omnipresent man of action. In the 'Pentagon' – the 'trust' of Pacellian Curial cardinals which weathered the good and bad times of the Church in the last decade of Pius XII's Pontificate – he always gave the job of making a final break to Ottaviani, his successor as Secretary of the Holy Office after having been Assessor and Pro-Secretary under Pizzardo. But during the pre-Council period Ottaviani, too, generally preferred action to public polemics; and so he remained in the Siri camp. My quotations from Siri are eloquent proof of a determination not to compromise, and to move into attack rather than remain on the defensive.

How much of this attitude of Siri's is due to personal factors rather than to a definite ideal is of course difficult to say. It is no secret that this former protégé of Pius XII – who made him Archbishop of so important and difficult a see as Genoa when he was only forty, and Cardinal at 47 – has been completely eclipsed by John XXIII's advent to the Pontificate. Indeed it was a masterpiece of diplomacy on Papa Roncalli's part to manage to set him on one side without removing him from a single one of the prominent positions that Siri held under Pacelli as president, simultaneously, of the Italian episcopal conference, the episcopal Commission for the higher control of Catholic Action, the social weeks for Italian Catholics, etc. It would be only natural that this should be a severe blow to the man who probably regarded himself as 'predestined' for higher things.

Several of the local clergy in Genoa frequently assured me, between 1955 and 1958, that Siri was seriously preparing himself for the succession to Pacelli both by keeping up his languages and by studying to remain abreast in all the necessary branches of knowledge. And there can be no doubt that had he been elected he would easily have proved a better '*doctor pentecostalis*' than his predecessor (he was particularly well up in international law and interested in various aspects of penal problems, though not so competent in theology), being inferior to him only, cold and stiff as he is, in personal charm.

After this preliminary skirmish it seems likely that Siri will reserve his weightier attacks for the Council itself; though I doubt whether he will agree to become leader of the opposition, especially there. His colleagues of the Pentagon would prevent it. 'Their natural shield and protector is Ottaviani,' Antimori says.

Rome, Monday, 8 October

This morning a plane landed at Fiumicino bringing what is probably the largest group of bishops ever to have embarked on a collective flight over so tremendous a distance. They came from the Far East and had with them two Cardinals, Thomas Tien-Ken-Sin from China and Peter Tatsuo Doi from Japan, together with 75 archbishops and bishops from Japan, Formosa and other Far Eastern countries.

While I was waiting for the plane to come in after it had touched down – I was in a group just behind the secretary of Cardinal Marella and the Chinese Nationalist Ambassador to the Holy See – I reflected that today you can fly to Rome from Tokyo in 48 hours, from New York in 5¾, from Buenos Aires in 23, from London in two and from Paris in one and a half. A century ago, at the time of Vatican I, the inconveniences of travel were very different – and not only for the bishops from overseas but also for the Europeans, whether they travelled by coach like most of the Italians and even the Hungarians, or by train. The trains of those days were both more uncomfortable and slower, and the Alps still constituted an insurmountable barrier. The first direct Paris-Rome train went through the Mont Cenis tunnel on 16 October 1871, more than a year after the Council closed; so that Cardinal Feltin's predecessor in Paris, Monsignor Darboy, after having spent 16½ hours on the journey between the capital and Saint-Jean-de-Maurienne, had to cross the pass in a snowstorm, which exhausted him so much that he had to stop some days in Turin after rejoining the train at Susa, eventually arriving at his destination after eleven days' travelling.

Even a century ago, however, dozens of Fathers came to Rome both from America and the Far East. The only thing missing among them was a coloured bishop. Today there are five cardinals and 200 bishops from the Afro-Asian countries. On the Boeing that I saw land this morning the Western prelates were actually an insignificant minority by comparison with the Asiatic ones. But naturally the attention of the bystanders was at once concentrated on the cardinals who were known to be in the group, though their everyday clothes made it difficult to identify them. Even Tatsuo Doi, the pocket or baby cardinal, was hardly distinguishable among the other Japanese bishops not much taller than he with their smiling ageless faces.

Tatsuo Doi only looks like a baby, for he is in fact just over 70. When seen close to, the colour of his hair and his wrinkles seem to give his face the look of a dramatic mask. In any case as a Cardinal he is very young indeed, for he was created only in March 1960, and it is said that he owes it in equal parts to the importance of his see and the efforts of Cardinal Marella, to whom he was personal secretary while the Cardinal was in Japan as Apostolic Delegate. In point of fact, however, the archbishopric of Tokyo was secured for him in December 1937, also by Marella, so Marella is his real 'creator *ex nihilo*', as he is wont to say, smiling and bowing. Indeed, since no Japanese before Tatsuo Doi had been Archbishop of Tokyo or Cardinal of the Holy Roman Church, all Catholic Japan owes a debt of national gratitude to the former Nuncio in Paris. The fact remains, in any case, that Tatsuo Doi has shown that he deserves both the confidence placed in him and the honours he has received, especially in the war and immediate post-war years when he constantly refused to compromise in a political situation that was extremely delicate and dangerous.

It seems one cannot say as much of his predecessor in the purple (since 1946) and travelling companion and contemporary, Tien-Ken-Sin. Or at any rate the circumstances seem to have been very mysterious which prevented Mao's troops from finding him in his see, or even in the country at all, when they made their triumphal entry into Pekin. Moreover, to all appearances those circumstances remained unconvincing, even to Rome, and in particular to Pius XII, who would not have objected to being able to count on a Chinese, or at least Oriental, Mindszenty. For some years, it is said, he refused to forgive Tien for having evaded a rôle which, while obviously uncomfortable, would have been very useful to the Church, and he banished him to Illinois Tech as if wanting to forget him. It is certainly strange that Pius XII kept silence about him even in official documents concerning the Church in China; this is the more marked when compared with the constant references he used to make to the other bishops 'prevented' from fulfilling their office by the Communist régimes, particularly if he had personally created them cardinals, as in Tien's case. It was not until 1957 that Pacelli decided to allow his rehabilitation and sent him on a journey of inspection to Nationalist China, to Formosa. Only in 1960 did John XXIII appoint him Apostolic Administrator of the Church there, thus freeing him at last from his American exile.

I don't know if Tien came to Rome before 1957, when he had to present his report. But at any rate it seems certain that both then and in the following year, for the Conclave, his visits to Rome were somewhat ill-fated. In 1957, he had at once to go into a nursing-home, and the following year he was actually carried into the Conclave on a litter, having broken several ribs and fractured his right arm in a motor accident. On the first day he could not even go to the Sistine Chapel for the voting and the 'nursing cardinals' had to go to his cell to collect his ballot slip, which must obviously have been filled in under secrecy by his secretary.

If what a Chinese priest told me about him some years ago is true, Cardinal Tien will certainly not be one of the members of the Sacred College who will stand out particularly because of his familiarity with Latin. But Tien is a member of the Order of the Divine Word, and the Verbites are not only one of the most numerous and best organized missionary institutions in the Catholic Church (with over 5,500 members) but also one with perhaps the best cultural and scientific background. He can therefore rely on good advisers to help him and can convey their views in his light twittering oriental voice, or more probably in writing.

Contrasts such as these between men even of the first rank can surprise only the simple-minded or the hypocritical. Every society is a mixture of the pure and the impure, the heroic and the timid, and there is no knowing whether when put to the test the former will show up better than the latter. Often what is taken for fear is really only uncertainty or hesitation, and heroism is sometimes just a more fleeting and provocative fanaticism. Some of the other arrivals in these last days raise similar and even more complex questions, in the face of which I notice that the Catholic journalists prefer to take refuge in silence or reticence. I refer to the arrival of the delegations from beyond the Iron Curtain, of which the papers have begun to speak almost furtively only in the last few days. Up till then nothing whatever was said about such arrivals, and now there is obvious embarrassment at having to admit a fact which has so often been denied for mere reasons of prejudice. It seems, indeed, that there will be present at the Council not only all the bishops of Yugoslavia and a good many of the Polish ones but also representatives of the episcopates of Czechoslovakia, Hungary, Bulgaria, and even the Baltic States under Soviet control.

The disappointment of those who up to the last believed this impossible expresses itself in petty cavilling such as the three-column headline in the Bologna *Avvenire d'Italia* of yesterday: 'The Hungarian Bishops will arrive in Rome without a penny'. Fortunately, however, more responsible thoughts are beginning to emerge, and not, I believe, by chance. The Milan *Italia,* for instance, which last Thursday reported without comment the departure of Fathers from some of the Eastern European countries, today abandons its reserve and instead of just publishing agency messages ventures on a report of its own which says among other things: 'The representation of bishops from beyond the Iron Curtain is, notwithstanding the comparisons between Utopia and reality, superior to what was expected . . . Obviously the absentees cause the attention of many, especially those interested politically, to be concentrated on the situation of the Church of Silence. But now bishops are coming from those countries too. That obviously does not imply, nor should it be argued therefrom, that the anti-religious struggle of the Communist Governments is on the wane; nor would it be right to judge the bishops who are coming to Rome with the permission of the "red politicians" on the rigid basis of their relations with the Communist authorities, without any understanding of the situation.'

I should very much like to have been at the station when the Hungarian bishops arrived. Antimori tells me there was only a group of compatriot priests and seminarists to meet them. The inquisitive who were attracted by the gathering were surprised to see that they were smiling and seemed quite excited, and they readily agreed to pose for the photographers in Via Marsala before the cars took them off.

I couldn't, either, manage to be there when Wyszynski arrived today. 'He looked older and more tired than usual but charming as ever,' Antimori told me. There were a thousand people on the platform, with flowers and photographers' magnesium flares and several high-ups: Dell'Acqua from the Vatican, Archbishop Gawlina from the Polish emigrants, the Ambassador of the Warsaw Government to the Quirinal (whom the *Osservatore Romano* carefully ignored in its report), and others.

When he came to Rome for the Conclave in 1958, the crowd almost called out 'Long live the Pope'. You could feel it in the air; and it was indeed a deep secret aspiration of the Poles that such a miracle might come about. Fortunately for his country's welfare, Wyszynski could not become Pope; but his presence was decisive at that time towards giving the Church and Poland the Pope best suited to the task. What influence will he and the Bishops from Eastern Europe exercise in the Council? This time Wyszynski had 13 bishops with him, about a quarter of the whole Polish episcopate. About as many again will be coming separately during the next few days, but the rest cannot leave the country.

A few papers comment severely on this. Not one of them recalls that in 1869 the Holy See tried in vain to persuade the Russians to allow the Polish bishops to come to Rome. The Vatican went so far as to release a Polish priest whose extradition from the Papal States was demanded by the Russians; the unfortunate man was sent off to the highly dubious fate awaiting him, but even this cowardly action failed to move the Tsar.

Two hours ago Monsignor Bontempi told me on the telephone that the Hungarian bishops were met in Vienna by a message of welcome from the Pope. Is this detail to be seen in relation to the barely disguised interest which the Hungarian leaders have shown for some time in reaching a *modus vivendi* with Rome? It seems not unlikely. Slavs and Orientals in general set much store by symbolism.

The Pope receives the Polish Bishops

Rome, Tuesday, 9 October

John XXIII has not waited 24 hours before receiving Cardinal Wyszynski and the Polish bishops (the other Iron Curtain prelates have already been notified about their audiences which will take place during the next few days with precedence, at the Pope's express and significant wish, over all the other groups). In receiving the representatives of the episcopate he wanted to show his sympathy not only with the Church but with the Polish nation. And in speaking of the past history of this martyred country whose territorial integrity has been violated through the centuries from both East and West, he referred to 'the Western territories of Poland recovered after centuries'.

The Archbishop of Warsaw had had the happy thought of reminding him that among the Italians who had espoused the cause of Polish independence there was one from the Pope's own region of Bergamo, Colonel Francesco Nullo, a follower of Garibaldi, who had defended the Roman Republic in 1849 and was killed fighting for Poland at Krzjkawka in 1863. John XXIII was delighted by this association and ended his little historical survey with the words: 'I have followed the efforts of your people in their struggle for liberty and the inviolability of your frontiers. I have followed with emotion all the heroic efforts of your people.'

The news of this speech will cause an outburst of enthusiasm among the Poles and will help to improve relations between the Church and the Communist Government. But there is also a danger that its contents may introduce a dangerous political element into the Council just at the delicate moment of its opening. A purely religious affair of such exceptional importance as Vatican II has nothing to gain from becoming involved in awkward temporal matters. I am told the Polish Ambassador was exultant: one may be equally sure that the German Ambassador to the Holy See will not pretend to ignore it for long; he may delay taking action until after the Council's opening ceremonies, but he cannot avoid doing so eventually. But can John XXIII have allowed himself such an 'imprudence' without some definite reason?

Towards midday, I went down to Via della Conciliazione to the

Press Office, but I was only in the 'organization and information' section. Antimori was waiting for me so that we could get hold of one or other of the bishops together, and there were dozens of them, Africans, Japanese, Indians, South Americans, Germans, and so on, queueing up at the various inquiry desks. We were just about to talk to some of them when a tremendously tall and energetic-looking prelate came into the room who at once reminded me of a well-known hero of Western films. I was just trying to think which (that kind of hero isn't a strong point with me) when someone behind me whispered: 'Here's Cardinal Gary Cooper'. I turned round, but the remark wasn't made to me but to a South American bishop by his secretary.

The new arrival was Cushing, Archbishop of Boston, the 'No. 2', after Spellman, of the U.S. episcopate. Unlike the heroes of Westerns, however, his manner was not swaggering or provocative, and he did not have that scornful indifference of someone whose one idea is to do down both enemies and friends. He wasn't left severely alone, either, but was at once surrounded by several prelates. As soon as he approached a queue people offered their place to him. But he refused and went to the end of the queue, saying with a smile, in Latin, 'We're all bishops here.'

Looking at him closely it is not difficult to discern beyond his vigorous and attractive features the signs of his origins. Sixty years ago (he is now 67), the son of humble Irish immigrants, he was a blacksmith's boy in his father's shop. When he decided to enter the priesthood it was not in order to better himself: he has always kept close links with the Boston working classes, and indeed the first action of his that gained widespread notoriety after he became Bishop was his organization of an annual dinner on Thanksgiving Day for thousands of poor and lonely people, at which he distributed presents after cutting the turkey. His faith was a very real thing with him, and he had no ambitions beyond that of a zealous apostolate. He had some experience in most of the branches of the pastoral ministry, while all the time his aspiration grew for that total apostolate which missionary work stood for in his mind. It was while he was devoting himself to the promotion of such missionary work in the diocese that to his astonishment he was appointed bishop of his own town, first as auxiliary and then as ordinary (from 1939-1944).

He was even more astonished to be elected Cardinal four years ago, at John XXIII's first Consistory. But he never regarded it as an insurmountable obstacle to pursuing his true vocation, and he has twice recently begged the Pope to let him go to Chile or Brazil as an ordinary missionary. I think John XXIII must have been tempted to grant so disinterested a wish: it would have been an invaluable example. His decision not to do so must have been because he was convinced that the American episcopate should not be deprived, especially at this particular moment, of a man like Cushing.

For some years Spellman's prestige has been in decline and the eyes of American Catholics and non-Catholics have turned more and more towards the Archbishop of Boston. This arises partly from the close links of friendship between Cushing and the Kennedys (the first words spoke by the President's father, Joe Kennedy, after his stroke were to Cushing when he went to visit him at Palm Beach; several of the Kennedys have been married by him and he christened Caroline and some of Joe's other grandchildren), but the deeper reason is that Cushing represents and personifies 'the Catholicism of tomorrow' in his country. If his programme is the very opposite of Spellman's, he certainly did not adopt it out of rivalry towards the Archbishop of New York. Indeed, though he had for years been opposed to any form of public subvention for Catholic schools, when Spellman asked Kennedy to grant it and it was refused he took no part whatever in the debate. The truth is that while Cushing fights for Negroes' rights, and opposes both right-wing anti-Communist movements and police brutality, and does everything he can to improve relations between Catholics and Jews, Protestants, and members of the Orthodox Church, this is all the result of something consistent in his whole character, not of any artificial improvisation on account of circumstances or, less still, of a sterile personal antagonism.

As for the Council and his ideas about it, it is clear from the statements he made to the press on arrival in Rome that John XXIII will have in him a strong supporter of his 'new line'. Cushing is in an unusual position in relation to the Curia: he is one of the few US bishops never to have done his theological studies in Rome and is therefore not permeated by the fatal Curial '*romanitas*'. It now remains to be seen how the big US contingent of 236 bishops will divide up – and whether the majority will be with him or with the representative of the 'old guard', Spellman.

Before leaving the Information Office Antimori and I looked in at the Press Office, where Cardinal Cerejeira, Patriarch of Lisbon and Primate of Portugal, was pointed out to us. He was sitting at a table preparing, so we were told, answers to questions for a Portuguese television programme and his secretary and some other Portuguese priests were keeping guard to see that no one disturbed him.

Even looking at him closely I would not have recognized him. The only time I ever met him was in Milan some years before the war. Cerejeira wanted to go to the Catholic University of the Sacred Heart to meet its Rector, Padre Agostino Gemelli, and it fell to me to accompany him. But the Franciscan Father could not at first be found, so I filled in the time by telling the Cardinal some of the anecdotes then current about him, as, for instance, that Padre Gemelli's not exactly serene temperament caused students to call him the 'magnificent terror' instead of the 'magnificent rector' (*rettore magnifico* being the usual Italian title for heads of universities). But I didn't suspect then that I was giving the Patriarch a good preparation for what was about to happen to him.

Padre Gemelli eventually arrived from the dark recesses of a long corridor, and it soon became apparent that we had come on one of his less fortunate days. He shook hands briefly and asked us into his study. There, after a somewhat disjointed explanation that he was in the middle of a difficult piece of research in his laboratory, he asked us to sit down and listened to what Cerejeira had to say. Rather intimidated by this unceremonious welcome, the Cardinal said he and other important people in Lisbon were very anxious for Padre Gemelli to give a lecture there. 'Quite impossible, quite impossible,' Gemelli replied brusquely, getting up. His guest tried to explain the importance of the occasion, but in vain: Padre Gemelli hadn't time. Cerejeira, still standing, brought out his final inducement: Padre Gemelli could make the journey both ways by air. The Father answered that he went by air practically every day because of his work. That finished it, and with the danger of the lecture averted the terrible Franciscan softened slightly and talked about some branch of scientific research the relevance of which must certainly have escaped the unfortunate Patriarch. Then Gemelli looked at his watch and prepared to say goodbye; this time, he even went so far as to make a sketchy attempt at kissing the episcopal ring.

Cerejeira must then have been about forty-six. Pius XI had appointed him to the see of Lisbon and to the purple in 1929, when he was barely forty-one, possibly because he knew that he had been a fellow-student of Salazar's at Coimbra and had always remained on close terms with him. Papa Ratti intended thus to bind the ex-seminarist dictator even more closely to him in view of the Concordat for which approaches were already being made. At the Conclave in March 1939 from which Pius XII emerged as Pope, Cerejeira was the only cardinal to travel by air: he landed at the Lido at Ostia in a hydroplane, and the papers were amazed at such daring on the part of a prince of the Church.

I reminded Antimori of all this. 'Those were far-off times,' he commented, 'when the dictatorships believed they could carry the Church along in their wake. Now not only the dictators but their ecclesiastical advisers too are a millstone round its neck.' And he referred me to the impression made by the collective letter from the Portuguese episcopate in defence of the Salazar policy in Angola. He may have raised his voice at the name of the unhappy colony, for the Patriarch's vigilant secretary stiffened and gave us an angry look. It certainly wasn't the most propitious introduction for a useful talk, and we decided to go.

I must confess that I had not noticed in the last few days the first advertisements in Latin in the *Osservatore Romano,* obviously meant for the Fathers and their suites. There is a mention of them in another paper today. For instance, a car-hire firm promises 'novae automobiles quacumque amplitudine omnibusque numeris absolutae etiam sine raedario' (i.e. without any obligation as to minimum journey, driver optional); a bank announces its readiness to establish 'peculiarem mensam argentariam apud additiciam procurationis sedem quae eorum necessitatibus inserviat' and recommends one of its branches 'quae cum ad petrianae basilicae forum prope adiaceat'.

These are not, however, the first advertisements of the kind. For example, *Meridiano II*, a monthly of the 'digest' variety run by the Salesian Fathers, has since last January published four whole pages of advertising for Air France in Latin. It even had a Latin explanation attached to the map of the world showing which of the company's airports have chapels where Mass can be celebrated.

Rome, Wednesday, 10 October

It is now less than twenty-four hours to the opening of the Council, and the great question on the far side of the Tiber is whether the rather uncertain weather will permit the procession of the Fathers to file across Piazza San Pietro tomorrow morning. 'A hundred years ago,' I read in today's papers, 'Vatican I both opened and closed in apocalyptic thunderstorms. Were the same to happen again . . . etc.'

Such meteorological conjectures create atnosphere but they leave me indifferent. Pastor R. was with me just now and we had a long talk about the observer delegates, so I am thinking much more about them at the moment. They will be in St Peter's tomorrow in their appointed places on the left as you face the Altar of the Confession waiting like everyone else for John XXIII's entry into the 'cathedral of the world'. According to the latest news there will be about 50 of them, including the eight 'guests of the Secretariat for Christian Unity'. I can imagine their embarrassment at finding themselves, for the first time both in their own lives and in the whole history of their Churches, taking part in an official ceremony like that of tomorrow.

To begin with, their numbers are so small and they will be so isolated – only fifty of them as compared with at least 20,000 people crowded into the basilica and another two or three hundred thousand outside in the piazza and the converging streets. And the 20,000 in the basilica represent the élite from all sorts of strata, diplomatists and statesmen, the aristocracy and representatives of public opinion, and above all thousands from the higher ranks of the Church which is their host: 80 Cardinals, over 2,500 archbishops and bishops, hundreds of prelates from the Curia, dozens of nuncios and heads of religious orders, hundreds of theologians and experts, dignitaries of all kinds, and priests, monks and nuns by the thousand. These figures suffice to give an impressive demonstration of the grandeur and power of the organization from which they alone, just those fifty delegates, are excluded, and towards which they must feel themselves at once attracted and repelled.

True, not all those present share the faith of the majority. Among the diplomatists, many do not even belong to the Christian faith, and many more belong to schismatic confessions, while among the nominally Catholic themselves quite a few are agnostic both in theory and in practice. The same is true for a large number of the aristocracy, intellectuals, and journalists present, but the very fact of finding themselves there beneath Michelangelo's vault expresses at least formally a positive agreement and participation on their part. As for the crowd outside, it is conscious of living through one of the most exceptional moments in history, and it expresses its jubilation in all sorts of comments, applause, and songs.

Finally, after the blast on the silver trumpets which will announce the entry of the 261st Pope to wear the tiara, one of the most magnificent choreographic spectacles of the whole Roman Church will be displayed before the observers' eyes. How can they help in their secret thoughts contrasting the size of their respective communities and structures with the proportions and structures of the Roman Church which is lording it almost menacingly over them in this hour of its glory?

Bit by bit their psychological embarrassment becomes even stronger than the physical embarrassment of their surroundings. True, these Orthodox, Anglicans, Lutherans, Baptists, Old Catholics, Quakers, and the rest are not the disarmed plenipotentiaries of conquered armies seeking to surrender. But there is a certain irony of history whereby those taking part in certain events can hardly avoid seeming in some sense victims. It is indeed impossible for them not to feel themselves, especially at a moment like this, the heirs of historical circumstances varying in importance but all characterized by revolt against the Church that is now their host; and inevitably they must feel themselves in some sense called to judgment by that history and that past. They cannot but feel conscious of the presence of their ancestors and recall their deeds and the crucial and dramatic moments through which they lived.

What will trouble them most will be their presence in the 'temple of superstition', in the heart of Rome, the 'new Babylon'. St Peter's according to their tradition stands for the temple of idolatry, and the man who will soon enter it borne along amid the ovations of a whole populace between the halberds and drawn swords of his guards of honour is the very personification of judgment placed above law, intolerance instead of freedom in faith, and an autocracy that penetrates even into the free community of believers. Certainly the face of the present Pope is simple and kindly, but the essence of the 'pontifex maximus' and his powers remains the same as it was eight or five or one centuries ago. In those days he aroused mistrust and fear on the shores of the Bosphorus, among the castles of the free cities of Germany, on the banks of the Thames and the Lake of Geneva. And now in idolatrously eloquent fashion they find themselves faced with the effigy in bronze of the first apostle, raised on a throne a few feet from them on the right-hand side of the basilica: the famous statue of St Peter, his right foot worn away by the kisses of the faithful, decked out for the occasion in mitre and cope like the Madonnas in villages of the South for their annual procession. Soon the Pope of Rome will traverse the whole length of what tomorrow will be the Council Hall to the sound of 'Tu es Petrus' and before the Altar of the Confession will turn left with his suite to reach his throne in the apse, and the gestatorial chair will pass above their heads, and they, the guests, can but bow in reverence before it.

What has changed between Rome and their Churches to justify their presence now? Nothing of any real substance. For all of them the theocratic apex of the Roman Church remains the prime obstacle, still standing four-square and untouched. For the great majority the dispute extends as well to the main fundamentals of theological and moral doctrine, affecting not only the doctrine of the priesthood and the episcopate, which they entirely reject, but also the doctrines of grace, of the sacraments, and of eschatology. Most of them do not even believe in the Councils, so that the presence of their delegates at Vatican II becomes, viewed from that angle, even more paradoxical.

But there are justifications all the same: in particular, the need to put an end to the scandal of hostile relations between the followers of one and the same founder, and the desirability of establishing a common religious front in a world becoming increasingly material. But are these reasons really such as to justify so embarrassing a participation in the inaugural ceremony? Given acceptance of the functions of the observer delegates, I think the answer is plainly yes: absence would take on an inevitably hostile significance. A little more foresight might have suggested putting off the arrival of the delegates till after the beginning of the Council; but that was obviously too much to ask.

The only ones who have managed to do so, after a splendidly skilful display of tergiversations and postponements up to the last moment, are the representatives from the Moscow Patriarchate. This morning, in fact, Cardinal Bea and Monsignor Willebrands have each received telegrams announcing that two observers are on the way from the Soviet capital but will reach Rome only the day after tomorrow. Moscow has once more avoided humiliating herself before her great antagonist.

PART II
THE COUNCIL

Rome, Thursday, 11 October

Millions of viewers on TV will long retain the memory of this morning's interminable white procession of 2,500 bishops as it emerged through the Bronze Door and traversed the Piazza San Pietro to wend its way into the Vatican Basilica. Skilful photography contrived, while registering the procession's frequent interruptions, to give the impression of an endless stream advancing wave upon wave. Never since 1 November 1950, when Pius XII proclaimed the doctrine of the Assumption, had so many bishops been seen within the embrace of the Bernini colonnades. Yet at that time only about a thousand were present, and it seemed unlikely that such a gathering would be witnessed again at least for many decades.

But it was only when the shots ranged over the whole piazza or large parts of it that the picture was purely spectacular and scenic. Sometimes, instead, the cameras halted at a group of prelates as if to scrutinize them one by one, or lingered almost compassionately on an old archbishop supported by a younger colleague or other attendants, or on one prelate who limped or another who let a yawn escape him and clumsily adjusted the cope on his shoulders: then the encounter between the spectators and the protagonists of the Council became suddenly human and revelatory. A faithful Catholic might not always have been able to pick out his own particular bishop, but he suddenly became aware at one and the same time of all the bishops. Indeed, paradoxically, within this immense and magnificent frame he discovered them in all their authentic individuality: accustomed to their isolation and pre-eminence, he now saw them reduced to mere faces and figures in a crowd, to common mass-produced men, with faces sometimes expressive but for the most part generic, shorn of the usual hieratical poses and the conscious attitudes of wielders of power.

The TV reporter tried to counteract this impression of a general levelling by mentioning the various ages and places of origin of some prelates, giving details about their far-off dioceses, or describing how they had become well known even outside their own countries. But all in vain: the visual impression was stronger than any words. In the eyes of the spectators the Council suddenly ceased to be a simple choreographic spectacle to become instead an inextricable mixture of questions and problems, of unknown quantities and hopes, of possibilities and setbacks. The future of the Church and of its influence on the world suddenly fell upon the shoulders of these mitred men, without their croziers here where all croziers yield to the sceptre of the tiara'd Pope: they might be too young or too old, too hesitating or too self-assured, some learned but most of them perhaps unequal to the weighty debates of the Council, ascetic or well-living, devoted to the interests of the Church but probably no less so, if not more, to those of their own people or stratum.

It is not for nothing that faith, in order to overcome the bewilderment of believers, invokes the Holy Spirit as the great and true bearer of responsibility for the Councils. In any case, however, the Fathers of the Council remain the organs of transmission and therefore, in proportion to their efficiency, the conditioning factors. And that they have often conditioned it, even to the point of silencing it altogether, the history of past Ecumenical Councils gives eloquent proof. Will that happen in the present instance too, or will this assembly of 2,500 stand out as a docile interpreter, as the ecclesiastical language has it, of the Holy Spirit's inspirations?

If anyone asked himself these questions as the procession filed past, he probably forgot all about them the moment the pontifical Mass began in St Peter's. Then the great nave, all white with the copes and mitres of the Fathers of the Council, and with the press cameras moving about at intervals from place to place, became no more than a scenographic detail of the great liturgy celebrated around the Altar of the Confession. All attention was centred on the papal throne and the man seated there, laden with the vestments and symbols of a superhuman power. The rhythm of the ceremonies blended with the voices' polyphony, concentrated on some detail of gesture or clothing, resounded in the echoes of the organ and the choirs, and emerged again in the voice, now firm now tremulous, of the celebrant. The whole spectacle, serene and sumptuous, orderly and overwhelming, wisely calculated in its breaks and pauses, unrivalled throughout the whole world, millennial yet ever new, tranquil in the sureness of its perpetuity, absorbed the imagination, suspending all vital rhythm and compelling aesthetic agreement even from those who strove to react against it on the ideological plane. And the vision of the Church through five continents came flowing back to its centre, its pivot, its touchstone and its stumbling-block: Rome, and papal supremacy.

The reporter, at the moment of preparing viewers for the appearance of the Pope at the entry to the Gallery of Tapestries, had repeated what the press had already been saying in the past few days, namely that John XXIII too, like all the other prelates, would make the transit from the Bronze Door to Piazza San Pietro on foot, so as not to humiliate, as he said, the bishops of all the world by allowing himself to be carried above them. And, as we saw, John XXIII – a little tired, a little awkward – did in fact descend the whole flight of steps on foot among his surrounding suite. But before he appeared on the threshold of the colonnade the group was suddenly held up, and the gestatorial chair was seen to advance towards it; a few seconds later John XXIII was borne high on the shoulders of his damask-clad bearers amid the slow swaying of the fan-shaped feathered standards hovering over the canopy above the chair.

Thus once again Papa Roncalli has had to give in to Court protocol. The compromise reached, that he should go on foot at least for the length of the gallery, had resolved itself into a humiliating bargain. Yet, in the light of sober reflection, even if he had had his way, the contrast with the triumphant rite of the ceremonies in the Basilica, and in particular with that of the 'obedience' of all the categories of church dignitaries to the single sovereign, would have remained, indeed would have been emphasized even more. It was the whole complex of ceremonial attending the opening of the Council that needed to be changed, not just some secondary if eloquent detail. But it would have been ingenuous to expect any such thing.

Lack of imagination and, even more, the arid religious sense of the hidebound courtiers, harassed by the idea of tens of thousands of TV sets in every continent and of 'Telstar' watching from outer space, prevented the world from witnessing the really revolutionary and sensational spectacle that would have been provided if the proudest and most magnificent spiritual hierarchy in the universe, preceded by its head and clothed in penitentiary robes, had entered to the sound of propitiatory prayers the hall of the Council's labours over which it was believed the Divine Spirit hovered. Even the most pessimistic might then have been startled out of their scepticism into thinking that the Council was about to prepare a radical regeneration of the Church and of Christianity.

When the service was approaching the singing of the Gospel I left the TV screen. I had happened to be in town and so had gone into the first café I found with a television set, and stayed there for a couple of hours with four middle-aged women and an old man who were also watching the ceremony. Now I wanted to see what was going on in the streets on this first day of the Council. I knew what would happen during the rest of the service in St Peter's, and the Pope's speech I preferred to read at leisure in the evening papers.

I came out and went along Via dei Serpenti to the Via Nazionale. The crowd, relaxed in the sunshine and warmth, sauntered or loitered in the streets in its usual aimless fashion. Anyone unaware of what day it was would never have guessed that a great ceremony was taking place little more than a mile away.

After going down to Piazza Venezia and along the Corso, up Via del Tritone towards the Trinità dei Monti, and then along Via del Babuino to Piazza del Popolo, I found another TV set so as to convince myself that the Council really was opening. As I was watching in a half-detached sort of way the last pictures of the Pope on the screen, I suddenly remembered something I had read in the papers the day after the Council was announced, on 26 January 1959. The report, which came from Venice and was attributed to certain circles in the patriarchal Curia, suggested Venice, 'the ideal bridge between East and West', as a likely choice for the seat of the Council: to be precise, the Council could be held on the island of St George, where, the article explained, the Conclave of 1799 was held and where Pius VII was crowned.

The article naturally did not mention the state of emergency prevailing when that Conclave met, nor how subdued and how dramatically prophetic that coronation ceremony was because of the Austrian Emperor's hostility to the newly elected Pope. But the very idea of opening the Council in the city on the lagoon aroused a shiver of apprehension: the sight of the Fathers in procession in hundreds of gondolas would surely have been bound to give a wrong impression of worldliness, not to say frivolity. I think today the Venetians can have no regrets about the failure of their attempt to secure the Vatican Council for their city but are convinced instead that St Peter's and its piazza provide the most suitable setting for it.

As soon as I read the Pope's speech in the special edition of the *Osservatore Romano*, all the pomp and splendour of the ceremonial purveyed through tens of thousands of TV sets throughout the world faded like a far-off memory gone out of focus.

This man of unpredictable surprises, who only an hour ago I had thought too weak to resist the intrigues of his courtiers, has suddenly grasped the helm of the Council. They tried to daze him by putting all the bishops of the world like a carpet at his feet, surrounding him with the diplomatic missions of 85 States, many of them without official relations with the Holy See and even of pagan religions, and trying to transform his speech into a complicated Ciceronian oration, making him declaim as if to an academy: *Gaudet Mater Ecclesia* . . . And instead, at the end of an exhausting ceremony his voice rang out strong and firm, and St Peter's, like Jehosophat, was suddenly stirred to amazement, where over on the left, transfixed by his warning against carping pessimism and the sloth of attachment to a waning past, the *rerum adversarum vaticinatores* – prophets of misfortune by inclination or profession – stood pilloried, *qui deteriora semper praenuntiant, quasi rerum exitium instet*.

Pope John decisively seized the banner of the Council from their hands and gave it to the waiting ranks ready to embark on innovation, to rejuvenate the Church and attempt a radical modernization in spreading the Gospel and initiating a frank and unprejudiced debate with the world. If even only a third of the 2,500 bishops sitting lined up side by side in what from tomorrow will be the Council hall could have understood the extraordinary message that assailed their unaccustomed ears, they would almost certainly have burst into applause and risen *en masse* in enthusiastic agreement. But the Pope's Italian pronunciation, and more especially the complicated *concinnitas* of his Curial Latin, prevented most of them from grasping the meaning of what they heard. And those who from long professional usage had no difficulty in understanding were certainly not the ones most readily moved to applause: the glances they exchanged conveyed their horrified dismay.

The discourse began, and continued for some minutes, like a typical official speech, adapted to the occasion and inspired by an inevitably panegyrical and conformist approach towards the event it was to inaugurate. The familiar superficial and uncritical exaltation of the Councils as 'shining highlights in the history of the Church', all unanimously and uniformly 'bearing clear witness to its vitality', sufficed to give that impression. But then, suddenly, just after the reference to 'the consoling fact of the happy circumstances in which the Ecumenical Council is opening', came the unexpected rebuke to the timorous *laudatores temporis acti*:

'In the daily exercise of Our pastoral ministry Our ear is sometimes offended by persons full of ardent zeal but not over-endowed with a sense of discretion and moderation. In our modern times they discern only prevarication and decay; they maintain that our era, by comparison with the past, is deteriorating; and they behave as if they had learnt nothing from history, which nevertheless is the teacher of life, and as if at the time of earlier Ecumenical Councils everything had proceeded under the triumphant auspices of the Christian idea and way of life and of due religious freedom. To Us it seems that We must dissent from these prophets of misfortune who continually announce baleful events as if the end of the world were impending.'

But this stern admonition, not to say open disapproval, as expressed in the Pope's explicit dissociation of himself from the standpoint of those he described, was not based on a generic judgment of a moral nature but rather was justified by historical reasons which the Pope surveyed in a passage showing complete agreement with the 'new order' emerging in the world:

'At the present historical moment Providence is leading us towards a new order in human relationships which, through the operation of men and, moreover, above and beyond their own expectations, are tending towards a fulfilment of higher and unforeseen designs; and everything, even human adversity, is ordered for the greater well-being of the Church.'

And the consequences were soon shown to be no less peremptory than the premises: no uncritical adherence to the past; preservation of the truth in its main substance, but reformulation and rethinking, and if need be modernization, as to its forms; abandonment of sterile denunciation and offensive and harmful anathematization; and effort towards a frank and confident approach to all, not only in reciprocal tolerance but also in the recognition of a fundamental freedom of conscience.

'Naturally', John XXIII continued, 'the twenty-first Ecumenical Council wishes to transmit pure and entire, without attenuation or distortion, that doctrine which throughout twenty centuries, and not without difficulties and disputes, has become the common patrimony of men.' Nevertheless, 'our duty is not only to guard this precious treasure as if our sole concern were with our ancient heritage, but also to dedicate ourselves readily and willingly and without fear to that work which our era demands, so continuing along the road the Church has pursued for twenty centuries.

'The salient point of this Council is therefore not the discussion of this or that theme of the Church's fundamental doctrine, repeating over and over again the teaching of the Fathers and the ancient and modern theologians which is supposed to be constantly present and familiar to our minds. There is no need of a Council for that. But, setting out from a renewed, serene, and tranquil adherence to all the teaching of the Church in all its entirety and precision, such as still shines forth from the Councils' records from Trent down to the First Vatican Council, the Catholic and apostolic Christian spirit of the whole world now awaits a leap forward towards a doctrinal penetration and a formation of consciences corresponding more completely and faithfully to the authentic doctrine, which itself should be explained and elucidated in accordance with the methods of research and literary formulation familiar to modern thought. It is one thing to have the substance of the ancient doctrine of the *depositum fidei* but quite another to formulate and reclothe it: and it is this that must – if need be with patience – be held of great importance, measuring everything according to the forms and proportions of a teacher of pre-eminently pastoral character.'

Widespread errors, though they may vary as much as fashion in opinion, are certainly an incontestable fact and 'the Church has always been opposed to them: it has often condemned them with the utmost severity. But now the Bride of Christ prefers to use the medicine of mercy rather than of severity. She believes that the needs of today can best be met by showing the validity of her doctrine rather than by further condemnation.'

But the methods used in the Council must be inspired by one axiom: that of that great opening towards all the needs of the world on which John XXIII insisted so strongly in his broadcast message of 11 September: 'the Catholic Church, in raising by means of this Ecumenical Council the torch of religious truth, wishes to show itself as the loving mother of all, benign, patient, full of mercy and goodness even towards those sons who are separated from it. To the human race, oppressed by so many difficulties, the Church, like Peter to the poor man asking for alms, says: "I have neither gold nor silver but I give you what I have: in the name of Jesus Christ of Nazareth, arise and walk".'

With all this there is no need to fear, according to the Pope, that the Council may become over-contemporary or make its horizons and programmes too perilously profane. The meeting of the Catholic Church with the world on the concrete ground of its problems, its accusations and its needs should be only a means in the debate to ensure that fundamental 'unity of the human family' which, according to the Pope, is 'the great mystery invoked with ardent prayer by Christ in the imminence of his sacrifice'. And for the first time John XXIII referred to a 'triple ray' of unity or universalism which should shine out from the Council: unity among Catholics; unity with the Christians separated from the Catholic Church; and unity with non-Christian peoples.

Naturally, John XXIII cannot conceive of these new openings other than from a Catholic standpoint, but the conservatives are not entirely wrong in fearing that the tenor of these various debates, by taking the Church out of its splendid isolation both in the ideological and in the spiritual and administrative spheres, may have the effect of laying it open to harmful infiltrations or alignments. But can one make history by putting oneself outside history? And did not Christ want His people to live in the world even though not of the world? John xxiii, against the super-cautious suggestions of many mentors around him, has chosen to imitate His daring and to range himself with the more courageous.

Rome, Friday, 12 October

In John xxiii's greeting at 7.15 yesterday evening to the 15,000 members of Catholic Action who thronged Piazza San Pietro bearing torches in celebration of the Council ('this is the *historic* contribution of the lay world to Vatican II,' the editor of a progressive Catholic review said to me bitterly as we watched the spectacle), the Pope once again expressed his confidence in the speedy conclusion of the Council. 'There is hope,' he said, so all the press agencies report, 'that it may finish before Christmas,' and added, 'but perhaps we shall have to come back again if we do not succeed in saying everything now.'

This evening the *Osservatore Romano* has once again corrected the Pope, and in so definite a way as not even to respect his style: 'The Council' – the paper makes him say – 'has begun, and we do not know when it will end. Should it not finish by Christmas, because perhaps we shall not manage to say everything and deal with all the various subjects by then, it will be necessary to have another meeting.'

This latest of many interventions over John xxiii's too impulsive pronouncements is perhaps the most innocent. But the fact of the impossible hope cherished by the Pope remains, especially after a speech like that of this morning. Can it be that the drafts drawn up by the Preparatory Commissions have already indicated a triumph for his 'line'? If so, the greatest optimism would be justified; but if not, it would be absurd to imagine that in ten weeks 2,500 Fathers can recast the greater part of the drafts. Moreover, quite apart from the dispute, referred to by the Pope himself, between conservatives and progressives, who could suppose that the Council could seriously discuss so much material in fifty-odd General Congregations? Since these questions are inescapable, Antimori prefers to think that the Pope cannot conceal his anxiety about the possible effects on the Fathers of a too prolonged stay in Rome, where the climate, both physical and moral, of the Eternal City might prove debilitating for many of them. In short he would like at all costs to preserve them from an imperceptible but irresistible process of 'Curialization' which would end by suffocating the Council.

This morning the Pope made another notable speech when he welcomed the representatives of 86 diplomatic missions in the Sistine Chapel, the chapel of the Conclaves, which is normally never used for secular occasions such as today's. But it was not chosen by chance, as he himself made clear at one point when, after recalling the nations' aspiration for peace and the duty of statesmen and their collaborators to do everything possible to achieve it, he suddenly confronted his listeners with Michelangelo's Christ as Judge. He did it, of course, in his own particular courteous and gentle way, avoiding any needless dramatic gesture and just saying with persuasive simplicity, 'Your Highnesses, your Excellencies, Gentlemen, we have before us in the Sistine Chapel that masterpiece of Michelangelo, the "Last Judgement", the solemnity of which must give us to think and reflect. Yes, we shall have to render account to God, we and all those who bear the responsibility for the nations' destinies.'

In the light of these words the assurances given earlier about the Church's true policy acquire a new significance and sincerity:

> Among men who would recognize no other relations but those of physical force, the duty of the Church is to reveal all the importance and efficacy of the moral force of Christianity, which is a message of integral truth, justice, and charity. These are the foundations on which the Pope must pledge himself to work in order to establish a true peace, destined to raise the peoples in the respect of human personality and to procure a just freedom of worship; a peace which furthers agreement between States even, it goes without saying, if it should demand some sacrifice from them. The natural consequences will be mutual love, fraternity, and the end of strife between men of different origins and mentality. This will also facilitate the provision of urgently needed aid for gradually developing nations and for their true welfare with 'the exclusion of any aim of domination' (*Mater et Magistra*). This is the great peace that all men await and for which they have suffered so much.

Similarly the exhortation that followed acquires a new force:

> Let all men know that they must one day answer for their actions to God the Creator, who will be their Supreme Judge. With their hand on their conscience, let them listen to the cry of anguish which from every part of the earth, from individuals to societies, rises up to heaven: peace, peace. Let the preoccupation with the final rendering be so strong that none will neglect the efforts to achieve this good, which is, on earth, the highest good above all others. Let them continue to meet, to discuss, and to reach loyal, generous, and just agreements. And let them be ready for the necessary sacrifices to save the peace of the world.

As a matter of fact the Council has begun at a time when the situation of international détente is more reassuring than at any other time, perhaps, since the end of World War II. The presence of 86 diplomatic delegations from different Powers constitutes in itself a fact that transcends the occasion of their meeting. But while it may be true that the Council has been favoured by the relative period of peace through which mankind is passing, John XXIII's words about the Council as a promoter of peace are not merely rhetorical, even though it must be emphasized that the Council will fulfil this function only according to the measure of its success in bringing reforms to the Church.

In the past the Catholic Church has only rarely been able to act as a curb to war through its diplomacy; and perhaps even less has it succeeded in curbing divisions between nations by means of its evangelical message. The Catholic nations even in recent times have certainly not been the least warlike. But if the Church's preaching is to be more evangelical its own visible structure and leading hierarchy must come to seem more detached from things temporal and, paradoxical as it may seem, more de-clericalized. If the Council can accelerate the Church's detachment from temporal affairs and restore the true original significance to its preaching, the world will have taken another step forward towards peace; if that does not happen, the blame for a lost opportunity will inevitably fall upon the Church.

Rome, Saturday, 13 October

The Council's first great event, the Pope's inaugural speech, is followed today by a second and in some ways even more surprising development: the refusal of Liénart, Frings, Koenig, and Alfrink – that is to say, of the leaders of the progressive episcopate – to proceed at once to voting for the members of the Council Commissions purely on the basis of the suggestions from the Curia.

This is such an important matter that I must devote more time and quiet to it than I can do today – especially as I shall not have the chance to talk it over with Antimori, Bontempi, and Martinez until tomorrow.

There have been other happenings worthy of notice today – the Pope's audience this morning with the journalists and that of this evening with the observer-delegates of the non-Catholic Christian confessions. The first was especially important because it took place just after the *coup de théâtre* in the Council Hall, about which the Pope must certainly have been told at once. Nevertheless when he appeared before the thousand and more journalists in the Sistine Chapel his imperturbable serenity, indeed his radiant satisfaction, gave no hint of any recent emotion. Is this another reason for believing that he is in agreement with what happened in the Council Hall? I rather think so.

In his speech to the press and television representatives he thanked them for the extensive treatment accorded during the past week both to his journey to Loreto and Assisi and to the Council's opening. He began by extolling again the dignity and influence of the press, and added a serious reminder of its responsibilities; he was able thus to indicate the particular kind of collaboration that he hopes for from journalists with regard to the Council.

A speech, in short, that would not in itself have escaped the sort of criticism made about his Secretary of State's speech a few days ago; but the Pope confined himself to a few particularly disarming themes and continued to make his requests as far as possible impersonal. Journalists, he said, had in the Council an exceptional opportunity to 'gain a real contact with the Church', to explore it beyond the range of certain prejudices that usually surround it, and thus to discover for themselves, and tell their readers, that in the Church 'political machinations do not exist', that 'it has nothing to hide; it follows a straight path without subterfuge; it desires nothing but the truth', and so on. A man-to-man talk, in short, which proved quite irresistible.

I have only heard what was broadcast on the Vatican radio about the Pope's audience for the observer-delegates but it seems to have been even more successful than that for the journalists. John XXIII is clearly never more at his ease than in extra-protocol situations; and this was certainly one of the most unforeseen and unpredictable occasions for a long time for the pontifical ceremonial department.

Towards the end of the eighteenth century, Popes in Rome sometimes received Mahomedan princes and sovereigns, and it excited a good deal of comment, but in fact on such occasions the Pope was usually eclipsed by the Head of State. Even visits from representatives of pagan religions such as that last July of the great dignitary and superior of the Shinto temple of Kenkun Jinja in Kyoto, though falling outside normal protocol, are brought under it by treating them in the same way as other visits from various categories of lay personalities. But heretic or schismatic Christians, especially if authoritative members and official representatives of rebel communities, under canon law are unapproachables for the faithful and ecclesiastics of the Roman Church, and if there is any ceremonial covering their case it is 'De auferenda excommunicatione', supposing they have made themselves worthy of it.

The precedents provided in recent years by the personal visits of Fisher, Lichtenberger, Jackson, Schlink, Craig, etc., have done away with the idea that there is anything shocking about such contacts and have indeed given them a symbolic significance (we have come a long way since Pius XI refused to see Gandhi because he insisted on wearing his native dress or since Pius XII's secret meeting in 1956 with Bishop Dibelius). But such visits are in no way comparable with today's, which was an official and collective visit of the representatives of a score of schismatic Churches to the Head of the Roman Church.

If John XXIII had received them seated on his throne in the hall of the Consistory no one could have raised any objection, since he is not only a religious but also a political soverign. But he refused to do that and instead had an armchair placed before the throne on a dais raised only a few inches above the floor. The gesture did not imply, nor could it be presumed to imply, any renunciation, but it was an ingenious symbol of readiness to make eventual if vague renunciations, and in this sense it was of an audacity without parallel. But John XXIII effaced himself, so to speak, as Pope not only from the throne but also in his speech; he let the private individual in him take over, pouring out reminiscences and personal confidences to make a conversation rather than a speech. Referring to his contacts, as apostolic delegate and nuncio, with Christians of other Churches in the East and West he made use at one stage of a phrase which perhaps provides the happiest description of today's meeting: 'We didn't debate, we talked; we didn't discuss, we made friends.'

At another point in his 'allocution' John XXIII described himself simply as priest and bishop, thus avoiding any implicit or explicit reference to the primacy. And in that particular passage the whole tone of what he said and the way he said it was so moving as to leave an unforgettable impression on his listeners: 'Your presence here, the emotion that fills my heart as priest – as bishop of the Church of God, as I said in the Council Assembly on Thursday – the emotion of my colleagues and of yourselves, I am sure, invite me to confide to you the desire of my heart which burns with longing to work and suffer so that the hour may draw near when there shall be accomplished for all the prayer of Jesus at the Last Supper.'

Rome, Sunday, 14 October

The first General Congregation[1] of the Council lasted – apart from the Mass, where the honour of first celebrant fell to the Archbishop of Florence, Florit – exactly 14 minutes.

It would be superfluous, however, to go by the Press Office communiqué, which could hardly have found a worse way to inaugurate the first session of the Council. It not only forgets to mention the 'enthronement' of the Gospel[2] but even neglects to say who presided over the assembly or how many were present. Even the information about the booklets which were to be distributed

[1] i. e. Plenary Session.

[2] This ceremony took place every day at the opening of the General Congregation, when the Gospel was placed on a special altar.

to the Council Fathers (there were three of them: 'the first, containing a complete list of the Council Fathers; the second, a list of the Fathers who were members or advisers of the Preparatory Commissions of the Council; the third, containing the ten forms, one for each Commission, on which voting for the 160 members will be registered') is either inaccurate or misleading. Inaccurate because, for instance, the first booklet contained a list of the Fathers having the right to participate in the Council, not of those who are in fact doing so (at least a couple of hundred were unable to come to Rome for health or other reasons); and misleading because it gives the impression that most of the Fathers had not received this material, or at least the first two booklets, whereas the case was the exact opposite. Finally, the communiqué does not trouble to explain what the first item on the assembly's agenda was, namely, a vote to appoint the 160 members of the ten Council Commissions who, the Rules of Procedure state, are to be elected by the Fathers, the remaining 80 being appointed by the Pope (this is a retrograde step as compared with Vatican I, where all the commissioners except those on the 'Commission for Initiatives' were elected by the Assembly).

Anyway, the colossal electronic brains of the computers, which should today have amused themselves with sorting out the voting among more than 400,000 names, have an unexpected rest until the next General Congregation, adjourned till three days hence. Instead, the technical device that dominated yesterday's short sitting was the solitary microphone, kept on the chairman's desk and used, after Cardinal Tisserant had called on them to speak, first by Cardinal Liénart and then by Cardinal Frings to make statements of an astonishing brevity which elicited a storm of applause.

For this first sitting when discussion was not expected, the Secretary-General of the Council had allowed television technicians to be present so that they might take shots of a General Congregation sitting. But everything happened so quickly that they nearly lost this exceptional opportunity, for they had expected it to go on for at least two hours and instead soon found the assembly moving out of the hall talking as excitedly as if something really dramatic had happened.

What in fact had happened? Simply that, in the words of the official communiqué, Liénart had presented 'a motion of adjournment, giving as reason the need for prior consultation, especially among the members of the different episcopal conferences, in order to allow the Fathers to obtain a better knowledge of the candidates'. After a resounding ovation, Frings in turn read a statement in which, in the names of his colleagues Doepfner and Koenig (but the communiqué left that out) as well as himself, he associated himself with the motion of the President of the Assembly of Cardinals and Archbishops of France. Both Liénart's motion and Fring's statement were quiet in tone and made no allusion to anything controversial, but their meaning was obvious: the episcopate refused to make a random choice of the members of the Commissions on the basis of the suggestions received from the Curia in the seemingly innocent little booklets placed at their disposal and had therefore, in order to make a wise and careful choice, decided to meet among themselves in episcopal conferences, whether severally or together.

The distribution of the second booklet to the voters was in fact undoubtedly intended to recall to their attention the ex-members or advisers of the Preparatory Commissions as persons worthy of special consideration since they were already familiar with the subjects coming before the Council for decision, having studied and discussed them and formulated the relevant drafts. Similarly it was implicit that their re-appointment was suggested partly as a demonstration of deference to him who had elected them to their previous office, in other words the Pope.

Now this was quite unacceptable, not only because the choice of the 800-odd members and advisers at the preparatory stage had been governed by much more complicated and less dispassionate motives, but also for a whole series of reasons which required the rotation of appointments rather than their confirmation. First and foremost, it would have been ill-advised of the Fathers to renounce the use of an already restricted right which had been recognized in the Rules of Procedure (especially since the percentage of appointments reserved to the Pope made it foreseeable that, but for exceptional cases, it would operate almost exclusively in favour of the Curials); secondly, it was obvious that the assembly would make use of men it knew and trusted to draw up its own records; and finally, above all, by leaving the situation unchanged the Council would have been transformed into a mere appendix to register approval of the work of the preparatory organizations.

Many Fathers had already discussed all these reasons in the preceding days, and some episcopates had held meetings to decide on the line to be adopted at the first General Congregation. Last Friday afternoon the French bishops met at San Luigi dei Francesi before going on to an official reception at the French Embassy to the Holy See at Villa Bonaparte in Via XX Settembre, the Dutch met in a hotel in Via Crescenzio, the Germans, Austrians, and Swiss at the College of Santa Maria dell'Anima, and the Belgians at their seminary in Via del Quirinale.

Each of these episcopates voted practically unanimously in favour of postponing the voting for the short time necessary to consider the possible candidates; they then worked out the best way of presenting the motion, or rather they approved the method already decided on in principle on 10 October by the Cardinals of the Western European countries (namely, that a motion should be presented by the President of the Assembly of Cardinals and Archbishops of France, with which immediately afterwards the President of the plenary Conference of the German dioceses would associate himself).

Thus it came about that some 200 Fathers as they approached St Peter's yesterday morning were already relishing in advance the *coup de théâtre* which was to make famous the first Congregation. In fact, Cardinal Liénart had barely finished reading his motion when an anticipatory outburst of applause drowned his last words, reinforced by a further wave from those who now learnt of the initiative for the first time and realized its importance. The applause that greeted Frings' adherence a few minutes later was not only a recognition of the two prelates' courage but an outburst of rejoicing on the part of the majority of the assembly, which congratulated itself on having succeeded in affirming its own autonomy by evading the Curia's attempt to dominate the Council.

In short, while ecclesiastical dignity and the appearances were duly preserved, nevertheless for the first time swords were crossed between the Curia and the Episcopate in the Council Hall yesterday. Everyone had been expecting this, but few thought it would happen so soon. The Curia is, in truth, the natural antagonist of the Episcopate. The two organs are, certainly, correlative and collateral, but that does not prevent the strength of the one being in direct proportion to the weakness or acquiescence of the other. Moreover throughout the last century the Curia, helped by exceptionally propitious circumstances, has imposed its will more and more despotically upon the bishops. And that was bound to bring about a reaction sooner or later.

We need only to recall in this connection the vicissitudes of the French episcopate. Usually only the most recent of them are cited as blatant examples: Rome's sabotage of many revolutionary or near-revolutionary apostolic initiatives which were approved in France, ranging from experiments with the liturgy to the new theology, the apostolate of the worker-priests, the so-called progressive catechism, etc. Earlier episodes under Pius XI's Pontificate are forgotten. In its first years alone there were several such: the disavowal, in 1923, of the collective pastoral which urged French Catholics to vote only for candidates who were 'determined to deny the laity'; in the next year, the approval of the diocesan associations, which the French episcopate opposed; in 1925, the disavowal of the declaration of the Assembly of Cardinals and Archbishops on the 'laws concerning the laity'; in 1926, the condemnation of *Action Française*; and so on. This black list of humiliations, it must be remembered, went back to Pius X, and to the morrow of the reconstitution, in 1906, of the Assembly of French Bishops, which had not met for 118 years, in other words since the French Revolution. In the eyes of Papa Sarto, it had committed the error of firmly refusing, at its first meeting, to go in for cultural associations (to which Pius XI later agreed) and he caused it to be suspended from all activities from 1907 onwards.

It is not surprising that all this could have happened. The only really efficient episcopate in Europe, and indeed in the world, between the two wars was the French. In the united Germany of those days Catholics represented barely a third of the population, and politically they ceased to count after the suppression of their party, the *Zentrum*; in England they were an even smaller minority; in Holland, though the Protestants practised birth-control the possibility was still remote that Catholics would ever outnumber evangelicals.

As for the feudal churches in the Eastern European countries, they and their prince-bishops continued to live a thousand years behind the rest of the continent. In Spain, the transition from monarchy to republic had brought with it a reduction in the

Church's power which was to be restored only with Franco's success in the civil war. In Italy, the bishops were heard of only as participating in Mussolini's 'Battle for Wheat' or handing over crucifixes and pastoral rings for the conquest of monophysite Abyssinia. And outside Europe there were only Churches in a coma, as in Latin America, or infant Churches, as in the United States, or mission Churches, as in all other parts of the world.

It was therefore easy for a Pope to treat the bishops *de haut en bas* and in cases of disobedience or errors to summon them peremptorily, as in the case of Cardinal Innitzer, 'ad audiendum verbum', or to compel them to surrender the cardinal's biretta, as in the case of Billot. And if in spite of everything an episcopate showed some backbone it was only natural that Rome should keep an eye on it.

Pius XI, in any case, acted in person. The Curia was little more than an instrument of his will. Pius XII, on the other hand, especially after that hyperbolical apotheosis of the Papacy and himself, the Holy Year of 1950, latterly came to content himself with the oratorical appanages of his mission, and the government of the Church fell increasingly into the hands of the Curia – or, more precisely, of a group of wellnigh omnipotent Curials, the famous Pentagon: Canali, Pizzardo, Micara, Piazza, and Ottaviani. In the last years of his Pontificate he actually ceased to receive bishops, even those making their regular visits *ad limina*; and the air of Rome became so unbreathable to them that Roncalli himself avoided coming there. The only satisfaction they obtained was to receive the salute of arms from the Swiss Guards' halberds at the Bronze Gateway. But once arrived in the offices of the papal Chamberlain they found they were looked upon in much the same way as the beggars in their own sees. If they then betook themselves to Trastevere, to the colossal ostentatious palazzi of the Congregations built by the pontifical-cum-Milanese firm of Castelli, they discovered that the most minor secretary could make them tremble more easily than the Great Inaccessible himself.

With the succession of John XXIII the bishops grasped that their hour had come. Papa Roncalli was, in fact, like many of them, a 'back-number' whom the Curia had sent to end his days in exile amid the decaying loveliness of the lagoon capital. It was true that he showed a willingness to share his favours equally between the Curia and the Episcopate. But the bishops felt themselves reanimated by the recognition he gave to the Episcopal Conferences, by his presence, for example at a meeting of the CELAM (the Latin American Conference), and his invitation to the Italian bishops to reconstitute the statute of their Episcopal Conference.

Certainty of decisive change came only with the announcement of the Council. The Council, as a legislative assembly of the whole episcopate, in a certain sense suspends the activities of the Curia and also, through its deliberations, conditions them for the future. The extraordinary power replaces the ordinary: and everything is possible so long as it continues to function. For this reason the Curia, especially in modern times, has always been hostile to Councils. It took a quarter of a century to summon the Council of Trent. And there was that famous remark of Cardinal Pitra's in 1867: 'But they'll turn our Congregations upside down!' (and there were thirty of them at the time). As for Cardinal Antonelli, Secretary of State of Pius IX, after having done all he could to delay Vatican I he just went away and ignored it.

Faced with the fact of John XXIII's gentle strength, the Curia had only one course open to it: to sabotage the Council; and they partly succeeded by securing that the pre-preparatory Commission should consist of regular secretaries or assessors of the Roman Congregations, and later on that the eleven Preparatory Commissions and the three secretariats should have as chairmen the prefects or secretaries of the parallel departments or other cardinals of the Curia. All these, as we know, have also remained at the head of the Council Commissions, so that there is good reason to wonder whether in the Council itself the bishops will succeed in storming this Curial fortress.

The *coup de théâtre* of 13 October is a point in their favour, but the Council promises to be long-drawn-out, and the bishops' remoteness from their own sees, their unfamiliarity in dealing with problems in which the Curials are born experts, and other such factors certainly do not operate to their advantage. In any case, one thing is certain, and that is, that the biggest battle will be fought when the draft 'De Ecclesia' comes to be discussed. Then the two protagonists will face each other at last without holds or barriers, and will cross swords to decide, perhaps for good, which of them will prevail in the government of the Church. The choice will be between a government that is monarchical or oligarchic, absolutist or democratic, personal or collegiate.

All divisions, whether national or ideological, will give way before this unique dualism of forces confronting each other which constitutes the great unknown quantity of the Council. Behind the episcopate stand reform and renovation, often in quite daring form and affecting all branches from theology to liturgy, defence of the pluralism of the Churches and of their relative autonomy, and perhaps even the possibility that the office of primate might be, to some slight extent at least, reorganized so as to make its proportions less overwhelming. Behind the Curia, on the other hand, stand the most tenacious conservatism, worship of tradition and of the whole system of the Papacy, centralization, the legalism of the Code of Canon Law, and so on.

The real difficulty is to know how far the world episcopate is penetrated by ideas of renovation or fossilized in accepted theological and legalistic conventions. It is easy to suppose, for example, that bishops coming from Afro-Asian countries will be automatically progressive; but is this really bound to be so? It is true that most of them are very young, but they are probably really too young – too young, that is, to divest themselves of that Roman, if not actually Curial, mentality with which they have become impregnated during their education at the Propaganda Fide college. It is a known fact – for they themselves have said so – that a good many of the priests trained there return to their countries so warped that they feel like strangers. What if this were also true of many bishops?

It must not be forgotten, either, that the Curia itself is in a tremendously strong position in the Council. Besides the dozens of actual members of the Curia who are present there as Fathers, there are also the nuncios and apostolic delegates, the Italian episcopate which is the nursery of the Curia, and a large part of the Spanish and Latin American episcopates, closely associated with it. But above all, whether one likes it or not, the Curia lies in a special relationship to the Pope. John XXIII is notoriously anti-bureaucratic and perhaps no one has ever shown less readiness to put up from sheer necessity with the *entourage* of the pontifical court. But a Pope cannot govern without the Curia, and he cannot tie its hands too tightly, however much he may wish to satisfy the legitimate claims of the episcopate. The Curia is, in fact, in a certain sense the projection of himself. A weak and humiliated Curia means that the Papacy itself is hampered or half-stifled. Yet another reason, then, for believing that the Pope remains the pivot of the whole Council Assembly, its natural mediator and indeed the decisive factor conditioning it. In short, it rests with him to act in such a way that the dialectic between the Pope and the Council shall not prove largely illusory and end in a vicious circle.

Rome, Monday, 15 October

In the radio, television, and newspaper reports the most popular figures of the moment in the religious sphere are the two elderly but indomitable cardinals who last Saturday by their resolute grasp of the helm seized the Council out of the hands of the Curia.

Up to 48 hours ago very little was known about either of them outside their own countries. Indeed even now, despite the journalists' efforts, only very meagre biographies have been produced. The solitary detail of interest, and even that going back to nearly 40 years ago, concerns Liénart and the reason why he was made cardinal at the age of 46, only a year and a half after his appointment as bishop (and bishop, moreover, of Lille, a very new diocese, constituted only in 1913, with no tradition as a recognized prelude to a cardinalate). Trade union strife had become particularly acute in Lille in 1929, and the most unpleasant feature about it for Catholics was that their trade unions were having to defend themselves against charges and denunciations brought against them by the Catholic conservatives. The latter relied for support on statements of Cardinal Charost, formerly Bishop of Lille and then promoted to Rennes, who had denounced the rural Catholic trade union movement of Abbé Mancel as a 'movement of class division and antagonism leading to inter-class strife'.

Liénart was appointed Bishop of Lille, which was, incidentally, his native town, on 6 October and consecrated on 8 December 1928. He lost no time in courageously taking the side of the workers, to the shocked astonishment of the whole of France. But in Rome Pius XI grasped that the young bishop had made the right choice and he supported him in it. Ever since 1924 the Congregation of the Council had put off dealing with a request from the French Catholic industrialist Eugène Mathou asking that Catholic trade unions should be condemned. In 1929 Pius XI had this request unearthed and the Congregation was asked instead to express an opinion in their favour. Then in June 1930 Papa Ratti awarded the purple to the Bishop of Lille, now known throughout France as 'the red bishop'. Liénart subsequently continued to adopt an advanced attitude on social questions as well as in apostolic and religious matters. He was one of the most convinced supporters of the experiment of the worker-priests, so much so indeed that when Pius XII reorganized the 'Mission de France' he called on Liénart to direct it as bishop of the diocese-extraordinary of Pontigny.

The piquant feature of the episode of 13 October is that the speaker to follow him was Frings, a man as far removed as possible from advanced positions especially in politics or social questions. There could be no clearer proof of this than his friendship for Adenauer and his unconditional support of him. His career, moreover, has been typically bureaucratic. Indeed Frings undoubtedly bears much if not most of the responsibility for the German Church's conservatism. His motto was 'reconstruction', and that at a time when a quite exceptional opportunity offered for something very different – a complete reorganization from the bottom upwards, conducted in a new spirit especially with regard to the future. But the pre-Nazi situation was restored and even widely consolidated, especially on the temporal side, though unfortunately without avoiding the danger of excessive concentration on organizational and administrative aspects.

But while Frings has always shown himself capable of taking only a strictly traditional view of Catholicism in his own country, he has proved unexpectedly anti-conformist and progressive in his conception of the duties of the Church in the world as a whole. A lecture which he gave in Genoa in 1961 on the Council and modern society aroused very considerable interest, and indeed few other statements on the subject by bishops, whether in Europe or beyond, can compare with it. An even more significant fact (and one which partly explains what happened on 13 October) is that Frings brought with him to Rome as theological adviser Joseph Ratzinger, a young 35-year-old disciple of Karl Rahner, professor of theology in the seminary of Cologne.

In any case, Liénart and Frings, at the present moment, whatever one may think of them personally, count not as individuals but as representatives of their respective ecclesiastical and national communities. In other words, they personify and express the views of Catholic France and Germany, and in so doing go beyond and perhaps even contradict their own personal convictions. It is not without significance, moreover, that two such countries as France and Germany should have, in a certain sense, seized the helm of the Council and steered it out into the open sea. This seems to me a decisive event for Vatican II.

I am thinking over what I wrote yesterday about the duel between Curia and Episcopate, and it seems to me that the most harmful thing about what people say or write on this subject is that they generally have no clear idea of either the technical or, still less, the sociological significance of these two terms. As far as the Curia is concerned, it is usually thought of as the central bureaucracy of Catholicism, identified with the personnel of the Vatican's departments and other organizations and institutions. This is perfectly correct as far as it goes, but it fails to give a true idea of the complexity of the phenomenon. The results can be seen in relation to the famous question of internationalization of the Curia.

The Roman Curia is, in fact, not only an administrative complex and a bureaucratic machine – in short, the central apparatus of the Church – but also, and primarily, a sociological entity linked with a definite ethnic and geographical area, that of the immediate hinterland of papal Rome, coinciding roughly with the territory of the former Papal States. Failure to grasp this fundamental fact not only makes it difficult to comprehend certain internal debates within the Church but also prevents an understanding of certain historical facts, such as the defence, tenacious to the point of absurdity, of the temporal power in the nineteenth century, the subsequent prolongation of the Roman Question (1870–1929), and above all, the continual efforts of the Vatican to assure for itself a privileged position in Italy such as the Holy See would never dream of claiming in any other country. Italy, in fact, is to the Catholic Church not unlike Israel in relation to ancient Judaism: a levitical land and population, constituting its most highly selected reserve of men whose loyalty and reliability can be counted on even when they are themselves uninterested or lacking in faith. (For if they lack the faith, they have something else equally effective, that sense of *romanitas*, of blind certainty in the destinies of the Church, which has become an instinctive part of their nature with Italians as with no other people.)

Centuries-old traditions, linked with a political and religious situation probably unique in history, whereby the State of the Church up to a century ago offered two parallel and often converging careers in office, the secular and the ecclesiastical, still continue today to favour the existence of a flourishing central Church bureaucracy. This is true in particular of Latium, but it applies also to all the territories of the old Papal States (the provinces of Central Italy from the Tyrrhenian coast to the Adriatic, down to Campobasso in the south and up to Bologna in the north) and to a much lesser but still perceptible extent to the other regions of the peninsula.

When we talk about internationalization of the Curia, therefore, we have to bear all this in mind in order to understand that it is not an operation that, like some others, can be carried out by means of a mere decree. It would come up against a passive resistance so solid as completely to vitiate any such measure for quite a considerable time. It is significant that the only such attempt to be made so far has been at the very top, in the Sacred College, and even there it is little more than symbolic. Yet another factor to be remembered, too, is the force of assimilation exercised by the Curial atmosphere, which in a short time radically transforms the whole way of behaviour and even the external attitude of all the foreign elements coming within it.

But if it is only a partial description of the Curia to call it the administrative arm of the Vatican departments, formerly in Trastevere and now in Piazza Pio XII, it is equally misleading to regard the episcopate merely as the sum total of the provincial officials of the Catholic Church. All the bishops certainly share this specific function of a peripheral bureaucracy but in such very different ways as to astonish the layman. These differences may depend on particular historical traditions, current political situations, or sometimes on ethnic or racial factors which may produce quite unsuspected sociological groupings, tantamount almost to islands, among this second group of the Church's élite. An example of this is the missionary branch.

This branch of the Church's work, often regarded as among its most idyllic and peaceful callings, is in fact often only superficially understood. Yet a moment's thought will serve to remind us that lands for missionary endeavour virtually no longer exist and will soon be reduced to a purely symbolic area. This is partly the consequence, at any rate in the Far East, of the advance of the Communist steamroller which has pulverized all the missionary organizations in China and the neighbouring countries; and partly of the autonomist movement among coloured peoples, which, particularly in Africa, has compelled the Church, in its anxiety to avoid seeming like a survivor of colonialism, to improvise a hurried framework of indigenous church organization with native bishops and clergy.

All these developments have forced the great Orders with missionary activities, from the Franciscans to the Jesuits, and the innumerable congregations which developed in the eighteenth and nineteenth centuries for purely missionary ends either to withdraw their forces altogether or, if they let them stay on, to recognize that they must henceforth occupy a subsidiary role in places where till yesterday they held the field; the only remaining alternative being to send them to other than 'missionary' fields in the classical sense, such as the Latin American countries. Some Western bishops have naturally stayed on until the coloured hierarchies become self-sufficient, but their prestige is in constant decline. Up to the first quarter of the present century there was no idea of having national bishops in missionary lands. Even the native clergy were in a subordinate position; they were given less training and inferior duties, and often were not even invited to the houses of white missionaries. The shock of seeing coloured bishops at the head of former missionary territories was too much for many Western missionaries and for certain institutes, some of which put up every kind of resistance and even refused to collaborate with them.

It is not difficult to imagine this state of mind, especially when taken in combination with the other shock of the colonial Powers' political withdrawal from the missionary lands. But the state of mind of some other missionaries cannot have been very different when they found themselves directed not to the long-dreamt-of missionary lands of old but to civilized countries like those of Latin America, where the adventure of bringing the Gospel loses all its romance and becomes merely a fresh version of the priestly apostolate in Christian regions where laxity or neo-paganism have entered in. Nor must it be forgotten that missionary work used to open up a relatively easy way to the episcopate: the mitre was an honour awarded not only to the individual but also to the Order or the Congregation. Now, instead, in the new Afro-Asian States it is becoming more and more an exclusive privilege of the natives of those countries; and in the same way Latin American governments are also becoming much less inclined to put up with diocesan heads of foreign origin.

It is therefore natural to wonder what line will be taken in the Council by the missionary bishops now retired or removed from their former territories when, for instance, the question arises of the autonomy of the churches in Afro-Asian countries, or of liturgical and canonical adaptations for the new continents.

Among these island-like sociological groupings of the clergy, another quite important question arises over the Fathers of the Church belonging to religious Orders. They number 940, or more than a third of the assembly, 75 being Franciscans, 56 Capuchins, 54 Jesuits, 50 Salesians, 40 of the Holy Ghost, 34 Dominicans, 33 Oblates of the Immaculate Heart of Mary, 24 of the Order of the Divine Word, 17 Passionists, etc. Will they be able to take an individually independent line within the Council, or will their attitude be conditioned, and, if so, to what extent, by the interests of their Order or Congregation? Or will it be determined by their country of origin or their particular branch of activity? Even confining the question to the influence of the religious Order on the Fathers, it is extremely difficult to foresee how much it will count for. The religious Orders are so numerous as to discourage any attempt at a precise answer, quite apart from the fact that within the Orders themselves there are often very different trends, especially in connection with things outside their particular scope.

How will the Uniate Bishops align themselves – the heads of the breakaway elements in the schismatic Eastern Churches which over the centuries have returned to unity with Rome? There is little point in their case in trying to work out their possible attitude towards conservatism or modernization. They have their own particular circumscribed problems to defend, mostly in the nature of claims for greater autonomy, and they will naturally end by allying themselves with those groups most likely to guarantee them effective support. Theoretically they could be regarded as possible mediators vis-à-vis the Orthodox world, but it must not be forgotten that in the event of a reconciliation of the ancient Eastern Patriarchs (those now Orthodox) with Rome, the fate of their Uniate counterparts would be sealed – with what results for them can easily be imagined.

Within the Catholic episcopate, and so within the Council, some degree of collaboration between bishops of the same region, race or language is not to be ruled out. It is very likely, for instance, that the Latin Americans may combine with the Spaniards, or the Italians among themselves, or the Africans with the Asiatics. The influence of the nationality factor is, in any case, disproved by some striking exceptions – for example, and to go no further, by the Franco-German 'axis'. The *rapprochement* of France and Germany within the sphere of the Catholic Church can surprise only laymen; it has been amply demonstrated, especially in the post-war period, in the history of all the *avant-garde* movements in the Catholic world (theological, liturgical, catechist, pastoral, etc.), which have at their head elements from the first rank in both countries. From this point of view France and Germany can really be regarded as two complementary communities, as was shown last Saturday. Their characteristic feature (and their ambition) is to be in advance of the other Churches and to stimulate their energies towards new and original modifications while always preserving a deep loyalty to the old beliefs. They would like to replace the leadership held by the American Church in the technical and organizational sphere by a theological and pastoral leadership based on a profoundly evangelical form of modernization.

One result of the prestige of this policy is that the Belgian, Dutch, Swiss, and Austrian episcopates have to some extent come to group themselves around the French and German episcopates and the Catholic intelligentsia of those two countries. European Catholicism, in short, gravitates for the most part, and, one may add, as to its best part, towards the Franco-German axis. But those other episcopates are all too small to be of sufficient help in ensuring a majority for their views in the Council. Those from the Afro-Asian countries might however conceivably ally themselves with the Western European episcopates: for instance, there is certain to be a marked gravitation of Black Africa towards Catholic France, and recently there has been a similar trend towards Germany because of the financial aid she has now begun to extend to under-developed countries.

And what about the influence in the Council of the major Powers in the political sphere? The Communist countries have realized the danger of their absence from it, and have arranged to fill the gap by an anti-canonical form of representation which has been accepted, *faute de mieux*, by the Church – by means of episcopal delegations (at Councils the bishops do not count as delegates of their countries' Churches but as representatives and impersonators of their own dioceses). But the small number of Fathers sent from these countries (around 50) means that they cannot exercise any determining influence.

The 250 bishops from the United States, on the other hand, represent an impressive shock force, though it is apparently no longer so compact as formerly. The American Church has developed from two different roots: Irish Catholicism and the American adaptation thereof. It owes its pervasive integralism to its descent from Irish immigrants, its technical modernism (what an encyclical of Leo XIII has termed 'Americanism') to its Yankee blood. It is a curious but effective mixture and one which American Catholics, headed by their hierarchy, imagined they could easily export after the Second World War together with Marshall Aid and the National Catholic Welfare Conference.

According to the more ingenuous and also more fanatical exponents of American Catholicism, not excluding part of the episcopate, the propulsive forces destined to guarantee the dynamism of the Church in the world should be provided largely by themselves, who are, they think, the only people able to train such forces and supply them with the necessary technical equipment. In their view, in fact, the leadership of the Roman Church belongs to the USA in the same way that the political leadership of the Western world is in its hands. In other words, the United Nations in the religious as well as the political sphere should be injected, for the good of the Church, with new blood from the most modern and powerful country in the world.

Nothing could be better calculated to send a shiver down the backs of the old European communities than an ingenuous claim like this, totally lacking in idealism and combining crude commercialism (the idea that aid implies ownership) with childish programmes of technical reform. But it aroused even more malicious and pitying smiles among the Roman Curia, accustomed to conducting their own particular traditional form of barter between financial aid and spiritual benefits without abandoning one jot of their prestige or autonomy. In any case past disillusionments might bring a desire for revenge, to be sought perhaps in the Council itself – but how? Here is yet another question mark.

Rome, Tuesday, 16 October

A minor battle this morning, before the voting in the second General Congregation. But even before that, a minor revenge for Monsignor Felici, the Secretary-General, to whom some people are beginning to give the perhaps exaggerated sobriquet of 'Monsignor Torquemada'. He asked the Fathers to refrain from applause in order still further to distinguish their assembly from an ordinary secular parliament. The request, which naturally could not be applauded, was greeted with a significant silence.

Then it was Cardinal Ottaviani's turn. Called on to speak by Tisserant, Dean of the Sacred College (who is at present for some reason acting as chairman), Ottaviani proposed that in order to save time and money – especially the Fathers' own private purses – voting should be by a relative rather than a two-thirds majority. It would, he said, be difficult to secure a two-thirds majority on the first vote, and consequently the start of the Council's real work would have had to be put off for at least another week, just in order to set up purely executive Commissions.

Apart from this rather slighting estimate of the Commissions' importance, the proposal would seem very sensible. But Ottaviani had made the mistake of not mentioning it beforehand to his friends, with the result that Roberti, chairman of the sub-committee on Rules of Procedure, feeling that this was his province, pointed out that the assembly could not modify the Rules of Procedure, since they were provided for by a pontifical law. That should have sufficed; but instead for some reason Cardinal Ruffini, former secretary of the Congregation of Seminaries and for the last twenty years Archbishop of Palermo, also wanted to have his say, which amounted to much the same as Roberti's. So the progressives enjoyed the unlooked-for spectacle of an internal skirmish among their adversaries, which served to convince them still further of the importance of their success of 13 October.

The skirmish was, in any case, quickly settled by a Solomon's judgment from the Presiding Council, which decided that for the time being voting should be in accordance with the Rules of Procedure, and the whole question should be at once placed 'coram Sanctissimo', in other words before the Pope. The President then made known the Pope's earlier decision as to the eligibility of Fathers of the Council for membership of a Commission: any Father (from a Cardinal to the Superior General of a religious Order) should be eligible provided he was not already a member of the Presiding Council or the Secretariat for Extraordinary Questions, or Chairman of a Commission, or a secretary-general or deputy secretary-general.

Lastly, a small printed booklet was distributed to each of the Fathers containing 34 lists giving the names proposed by the various episcopal conferences and the Generals of the Religious Orders, the individual Fathers remaining free to vote according to their consciences.

This booklet, the result of feverish labours, is typical of the way the Council has functioned so far not only on the technical side but also in its indirect anticipation of certain conclusions of a theological nature concerning episcopal power.

Liénart's request of last Saturday at once set in motion all the existing episcopal organizations and speeded up the formation of others which till then had not been established. The *Annuario Pontificio* lists 44 Episcopal Conferences on a national basis as in existence before the Council opened (some countries, however, have more than one, as for instance Germany, which has four, one federal and three regional): twenty of them American, twelve European, six African, five Asian, one Australian, and one conference on a continental basis for Latin America, the Consejo Episcopal or CELAM. Many of the early national conferences go back for decades or even to the last century, but the majority had fallen into disuse and were revived after the last war; about half of them were established from 1955 onwards (twelve under the Pontificate of Pius XII, six under that of John XXIII).

The movement for episcopal federation within the individual countries was welcomed the more readily under Pius XII inasmuch as the conferences had a purely moral authority and their statutes, which were recognized or accepted by Rome, were all without exception unlikely to disturb the Curia (this was so much the case with the Italian one that John XXIII had it altered as soon as he became Pope). Moreover the Code of Canon Law ignores any such organs existing prior to 1917, the date of its own promulgation. Thus they are being accorded a second and more significant recognition now: indeed, paradoxically, a self-recognition. The Council, in fact, intends for the present to divide itself, *extra sedem*, into episcopal groups, in order later on itself to sanction their form and attributes under general criteria which the new Code of Canon Law will have to define and make operative.

It is obvious – and the consequences of 13 October (I was about to say 'the revolution of 13 October', a very pertinent lapse of the pen) become increasingly clear – that any strengthening of the Episcopal Conferences means a beginning of decentralization of the Church's administrative apparatus which is certainly not likely to further the Curia's privileges; and it is equally obvious that now the movement has been started, it seems likely to go forward irresistibly.

What has happened so far is that in the last ten days all the existing Episcopal Conferences have come into operation – first and foremost that of the French, which is particularly anxious, as Cardinal Liénart promised the Pope last Sunday, to do away with the impression that the French bishops want to form a bloc within the Council rather than promoting its unity. In fact a communiqué saying this was issued by Abbé Hauptmann, head of the Bureau de l'Information Réligieuse. Two hundred Brazilian bishops met yesterday morning at the 'Domus Pacis' in Via Aurelia, and 400 Italians in the afternoon.

It would not be too much to describe that last meeting as a historic event, for never since the unification of Italy in 1861, in other words since she became an independent modern country, has there been a plenary meeting of the Italian episcopate. It was only in 1953 that the Assembly of the Presidents of the Italian regional episcopal conferences met for the first time (20 of them, including Rome and the suburbicarian sees), but the event was kept completely secret. The second meeting, on the other hand, at Pompeii on 1 and 2 February 1954, was made public, partly because a collective letter was issued at it, dedicated to unity among Catholics and their attitude towards social problems. The object of the two meetings was to prepare the draft statutes of the future Episcopal Conference, which virtually came into existence with the approval *ad experimentum* of the Consistorial Congregation on 1 August 1954. But the Italian Episcopal Conference was little more than a ghost. Its only public action was to issue a laconic and peremptory pre-electoral communiqué on 3 May 1958. After its statutes were altered under John XXIII it took on a new lease of life: it became subdivided into episcopal committees and publicly announced its meetings, though for some reason it continued to maintain complete secrecy about its organization. For such an organ to be truly representative of the episcopate it would be necessary for each region to hold an annual conference, so that the regional chairmen could really act as interpreters of their respective regions' views within the Italian Episcopal Conference; no one outside the Consistorial Congregation knows whether this really happens or not. In any case, one document was solemnly signed by all the 300 Italian bishops, headed by the 13 Cardinals (including the six from the suburbicarian dioceses, the Frenchman Cardinal Tisserant among them): this was the pastoral letter addressed to the clergy on secularism, dated 25 March 1960 and published on 14 April 1960. Yet even on that occasion no general convocation of the episcopate was held, each bishop being instead consulted in his own see.

Two other individual groups have held meetings in the last few days: the Uniate patriarchs of the Eastern Catholic rite, and the 69 superiors-general of various religious Orders. As for the 34 lists issued with such haste, they differ both in the nominations put forward and in their actual contents. While some episcopal conferences have proposed nominations for all the 160 candidatures, others have put forward only a few, and yet others, like the superiors of religious Orders, have done so for one Commission only. Certain episcopates have also combined together in preparing their lists (for instance, those of Germany, Austria, Holland, Belgium, and Switzerland), and others have communicated their respective choices to each other so as to be able to agree on eventual substitutions. Some episcopates after comparing their lists have completely recast them, as did the Italians, whose second and final version was distributed to the Fathers only this morning in Piazza San Pietro just as they were entering the hall.

In practice, in any case, two main lists have emerged: the so-called Western and Central European list (supported by the French, German, Belgian, Dutch, Austrian, Swiss, Yugoslav, etc. episcopates), and the Italian.

Yesterday evening I managed to get hold of Monsignor Bontempi on the telephone. He had just come back from the Domus Mariae and was absolutely worn out. 'They insisted on including me,' he said in genuine distress; 'it was no good refusing.' All he could tell me was that the situation is very confused, both because of the great number of Italian bishops and because of the complete novelty of such a meeting for nine-tenths of them. Moreover, there is no recognized leader. Siri is the official head, but many look to Montini, who, however, seems to take little interest in it all. Urbani and Lercaro, with the air of acting as mediators, support the positions that should really be supported by Montini. But Siri is extremely clever, and then too he has a supporter even cleverer than himself, Ruffini. Finally, to complicate matters still further there is the inconvenient presence of the so-called 'mute cardinals' such as Castaldo and Fossati.

Rome, Wednesday, 17 October

This morning, for the second time in 24 hours, Monsignor Dell'Acqua received the German Ambassador to the Holy See, Dr Hilger A. von Scherpenberg. Yesterday's meeting was at the Ambassador's request, while today's was decided on by the Deputy Secretary of State.

As was to be foreseen, news of the Pope's speech to the Polish bishops, which I reported on the 9th, quickly reached the German Embassy and was passed on to Bonn, where it caused surprise and resentment in the German Government. What was not to be foreseen, however, was that the report of the speech was distributed on paper bearing the heading of the Vatican Council Press Office. Hence the mobilization of the Ambassador to make a formal protest, and the equally formal reply of the Deputy Secretary of State,

Dell'Acqua, that the standpoint of the Holy See concerning the territories in dispute between Germany and Poland remains unchanged: no objection can be taken to John XXIII's speech for the reason that any conversation between the Pope and the Fathers of the Council comes under the rule of secrecy, and indiscretions cannot be taken into serious consideration.

Since the German Ambassador, speaking also in the name of his Government, professed himself satisfied, the little drama of the speech has ended by pleasing everyone: the Poles, the Germans, and the Holy See. Nothing has changed, except that the Poles now have the feeling that the Holy See is more favourably inclined towards them than towards the Germans: while the Germans, for their part, are convinced that they are too important for the Holy See to allow itself to do more than throw a few kind words to the Poles. How true it is that the greatest happiness comes from cherished illusions.

The Secretariat of State has naturally announced that it will institute an official enquiry to discover who was responsible for the use of the Council Press Office's headed paper; but it is obvious that it cannot discover what it knows perfectly well and has no intention of revealing. The fact of adducing the secret character of the Council certainly constitutes a find in diplomatic practice; but it shows a surprising openmindedness, if not cynicism, to be prepared to swallow so serious an infraction of the rule of secrecy. Considering that there were at least some thirty people at the audience of 8 October, one wonders what will happen in an assembly of 2,500.

True, the texts of the drafts have been kept secret so far, but only in the sense that hitherto no one has managed to publish them, as happened at Vatican I. But the technical details about them – the number of pages and notes, their essential structure, some of their topics, even some passages of the original Latin – are a mystery to no one. And only yesterday Don Silvestri told me that he had read the lot, or rather the seven so far issued in book form, thanks to the confidence placed in him by an old missionary bishop.

This evening at about 9 o'clock I ran into Renzo Egidi in the Galleria Colonna. I went with him to his hotel, the Minerva, in

Piazza Minerva. This hotel used to be the meeting place of the Christian Democrats in their very early days, while the Catholic integralists used to frequent the Santa Chiara, a few steps away. The Minerva preserves quite a number of relics and memories of its past in the rooms off its horrible hall on the ground floor. Both it and the Santa Chiara are still used chiefly by prelates and members of Catholic Action or the Christian Democrat party. And not just Italians either – years ago I met Henri Daniel-Rops there.

Egidi was a little worried that he might be seen in my company by Monsignor Pisoni, former editor of the Milan *Italia*, or, worse still, by Monsignor Spada, editor of the *Eco di Bergamo*. However, he calmed down eventually; but he kept on reverting to Spada for a quite different reason. 'It's their hour,' he said after a pause in the conservation. He meant the hour of the *Bergamaschi*, the men from Bergamo. Monsignor Spada would never in fact have been a member or even an adviser of the Secretariat for Press and Entertainment, and later an 'expert' to the Council, but for the patriotic nepotism of John XXIII (Popes must have some sort of nepotism, and Papa Roncalli, unusual in everything, even has two: for the *Bergamaschi* and the Venetians). As for the *Eco di Bergamo*, it is a small provincial paper (and of a province both mountainous and revolutionary) which has improved its quality somewhat under the episcopate of Monsignor Adriano Bernareggi, a Milanese bishop of vast erudition who is also responsible for a useful *Enciclopedia ecclesiastica*; but even now few people in Italy are aware of its existence. The same was true of its editor until John XXIII dragged him from obscurity by these unhoped-for promotions.

We didn't spend long discussing Monsignor Spada and Bergamo's representatives in the Council. I was much more interested to learn how the delegates from behind the Iron Curtain are regarded in the Vatican and in Council circles. Egidi said at once that outwardly they were being overwhelmed with courtesies, but underneath people were very cautious about them. He gave me the reasons for this, consulting his little notebook the while. 'Canon Stankevicius', he said, 'seems to have been the one who accused Bishop Stefanovicius to the Lithuanian Communist leaders. Among the Czechs, only Monsignor Frantisek Tomasek, titular Bishop of Buto, enjoys complete confidence: but people don't at all know what to make of the two apostolic administrators (of Trnava and Nitra). The head of the Hungarian delegation and present chairman of the Hungarian episcopate, Monsignor Hamvas, besides having a remote past over which a veil might be drawn, seems to be an ardent collaborator of the Hungarian Communists even down to their youth festivals. He has been awarded one of the régime's greatest honours, the gold medal of the People's Republic. Then Monsignor Pal Brezonoczy is constantly going backwards and forwards between Budapest and Moscow. And if one can suspend judgment about the bishops, it is not so easy to do so about their train of priests and laymen, all of them loyal to the Government and charged with the duty of keeping watch over their ecclesiastical superiors.'

This news is on the whole anything but reassuring; and what counts about it is that it comes from someone who, like Egidi, frequents the Secretariat of State and Curia circles. In any case his last remark fits in perfectly with what Monsignor Bontempi told me yesterday *à propos* of the Czechoslovak bishops, that they had declined the invitation to stay at the Nepomuk College so as not to have to take with them their guard of eight priests, who couldn't be left behind and would certainly have disturbed the atmosphere of the college.

The greatest unknown quantity are the two delegates from the Moscow Patriarchate. Their arrival, Bontempi told me, was uncertain right up to the last moment. Discussions between the Secretariat for Union and Monsignor Nicodemus had been going on for months. When the Archbishop of Canterbury, Dr Ramsey, went to Moscow at the end of July he is said to have taken soundings in this connection, and the report he gave at Lambeth on 5 August to Cardinal Bea, chairman of the Secretariat, when he came to London was on the whole positive.

Bea could have stopped in Paris, where Monsignor Nicodemus, who is in charge of the Moscow Patriarchate's foreign relations, was about to arrive to take part in the meeting of the central committee of the World Council of Churches. But his presence there could not have escaped notice. Besides, the secretary of the Secretariat for Union, Monsignor Willebrands, was also expected in Paris; and it was with him that Monsignor Nicodemus had had a number of meetings. When Nicodemus heard that Cardinal Tisserant was in France, he made no secret of his wish to meet him. A meeting was arranged but, for reasons of prudence, not in Paris but on the Franco-Belgian border near Metz, at Les Bordes, where Abbé Lagarde, a great enthusiast for the ecumenical movement, is chaplain to the Little Sisters of the Poor.

At Metz Monsignor Nicodemus was even more positive about the possibility of the Moscow Patriarchate's delegates' presence in Rome, but he said the invitation must be brought to the Patriarch in person and to the Holy Synod, and the messenger from the Holy See would have to give an official guarantee of the completely a-political nature of the Vatican Council.

When Tisserant returned to Rome from France he took this proposal with him, having already notified Cardinal Cicognani and Cardinal Bea about its main lines. But the Vatican took a long time to decide, partly because of the conservatives' objections, partly from natural caution in weighing the pros and cons of such a step. In particular, the Pope was much disturbed at the prospect that Moscow might step in ahead of Constantinople, even though Constantinople, despite many expressions of good will, had shown that she was finding it difficult to make a decision because of her unwillingness to confuse, as she said, the already difficult conditions in which the Pan-Orthodox Council was being prepared. Attempts were made to get Constantinople to understand that there might be some surprise developments on the part of 'some other patriarchate', carefully avoiding the direct insinuation that Moscow was meant, especially since, according to Monsignor Nicodemus, the Patriarch of Constantinople, Athenagoras, while keeping Moscow informed of his frequent contacts with the Holy See, had never actually mentioned that the latter had given a definite invitation to all the Orthodox patriarchates. In the end, as no decision could be obtained from Constantinople, it was decided that Willebrands should go to Moscow.

The communiqué issued by the Secretariat for Christian Union stated, as if it was the most natural thing in the world, that 'after the contacts which have been going on for some months between the Secretariat for Christian Union and some personalities of the Moscow patriarchate, Monsignor Willebrands, Secretary of the above Secretariat, took the initiative of going to Moscow from 27 September to 2 October 1962, in order to give the patriarchal authorities first-hand information about the Ecumenical Council Vatican II'. The telegram announcing Willebrands' arrival on the morrow reached the Moscow Patriarchate, after more than a month's silence, on 26 September. He was very cordially received and stayed till 2 October; he was housed in the monastery of Zagorsk, the seat of the Patriarchate, and when not occupied in official talks was taken to visit other monasteries. But he did not see either the Patriarch Alexis, who was in his summer residence at Odessa, or all the members of the Holy Synod.

Monsignor Willebrands had not in fact brought with him the formal invitation of which Tisserant had spoken to Nicodemus. Thus Rome's prudence matched the even greater traditional caution of the Moscow Orthodox. However, the Willebrands mission succeeded within the limits envisaged by both sides. The leaders of the Patriarchate became convinced that the Council in Rome would not embarrass their delegates in any way by taking up a political (i.e. anti-Soviet) standpoint, and Monsignor Nicodemus promised to get the Holy Synod to meet as soon as he received an official invitation from the Holy See. That meeting took place on 10 October, and on the afternoon of the 12th the two delegates from Moscow, travelling by Caravel from Paris, landed at Fiumicino.

They were, as we now know, Archpriest Vitali Borovoi, aged 46, a former teacher in the Theological Academy at Leningrad and provisional representative of the Russian Orthodox Church at the World Council of Churches in Geneva; and Archimandrite Vladimir Kotliarov, aged 32, Vice-President of the Orthodox Russian Committee in Jerusalem. But who were these people really, apart from the official data about them? As soon as their names were known, Cardinal Cicognani was besieged with such questions by many Cardinals of the Curia (nearly all of the conservative trend), who asked him not only to furnish precise information about them to all the members of the Congregation for Special Ecclesiastical Affairs but also to take measures to guarantee that they and their suites would be watched both in the Council itself (by the Vatican Secret Service) and in the city of Rome (by the Italian counter-espionage service). The Secretary of State also received an incredible number of similar requests from private individuals or organizations, most of them emanating from

Russian or other émigré circles or from the various anti-Communist world organizations.

It is too soon yet to know how the Secretary of State will react to the requests from members of the Sacred College. But tactful feelers have been put out to some members of the World Council of Churches now in Rome in an effort to learn more about Archpriest Borovoi. He is, as a matter of fact, already an old acquaintance of Willebrands', for he acted as interpreter in Paris last August between the latter and Monsignor Nicodemus, and Willebrands found him once more at his side in Moscow.

As for Kotliarov, the Secretariat of State must already have a pretty full dossier about him, for it follows every movement of the Moscow's Patriarchate's representatives in Jerusalem. This is the job not only of the Apostolic Delegate, Monsignor Giuseppe Sensi, who has held that office fourteen years, but also of monks of various orders seconded to the office of the Guardian of the Holy Land and other monastic houses to follow the activities and mutual relations of the dissident communities. It seems, however, that those who were most suspicious of him are destined to be disappointed, since apparently he has for some time been in confidential relations with Monsignor Sensi.

In any case, it appears that the Pope is extremely pleased about what has happened. The mission from Moscow has, if nothing else, at least counterbalanced his disappointment about the cypher telegram which Cardinal Bea received from Athenagoras conveying the refusal of the Orthodox Church of Constantinople 'together with the other national Orthodox Churches'.

But Athenagoras' Byzantine methods have in fact reaped what they had sown. The Moscow Patriarchate recognizes only an honorary primacy on the part of Constantinople; it has every right to act autonomously when it thinks fit. Moreover in 1948 the Patriarchate of Constantinople adhered to the World Council of Churches although that of Moscow either could not or would not do so. There is consequently something rather theatrical about the protests that Bishop Emilianos Timiadis, representative of the Orthodox Patriarchate of Constantinople in Geneva, hastened to present to Cardinal Bea because the Vatican had negotiated separately with Moscow.

Anyway, sooner or later – though for obvious reasons of prestige not immediately – Constantinople too will decide to send its own delegates to Rome. The step taken by Moscow will really make it easier for them to do so.

It is certainly not easy to explain Moscow's change of mind, especially when one recalls the uncompromising 'Non possumus' pronounced by the Patriarchate's periodical in May 1961. That particular article was doubtless the result of temporary causes (newspaper reports, which Moscow regarded as untrue, of contacts between the Nuncio in Vienna and certain Orthodox bishops, etc.); but also the political and ideological situation then was very different from that of today. Moreover the article, though unsigned (the author is now known to have been A. Vedernikov), was not an editorial, and cannot therefore be taken as an official expression of the Patriarchate's opinion.

Rome, Thursday, 18 October

This morning I went to visit Monsignor Bukavu at the Albergo delle Anfore on the slopes of Monte Mario (this is the hotel where the six cardinals, thirty bishops, and six auxiliaries from the former Belgian Congo are staying) and so I learnt by chance that today is Africa day.

For today both the various African episcopal conferences (fifteen, I was told, including those already in existence and others formed in the last few days or in course of formation) and their chairmen have met in order to create a permanent pan-African Secretariat, which will presumably be presided over by Cardinal Rugambwa.

Monsignor Bukavu is one of the ten native bishops from the Congo, and, like all of them, has only very recently come to wear the violet *zucchetto* – when he does wear it, for more often he sticks it in his pocket. We have known each other since he was made a bishop, and about three or four times a year we write to exchange news and information.

He was in a great state, partly because he hadn't been able to let me know about putting off our meeting for today, but particularly because while nearly all the African bishops seem eager to combine, their white colleagues of the Congo will have nothing to do with it. 'It's as bad as the Salazar people in Angola and Mozambique,' he lamented. He hopes, but without much conviction, for a last-minute compromise.

Before I left he went up to his room and fetched a bundle of the usual kind of material he sends me: some pastoral letters of his colleagues, some diocesan bulletins, a book for private circulation only, which I have to give back in two days (it is a collection, printed in a limited number of copies and intended only for the Fathers of the Council, of the first replies to a questionnaire conducted among African priests and laymen by *Présence Africaine*), and a 'historical document', also confidential and to be returned. This last is a document summarizing the various phases of the attempts made by the African bishops to meet together before the Council. Because of their unusual nature Propaganda Fide considered such meetings inopportune, whether in Africa or in Rome just before the Council. The document is very detailed but doesn't really tell me anything I didn't know already, even about the real purpose of Cardinal Montini's journey to Africa, which was arranged by Monsignor Pignedoli and his colleagues Monsignori Del Mestri and McGeough, Apostolic Delegates respectively of East Africa and South Africa.

When I got home I had a look at the pastoral letters. The one that struck me most was by a European bishop, Monsignor Copard-Lallier, apostolic prefect of Paraku in Dahomey. It is of very recent date, just before its author left for Rome, and contains the following passage:

> We here can be said to be in the first century of Christianity, with one, two, or three generations of Christians. The heritage of the faith has been faithfully transmitted and received: a heritage more elaborate than the theology of the New Testament at the time of St Ireneus or St Cyprian; a heritage bearing even more the stamp of the West. Now, in the first centuries of Christianity the apostles from the East found followers from Asia, from the West, from Greece, from Rome to carry on their ministry. With these new spiritual leaders it was easy to bring together Councils: on the basis of the faith, such as belief in the Trinity, and on the basis of morality in face of pagan customs. The Church, faithful to itself, does not welcome new peoples without making them participate in its inner life: it is not enough for it merely to remove the dangers of separate Churches; it wants to become more and more Catholic. Now, has it been sufficiently stressed that this Vatican Council will be the Council of the first century for the Church of Black Africa?

It could hardly find an apter definition. In 1869, when the first Vatican Council opened, the evangelization of Black Africa had barely begun. Only a year earlier Cardinal Lavigerie had founded the society of those White Fathers who were one day to convert the family of the future Cardinal Rugambwa, baptized by them when he was eight years old. The African continent was not officially opened to Catholic and Protestant missions until 1885, after the Congress of Berlin. Even in 1900 there were only just over half a million Catholics there. The first apostolic delegation dates from 1922; the first two negro bishops of Latin rite (one for Uganda, the other for Madagascar) were consecrated in 1939. The first ordinary Church hierarchies were established in 1950.

This change-over from missionary to ordinary ecclesiastical administration is itself an indication of the age of the Church in Black Africa. It has come about entirely in the last twelve years. It began in 1950 with Ghana, the Cameroons, Nigeria, and Sierra Leone; Basutoland, Swaziland and South Africa followed in 1951; Kenya, Tanganyika, and Uganda in 1953; French Equatorial and West Africa, French Cameroons, Madagascar, Morocco, the Sahara, French Somaliland, and Southern Rhodesia in 1955.

Today the Catholics of Black Africa number some 24 million, native priests (only 94 in 1912) about 2,500, bishops (17 at the end of 1956) 67, and ecclesiastical territorial divisions of Latin rite 262 (of Eastern rite 10). In short the development of the Church in Black Africa has been vertiginously, incredibly, almost absurdly, rapid, full of pitfalls and dangers, and Rome is well aware of it. The more so since everything has had to be improvised and is therefore highly precarious, because in general it was historical circumstances – often ill-foreseen and ill-understood – that forced the Church's hand. The hurried creation of the hierarchy in the ex-Belgian Congo when that country's independence was already impending (and this was the most Catholic country of all Black Africa, contributing about a quarter of the total African Catholic population) is a classic example the consequences of which have been seen only too clearly.

Nothing, then, could be more natural than that this Church should, so to say, stammer rather than speak. Though it has tried to build up a lay élite it is largely a Church of clerical cadres in which, by force of circumstances, non-native and partially assimilated elements predominate, many of them sensitive to the situation but sometimes reserved and even hostile. This explains why after the announcement of the Council and for the next two years the Church in Africa seemed to take no interest in it. The awakening came only in the last twelve months; and it is therefore extremely difficult to tell how much its bishops will count in the great assembly in Rome. The danger that a split, if not direct opposition, may develop between the black episcopate and the white missionary episcopate is very serious and might lead to unpleasant revivals of colonialism and racial strife. Another and possibly even more difficult problem is the lack of adequate theological preparation. And supposing native and Western representatives do agree, will it really be about essentials?

The fundamental problem for the Catholics of Black Africa, as Father Hebga aptly says in the volume lent me by Monsignor Bukavu, is this: 'What is, and what will henceforth be, the status of the African community in world Christianity? What is, and what will be, the attitude of Christianity towards men of a non-European culture?' Or, as Abbé Sastre rightly observes: 'It seems to me that the Council opens up an era of responsibility and initiative for the African Church. But is it ready to embark on this era? That is the question.' And Mark Ela: 'For the African Church, after the disastrous period of *adaptation,* it is not a question of reforms or *restoration* but of creation, or initiating a radical novelty, and of instilling Christianity into mentalities lacking in Christian traditions.'

There can be no doubt that the African dimension of the Council is among the most difficult of all. What will be its fate? Will the 300 bishops from the Black continent succeed in making their problems heard, and will the other 2,000 succeed in understanding their significance after almost a century of missionary incomprehension?

The day before yesterday I heard something that suggests that at least a partially optimistic answer might be given. Monsignor Jérome Rakotomalala, a young coloured priest who in 1960 at the age of 46 became Bishop of Tananarive, one of the three metropolitan sees of Madagascar and also its capital, asked the celebrated Dominican theologian Chenu, whose pupil he was, to be his theological adviser, indeed the theological adviser of his country's whole episcopate, and Père Chenu accepted. I don't know which to admire most: the courage of this young Negro bishop, who by this request in a certain sense challenged the conformity that prevented Chenu from being chosen as one of the Council's experts after having also been excluded from taking part as member or adviser in the preparatory stage (perhaps largely because a book edited by him, on the famous Dominican school of Le Saulchoir, has been put on the Index); or that splendid, indomitable old theologian of the French Church, who has willingly agreed to act as simple adviser to a young Negro bishop who till a few years ago was still a subject of one of his country's lesser colonies.

10 p.m.

As he promised, Monsignor Bukavu has just telephoned to tell me that the Pan-African Secretariat is now an accomplished fact – that the Congolese conference has joined it – and that Rugambwa is its President.

I wonder whether today's events, if only on the fringes of officialdom, will make it not only Africa's day at the Council but also a historic day for the African Church?

Rome, Friday, 19 October

I read in today's *Avvenire d'Italia* a letter to the editor which calls attention to the inaccuracy of the Italian translation (published in the *Osservatore Romano*) of the Pope's speech of 11 October. The editor in his reply is at pains to go one further than his correspondent in affirming that 'a careful examination will show even more places where the Italian version may seem less precise and felicitous than the original Latin', and he goes on to list several of them (but he is so kind as to consider innocuous the Latin translator's omission of the phrase affirming that the presentation of the authentic doctrine should be effected according to 'the methods of research and literary formulation familiar to modern thought'!). For him, in short, it is merely a question of 'the inevitable circumlocutions of any translation'. Obviously he has no suspicion that the original text is the Italian, drawn up by John XXIII himself, and that the problem therefore is to decide which of the two texts should be considered final in case of doubt or dispute.

Normally, the official text of the records of the Roman Curia is the Latin one – providing, of course, that such exists, for some pontifical documents, even encyclicals, are drawn up only in the vernacular. That is why the *Osservatore Romano*, and also the *Acta Apostolicae Sedis*, always print the Latin version before the Italian or other versions. Indeed in the *Osservatore* the Italian text is always preceded by the words 'The following is our Italian translation...'

Well, in the case of the speech of 11 October (though not in that case alone) that formula is obviously incorrect. No particular familiarity with the often highly personal style of John XXIII is needed in order to perceive that the Italian text is not a translation made by anonymous officials of the Secretariat for Latin Studies or by a sub-editor on the Vatican daily, but the original version prepared by the Pope himself. The use of certain archaisms, the choice of adjectives, certain unaccustomed transpositions, the number of exclamations and interjections, as well as, of course, the preference for certain expressions and words, all confirm this view. But if this is so, there is no doubt whatever that the Latin translators have not infrequently taken excessive liberties in their work. A good translation should not be first elegant and then faithful, but the other way round. The precedence given to elegance might be allowed and even appreciated in the case of a work of narrative or biography or a panegyric of some particular person, but it is absolutely inadmissible in a text expounding a programme or policy, especially if the matter is ideological, where the preciseness of the concept and the nuances are bound to be of the greatest importance.

An examination of the two versions of the inaugural speech at the Council at once excludes any idea of manipulation for a definite purpose, but it nevertheless shows a dangerously light-hearted approach and too little sense of literary style. In order to convince ourselves that there was no intentional attempt to tone down some of John XXIII's open and vigorous criticisms of the conservatives, it will suffice to notice that the Latin expressions used in relation to them are sometimes stronger than the Italian. We can find more than one example of this in, for instance, the passage about the 'prophets of misfortune'. It is much more stern to say 'non sine aurium Nostrarum offensione' than 'ci ferisce talora l'orecchio' (our ear is sometimes offended); and the word 'voces', the subject of the phrase, is more severe than the vaguer 'suggestions' used by the Pope; and 'a Noi sembra di dover dissentire' ('To Us it seems that we must dissent') becomes nothing less than 'at Nobis *plane* dissentiendum esse videtur'.

Immediately afterwards, it is true, in the even more fundamental paragraph on the relation between modern times and the action of Divine Providence, the by now famous paragraph on the 'new order', the Latin version instead tones down the Pope's clear-cut assertion. 'Nel presente momento storico, la Provvidenza ci sta conducendo ad un nuovo ordine di rapporti umani . . .' ('At the present historical moment Providence is leading us towards a new order in human relationships . . .') becomes 'In praesenti humanorum eventuum cursu, quo hominum societas novum rerum ordinem ingredi videtur, potius arcana Divinae Providentiae consilia agnoscenda sunt . . .': which certainly does not alter the substance of the thought, but weakens it by departing too arbitrarily from the original formulation. The same thing happens over the no less famous 'balzo innanzi' – the 'leap forward towards a doctrinal penetration and a formation of consciences' – and indeed over that whole long paragraph, where we find the same arbitrary departure from the original text, even to the point of excluding the idea of the 'leap forward', which is certainly not recognizable in the vague expression 'eadem doctrina amplius et altius cognoscatur'.

These difficulties not only give rise to unnecessary and unworthy disputes but also pose, or run the risk of making it necessary to pose, problems of real textual criticism essential for an effective evaluation of the meaning of the Pope's pronouncements. It is true that the Pope by accepting publication of the Latin version of one of his own texts, or even reading it in public, makes that version his own and gives it an official stamp; but in cases of dispute or differences between the text (on occasions when, of course, the Italian is undoubtedly his own version) the presumption must inevitably be in favour of the original.

All this would undoubtedly be much simpler if the Secretariat for Latin Studies functioned properly. Instead, there seem to be recurrent cases of this kind. I noted in my diary at the time a similar occurrence over the encyclical *Mater et Magistra*. I find I made no detailed note of the variation arising in the Latin text of *Aeterna Dei sapientia*, the encyclical which John XXIII dedicated to

St Leo Magnus at the end of 1961. But at a certain point that encyclical refers to the friendly relations between Pope Leo and St Prosper of Aquitaine, who despite the office he held in the papal chancellery was a layman. Well, the Latin text makes him a bishop – 'cum Santo Prospero Aquitanorum Episcopo' – whereas the Italian text simply says 'San Prospero di Aquitania'.

As a matter of fact, much the same sort of thing is liable to happen in all the Roman Congregations as well as in the papal Secretariat for Latin Studies. For example, the *Acta Apostolicae Sedis* of May 1958 published a Latin text of the letter sent on 27 October 1957 by Cardinal Pizzardo to the bishops of all the world which differed perceptibly from that received by the bishops: in this case, obviously, it was a question of a different version from the original.

These facts were probably not known to the judges of the American Institute of Management who gave the Holy See the first prize for efficiency of organization and results.

Rome, Saturday, 20 October

The run of ill luck for the Curiali and their supporters seems not yet to be at an end. The third General Congregation this morning produced yet another bad day for them. ('A double misfire today!', called Antimori over the telephone, as if he was speaking to me not from the Press Office but from the Maremma, where at this time of the year he is usually boar-hunting.) The results of voting for the Commissions, though still incomplete, show a definite defeat for the Curali; and they have also been compelled to give unanimous approval to a Message of the Fathers to the world which up to the last moment they had striven to oppose.

Their leaders had already realized by yesterday evening that the Pope's acceptance of Ottaviani's proposal had removed any hope of recovering their position through a second vote. They knew, too, that what had most influenced the Pope's decision was the fact that most of those elected had obtained an absolute majority. In any case, yesterday evening they fought with all the determination that the situation in their view demanded. It was a question of regaining the prestige damaged by their opponents' electoral success, in order to prevent the presentation to the

Assembly of the Message which a group of Cardinals – Liénart, Doepfner, Léger, Alfrink, and Montini – had compiled on the basis of a text drawn up by Chenu and Congar and presented to the Pope. They had entrusted the final effort to Monsignor Felici and then went to wait for the result in a room in the Palazzo of the Holy Office. Finally, about 8 pm, the Secretary-General telephoned to say there was nothing to be done: the Pope wanted the message to be presented to the Assembly the next day and approved by standing or sitting, so that at the fourth Congregation on the 23rd the Assembly could embark on the real labours of the Council.

The only thing left to do for the Curiali was to decide what line they should take during the discussion of the Message: should they give battle, or let it go as if nothing had happened? In their view the 'unfortunate' document was political, not to say demagogic, rather than religious, and in addition to adopting the fundamental themes of Communist propaganda (demands for greater social justice, calls for peace, affirmations of anti-racialism and anti-colonialism, etc.) it also committed the unforgivable error of forgetting to mention the Churches of Silence scattered from Europe to Asia in the countries oppressed by international Communism. To submit to it would mean accepting that a similar outlook should influence the Council's drafts, and that was intolerable. But could they run the risk of another defeat, which was quite likely to happen given the progressives' present state of euphoria? They therefore chose a middle course: none of the cardinals who had originally attacked the document would speak now; the opposition was to be entrusted to the bishops alone, and in particular to the Ukrainian exiles.[1]

These tactics were put into effect this morning after Monsignor Felici had read the text of the Message, which he presented to the Assembly as having been proposed by the Presiding Council with the Pope's approval. The sitting was suspended for half-an-hour's reflection and then five cardinals rose to speak (Bacci, Wyzsynski, Ferretto, Cicognani, and Léger), followed by the Patriarch Saigh and 31 archbishops and bishops, 11 of them Italian (among whom, significantly, were Parente, assessor of the Holy Office and

[1] There are now some 2 million Ukrainians in exile, including 600,000 in the United States and 20,000 in Britain; they began to emigrate at the end of the nineteenth century. None of the fifteen Ukrainian bishops in exile has ever lived in the Ukraine except Monsignor Bucko, Apostolic Visitor for the Ukrainians in Eastern Europe.

Ottaviani's right-hand man, and Fiordelli, who became notorious in 1958 for having sent the Vatican and the whole country into mourning after his condemnation by the Florence tribunal: he had been summoned by a married couple of Prato whom he had described in a public document as living in concubinage because they had been married by civil rite alone).

In short, it was a sort of dress rehearsal of all countries and ranks, especially of those with merely walking-on parts. And, as if sticking to the dress-rehearsal idea, the speakers got no publicity: the third communiqué of the Council Press Office mentioned no names and did not even say how many Fathers spoke. The debate in fact produced no significant criticisms or suggestions apart from pointing out the absence of any reference to the Churches of Silence or the Madonna. The first of these two criticisms was given especially lively and passionate expression by the most authoritative of the Ukrainian episcopate in exile, Monsignor Hermaniuk, Metropolitan of Winnipeg. But the effect was blunted by the dignified and diplomatic contribution of the head of the Hungarian episcopal conference, Monsignor Hamvas, who said, and was supported in this by others including Monsignor Fiordelli, that the best service the Council could render to the Eastern Catholics was to refrain from talking about them.

As to the question of devotion to the Madonna, it would have been very embarrassing to resist its claims: the compilers of the Message let it be known, however, that their chief concern had been to draw up a text which would be exemplary from the Biblical angle and therefore particularly acceptable and comprehensible to evangelical readers. The objection was raised, and with some justification, that, far from doing honour to the Bible, it was irreverent to make use of it in order to disguise rather than stress a dogmatic tenet, especially in this particular case of the Madonna whom the Bible unquestionably honours and exalts. The situation was saved by Monsignor Ancel, Auxiliary of Lyons, who counselled the insertion of a scriptural text making mention of the Madonna (the passage in the Acts of the Apostles referring to her presence at the Last Supper among the Twelve), and this was done.

All the attacks on the Message on grounds of its too penitential or 'too terrestrial' tone collapsed, however, in face of its explicit references to the Pope's broadcast message of 11 September. And in fact the virtues of this skilfully drafted Message of the Fathers lie precisely in its combination of frank and impassioned religious inspiration with an open recognition, on the one hand, of the 'human values' ('the discoveries of science, technical progress, and the diffusion of culture') and, on the other, of the urgency of finding agreed solutions for the most pressing 'material and spiritual' needs of all peoples, especially 'of the humblest, poorest, and weakest' among them, beginning with the consolidation of peace and the defence of the fundamental demands of social justice. Lastly, in happy harmony with the humble tone adopted by the Fathers was the direct appeal 'to all brothers who believe in Christ' and 'also to all men of good will' to labour together to 'build in this world a more just and more fraternal city'.

At the same time it was obvious that many of the Fathers, and especially the representatives of the Curia, accustomed to the supremely pontifical and absolutist, not to say triumphal, documents of the Pacelli era on the Church's mission in the world, were shocked by a text like this which repudiated both the thunderbolts of the *Sillabo* and the leadership of Roman Catholicism in the world. Be that as it may, when the time came to vote by standing or sitting (and not, as the Press Office bulletin says, 'by a show of hands'), only a few Fathers apart from the 14 or 15 Ukrainians had the courage to remain seated. Several decided to rise only after an anxious look around them, but still they did so in the end. The Message was thus declared unanimously approved.

Discussion of the voting results which were announced at the opening of the sitting by the Secretary-General (in relation to the first seven Commissions, for voting for the last three is still going on) caused most people to feel that the episode of the Message was closed, especially as the Pope had let it be known that these results were to be regarded as final and had at once notified the eight members of the Commission on Liturgy (the first to start functioning), whose appointment was, according to the Rules of Procedure, reserved to himself. Yet another fact that was anything but pleasing to the conservatives, but, who knows, perhaps one misfortune cancels out another. During the debate on the Message a good many Fathers had been indulging in some calculations and now as they streamed out of the hall they formed little groups to compare notes.

An examination of the list voted by the episcopates gravitating round the Franco-German axis (i.e. the majority of the French, Canadian, Belgian, Dutch, British, Scandinavian, German, Austrian, Swiss, Polish, Yugoslav, etc.) shows that out of the 16 members elected to each Commission, the successful candidates from the progressives' list numbered 8 on the Missions Commission, 9 each on the Theological Commission and the Commissions on the Bishops and the Clergy, 10 on the Commissions for the Eastern Churches and for the Laity, and as many as 11 on that for the Liturgy. It was especially interesting to see how many of the progressives figured high up on the list for each Commission. Of the eight Frenchmen, two occupied first places, two came in second, two fourth, and one fourteenth; of the seven Germans elected, two got first places, two came in second, two third, and one fifth; the three Austrians came in first, third, and sixth; the three English, fifth, sixth, and ninth; of the three Belgians one got a third place, of the three Dutch one got a fourth; the two Canadians, sixth and seventh.

The ratio of representation was also significant. Luxembourg won a place (a fifth place) for its single bishop; Holland and Belgium, with only seven dioceses apiece, and Austria with nine, each got three places. The winning list, moreover, had included three Italian bishops not appearing in the list of the Italian Episcopal Conference (these were Lercaro, Gargitter, and Minisci) with the result that only twelve out of the 49 on the latter's list of candidates were appointed members of Vatican II Commissions.

The unsuccessful candidates were not in the best position to understand the reason for their failure and for the success of what had been regarded as the minority list. But an outsider can easily guess which were the two decisive factors in its victory: first, its choice of candidates covered a wide and nationally representative range of high quality, and secondly, only men of undoubted competence were put forward. The large number of episcopates gravitating round the Franco-German axis undoubtedly made it easier to give this list its ecumenical character, but no less striking is the opportunity it offered to small countries, such as, within Europe alone, Belgium, Holland, Austria, Switzerland, and even little Luxembourg.

First Subject Discussed: The Liturgy

Rome, Sunday, 21 October

Tomorrow discussion begins in St Peter's of the draft text 'De Sacra Liturgia' which John XXIII has chosen from among the seven distributed to the Fathers. The choice of this draft (which incidentally appeared fifth in the volume of drafts) does not correspond to any criterion of order, and appears to have been fortuitous. There seems in fact little doubt that the Council has never had a pre-arranged plan: the guiding lines will emerge gradually as the debate proceeds and will suggest a suitable arrangement of the material to be dealt with under the main headings.

It was decided to take the Liturgy as the first subject, partly in order to avoid an immediate clash between conservatives and progressives on the theological plane (because of its inevitable repercussions especially on public opinion) and partly because the complexity of the solutions it calls for will compel the Fathers to tackle from a practical angle major problems (such as the need to widen the powers of the bishops and hence to decentralize Church administration) for which a solution on principle will eventually be sought on the theological plane.

There are various different ways of approaching the Liturgy, but two stand out particularly: either it can be treated as the whole combination of outward and visible rites which constitute the official method of prayer of the Church (*lex orandi*), or it can be considered from the angle of its doctrinal context in relation to the mystery of divine action which should inspire the rites themselves (*lex credendi*). In the second case, for instance, it would be of minor importance to know whether or not the Eucharist should be the centre of liturgical life: the important thing would be to define the essential nature of the Mass (commemoration, or actual sacrifice?) and the significance of the Eucharist (a symbol of the sacrificial presence of Christ, or His authentic presence through transubstantiation, etc.?).

Since the real theological questions are dealt with in specific drafts, it would seem that the Liturgical draft ought to be of an eminently practical character. But precisely from this angle it connects up with the liturgical movement which, originating in the last century, received a legitimate status in a document of Pius X ('Inter sollicitudines', of 22 November 1903) and which has since then become widely diffused with varying success throughout Christianity. A far more important detail is the fact that the liturgical movement preceded and – owing to the place occupied by the Bible and the writings of the Fathers of the Church in the Catholic liturgy, especially in the Mass and the Divine Office – in part inspired the biblical and patristic and also the catechistic movements, thus lying at the root of the fundamental demands of the 'new theology', preceded some years earlier – and not by chance – by kerygmatic theology, or the theology of preaching.

In other words, the draft 'De Sacra Liturgia' not only impinges on the most vital questions debated in recent years among practically all the *avant-garde* movements of Catholicism but it also goes right to the heart of the fundamental conflict that overhangs the Council: a conflict which does not concern any one particular dogma, for no dogma is directly in question, but which will end by challenging the whole of theology as a science or sacred discipline, demanding a definition and instrumentation of it which will be at once more modern and more ancient. It is, in short, not so much the *content* – which no one at present thinks of submitting to fresh examination – as the *container,* the instrument for preserving and transmitting the so-called 'revealed truths', that the Council, under the impulse of the theologians and with the full approval of John XXIII, aims at modernizing and renovating.

It is therefore easy to see that since dogmatic, sacramental, pastoral, and catechistic theology, canonical and moral discipline, etc. all converge in the liturgy, the Liturgical draft seemed the ideal draft to be discussed first, and for two reasons. First, it can serve as a most useful way of initiating the Fathers, especially the newcomers, in their early exercises in parliamentary debate, for they will be the more eager to tackle it because of their particular interest in liturgical reforms; and secondly, it will serve to bring out both the trends of the various groups and the kinds of problems that will emerge in the Council. I imagine that after the debate on 'De Sacra Liturgia' the fundamental characteristics of the Council and the typical features of its major trends should no longer prove an enigma.

Rome, Monday, 22 October

This morning in the Council Hall, under the chairmanship of the

Archbishop of Sidney, Cardinal Gilroy, the names were announced of the last 48 members of Commissions elected by the Assembly on the 16th, and the debate on the Liturgical draft began.

The latest election results (for the Commissions on Discipline and the Sacraments, on members of the Religious Orders and on Seminaries) have given yet another proof of the strength of support for the Western and Central European list; though the hitherto dim and impersonal bulletin of the Press Office shows an unexpected fighting spirit in inveighing against certain newspapers which, it alleges, have shown themselves 'followers of phantoms rather than objective channels of truthful information'. Ten out of the sixteen places on the Sacraments Commission, and eight on each of the two Commissions for Seminaries and the Religious Orders, have gone to candidates from that list. Moreover, in the first of those Commissions they got the first four places, the sixth, and the ninth; in the second, the first two, fourth, fifth, sixth; and in the third, the first three, sixth, and seventh places.

Now that we have the whole picture of the results before us, it becomes quite clear that the aim of the Western and Central European list was not to get its own men in at all costs, but to support only the best candidates whatever their provenance. In fact, the Frenchmen elected number only 12 (Guerry, Veuillot, Mazerat, Marty, Jenny, Garrone, Riobé, Ménager, Renard, Puech, Huyghe, and Urtasun), the Germans 11 (Schäufele, Bengsch, Janssen, Spuelbeck, Schröffer, Hoech, Hengsbach, Schneider, Leiprecht, Reetz, and Hoeffner), the English 4 (Dwyer, Grimshaw, Petit, and Beck), the Belgians 4 (Van Zuylen, Clewaert, Charue, and Daem), the Austrians 3 (Zauner, Koenig, Laszlo), and the Dutch 3 (Van Dodewaard, Jansen, and De Wet): 37 in all.

The 160 Commission members elected by the Assembly can be grouped as follows:

Europe	= 84	(Italy 20, France 16, Germany 11, Spain 10, Eastern Europe 9, Belgium 4, England 4, Austria 3, Holland 3, and Switzerland, Ireland, Portugal, and Luxembourg one each).
America	= 53	(USA 18, Canada 9, Latin America 26).
Asia	= 14	(of whom 2 from the Middle East).
Africa	= 7	
Australia	= 2	

Ninety-two of them had already taken part in the Preparatory Commissions; but several of those who were formerly on the Central Commission in virtue of their position as Chairmen of Episcopal Conferences are now to be put on Commissions corresponding to their particular qualifications. Only 61 have returned to the same Commission as before.

As for the opening of the discussion on the Liturgical draft, the official communiqué describes how it was presented by Cardinal Larraona, chairman of the Liturgical Commission (which met for the first time yesterday morning in the Palazzo of the Congregation of Rites) and accompanied by a report from Padre Antonelli, Rector of the Antonianum (the theological university of the Franciscans), 'general promoter of the faith' and since yesterday secretary of the Liturgical Commission. The bulletin, fearing to violate the secrecy of the Council by revealing the length of the draft – a Preamble and eight chapters – only says that it is 'very long' and that 'beginning with the definition and nature (of the liturgy), it considers the mystery of the Eucharist, the Sacraments, the Divine Office, the Sacramental Rites, the Liturgical Year, Sacred Music and Art, the Liturgical Books, the present liturgical movement, and the need for a sound education in liturgical piety'. (The chapter headings are in fact as follows: 1) General principles for liturgical renewal; 2) The Mystery of the Eucharist; 3) The Sacraments and the Sacramental Rites; 4) The Divine Office; 5) The Liturgical Year; 6) Liturgical clothing and objects of worship; 7) Religious music; and 8) Religious art.)

The communiqué does not hesitate, however, to give an opinion on that controversial subject, why preference was given to this particular topic for debate in the Council: it was, it avers, the one most in harmony with the Council's aims since it 'tended primarily towards an inner renewal of the Church'.

A historic event: for the first time the bulletin gives the names of those taking part in the debate, distinguishing them by rank but mentioning only the surnames (with the result that it is sometimes impossible to tell who is meant, as in the case of the two Hurleys), forgetting Cardinal Rugambwa, and adding laconically that twenty (should be 21) Fathers spoke, 'some to defend the draft, others to attack it'. For the record, the speakers were nine

Cardinals (Frings, Ruffini, Lercaro, Montini, Spellman, Doepfner, Tatsuo Doi, Silva, Enriquez, and Rugambwa), a Patriarch (Paul II Cheikho, of Babylon of the Chaldaeans), six Archbishops (Vagnozzi, Hurley, Young, Del Rosario, Scapinelli, Dante), and five bishops (Garcia, Saboia Bandeira de Mello, Kempf, Ungarelli, and Hervas).

The discussion is however known to have covered the whole ground of the draft. It is significant that at this first sitting, apart from the Apostolic Delegate in Washington, Vagnozzi, and the assessor of the Eastern Congregation, Scapinelli, no theologians spoke but only pastors. Moreover the nine Cardinals mentioned are all residential bishops.

There was much more praise than criticism, the latter coming mainly from Ruffini, Spellman, Silva Enriquez, and Dante. Enthusiastic supporters of the draft were Frings, Lercaro, Montini, Doepfner, Tatsuo Doi, Rugambwa, and others. Montini, for example, outlined his view of the criteria which should govern a fruitful modernization of the liturgy: these were, in order of importance, retention where suitable; comprehensibility; simplification (or, if need be, expansion); and the question of the authorities responsible for the reforms. He also referred to the use of the Latin language, which should, in his view, certainly be retained for use by the priest but might well be replaced in the didactic parts of the service. On the last point, that of who should be responsible for the reforms, he advanced the opinion that while the Holy See should remain the supreme legislator, the episcopal conferences should have wider powers. Monsignor Dante, secretary of the Congregation of Rites, even read a list of eleven lengthy admonitions.

In general, judging by the speeches, the draft seems to have been definitely progressive in tone. The fundamental criteria inspiring criticism or praise virtually coincide with the two recognized groupings among liturgical scholars: on the one hand, those who support the sacrosanctity of the liturgical patrimony as it has come down to us today, defending even its obscurity and incomprehensibility as a fascinating and unalterable part of sacred rite; and, on the other hand, those who deplore the accretions, and would like to restore the liturgy to its original simplicity and communicative efficacy. But clearly the Fathers of the Council cannot concern themselves only with antiquarian aspects or with restoration; they have to provide an answer to precise questions of a pastoral character, drawing their inspiration from theological criteria which define the nature and functions of the liturgy. Among such questions, the most important and all-embracing is whether the liturgy is the communal expression of the Church's cult, of its faith and hopes, and above all whether it is the expression of the combined participation of its members in the sacramental act deriving from its founder, and whether or not it needs to have simplicity and popular appeal and to correspond to the psychological characteristics of the people who are called on to share in it and not merely be present as if at a spectacle.

According to the Fathers of the conservative trend, the answer is decidedly in the negative: the liturgy, according to them, is not and cannot be, so to speak, a popular phenomenon: it achieves its own perfection solely in the priestly celebration above and beyond what can be understood by the faithful. For the progressive Fathers, on the other hand, this signifies an inadmissible intrusion of class or caste: the Church, a mystical body, is composed not only of priests but also of worshippers; indeed the priests are there primarily in the service of the worshippers. A form of language or collection of rites which are obscure and incomprehensible, hardly to be understood even by the intellectual few, alienates the more intelligent people if it does not cause them to be lost altogether; quite apart from the fact that, just as in the first centuries of the Church widely differing liturgies were evolved by various peoples, so today, especially since the entry into the Church of new civilizations and new traditions (the Afro-Asian peoples), it has become an urgent necessity to give them the possibility to evolve their own liturgical forms in complete, if obviously controlled, freedom.

Rome, Tuesday, 23 October

The question of Cuba, which for ten days has hung like a dark cloud over the Council, has in the last day or so become more acute. Plainly if the situation were to get much worse it might cause a number of Fathers from the United States and the Caribbean countries to have to leave the Council and go home; and if it really were to explode into armed conflict on an international scale, the work of the Council would have to be suspended. Moreover, Cuba is not the only explosive question of the moment. On the frontiers of India threatening Chinese troop movements are going on.

Antimori told me yesterday that the Secretariat of State is constantly having to defend itself against pressures of a political nature which are trying to influence the Council. As well as the ever-restless Poles there are now the Angolans, including a number of native priests or missionaries expelled from that colony by the Salazar authorities and interned in Portugal. Even more difficult to hold in check are the Ukrainians in exile, who might seek support from the episcopates of the countries (mainly in Europe and America) in which they now live scattered, and above all from some members of the Sacred College. Up till now the efforts of the Secretariat of State have proved effective, but Cicognani lives in a constant state of alarm lest this should not last. Antimori thinks that the Pope wants to intervene personally, especially through the special audiences for the individual episcopates.

If the international situation should continue to provoke the feverish reactions of these last days, it would be difficult for the Council to keep itself free from disturbances of a political kind, especially in the anti-Communist direction. And clearly the situation of the observer-delegates of the Moscow Patriarchate might become untenable.

I received today the first bulletin of the Press and Information Service of the Federal Council of the Evangelical Churches in Italy. Unfortunately, as a notice in it states, its publication has been made possible only 'thanks to the direct interest of the World Reformed Alliance, the Netherlands Protestant Convent of Utrecht, and the Commission on Ecumenical Mission and Relations of the Presbyterian Church in the United States'. I thought the time was over when Italian Protestants had to seek help from abroad even for relatively modest enterprises like this.

This first issue is rather thin and disappointing except for the 'Annexes', which contain texts of the speeches given by Bea and Schlink at the first 'Tuesday meeting' between the observer-delegates and the members of the Secretariat for Christian Union, and of other speeches made by Skydsgaard, Cullmann, and Rostan at the reception given by the Federal Council of the Evangelical Churches in Italy in the big hall of the Waldensian Faculty of Theology on 18 October. Apart from reporting these two events it devotes only about twenty lines to the inauguration of Vatican II. Oddly enough, however, the only judgment it expresses about it is much more generous than that of a good deal of the Catholic press or even of a good many bishops. This is what it says:

> The magnificence of the ceremony may have caused some people to feel a jarring contrast between such sumptuousness and the simplicity of the primitive Christian assemblies or the sobriety of the official gatherings of the Churches born of the Reformation. But the grandeur and splendour may have aroused a genuine emotion in those who feel themselves more drawn to a glamorous style of ceremony such as that of the Church of Rome. The pomp of so splendid a ritual is, in fact, designed to attest the independence, the supra-terrestrial and eternal character, the presence, and the memory of the Roman Church in the world.

The first Tuesday meeting initiated a series of high-level talks between the members of the Secretariat for Christian Union and its Protestant and Orthodox guests, the importance of which needs no comment. A second meeting took place yesterday, and I imagine dealt more directly with the questions that have emerged so far in the General Congregations: the autonomy and liberty of the Council, the role of the Episcopate especially through the Episcopal Conferences, and the importance of the liturgical problem.

At the Council, obviously, the observers are not able to speak. But that does not mean they are inactive. Their very presence constitutes a warning and a stimulus for the Fathers: a warning to avoid any argument or expression which might prove unfortunate or offend against charity and so aggravate relations with the separated Christian confessions; and a stimulus to adapt as far as possible the way in which problems are posed and solved to the needs of the other Christian churches.

The observers, for their part, by courtesy of the Pope have received the volume of drafts prepared by the Commissions and are helped in every way in such matters as translation of speeches and explanation of what is said or done in the Council Hall. Later on there will be special sessions at which they will study the drafts and speeches among themselves and at the 'Tuesday meetings' they will be perfectly free to put their points of view to the Secretariat for Christian Union or discuss them with the specialists it may summon. Thus through the channel of the Secretariat the observers' criticisms, requests, or approval can be conveyed to the Council, and this can often be very important, though naturally such views commit no one but the individual observers.

I went to the first of these meetings on Tuesday the 15th at the Hotel Columbus in Via della Conciliazione, where they are being held. The Columbus is just opposite the Palazzo dei Convertendi, headquarters of the Eastern Congregation and also of the Secretariat for Christian Union. I was going to meet there a young Protestant pastor from Heidelberg who, having taken his degree, is continuing his historical researches here in Rome. We suddenly found ourselves opposite a little group of ecclesiastics who were crossing the road in the direction of the hotel. In their midst, between Monsignor Willebrands and Father Schmit, I at once recognized Cardinal Bea. Except for the red and gold cords on his hat and the flash of purple from his *zucchetto* showing beneath it, he looked exactly the same as when I used to see him sometimes in the last years of Pius XII's Pontificate coming out of the Biblicum, generally on a Saturday evening, and getting into a Vatican car in which he drove off to the papal apartments in the Sacred Palaces to hear the confessions of the Pope, his German housekeeper Suor Pasqualina, and the other two German nuns who looked after him. Perhaps his shoulders were a little more bowed, his eyes more sunken, but his limpid, gentle gaze was the same as ever but for an added luminous quality.

On my way home I was still thinking about this astonishing old man. Two very different Popes have both made use of him, the one to confide to him the secrets of his own conscience, already become slightly alien and impersonal because expressed in German, and the other to send him all over the world as a peaceful herald of the crusade for unity – two completely different rôles, yet each chosen with immense perspicacity. Who, indeed, would ever have thought of turning a world-famous biblical scholar into a confessor? Obviously, if Bea had not been a true ascetic, Pope Pius would never have given him that office, for he was always meticulously careful in choices that closely concerned himself.

All the same, I would say that Pope John showed even greater perspicacity when he entrusted this indomitable octogenarian with the cause of the newborn Catholic ecumenicalism. He did so regardless of Bea's age, habits, and inclinations, not easy to change so late in life. It has been suggested that in choosing several men of his own age or even older among his new Cardinals Papa Roncalli intended to make it easier for his successor to build up a new Sacred College according to his own views and preferences. But it is nevertheless true that several of the octogenarians whom he promoted to the purple have revealed an astonishing youthfulness of spirit and power of physical resistance.

Who, for instance, could have looked for such adaptability from Cardinal Bea? At an age when men usually think of putting on their slippers and leaning on a stick, he suddenly became the most dynamic member of the Curia. True, he had not led a purely sedentary life in the past. During the twenty years that he was Rector of the Biblicum he several times went to Palestine and the Middle East, including Arabia and Egypt, and in 1929, I think it was, he set forth on a special mission to Japan to reorganize the Catholic University in Tokyo founded by his Order, the Jesuits. That journey, which lasted six months including his stay in Tokyo, was certainly his most adventurous. Setting out from Berlin, he stopped in Warsaw and Moscow and then crossed Siberia to Korea, from where he travelled by sea to Japan; on the return journey he went via Shanghai and Hong Kong to Java and Ceylon, in both of which he stayed, finally going through the Red Sea to the Mediterranean. But the most interesting thing about it was that though by his own wish he travelled through the Soviet Union he did not go incognito, though of course he was not wearing full canonical dress: the Russian Legation in Berlin was duly informed before he set out that a German Jesuit proposed to make this journey, and he was given a visa without much difficulty.

But in 1961 all this belonged to the remote past, and now the octogenarian Chairman of the Secretariat for Christian Union became in a certain sense its diplomatic messenger. Speaking as guest of the Foreign Press Association in Rome in April 1962 Cardinal Bea gave some details about his work: in 1961 alone two thousand letters had gone out to the 'separated brethren' and some five hundred visits to leaders of the different confessions had been arranged. He said nothing about his own journeys, probably because everyone knew about them already, but if he had mentioned those of only the previous three months he would have told of lectures in January in Berne, Bâle, Strasbourg, and Paris, in February at Heidelberg and Tübingen Universities, and in March at Essen and in Berlin – in other words, in places where no Roman Cardinal had spoken or set foot since the Reformation. Moreover he not only went to West Berlin but to East Berlin as well. There, all in the space of a few hours, he was present at the closing session of the Episcopal Conference of the East German bishops, addressed a special meeting of the clergy, preached to over two thousand people in the Church of Corpus Christi, and met the two main personalities of the German Protestant world, Dr Otto Dibelius (who in 1956 had an almost chance meeting with Pius XII) and Dr Kurt Scharf, President of the Evangelical Church in Germany.

The ecumenical movement, as everyone knows, is Protestant in origin, and the Popes up to John XXIII made the great mistake of underestimating it. Papa Roncalli, certainly not merely for calculated reasons, felt the urgent need to make up for lost time. This probably explains the feverish activity of Cardinal Bea and his efforts to keep up with the insistent initiative of the non-Catholics, as shown in the Pan-Orthodox Conference in Rhodes, the General Assembly of the World Council of Churches in New Delhi, the Bulgarian Patriarch's journey to the Middle East, exchanges of visits between Geneva and Moscow, and so on.

Some months ago, when it was announced that the Anglican Archbishop, Dr Ramsey, after visiting Istanbul and Athens in March would go on to Moscow, some people talked of an 'Anglican démarche' and suggested that this time Bea had missed the bus. But immediately afterwards a communication issued by the Catholic Archbishop of Liverpool, Monsignor Heenan, announced that Cardinal Bea was coming to England at his invitation from 6 to 10 August to give a lecture. At the same time a communiqué from Lambeth Palace stated that Cardinal Bea would pay a courtesy visit to Dr Ramsey soon after the latter's return from Moscow.

There is something really amazing about all this when one

recalls that at the age of eleven little Augustin Bea was thought to be at death's door with TB. This was not a wrong diagnosis, either, merely an over-pessimistic one. He had several subsequent relapses and once had to enter a sanatorium. But, as with so many other exceptional men, Bea's life, though mainly that of a typical scholar and university professor, is full of unexpected happenings. Perhaps the most unforeseen of all was the choice of his religious Order. He was at first attracted by the Capuchins, whose public preaching made a great impression on him; later on, especially after a visit to the famous abbey of Beuron, the Benedictines began to exercise a strong appeal, but here his difficulty was that he couldn't sing, and singing plays a large part in Benedictine services. What decided him in favour of the Jesuits was his discovery of their well-known periodical, *Stimmen der Zeit*. He had no cause to repent his choice. Though, all the same, one day in Rome after attending the pontifical Mass of a Benedictine Abbot not particularly brilliant at plainsong, he was heard to say with his typical twist of humour that perhaps he had been over-precipitate in giving up the Benedictines just because he hadn't a musical ear.

For the whole of the past century no Curia Cardinal had ever before been known to travel so frequently outside Rome, let alone outside Italy and Europe; and even in these days of television no other Cardinal who was head of a central organization of the Roman Church had broadcast and spoken in public so frequently, presided so often over unofficial meetings with members of widely different confessions, or given so many press interviews, freely describing his own activities and those of his department. But the greatest revolution brought about by Bea went far beyond his own personal dynamic quality to the character he gave to the Secretariat for Christian Union.

Almost all the other Preparatory Commissions of the Council carried out their work exclusively in their own headquarters in Rome. The Secretariat for Christian Union, however, held several meetings of some of its members abroad and even had a plenary meeting in Germany, at Bühl, at the headquarters of the annual Fulda conferences of the German episcopate. Its individual members have also travelled about a great deal, so much so, indeed, that they are often called the 'racing champions' and their organization is known as the 'Champion Secretariat' ('Il Segretariato dei Corridori' – they have their headquarters in Via dei Corridori, and the name obviously refers both to that and to their own dynamic character). The same palazzo also houses the Commission for the Eastern Churches, as guest of the Eastern Congregation; but when it is a question of travelling about in the Middle East, as in March 1962 to Istanbul and Athens to make arrangements for attendance at the Council, it is always the members of the Secretariat who do the travelling.

There are naturally varying opinions about the 'new look' given to the Secretariat by Bea. The more spiteful say that he has just imitated the World Council of Churches in Geneva, which is well known to be an eminently dynamic organization. But such critics are alarmed less about the present than the future if, as is thought certain, the Secretariat continues in one form or another after the Council is over. They fear that the passion for travel might attack other Congregations and not only disturb their slow and solemn rhythm but also reduce their prestige, turning their officials into mere messengers in the service of the Churches abroad, whereas their practice hitherto has always been to receive visitors from outside at their own headquarters.

But young priests with different ideas look with gratitude to Bea as to one who has revolutionized the Curia before any organic reform was even considered.

Rome, Wednesday, 24 October

When I left the house yesterday for my usual early morning walk with my dog, Leila, I saw outside the Convent of the Salvatorian Sisters (Sorores Divini Salvatoris) the big black limousine of the Patriarch of Antioch, Maximus IV Saigh, and his colleagues of the Eastern Church, who are staying there. Shortly before, another car had arrived with some German prelates (the Sisters are a religious order of German foundation).

There must be at least ten Fathers staying at the Convent, the two most important being Cardinal Koenig and the Patriarch of the Melchites. Up at Monteverde there must be at least a hundred Fathers of the Council within a radius of quarter of a mile, as a tour of the local monasteries and religious dependencies would show. It would have been even easier to tell a fortnight ago, when the Council opened, for on 11 and 12 October every religious house in the neighbourhood had a couple of carabinieri stationed in front of it as guard of honour and symbolical guarantee of vigilance for the safety of the Fathers staying there.

At the present moment I believe about 90 hotels or ecclesiastical institutions and religious houses, both male and female, are providing hospitality for the Fathers. Members of religious Orders are usually guests of their Generalates or of other institutions of their Order. The Salesians, for example, including their Rector, are staying at the Istituto Torlonia in Via Nomentana.

Some of the Fathers are living in very modest hotels, and some bishops are said to do their own laundry to save expense. Dozens of Asiatics have been put in an hotel about five or six miles away from St Peter's over a cinema where the loudspeakers go on till late at night. Some have not yet found a home anywhere – they are a sort of modern version of the wandering friars. The proprietress of a *pensione* in the Prati to which I occasionally send people told me that a few days ago two Brazilian bishops turned up on her doorstep, while two others waited in the street, offering in exchange for board and lodging goodness knows how many suitcases full of coffee which they were evidently using as currency after getting it free through the Customs.

To go back to the Convent of the Salvatorian Sisters, it has beside it, standing in a magnificent garden, one of Rome's most fashionable and expensive clinics, the Salvator Mundi, frequented by actors and actresses as well as by officials of the diplomatic service and high-up members of the Vatican hierarchy. Some months ago Elizabeth Taylor was brought there in a great hurry with food-poisoning, and throughout her stay dozens of journalists and photographers mounted guard outside the gates. At about the same time Cardinal Acacio Coussa was sent there, only six months after becoming a Cardinal. He had an operation but got worse and died. John XXIII went to visit him in person in the clinic; the visit was so discreetly arranged that no one noticed it, though I could have seen him arrive from my study window. From another window at the back of the house, though, I sometimes see Cardinal Koenig or one of the German bishops walking about in the Sisters' garden, usually reading a breviary. I imagine that from a different angle the poet Bertolucci, the novelist Pasolini, and the actress Liana Orfei can do the same, for their apartments overlook Via Carini on one side and the Sisters' garden on the other.

Anyway, when I ran into Maximus IV yesterday I certainly wasn't expecting to see his name that same afternoon among those who spoke in the debate on the Liturgical draft, which has now moved on from the stage of general discussion to discussion of the Preface. The odd thing is that Maximos IV spoke in French. Antimori told me so, adding that it was the second time this had happened, for in the debate about the Fathers' Message the Patriarch of the Melchites also refused to speak in Latin. Antimori also told me that Maximos IV was the great absentee-from-protest at the opening ceremony on 11 October because he objected to the Cardinals being given precedence over the Patriarchs. The Presiding Council turned a blind eye, partly out of regard for the Patriarch's age (he is 84) and personality but even more because of the prestige he enjoys as leader of the Catholic Churches of the East (the Uniates) upon which the eyes of Orthodox observers – whether or not present in St Peter's – are fixed.

Maximos IV, bishop of Tyre in 1919, then of Beirut from 1933 and Patriarch since 1947, is not the only Uniate patriarch, indeed he is not the only Patriarch of Antioch, as his title would suggest, though he has another personal title as well, that of Patriarch of Alexandria and Jerusalem. But there are three other Catholic Patriarchs in Antioch: those, respectively, of the Syrians (Cardinal Tappouni), of those of Latin rite (at present vacant), and of the Maronites (Pierre Paul Meouchi). In addition, there are also in the Middle East the Patriarchs of Alexandria (Coptic: Stephanos I Sidarouss), Jerusalem (Latin: Alberto Gori), Babylon of the Chaldaeans (Paul II Cheikho), and Cilicia of the Armenians (Ignace Pierre XVI Batanian) – in short, twelve patriarchs in all, some of whom, like Maximos IV Saigh, occupy more than one see, while some sees are vacant at the moment.

Latin Catholics in general know little or nothing about these numerous Middle Eastern bishoprics (and in addition to the Catholic sees there are also the Orthodox, corresponding to the original historical titles, so that in certain towns patriarchal mitres are almost more common than minarets); and they have even vaguer ideas about the importance of the Uniate Church. For the majority of people who watched the procession of the Fathers on television on 11 October the presence of so many prelates in Eastern vestments mingling among the Latin Fathers came as a genuine surprise. According to the statistics I have by me, there are over 120 Eastern bishops in Rome at present: a Cardinal, 5 Patriarchs, 28 residential and titular archbishops, 42 residential and titular bishops, and 11 Superiors General of Orders. Their followers throughout the world number about 10 million, mainly in the Middle East but also in Africa, India, and among the emigrants to Europe and America.

Even those who think they know something about the Uniate Churches are inclined to take the ingenuous or romantic view of them as a bridge between the Orthodox and the Catholics. The situation is in fact quite different. Maximos IV Saigh himself emphatically refuted this view in a lecture at Düsseldorf in August 1960 which made a considerable impression in the Central European countries. 'By stretching a point,' he said, 'it could well be maintained that the definite break in relations between the Roman Church and the various Eastern Churches occurred only on the day when Rome, impatient or disillusioned about the possibility of a world-wide union of the Churches, admitted within her own unity various separated Eastern groups, for that put an end to the attempts at world-wide union between East and West.' 'Indeed', he added, 'we can ask ourselves the theoretical question whether the establishment of the Uniate Churches was a good or a bad thing for world union.'

The Orthodox, in fact, regard the Uniate Churches as an element definitely hostile to union and actually destructive of Orthodoxy, rather as an instrument made use of by the Catholic Church for the purpose of undermining Orthodoxy. Indeed, according to them the Uniate creed not only militates towards the destruction of Orthodoxy but also serves as the instrument for gradually bringing the Eastern Churches under the domination of the Latins, whose ultimate aim is the eventual suppression of the great Eastern forms of Christianity, the original cradle of the Christian faith.

While the first of these views is probably based chiefly on prejudice, there is unfortunately a good deal more foundation for the second. The history of relations between the Catholic Church and the East, and between Orthodox and Uniates, from Innocent III to Pius IX undoubtedly supports it. True, Pius IX in 1862 founded the Sacred Congregation for the Eastern Churches; but he made it subordinate to the Propaganda Fide, and his unfortunately framed invitation to the Orthodox on the eve of the first Vatican Council included the demand that in order to take part in it they should admit their schismatic responsibilities and revise their 'errors'. In any case, the policy of assimilation and Latinization hitherto adopted in relation to the Eastern Churches officially came to an end under Pius IX and Leo XIII. And Benedict XV, by giving full autonomy to the Eastern Congregation in 1917, removed a further misapprehension, that of seeming to equate the Church's action in the Christian-Orthodox East with its missionary activity in pagan continents.

But there is no doubt that in general all those Popes I have mentioned and their Curias had very imperfect ideas about the orientalism of the Uniate Churches, which they thought of largely as a matter of rites. It is a fact, moreover, that even since the reform of Pius XI in 1938 the Eastern Congregation still lacks competency to act not only in diplomatic questions, canonization proceedings, or matters coming under the Holy Office but also in matters subject to the authority of the Sacred Penitentiary or even of the Congregation of Seminaries and of Theological Universities. 'Knowledge,' Pius XI once said, 'is neither Eastern nor Western, it is universal, and the same everywhere': this, it goes without saying, was an astonishing way of simplifying but at the same time muddling things, somewhat disconcerting to find in a scholar such as he.

It was the promulgation of the New Code of Eastern Law that showed up clearly how far Rome was prepared to go in recognizing the Uniate Churches' autonomy. The preparation of this Code was entrusted to a special Codification commission which began work in 1929-30. The first results appeared only twenty years later, with the publication of the canons relating to marriage (in 1949), ecclesiastical tribunals (1950), and members of religious Orders and administration of Church property (1952). Although the obvious model for these canons was the Latin Code of Canon Law, the first ones to appear aroused no serious opposition. But there was a positive outburst of protest in August 1957 when Papa Pacelli promulgated the section relating to legal 'persons' (that is to say to communities, those performing rites, ecclesiastical communities and their powers, etc.) and the most alarming feature for Rome was that the insurrection was not undisciplined but official and controlled in a dignified way under the supreme responsibility of Maximos IV.

The Patriarch of the Melchites placed consideration of this last section of the Code on the agenda of a synod of his Church which was held in Cairo (instead of its usual meeting-place, Ain Traz) from 6 to 11 February 1958. On 9 February, during a solemn liturgy in the Cathedral, he gave public if restrained and moderate expression to his disappointment about it, declaring roundly that some of its provisions established an unacceptable supremacy of the Latin Church over the Eastern Churches not only on the part of the Pope – which obviously could not be a subject of dispute – but also of the Latin Church as such.

In a subsequent lecture (published by the official review of the Patriarchate) Monsignor Pierre K. Medawaar, his auxiliary bishop, specified the more delicate points in the dispute. The first of these was the attack on the Oriental rites themselves. As he pointed out, the old regulation confirmed by Leo XIII in his encyclical *Orientalium dignitas*, on the basis of which all schismatics of Oriental rite who returned to the Roman Church were to retain their own rite, was simply abrogated under the new Code and replaced by a new regulation decreeing that an Eastern non-Catholic returning to the Catholic Church was free to choose whatever rite he pleased. 'What makes this measure the more vexatious,' added Monsignor Medawaar, 'is that it implies a quite inadmissible segregation as between the Catholic rites. In fact, this measure can operate only to the disadvantage of the rights of the Eastern Church and the advantage of the Latin: paragraph 1 of Canon 11, granting freedom in the choice of rite, concerns only "baptized non-Catholics" of Eastern rite who wish to be admitted to the Catholic Church. It can therefore be deduced that Protestants, since they do not belong to the Eastern rite, have no choice as to the rite they will adopt: if they become Catholics they must be Latin Catholics. Why this strident inequality, this intolerable partiality?'

In short, 'the provision of para. 1 of Canon 11 is a blow to the development and even the maintenance of an Eastern Church within the bosom of Catholicism'. And Monsignor Medawaar revealed that when the Eastern protest was conveyed to Rome it received an astonishing answer: 'Rome explained that the new regulation was adopted at the request of the American bishops, and gave us to understand that it was not to be applied in the East, where Leo XIII's provisions would remain in force. But in this way even in America the rights of the Eastern Church are violated in favour of the Latin Church, whereas no discrimination between rites should be tolerated.'

The second subject of dispute, a no less burning one if now no longer so for the Eastern Churches, concerns the low position given by the new Code to their Patriarchs. This was done despite the fact that the history of antiquity, indeed of the whole first millennium of Christianity, shows how the Eastern patriarchs shared with Rome the government of the Church in the world, and Rome itself recognized their right to first place 'without intermediaries' immediately after the Pope. 'But', Monsignor Medawaar went on, 'the new Canon Law, instead of demonstrating to the Orthodox world this position to which it has a right in the reunified Church, presents its patriarchs as reduced in status, conceding, it is true, recognition of certain privileges of a purely historical nature, but making the most important of them dependent on earlier authorizations or later confirmation. Granted such a conception of the patriarchal institution, it was only natural to assign them a place far removed from the Pope in the order of precedence . . .' In fact, 'regardless of all this holy and honourable inheritance and of all that the Patriarchs have stood for in the past and the great hope they represent for the future, the new Canon Law relegates them to a place not only after the 70 Roman Cardinals but also after the hundreds of Apostolic Delegates, even if the latter are merely ordinary priests, and sometimes even after the mere bishops of Latin rite!'

Maximos IV's auxiliary concluded with the words: 'Those who have not in their blood this tradition I have described, those who are not united by a thousand links to the 250 million Orthodox scattered throughout the world, cannot feel, as we feel, the immense grief which legislation of this kind causes to the Eastern Churches, or estimate the depth of the new breach it creates between them and the Catholic Church. But we who are Greek-Melchite Catholics cannot remain insensible to this disaster and we cannot fail to react. This reaction we have made plain in our Synod.'

Maximos IV in his speech at Düsseldorf also referred to the new Code and made the following grave assertion: 'We have seen to our great regret that, despite a formidable critical apparatus and a terminology drawn from Eastern sources, and despite all the highly meritorious work done on it, the basis of the codification still remains unfortunately very Latinized. This was not always the fault of the experts who worked on it but rather of the spirit pervading the circles in which the work was done. For these circles, the supreme ideal is still to bring both the substance and the form of our Code as close as possible to the law of the Latin Church.'

Rome naturally succeeded in finding allies among the Uniates themselves, not only in the preparation of the reforms, but also, and more especially, in getting them carried out; and the outcome of the Curia's efforts was, he said, that 'in the majority of Eastern Catholic communities, except for the liturgical rites (and not always those), nothing could more closely resemble the West than this united East'. This state of affairs could only serve to justify the harsh judgments of the Orthodox. In order to bring about a change in the situation the only course open to the authentic Uniates was to adopt a different attitude towards Rome, abandoning submissive compliance in favour of conscious and dignified resistance. In other words, they had to realize and put into practice a dual and equal loyalty, to Catholicism and to the East. 'Any deviation to either side', as Maximos IV said in that lecture of 1960, 'would signify compromising the cause of unity.'

But loyalty to the East, he went on, implied not only a question of rites but also of ecclesiological structures. The East was a world in itself just as much as the West, and like the West it must preserve its own characteristics, remaining conscious of them and living in accordance with them on a basis of complete equality. 'Union,' Maximos IV, admitted, 'has in general meant enrichment for us, but an enrichment often followed by the fruitless loss of nearly all the East's own spiritual values. And from that point of view it was a considerable impoverishment.'

It is easy to see how the recognition of this plurality of ecclesiological worlds – in fact of Churches – is based on a conception of juxtaposition rather than centralization, of autonomy rather than dependence, except for the respect due to the supreme authority of the representative of Peter (but of a Peter who governs together with the other patriarchs, while still remaining the first among them and the final court of appeal). Hence the importance of the patriarch's role, which the Uniates maintain not merely in order to defend the rights of their Churches' leaders but also with a view to the return of the Orthodox to unity. For then the Uniates will be destined to disappear, and there will be only one East, of which they merely aspire now to provide an anticipatory image.

In coming to Rome for the Council, the Uniates, and in particular their moral leader Maximos IV Saigh, clearly intended first and foremost to reaffirm these profound convictions of theirs. Any possible doubts about this are removed by a recent interview given by the Patriarch of the Melchites. After expressing his satisfaction that, through the personal merits of John XXIII, the Catholics had at last begun to adopt the right course in their relations with the Orthodox – by ceasing to regard them as solely responsible for the schism and guilty of heresy – he made some important statements, from which I give the following extracts:

'The greatest difficulty for the Latin Catholics is to grasp that, both theoretically and in practice, union does not mean uniformity, or the absorption of others, or a means for wider domination. The Eastern Catholic Churches are a testing ground for the Roman Church. According to the way in which they are treated within Catholicism, the Orthodox will judge how they can expect to be treated if union is restored.'

'While recognizing all the advantages and benefits we have derived from union, it must also be recognized that our Eastern Catholic Churches have not yet found within Catholicism a place worthy of themselves.'

'This Council will certainly have a decisive influence on union; but in what direction it is difficult to say. It can open the way to union, but it can also definitely close it by giving the Orthodox brethren the conviction – which God forbid – that there is no room for them in the Catholic Church except through their absorption and the dissolution of their own being in Latinism, which is wrongly identified with Catholicism.'

'Our Orthodox brethren want to see in us (Uniates) an example, not of a "Latin" Catholicism, but of how it is practically possible to be Catholics and Orientals at the same time.'

Lastly, he listed a number of problems which the Uniates are determined to bring forward at the Council. The main ones are: 'A clearer definition of the divine origin of the episcopate and its powers; wider disciplinary autonomy for the Eastern Churches; a revaluation of the institution of the Patriarchate in Catholicism; steps to be taken against the Latinization of the East; unification of the date of Easter; creation in the Roman Curia of a permanent department for ecumenicalism; administrative decentralization; internationalization of the Roman Curia and the representation of the Holy See; re-establishment of the office of deacon for life; association of the Eastern Catholic Churches with the work of the missions (especially in North Africa, Ethiopia, and India); improvement of the position of the laity in the Church's apostolate, not only as objects of sanctification but also as authentic and important collaborators in the work of world evangelization.'

Both because of the part he intends to play – less for himself than for the Churches he represents – especially in solving the problem of reunification between the Orthodox and Rome, and because of his personal ascendancy and indomitable temperament, it seems to me beyond doubt that Maximos IV must be regarded as one of the most outstanding key personalities of the Council.

Rome, Thursday, 25 October

At midday today John XXIII read over the radio in French a broadcast message exhorting the Heads of State to pause in time before running into war. The danger is extremely serious, but there may be some justification for the relative optimism of those most responsible, given the obvious futility of a recourse to war in the conditions of today.

Cuba's four bishops (out of its total six) who are present at the Council – including the exiled Monsignor Bozza Masvidal – are carrying on with their work to all appearances quite calmly, avoiding as best they can the journalists who since early October have given them no peace. By definite orders from the Holy See, the two other Cuban bishops left behind to hold the fort are also apparently maintaining silence. One who would probably be glad to speak, but fortunately cannot do so, is Cardinal Arteaga y Betancourt, Archbishop of San Cristobal in Havana, who for the last two years has taken refuge in the Argentine Embassy in Cuba, but the Holy See has taken good care not to let him be turned into another Mindszenty. This is not surprising, given the new mild and conciliatory tone adopted by the Secretary of State, at John XXIII's wish, towards all the countries in difficult relations with the Church or even actually persecuting it. What is stranger, however, is that even those who might be regarded as of similar trend in the Sacred College regularly avoid any mention of him, and make no reference at all to his absence from the opening of the Council. I think they must have good reason to believe that his presence in Rome would not have helped their cause much and might even have harmed it: the testimony of so pre-historic and plethoric a prince-bishop, scion of a noble family and involved from youth in the factious struggles that divide his country, a hidebound conservative and unwise supporter of dictators, especially of Batista, might well have proved provocative.

Rome, Friday, 26 October

This morning, for the first time since the Council began, I went to Piazza San Pietro. It was a few minutes before midday when I parked my car in Via della Conciliazione. In a quarter of an hour or half an hour at most, the doors of the Basilica, kept inexorably closed during the General Congregations, would open to release the stream of over two thousand Fathers. This still unaccustomed spectacle attracts hundreds of Romans and tourists, among whom I mingled.

But it is impossible to go much beyond the Palazzi of the Propilei. Wooden barriers prevent access to the piazza and the Bernini colonnades; and there are cordons of carabinieri and plain-clothes police with strict orders to let no one pass. In fact it is just like what happens on the occasion of official visits of Heads of State to the Vatican. Under the Concordat of 1929, Piazza San Pietro and the Bernini colonnades are an extra-territorial zone, an internal piazza or courtyard of the Vatican, just as much as the other piazzas of San Damaso, the Pigna, or the Belvedere. Normally, the frontier between the Italian State and the State of the Vatican City reaches as far as the threshold of St Peter's; but on official occasions the pontifical corps of guards have to execute manoeuvres in the piazza to do honour to the guests, and the demarcation line is moved to the limit of the colonnade and its theoretical completion.

In these days of the Council's sessions, however, there are no pontifical guards on manoeuvre in the piazza but dozens and dozens of charabancs and hundreds of private cars standing there as if in a vast car park. These are the Cardinals' cars, put at their disposal by the Holy See and therefore bearing the number-plate SCV (Santissima Città Vaticana), those of such bishops as have managed to get hold of them, and, lastly, the charabancs of the 'Peregrinatio Romana'. (All the cars of the Fathers have a special round metal plaque bearing within a crown of olives and oak the words 'Ecumenical Council Vatican II'.)

So the curious throng behind the barriers waiting for the doors of St Peter's to open and the first bishops to come out. Today the first prelate to come down towards the piazza appeared punctually at 12.30; and he was a boyish-looking Negro in the middle thirties. He was at first visible only sideview as he was talking to a colleague behind him. When the latter emerged he proved to be an Asiatic. First appearance to the Afro-Asians.

A few minutes later, hundreds of Fathers were scattered about the forecourt, some talking together, others hurrying to their cars. It was a quite fascinating galaxy of colour. Capes in every gradation of brilliant red, some of them even white or grey (these were bishops belonging to the religious Orders and therefore wearing the colour of their Order), the wide black bell-shaped tunics of the Eastern bishops, glittering with pastoral crosses and medallions, wove their way about the piazza making an ever-changing rippling pattern.

Naturally, the moment when the Fathers emerge is the great time to waylay them. Some few can go and wait for them within the confines of the piazza itself, and these are the journalists with a special pass; others, such as real or would-be acquaintances, have to wait for the cars to come out, or the prelates themselves who don't use cars but prefer to return to their lodgings on foot or use the same means of transport as ordinary mortals (having, however, first taken off their cloaks and put on some more convenient covering). But some crafty press-agent may also try to insinuate a film actress among the throng of the Fathers, and one or two have succeeded. A picture has already appeared in the papers of Claudia Cardinale, tranquil and radiant as ever, standing beside the quite unperturbed and equally radiant bishop of Kandy, in Ceylon, Monsignor Leo Nanayakkara, a sturdy fifty-year-old prelate with a bronzed olive complexion.

The Fathers must all have left the Hall and the Basilica by 1 pm, for then the doors are shut once more. They will not open again until next morning, a little before 8 o'clock, for the next General Congregation. Yesterday, Thursday, they remained shut all day, as they are every afternoon and on all the days when the Congregation does not meet. That might have been the rule in any case, but the bomb attempt of 22 September has certainly caused the Vatican to tighten up regulations. The lock-up at St Peter's has in fact been going on ever since 27 September.

Rome, Saturday, 27 October

A whole collection of *bons mots* could be made about the collaboration of the Holy Ghost in the Councils. At the Council of Trent, when the messengers of the Holy See arrived there from Rome with their horses still steaming, the wits used to comment: 'Here's the Holy Ghost arriving in the baggage from Rome.' At Vatican I the *Correspondent*'s reporter explained to its readers that discussion at a Council had to be lengthy 'in order to give the Holy Ghost time to form an opinion'.

This, it seems, is exactly what is happening at this first session of its successor. Discussion of a subject carries on from one sitting to the next. This morning, at the eighth General Congregation, they were still struggling with the first chapter of the draft. True, it is an exceptionally long chapter, amounting to a third of the whole draft, and summarizing the general principles which, once agreed on, will or should be applied automatically to the cases dealt with in the subsequent chapters; but in any case it looks as if the Council will go on for a long time. Yesterday the Presiding Council had a joint meeting with the Secretariat for Extraordinary Affairs in order to 'study questions arising out of the development of the Council's work'. It is therefore easy to foresee that, without infringing on the freedom of discussion, there may be some quite considerable modifications in its methods.

But, as the Benedictine Dom Oliver Rousseau said to Monsignor Martinez, it will not be easy: 'Once more than a certain number take part in a debate, a simple meeting becomes an auditorium and eventually a vast public assembly.' 'This is the price that has to be paid for freedom,' Père Congar added, and, allowing for exaggeration, he is right.

Unfortunately, I gather from my informants, the bottleneck has arisen around the question of the use of Latin and the vernacular in the liturgy. This corresponds in the draft to para. C. of the draft's 3rd article, which seems to have proved a real stumbling-block.

Yesterday's communiqué on the seventh General Congregation enlarged quite objectively on the contrasting views in the assembly, illustrated more or less amicably or vigorously by the various speeches. 'There are reasons,' it stated, 'militating in favour of Latin, since its adoption would have not merely a traditional significance but also a unifying influence; moreover, because of its logical precision and legal concreteness it lends itself particularly to theological and dogmatic subjects. It also has considerable psychological and ascetic value; the Latin language, by imposing a logical and rational discipline and usage, prevents excursions into sentiment or romanticism and induces concreteness both in expression and in practice.

'On the other hand, the reasons in favour of the use of the vernacular languages in religious services are by no means negligible. The first and most important is their ability to make the liturgical rites accessible to the community of the faithful and so to further their active participation in the celebrations. The use of the vernacular languages, moreover, demonstrates visibly the universal character of Christianity, at once immutable and yet capable of assuming the values and traditions of the individual peoples of all latitudes and times, including the modern era and times to come.'

In practice, however, it is somewhat different. There are not just two but three trends competing with each other in the Council hall. In addition to the extremists of right and left – the minorities opposing, respectively, the vernacular languages or Latin – there is apparently a considerably larger centre group which is inclined to retain Latin, especially at the culminating stages of the various rites (those where the priest plays a major part), but which at the same time would like to open the door to the vernacular languages if the liturgy is to be truly, as it must be, a celebration of 'the blessed people of God'. In short, if it is not too soon to make prophecies, it seems that the Council is well on its way to adopting the middle course of liturgical bilingualism.

Monsignor Martinez has been talking to me about Padre Bugnini, who was turned out of both the secretaryship of the Preparatory Commission for the Sacred Liturgy and the Chair of Liturgy at the Pontifical University of the Vatican: a twofold eviction which aroused a good deal of talk since it is the only instance of its kind to affect so highly qualified a member of the Council. The *discedat* was of course signed by Cardinal Larraona, chairman of that Commission for the past few months, but the step is said to have been taken at the instigation of elements in the Lateran Athenaeum and of their exalted protectors in the 'Pentagon'.

Bugnini is an Umbrian monk in the early fifties belonging to the Congregation of the Mission, who began to devote himself to the study of the liturgy around the beginning of World War II. By 1947 he was already editor of one of the best-known Italian liturgical reviews, *Ephemerides Liturgicae*, and in the following year he became secretary of the Pontifical Commission in the Athenaeum of the Propaganda Fide. From there in 1957 he went on to the Lateran University, after having become adviser to the Congregation of Rites the year before.

This was perhaps rather too rapid a career, but not without background, for Bugnini's preparation for specialization in liturgical matters went back to the period of his studies at the Pontifical Institute of Christian Archaeology in Rome. And if the patronage of Cardinal Cicognani, Prefect of the Congregation of Rites, was a decisive factor, it was certainly no substitute for Bugnini's own undoubted competence as demonstrated in some scholarly works of high quality, for instance his two-volume *Documenta Pontificia ad institutionem liturgicam spectantia,* 1953-1959, and by a number of successful works of popularization (his book on the Mass, *La Nostra Messa,* has sold over a million copies since 1949, including foreign editions).

But Padre Bugnini, while courageous in his plans for modernization, possibly lacked the necessary diplomacy and failed to avoid difficulties and disputes with his theological colleagues. The latter, fortified by protection from high quarters in the Holy Office, seized the unexpected opportunity of his protector's death to get rid of him as secretary of the Preparatory Commission and put an end to his teaching at the university. All the same, Bugnini managed to get his draft through as far as the Council, and now it will be interesting to see if it is passed, and even more so if the draft scheme of the proscribed Secretary of the Liturgical Commission should open the way for the success of other drafts of a progressive character.

Rome, Monday, 29 October

At last, today there was a little *coup de théâtre* in St Peter's in favour of the conservatives, and in particular the Curia. What is still more surprising is that the author was the Pope himself.

At the opening of the Congregation Monsignor Felici made known the names of the members appointed by the Pope to the Commissions of the Council (90 of them instead of 80, as the Rules of Procedure had stated). Among them are all the secretaries and assessors of the departments of the Curia, as the Pope had promised the episcopate in September to give them the right to membership of the Council; also the heads of the two first sections of the Secretariat of State (Samoré and Dell'Acqua) and four Curial Cardinals (Browne, Giobbe, Jullien, and Albareda): in short, the entire leadership of the department.

This batch of Curial appointments, though foreseen and feared, has come as something of a surprise. In fact it was only decided on in the last few days. An indirect proof of this is that when the Liturgical Commission was to be completed John XXIII appointed only eight members instead of nine (Monsignor Dante, Secretary of the Congregation of Rites, was added only today). According to Monsignor Martinez, the formal request for the inclusion of the secretaries and assessors was put forward as a counterpoise to the Pope's request to them to intervene only with the utmost discretion in the Council's sittings.

Also according to Monsignor Martinez, it was the inclusion of the Curia leaders that prompted the Pope to alter the number of members on each individual Commission, raising it to 25 instead of 24; and the odd number of members will make voting easier.

There were two other main reasons governing the choice of the pontifically-nominated members: first, to allow for representation of all the countries who up till then had no representative on the Commissions (these were Cuba, San Domingo, the Ivory Coast, Burma, Thailand, Malaya, Pakistan, and Formosa), and secondly, to put in the right perspective the representation of prelates of Spanish nationality, which had been thought by some to be inadequate and discriminatory.

The most discussed appointments after those from the Curia are those of the five Eastern (Uniate) patriarchs, co-opted on to the Commission for Eastern Churches; that of the Patriarch of Lisbon, Cerejeira, the author and apologist of the much-discussed missionary agreement of 1940 between Portugal and the Holy See, who is included on the Missions Commission; and, lastly, that of the 'Black Pope', the Jesuit Janssens, on the Commission for Religious Orders. The high proportion of Italians – 24 out of 90 – has also been noted.

À propos of Janssens, some days ago he was said to have had a plan for a meeting of the superiors of Religious Orders and Congregations present at the Council (according to the current statistics there are 97 of them). In itself, nothing could be more reasonable and harmless; the only thing is that it seems impossible to attribute modest or ingenuous schemes to the 'Black Pope'. Certain newspapers consequently transformed his idea into a dark and ambitious plan to get control of all the sections of the episcopate coming from the Religious Orders (corresponding to about a third of all the Fathers present at the Council) under the pretext of creating a neutral 'third force' between the Curials and the episcopate. The story seemed to be successfully launched, but instead it never got beyond the first instalment.

This is really very odd, for it had all the makings of a good story: the small account taken by the forthright and peace-loving Pope of the semi-secret army established by Loyola for the Popes' personal service (John XXIII has had no Jesuit advisers close to him, as had both Ratti and Pacelli); the exclusion of the Jesuits from vital and leading administrative positions in the Council (with the merely apparent exception of Cardinal Bea on the Secretariat for Christian Union, for it is known that Bea's views and those of Janssens differ considerably on various points);

the disavowal of Padre Lombardi, after his attempt to influence the Council through a book of his since he could not do so from within[1]; and so on.

But Vatican II is obviously in itself an event so complex and rich in drama that there is no need to seek for too far-fetched an interpretation.

Rome, Tuesday, 30 October

Up till now I have heard only contradictory reports as to whether the Council has discussed the possibility of using women in sacred or at least in para-liturgical offices. But if the matter has not been raised yet, it certainly will be, quite apart from the question of the suitability of women for the priesthood, which has apparently already been settled uncompromisingly in the negative in one of the drafts of either the Theological or the Sacraments Commissions.

It is, however, a fact that a couple of weeks ago several Fathers, as well as, of course, the General Secretariat of the Council received a pamphlet from Frau Gertrud Heinzelmann, President of the Zürich Association for Women's Suffrage and a lawyer by profession, entitled *The Place of Women in the Church*. The authoress begins by making the statement, an awkward one from the point of view of the Fathers in general, that the idea of women in the Catholic Church has not moved beyond the theories of St Thomas Aquinas, which were declared official by Leo XIII in the famous encyclical *Aeterni Patris* of 1891. According to the great mediaeval theologian, Frau Heinzelmann says, woman is by nature weak, born to be subject to man within the family circle of which he is the head. These ideas, she continues, have now been both superseded through the advances in biological and psychological knowledge and also rejected from most legal and social points of view in modern countries. The Council should see to it

[1] Padre Riccardo Lombardi, a writer in *Civiltà Cattolica,* leapt into sudden notoriety after the Second World War as a mass preacher – he was known as the 'microfono di Dio'. In 1952 he started, with the approval of Pius XII, a 'Movement for a Better World' which gained wide popularity in Italy and abroad. John XXIII was more sceptical about the value of Padre Lombardi's activities and did not make him an adviser to the Council. But Padre Lombardi attempted to influence the Council's work through a lengthy volume published in 1961, called *Concilio: Per una riforma nella Carità*.

that they are brought up to date with all the necessary objectivity. One consequence of the desired new approach – a consequence justified by the equal dignity of the human soul in both sexes and the identical elevation of man and woman to the supernatural state – would be the extension of the priestly office to women, as has already been done in some Protestant Churches.

Whatever may be the outcome of this Swiss champion's efforts in favour of women in the priesthood, it is a curious fact that the same question has been raised during the last few weeks in a number of letters to the papers, thus constituting a sort of secular sideline to the Council. The phenomenon is the stranger because it is quite spontaneous, and the idea seems to be advanced with greater seriousness and sincerity than was the case in the drawing-rooms of certain aristocratic Roman ladies, the famous 'matriarchs' of Padre Bresciani,[1] at the time of Vatican I. In the Turin *Stampa* alone, I have seen in the last few days both a letter from Atlanta, USA, on the problem of ecclesiastical celibacy, stressing in particular the rôle a clergyman's wife can play (it was signed by a Dr Elio Eynard who must, I think, be a Waldensian) and also several letters on the subject from women readers. Here is one:

> Female religious vocations are on the decline because many educated young girls, though enthusiastic about the Christian mission, renounce the veil because as nuns they cannot participate in the spiritual privilege and moral prestige reserved for the priest alone. Priests can act with a certain freedom in the difficult society of today, whereas nuns, who, as Padre Rotondi says, 'carry in their hearts the sign of a martyrdom, a loneliness, and a sacrifice ignored by all', leave young aspirants uncertain and perplexed because of the limitations imposed on their sex.
>
> Today women are making their mark in the universities and in all spheres of social life. It is therefore natural that they should want to be able to play a part with prestige and freedom of conscience in religious life too.
>
> The raising of women to the priesthood might have fruitful developments, and if there were a female seminary it would certainly receive within it many educated and virtuous young girls who, besides furthering the cause of Christianity, could contribute to the evolution of the coloured or backward peoples and redeem the prob-

[1] One of the main early writers in *Civiltà Cattolica* immediately after its foundation in 1850; he was especially famous for his short stories.

lem of sex which is at the bottom of so much misery and human suffering.

The letter ends: 'May the dove of the Holy Spirit (female symbol of the wisdom and intuition of the Kingdom of God on earth) illuminate the Council on this most important problem of the raising of women to the priesthood.'

Rome, Wednesday, 31 October

Yesterday, a quarter of an hour after the end of the tenth General Congregation, all Rome knew about the encounter between Alfrink and Ottaviani. It will probably not be mentioned in any communiqué, but all the same it seems pretty important. Today Ottaviani's seat at the Council was empty, but even tonight's bulletin makes no reference to it.

A week ago, when there was some misunderstanding about an alleged remark by the Archbishop of Westminster, the Council's Press Office did not wait 24 hours to publish an explanation on the front page of the *Osservatore Romano*. But the Alfrink-Ottaviani episode is of quite a different order, and it is easy to understand that the Council authorities are doing everything to avoid repercussions. It shows how tense, despite outward appearances, the atmosphere is in the Council hall. Even though the provocation and the original mistake came from the Secretary of the Holy Office, the obvious manifestation of feeling in relation to him is quite out of proportion and very embarrassing. But it is clear that certain personalities at the Council are no longer regarded merely as themselves and as individuals but have come to be looked on as symbols and treated as such. In an assembly like that at St Peter's, where the members cannot form groups according to their respective trends but have to remain isolated from each other, all mixed up together in accordance with an artificial hierarchy of rank and precedence, a strongly felt need develops to give a name and a face to the various groupings. And just as Liénart, Frings, Alfrink, and others stand for the progressives, so Ottaviani is the symbol of the conservatives – with the difference, however, that Liénart has come to occupy the position he holds in the course of the Council, whereas Ottaviani was regarded as the Curia's outstanding man long before.

Rightly or wrongly so? Probably more rightly than wrongly, but also exaggeratedly, at any rate in the sense of identifying the man with the office or some of his actions with his whole nature. For it is certainly an exaggeration to suggest that Ottaviani deserves the rather sinister reputation usually attributed to him. If the dark picture generally painted of him were true, there would be no place for other undeniable characteristics in his nature, such as his simplicity, his childlike ingenuousness, and his kindly generosity.

Monsignor Bontempi, who succeeded Ottaviani at the Nepomuk College and frequently goes to see him at the Holy Office and is therefore in a position to know him well, has helped me to understand him better. Although Bontempi does not share all his views and particularly disagrees with the manner of his attitude on several points, he is well aware of the attractive sides of his character: his quite exceptional intelligence, assisted by a wellnigh infallible memory, and also, and more especially, his simplicity and kindliness. He has often told me what a moving sight it is to see Ottaviani of a Sunday morning mingling in his clumsy, awkward way, and in spite of his bad sight, with the boys at play at the St Peter's club and talking to them like a father.

According to Bontempi, you cannot understand Ottaviani unless you remember his Trastevere origins. He was the son of a baker in Via della Lungaretta, in the poor quarter of Rome across the Tiber, and one of his brothers still carries on his father's shop there; Ottaviani still goes back whenever he can to the streets of his old neighbourhood to steep himself in its homely workaday atmosphere. As far as his own personal character is concerned, he is first and foremost quite simply a good man, a man, that is to say, who not only desires but has an active need to like people and do good among them; and, as an example of this, he has opened an orphanage for little girls at Frascati and put his sister Rosvilde in charge of it.

At the same time, however, with just the same authenticity and spontaneity and uprightness, Ottaviani is an idealist, and an idealist called upon by the office of 'Defender of the Faith', entrusted to him by Pius XII and confirmed by John XXIII, to act with a consistency and intransigence the effects of which he is himself incapable of realizing. He has, in fact, the typical abstract consistency of the intellectual or the pedant who thinks he can pigeonhole the world and its happenings within the geometrical framework of his own ideological schemes but who lacks the feeling for adaptability and understanding of circumstances, in a word the suppleness, typical of the man of action and especially of the diplomatist.

The odd thing is that, incredible as it may seem, Ottaviani was not only in the Vatican diplomatic service but was actually a high official in the Secretariat of State for seven years, first as under-secretary of the Congregation for Extraordinary Ecclesiastical Affairs and then as deputy in the Secretariat of State. But, in addition to the fact that under Pius XI no one close to the Pope had the right to entertain ideas of his own, that was the result partly of the protection of Cardinal Gasparri, who thought much of his legal ability, and partly to that of Monsignor Pizzardo, with whom he has since worked side by side. In any case, Papa Ratti ended by preferring the sterner and more impenetrable Montini, and moved Ottaviani over to the assessor's office of the Supreme Congregation of the Holy Office, of which he was later to become pro-Secretary and eventually Secretary.

Until he became a Cardinal (on 12 January 1953) and was given virtually the main responsibility for running the Inquisition, Ottaviani always remained discreetly reserved. From that moment, however, he was continually making statements and adopting definite standpoints about all sorts of matters. He had been Cardinal barely two months when, having been invited to Bologna to speak on relations between State and Church, he declared it to be 'a certain and indisputable truth according to the principles of public and ecclesiastical law that in a State composed almost entirely of Catholics and consistently governed by Catholics it is the duty of the leaders to give a Catholic tone to the legislation. That implies (he explained) three immediate consequences: the corporate profession, in public as well as in private, of the religion of the people; the Christian inspiration of the legislation; and the defence of the religious patrimony of the people against every attempt to deprive them of the treasure of their faith and their religious inheritance'. And replying to those who were shocked because Catholics demanded from the Government 'the exclusive protection of the Catholic religion', he added: 'Men who feel themselves in sure possession of truth and justice do not descend to transactions. They demand full respect for their rights.' Claims which, it goes without saying, Bea, barely ten years later, has completely turned upside down and discarded.

In February 1954 Ottaviani took over the official protection of a French Order in Rome. This was an eminently academic occasion, but he seized the opportunity to give his views on the difficult problem of the worker-priests which was then causing anxiety not only in the Church in France but virtually throughout the world (1 March was the time-limit for the 'surrender' of the worker-priests, requested by the French episcopate at the orders of the Holy See). Ottaviani's comment was that if the generosity of the priests' ardour was typically French, no less French was the generosity of the obedience required from them.

It was customary at that time to say that the main task of the worker-priests was to provide an example of Christian living, and so he praised the monks whose protector he had become because, he said, 'they show that they know how to adapt the traditional methods to modern needs without exposing themselves to leaps in the dark or employing methods that are spectacular rather than of sure effect from the priestly point of view, in order to make the best use of those gifts of supernatural grace of which we must be not only the living witnesses but also the ministers.' After criticizing the idea of creating purely working-class parishes, he went on to deplore the fact that 'under the pretext of making closer contact with men whose only desire is earthly prosperity, the reformers of the apostolate today speak more of temporal than celestial bread, and have little to say of Christ and His Cross; they no longer remember that when the teaching of Christ was preached it seemed both shocking and foolish, yet it continued to be preached and it conquered'. His last words were directed to the faithful: 'All that is most saintly and pure, that is both apostolic and modern in the Church, all that is pleasing to the heart of God and salutary for the heart of man, all this you will not abandon, nor let yourselves be deceived by the apostles of hatred, the theoreticians of fraud, or the preachers of violence.'

In this speech of Ottaviani's his optimistically controversial style had already become more highly coloured and picturesque than in the past. In subsequent years he was to give much more eloquent proof of this picturesque, impassioned, and bellicose style, whether in speaking to a restricted and selected audience of, for example, Catholic book reviewers, or to a wider public in the columns of the popular press. But the non-party press does not customarily take much notice of the attitudes adopted by members of the ecclesiastical hierarchy unless they actually intervene in politics. Thus the widest echo to be achieved by Ottaviani's writings occurred some years later in an editorial entitled 'To serve the Church or to make use of it', published in the *Quotidiano* of 21 January 1958 and directed partly towards the political intrigues among the Christian Democrats and partly to the party's progressives and those favouring a relaxation of political rigidity, such as, for instance, the Cabinet Minister Del Bo. 'Certain men,' this article said, 'who have received from the Catholics the mandate to safeguard in public life the Christian principles proclaimed in their organizations, often demonstrate in practice that they have at heart their own ambitions, political fortunes, or worldly dignity rather than progress towards that better world to which the Church desires to lead humanity.' And again: 'There are even some Catholics who from a position of political authority dare to take the part of those who not only offend but actually massacre the Church! And at the same time people go running to the priests to get them to act as intermediaries with the authorities, and in this way the country gets tired of the men whose profession is eternity but who are thus transformed into agents in purely temporal matters. This is not the way to honour the Church but rather to dishonour it. It is not serving the Church, but simply making use of it.'

In this implicit affirmation of anti-Communist intolerance there was a foretaste of the attack that Ottaviani was to launch on 7 January 1960, in a sermon in Santa Maria Maggiore during a Mass for the Church of Silence, upon no less a person than the President of the Italian Republic who was then about to set out for Moscow. He had already, in April 1959, caused a decree to be published by the Holy See extending the prohibition against political collaboration with the Communists to apply to collaboration with their Socialist allies as well.

In this and innumerable other avowals of his standpoint, it would be merely prejudice not to recognize a sincerity and uprightness that place them entirely beyond suspicion. But good intentions do not pave the way to Paradise, and what is subjectively good is not always objectively so; in particular, while a thing may be good in the abstract it is not necessarily good in relation to the actual circumstances. On the other hand, Silvio Negro's comment on Ottaviani, in a profile written at the time of the Conclave in 1958, was untrue of him then and is even more so today: he described him as 'by nature gentle and shy, keeping himself apart from all ecclesiastical or political cliques'. He is in fact not only, as a member of the Pacellian Pentagon, the spearhead of the Curial-conservative trend but also has notorious contacts with Right-wing circles, has been known to praise dictatorial régimes such as that of Franco, and has established the Pius v Institute which is no longer quite so mysterious as it was since some curious facts came out about its sources of finance.[1]

All this is familiar to some but by no means all of the Council Fathers; but what is known to all of them is the harshness of the methods he has used as inquisitor of the Holy Office. Within the walls of the Vatican basilica, in fact, the figure of Ottaviani inevitably evokes ominous memories, past and present, of one of the most ill-famed institutions of the Catholic Church.

The Council did not meet on 1 to 4 November, days which included All Saints' and All Souls' Days, 1 and 2 November.

Rome, Saturday, 3 November

I had a brief meeting today, thanks to Monsignor Bukavu, with Monsignor Zoa at the headquarters of the White Fathers in Via Aurelia. Monsignor Zoa is one of the two secretaries of the Pan-African Secretariat; he looks after the French-speaking side while his colleague Monsignor Blomjous does the same for the English.

I just missed meeting Cardinal Rugambwa, whom I should have liked to ask about the activities of the National Union of St Augustine for the formation of a Catholic lay élite, of which I understand he is the founder. I would have welcomed the opportunity to discuss with him the Catholic Church's urgent need of laymen capable of taking on leadership in economic, cultural, and political affairs in the African countries, and to get some idea of the present situation in Catholic Africa in this particular connection, especially in relation to other religions and ideologies.

[1] It was founded by Ottaviani to collect funds for distribution in order to sustain the defence of religion especially against Communist attacks.

But in any case I was able to observe him at close quarters for a few minutes, and to note his distinctive bearing, resembling that of a Western prelate, and the calm assurance of his manner in speaking to some of the Western priests in his group. I remember reading in 1960, when he was among the Cardinals-elect at the Consistory of that year, that he came of a noble family. The significance of that may be more or less relative, especially in the case of continents or populations of a wellnigh primitive civilization. In any case, today it is not his noble ancestry or pure blood that come out most strongly in his faultless manner, for that was plainly acquired in typical ecclesiastic circles.

Monsignor Bukavu had already told me a certain amount about Monsignor Zoa, some of which I had also confirmed from the *Annuario Pontificio* (that he has been Archbishop of Yaoundé, capital of Cameroon, for just over a year, and is only 38 years old) and from a PIME[1] missionary who said that but for chance Zoa might have been a leading figure in the Protestant Church rather than of the African Catholics. It all depended on which part of the Cameroons his family lived in. The Germans, who were originally responsible for the protectorate, to avoid rivalry between Catholic and evangelical missionaries divided the whole area between the two, and his family happened to live in the area allotted to the Catholics. Another curious detail is that his father, when he became converted to the new Western faith, had his son baptized at the age of ten but could not be baptized himself because he was involved in some complicated situation of polygamy.

Monsignor Bukavu told me in addition that Zoa's astonishing intelligence, his diplomatic ability, and his capacity for organization all went to explain the brilliant career he had achieved, despite the fact that when he was studying at the Urbanian College of the Propaganda Fide he was regarded with some suspicion because of his restless and anti-conformist spirit.

It was precisely this that struck me at once when I met him. Of less than middle height and rather thickset, something of a poseur but without affectation, he exuded an indomitable but controlled vitality, especially in the look of his eyes, sometimes vivid and steady, sometimes darting all over the place in insistent and disconcerting scrutiny, and in the slightly ironical manner often found in people of quick intelligence and decisive action. You could read

[1] *Pontificio Istituto delle Missioni Estere,* or Pontifical Institute for Foreign Missions.

in that incredibly black face of his a sense of pride at being first an African and then one of the foremost bishops in his continent.

He spoke to me in fluent and brilliant French with only a slight exotic accent. I had told him that I would be satisfied with an exhaustive answer to one question only, but one which I realized was of a somewhat embarrassing nature, namely, what sort of relations prevailed in the Council between the native bishops of Black Africa and the Western bishops who had remained at the head of African dioceses? A twinkle of the eye and his answer came at once, precise and unhesitating: one need only recall, he said, the composition of the Pan-African Secretariat, where no distinction was made between black and white bishops and where, though the former might be in a minority numerically, the latter were glad that they should carry a moral weight superior to their actual numbers. Moreover, his colleague, Monsignor Blomjous, Bishop of Mwanga in Tanganyika, was white, a European and a Dutchman. Because of his age (54) he certainly could not be reckoned among the missionary recruits; but he was nevertheless one of the first to favour an autochthonous laity in Africa. Today, in any case, said Zoa, Monsignor Blomjous was no longer the exception that he was ten years ago: the situation had greatly changed except for a few areas. In short, as he concluded with a decisive 'Oui, sans doute,' he is optimistic.

Rome, Sunday, 4 November

The sitting of 31 October witnessed the greatest number of interventions in the actual Council debates so far (in the debate on the Message to the World 37 Fathers spoke).

This is no doubt partly due to a sort of natural speeding-up before the four days' vacation which ended this evening with the reception for the Fathers given in the Campidoglio by the City of Rome. Five days ago there was a party for them in the Quirinal which would have been a fantastic spectacle if it could have been held in the gardens instead of in the rooms in the reception wing, which are magnificent but stifling for 4,000 guests. As it was, the spectacle was impressive enough not only for its colour, from the prelates' robes to the academic and military uniforms, but also because of the ritual ceremonies attending the arrival and departure of the Cardinals, the Grand Master of the Order of Malta, and the Prince Custodians of the Council, accompanied by Masters of the Ceremonies and attendants bearing lighted torches.

A century ago in the Campidoglio and at the Quirinal the Fathers of Vatican I met, instead of the hospitable representatives of a foreign if friendly Power, the sovereign himself, the Pope (or his representatives) who in the Basilica of St Peter's was the head and symbol of their faith, and on whom they were preparing to confer the most dazzling and debated crown in the world, that of infallibility. That last has survived; but the temporal crown was to vanish a few months after the Council's suspension, on 18 July 1870, as a result of the Franco-Prussian war. Another sixty years and the Roman Question itself would be forgotten, while the international sovereignty of the Papacy would content itself with a symbolical territory little larger than the Vatican itself.

How many years or decades must go by before that same papal theocracy accepts in a spirit of sacrifice, or joyfully offers, the renunciation of Pius IX's dogma of papal infallibility, thus placing itself at the centre of an international federation of Christian Churches which will perhaps constitute the first step towards a universal federation of religions?

This morning in St Peter's, almost as if to belie my premature hopes, John XXIII celebrated the fourth anniversary of his coronation. Not far from him, perhaps among those officiating at the altar, perhaps sitting in the stalls of the Cardinals or the Patriarchs, Archbishops, or Bishops, was his unknown successor; perhaps even his successor's successor.

In those four years, Pope John has created an opening in the Catholic Church towards the religious and civil world such as has never before been realized in the past. But is there not perhaps in the history of the Church something like a mysterious continuation of the myth of Penelope? Is there not, in its alternation of leaders, an inevitable and persistent design to balance the new and the old, restricting every development to the minimum necessary to prevent decrepitude and decay in an institution now wellnigh two thousand years old?

Rome, Monday, 5 November

Between 31 October and today, as a result of the occupation of part of their country's territory by the Chinese, Cardinal Gracias, Archbishop of Bombay, and two Indian bishops have temporarily left the Council. Gracias is to come back as soon as possible, but the return of the two bishops will depend on the fate of the occupied territories.

Cardinal Cushing's return home, on the other hand, seems to be both a polemical and a definitive act, at any rate as far as this first session is concerned. The Archbishop of Boston has tried in vain to persuade the Pope, the Presiding Council, and the Secretariat for Extraordinary Affairs to adopt at least a system of simultaneous translation of the speeches made in the Council Hall. To listen for hours each day to a sequence of practically incomprehensible speeches, when he had so much else to do in his diocese at home, was something he could no longer stomach. He had no objection to Latin as such, though his relations with the language were somewhat strained; but he did object to this absurd imposition which does not even permit of ordinary translations, in an assembly where certainly many of the Fathers are as much at a disadvantage as he is, if not more so. So he preferred to pack his bags and go.

The news of this departure has caused me to try to compare the number of Fathers now present (2,196) and the number participating in the first General Congregation, but I have come up against unexpected difficulties. The Press Office's communiqués for some reason began to give the numbers of those present only from 23 October, i.e. from the fifth General Congregation, onwards. Luckily Antimori has managed to give me the figures for all the other dates except 13 October. According to these figures, which he guarantees as coming from the Council's meccanographical centre, the second Congregation, the one when the voting took place, reached the record number of attendances to date, 2,381; at the third and fourth there were, respectively, 2,379 and 2,340. Subsequently, except for a temporary recovery to 2,363 on 23 October (the fifth General Congregation), the curve descends; in fact, on the 24th there were 2,337, on the 26th 2,323 (the missing days are Thursdays and Sundays, days on which the Fathers do not meet in full session), 2,302 on the 27th, 2,277 on the 28th, 2,257 on the 29th, and 2,230 on the 31st.

Perhaps there is no need to attach too much importance to today's further fall in numbers, even if it is rather more marked than before. A good many bishops, especially among the Italians, have profited by these four days' pause to return to their sees to despatch urgent business. Tomorrow and in the following days the numbers may go up again. But in any case, apart from today, the fact remains that between 16 and 31 October 151 Fathers have absented themselves from the Council or left it altogether.

How is this to be explained? By a desire for a little amusement and the inability of many of the bishops to resist the magical fascination of Rome and Italy? But the Fathers have every afternoon and two whole days in each week free; in addition to which they were told long ago of the pause from 1 to 4 November.

Is it a question, then, of their tiring journeys, the change of climate, or maladies attendant on the early autumn season? There is undoubtedly something in all these reasons, especially considering the advanced age of over 50 per cent of the Fathers. The three deaths that occurred in a single week, on 16, 21, and 24 October, are significant in this connection and have, strangely enough, been practically passed over in silence. The first was the 76-year-old Bishop of Buffalo, Monsignor Joseph A. Burke, followed by Monsignor Edoardo Facchini, Bishop of Alatri, also of the same age; the third was the Bishop, or rather titular Archbishop, of Velebusdo, previously head of the missionary archdiocese of Salisbury, Southern Rhodesia, an 83-year-old Jesuit, Monsignor Aston Chichester. I don't know how the first one died; the second had a heart attack in a bus; the third collapsed at the entrance to St Peter's while on his way into the sixth General Congregation.

In any case, I cannot think that reasons of health suffice to explain this high and progressive absenteeism. Rumours agree that as the days go on the seats in the Council Hall become steadily emptier, especially after the first hour of a sitting, while an increasing number of Fathers can be seen walking about in the neighbourhood or sitting at the two cafés.

Rome, Wednesday, 7 November

Ottaviani continues to be absent from the Council Hall. According to Monsignor Martinez, some of the Curia expected the day before yesterday that Liénart, whose turn it was to be chairman that day, noticing his empty seat would make some official expression of regret about what happened on 30 October. But neither Liénart nor yesterday's chairman, Tappouni, nor Gilroy today have said anything. So it seems that some members of Ottaviani's trend have decided to absent themselves too as a demonstration of solidarity. In any case, in the past two days attendances have risen by only eight.

The Presiding Council has at last succeeded in launching the new arrangements for speakers in the Hall: Fathers who wish to speak must henceforth accompany their request by a brief summary of what they propose to say; and after speaking they must give the Secretary-General two copies of their speech, one for the archives and one for the relevant Commission.

In addition, as Monsignor Felici announced yesterday, 'the Holy Father has deigned to grant the Presiding Council the faculty of proposing to the General Congregation that discussion of a chapter should be terminated at the Chairman's judgment when it has been sufficiently debated and illustrated. In that case, the Presiding Council will put the proposal to the vote and the Fathers can accept or reject it, voting by standing or sitting.'

Monsignor Felici also announced today that, in contrast to what he said yesterday, in order further to speed up work chapters 5-8 of the Liturgical draft will be discussed all together, after which discussion will begin on the draft 'De Fontibus Revelationis'.

Yesterday's chairman, the Middle Easterner Tappouni, followed this up by at once putting to the vote the proposal to end the discussion of the second chapter. This was agreed to and the assembly then went on to discuss chapter 3, on the sacraments and sacramental rites. The debate on that ended today and discussion of the fourth chapter, on the Divine Office, began. But even with this speeding-up it will be difficult for the whole of 'De Sacra Liturgia' to be examined in less than a week; and that means that if, as seems likely, the first session of the Council ends on the Feast of the Immaculate Conception (8 December), more than half of its time will have been spent on just one of the 69 drafts drawn up by the Preparatory Commissions. At that rate Vatican II will take about ten years.

I feel I should say something about the various reports I have heard concerning the substance of the debates so far, but I can't decide how to set about it. A purely external approach, though not so superficial as it might at first seem, would be to highlight certain typical days of the debate: 22 and 24 October, for example, have been described by some as the Curia's days, 26 October the day of the Benedictines, etc. On that day, in fact, there spoke for the first time and in quick succession three Abbots General of the Order, those of the Congregations in England, Beuron (Germany) and France. But it was to be expected that the Benedictines would take a particularly prominent part in the discussion of the Liturgical draft.

It was also foreseeable that the 'pezzi grossi', the big shots, of the Curia would throw their weight about a bit. In fact they did so quite early on. On the 22nd, at the fourth General Congregation and the first day of actual discussion, three of them spoke, Vagnozzi, Scapinelli, and Dante, and two days later four more, Van Lierde, Zanini, Parente, and Staffa; not to mention the occasional Cardinal. This was obviously too much; complaints rained down on the Chairman's desk, and the Pope when he heard of it intervened unofficially, as I mentioned earlier. It is difficult to say whether he did the same about the Curia Cardinals; given the recognized privileges of the members of the Sacred College, I would be inclined to think not. Besides, up till now the Cardinals of the Curia have been quite restrained; against two interventions each from Bea and Bacci, there have also been two each from Lercaro, Spellman, Gracias, and Godfrey, all of them residential bishops, and as many as four from Cardinal Ruffini, Archbishop of Palermo (who, however, is after all an ex-Curial).

There is also another way to peer behind the scenes of the Council, and that is to attend the press conferences that the Fathers seem eager to give. The most lively centre for these so far seems to be with the Verbites, the Order of the Divine Word, who have made their temporary headquarters with the Salvatorians in their Generalate in Via della Conciliazione. During the past fortnight speakers there have included the Indian Monsignor D'Zouza, the Argentinian Monsignor Kemerer, the Filippine Monsignor Duschak, and the Dutch bishop of an Indonesian see, Monsignor Van Bekkum. As I was unable to go to his press conference I haven't been able to make out from the newspaper reports exactly what Monsignor Duschak had in mind with his idea of an 'ecumenical Mass', which would, according to him, be complementary to, but not replace, the present Latin rite: he seems to be thinking of a rite stripped of all historical superstructure and reduced to the essence of the sacrifice of the Last Supper as described in the Gospels.

Monsignor D'Zouza maintained the need to grant the Church of Latin rite in India the possibility (which the Catholic Church of Syrian-Malabar rite already has) of celebrating the Mass in the vernacular and of introducing adaptations of the numerous and picturesque traditional Indian rites and customs. This he suggests because 'the oriental liturgy is in general richer and more attractive when it is closer to the native tradition'.

Monsignor Van Bekkum said he was converted to the liturgy only in 1952, during a long stay in Holland when he came into contact with the Benedictines and had the opportunity to meditate on Pius XII's encyclical *Mediator Dei*. After a period of reflection and theoretical planning, which he described at an Assisi congress in 1956, he moved on to the experimental stage. Today he is convinced that in regions like Indonesia the most direct way of spreading the Gospel is to penetrate the local rites, which means in practice the local festivals: these festivals generally last for several days during which there are songs, dancing, processions, theatrical representations, and games etc., but all with strictly religious significance and allusions. It is not a question of Christianizing all this, 'but rather of abolishing all immorality and then of adopting Christian prayers, expressed, however, in local dialects and forms, and giving the dances, songs, and so on a Christian symbolism'. 'Paganism is really the absence of Christ: where Christ is there can no longer be any thought of paganism.'

Today I went to the press conference of Monsignor De Castro Mayer, Bishop of Campos. It was an unexpected experience, for this Brazilian bishop is a convinced and consistent champion of rigid traditionalism. In his view, it may be all very fine to give the faithful missals and expect them to take a more active part in the Mass but, apart from the difficulty of making such innovations on a universal scale, he does not see what use they are in promoting a sense of holiness since 'the more secret a service is, the more evocative it becomes' and 'the atmosphere of mystery adds to the sensation of the divine'. These are trite commonplaces to which the lecturer's Iberian eloquence failed to lend conviction; but Monsignor De Castro did succeed in being original in his own particular way when answering the question whether he did not think the aristocratic nature of Latin might carry a risk of social discrimination between the educated classes and the rest. He simply blew up, affirming with some heat that just because Latin was an aristocratic language he saw good reason to preserve its ritual use, 'since it is a means of accustoming men to realize and recognize the natural stratifications which must exist in society'. Latin, in fact, fulfilled 'the pedagogic function of reminding people that despite the equality of all men in the face of God different social strata do nevertheless exist'.

The Press Office also arranged two press conferences to which they invited expert speakers, not Fathers: these were the Jesuit Hermann Schmidt, Professor at the Gregorian University, who is said to be responsible for the rough draft of the Liturgical draft, and the Benedictine Salvatore Marsili, President of the International Liturgical Pontifical Institute of St Anselmo. Everybody present was impressed by the broadmindedness, ease of manner, and liveliness of these two experts. Father Schmidt's exposition was perhaps the more classical in form: in it he explained that the task before the Fathers was to weigh up the proposals presented to the Council, pass judgment on the reforms introduced in recent years, and decide on the general measures which the appropriate authorities will eventually put into practical application. The overall aim should be that the liturgy should cease to be something purely marginal in the life of the faithful and become instead an organic, formative, and guiding element. Also of interest were his contention that a close link exists between cult and culture, and his analysis of the present paradoxical situation, characterized, so he said, by the two opposing phenomena of Western predominance and the decline of colonialism. It is a fact that while on the one hand new regional liturgies are being sought and there is a reaction against Western influence, on the other hand Western culture is being assimilated everywhere – so much so, indeed, that while farsighted Westerners are advocating de-Westernization for the other peoples, those peoples themselves are striving by every means to become Westernized.

The speech of the Benedictine monk Dom Marsili astonished everyone both for its brilliant language and its openmindedness.

Briefly, he maintained that in the liturgical sphere the Council should strive to give a deeper doctrinal significance to the various dogmatic concepts from which official prayer in the Church today draws its inspiration; it should then define the scope and methods of the proposed modernizations; and lastly it should decide on the reforms to be carried out. These last, in his view, should include both the elimination of outworn accretions and superstructures and the provision of new ritual formulae.

Referring to certain 'archaeological remains' which had been preserved merely in order to perpetuate a 'feeble and forced' symbolism, Dom Marsili declared that the liturgy could not but gain in intelligibility and seriousness by their abolition (he mentioned as an example the rite of purifying the hands during liturgical ceremonies). He deplored the fact that many people had an almost idolatrous veneration for the letter of the rubrics even when they verged on the absurd (as, for instance, in the invitation to leave the Church – the 'Ite, Missa est' – long before the Mass is over). To him, incrustations are never, despite appearances to the contrary, really ancient or venerable, and he pointed to all the 'dressing up and undressing', to use his own words (the putting-on and taking-off of sacred vestments in a Pontifical Mass) or to the excessive and even controversial moving-about of sacred objects (the continual changing of mitres, handing of missals, exchanging the missal for the canon and vice versa, etc.). He, too, spoke of class differences but in exactly the opposite sense from Monsignor De Castro, referring, for instance, to the custom of distributing pre-consecrated particles of the Host to the faithful while the celebrant of the Mass reserves to himself the consumption of the newly-consecrated 'hostia magna'.

The majority of his listeners must have seen in Dom Marsili a modernist[1] come to life again. But as an antidote to this impression came his attack on certain 'nouvelles vagues' trends desirous of introducing such absurd innovations as, for instance, the proposal of a French group to replace 'Dominus vobiscum' by 'Salut, camarades!'

I see today that the Kipa agency on 30 October reported the

[1] Modernism was the name given by Pius x to the movement for modernizing the Church, promoted by various theologians around the turn of the century (e.g. Buonaiuti in Italy, Loisy in France, Tyrrell in England).

following words of praise for the Bugnini draft[1] from Canon A. G. Martimort, head of the Centre de Pastorale Liturgique and an ex-adviser of the Council: 'A new theological language, a new ecclesiastical style has been created, and we find it in the Liturgical draft alone. Theological style used to be scholastic in character, and it is that style that still recurs in all the other drafts. But the style of the Liturgical draft is biblical and patristic, completely orientated in the direction of the pastoral letter. Such a style can be understood by the people and will touch men deeply. It is a style widely used among Orthodox, Protestants, and even pagans.'

Rome, Thursday, 8 November

At the general audience yesterday the Pope made a notable re-affirmation of the progressive aims of the Council. After saying, as usual very generously, that the Council's labours were 'proceeding at a resolute but calm pace' and were 'going forward with decision and clarity, with the aim of causing the truth, enunciated and repeated in varying forms, to penetrate into each man's mind', he added (I quote from the *Osservatore Romano*):

> The life of a Christian is not a survey of antiquity. It is not a question of studying some museum or academy of the past; that can doubtless be useful, as a visit to monuments of the past is useful, but it is not enough. We live to advance, making use of what the past has to offer us in practice and experience, in order to go ever onwards along the paths Our Lord has shown us.

Rome, Friday, 9 November

During the first week in November various episcopates have met to study together the problems under discussion at the Council and some of them have decided to publish collective documents which will certainly have an influence on its work. Thus, for example, the Indian bishops before Gracias' departure signed a statement declaring themselves in favour of a lesser use of the Latin language in liturgical celebrations and especially in some parts of the Mass, and copies of it have been sent to all the other episcopal con-

[1] See above p. 224

ferences. A similar statement has also been drawn up by the African episcopate, emphasizing how in that continent almost everyone is illiterate and popular civilization is based on an oral tradition. Lastly, the Japanese bishops have pronounced themselves in the same sense, pointing out in their memorandum to the Presiding Council how Latin and Greek are completely foreign to the Japanese cultural tradition, even among educated people.

It is a perfectly normal procedure to make declarations of this kind, and these episodes have evoked no protest. On the other hand, so Bontempi and Martinez tell me, some irritation has been aroused by something which many have interpreted as an attempt to sabotage the draft 'De Fontibus Revelationis', which is to be discussed in a few days. This is itself a draft entitled 'Revelation concerning God and Man as shown by Jesus Christ'; it begins thus: 'Since it appears impossible for the Council to discuss all the drafts prepared and express a vote on them, it has been thought necessary to omit some and shorten or combine others. It is for this reason that the Chairmen of the Episcopal Conferences of Austria, Belgium, France, Germany, and Holland venture to propose as a point of departure for the discussion the following text, being a résumé of the material contained in the two first drafts but expressed in a more positive and more pastoral style.'

The important thing, as can easily be imagined, is the support given to this draft – which undoubtedly bears the marks of Rahner's influence – by the five most progressive episcopates in Europe; but a perusal of its contents shows convincingly that it cannot have been quickly improvised for mere tactical reasons but is rather the fruit of long and patient elaboration, most probably initiated before the Council started. This seems the more likely since the Council was originally to have begun by discussing the theological drafts.

It is probably the distribution of this text among the Fathers that has prompted the launching of a counter-pamphlet entitled *Rationalism, Catholic Exegesis, and Teaching*. True, the pamphlet is signed by a private individual, an ex-member of the Preparatory Commission on Studies and Seminaries, but that individual is none other than one – if the most modest – of the protagonists in a celebrated dispute which a year ago stirred all the cultural circles of the Catholic ecclesiastical world, setting in opposition against each other the Lateran Biblical School and the Pontifical Biblical Institute. The risk of reopening this controversy is obvious, even though the pamphlet in question is in fact merely an extract from the volume *Saggi di critica ed esegesi biblica,* by Monsignor Francesco Spadafora, which came out a few days ago in the 'Lateranum' series (it appears there as a reprint of an article, polemical in subject but moderate in tone, which originally appeared in *Palestra del clero* of 15 September 1961).

I think, therefore, that it may be useful to give some account of this remarkable dispute, for at any moment we may find ourselves involved in a battle with no holds barred, as happened in eminently unedifying circumstances in Vatican I. But at that time the struggle against the doctrine of papal infallibility conditioned the means and methods adopted by the opposing sides without involving any real competition between the theological schools. And in any case in 1869-70 the Roman theological schools were completely at one in their opposition to the schools beyond the Alps. Stranger still, they submitted docilely to the leadership of the Collegio Romano, the Jesuit University, rechristened the Gregoriana after the occupation of Rome by Italian forces. The theologians of the Council were in fact at that time nearly all teachers at that college.

The situation is quite different today. Among the fourteen ecclesiastical academies in Rome, half of which are really just for show and do nothing but train the personnel of the religious Orders that run them, two alone, the Gregorian and the Lateran Universities, vie with each other to secure the secular (diocesan) clergy from all parts of the world, only a very small proportion of whom go to the Angelicum or other universities; though the Urbanian College of the Propaganda Fide is really also an academy for secular clergy, most of them from Afro-Asian countries, and is indeed the only one besides the Lateran University to be run by them.

Among all these universities there is no real rivalry: none of them, for instance, thinks of supplanting the Gregorian University, which is both the most efficient and the one with the oldest traditions. This is not the case, however, with the Pontifical Biblical Institute and the Pontifical Eastern Institute, both of recent foundation by, respectively, Pius X and Benedict XV and placed by those Popes under the direction of the Company of Jesus. Given their association with the Gregoriana, though they are formally subject to the Curia they escape its direct control, despite their importance and purpose.

Up to the present time – that is to say, in a period of ecumenical isolation, if not of official anti-ecumenicalism – the Pontifical Eastern Institute has not amounted to much and has therefore aroused no particular ambitions on the part of others. With the Biblical Institute, however, it is a different matter, for it monopolizes and in a certain sense conditions, together with its branch in Jerusalem, the whole movement for biblical studies throughout the Catholic world. Consequently both the Sacred Congregation for Seminaries and Universities of Studies and the heads of the Lateran University and the Urbanian College have for some time cherished the project of securing its gradual 'secularization'.

Under Pius XII, however, nothing of the kind was to be hoped for, for he inherited his predecessors' weakness for the Jesuits even to the point of setting up a special private secretariat composed of some members of the Company. It was already something that the integralist trends in the Holy Office, the Congregation for Seminaries, and the two academies had managed in 1950 to get inserted in the encyclical *Humani Generis* some directives toning down the opening of the *Divino afflante Spiritu*, the biblical encyclical of 1943. Father Bea, the main inspirer of the latter, had ceased to be head of the Biblicum the year before and though his opinion had been asked he had not managed to make it prevail although he had been the Pope's confessor since 1945. The Rector at that time, Father Vogt, not foreseeing the abuses that were to arise in interpreting the new passages of the encyclical, found no particular difficulty in letting them pass.

The advent to the Pontificate of John XXIII put an end to the directorial supremacy of the Company of Jesus and thus offered the possibility, or at least better prospects, of a conquest of the Biblicum by the Curia and the secular clergy. It was only then, too, that the combination of forces to conduct the attack was completed. The Pizzardo-Ottaviani tandem, formed in the Secretariat of State, had been strengthened and reinforced after the reconstitution of the Holy Office, soon extending its influence to the Congregation for Seminaries as well. But it needed the right men to carry out its plans, and these were soon found. They were

Parente, Garofalo, and Piolanti, respectively an Apulian, a Neapolitan, and a man from the Romagna, all three of whom had ended up on the staff of the Urbanian College of the Propaganda Fide (Parente, indeed, was formerly its Rector) and were linked by ties of both friendship and common ideological aims. Parente was presented by Garofalo and Piolanti, his two disciples (the former in the strict sense of the word, the latter morally), as the 'theologus princeps' of the Roman universities; Garofalo passed for the foremost Italian biblical scholar since the publisher Marietti had entrusted to him, rather than to Ricciotti, the compilation of a big annotated edition of the Bible; and Piolanti was a specialist in sacramental theology, a terrific worker who produced book after book with a positively Teutonic attention to detail.

In reality all three were little more than scholarly pedants, doubtless quite competent as far as they went, but all the more determined to defend their limited horizon, entrenching themselves in a militant integralism ready to adopt measures against the 'rerum theologicarum novatores'. The most personable and the cleverest of the three was undoubtedly Garofalo, but he was also too astute not to realize that his future in Rome could lie only among the standard-bearers of official traditionalism.

The post-war aims of this pair of Cardinals and trio of prelates included, in addition to the out-and-out defence of traditional doctrines, the direct or indirect control of the pontifical universities for secular clergy and of high-class ecclesiastical publishing in Rome, and also the strengthening of the Roman Pontifical Academy. In their defence of traditionalism they were busily occupied from 1946 onwards against, in particular, the French school of the 'nouvelle théologie', which they succeeded in getting condemned, together with a certain exegetic liberalism, in the encyclical *Humani generis* of 1950. In the following year Piolanti left the Urbanian College and entered the Lateran University, sure that he would easily effect its conquest soon. This he achieved in 1957, shortly before Garofalo became in his turn Rector of the Urbanian College of the Propaganda Fide. Almost simultaneously, Parente was recalled to Rome by Ottaviani after an unexpected pastoral interlude in Perugia as the result of the veto advanced in 1955 by the French Ambassador to the Holy See against his appointment as assessor to the Holy Office. The French Ambassador had, in fact, taken similar swift action in 1959, once again as the result of a timely warning from the French episcopate, to avert the same threat, but when he arrived at the Vatican for the pontifical audience Ottaviani was just coming out of the Pope's apartment bearing the long-awaited signature.[1]

In the sphere of control of Roman religious publishing, the integralists' greatest achievement certainly lay in their seizure of the *Enciclopedia Cattolica* out of the hands of its original proposers and organizers, Monsignor Barbieri and Abbot Ricciotti; in 1948 they placed it under an editorial organization of their own, presided over by Pizzardo and run by the then Rector of the Lateran University, Monsignor Pio Paschini. At the same time, moreover, the trio of prelates skilfully penetrated into the Studium publishing house of the Italian Catholic Graduates' Movement, not only writing some volumes of its 'Biblioteca Universale' but also jointly editing a *Dictionary of Dogmatic Theology* (which was soon followed by the *Biblical Dictionary* edited by Monsignor Spadaforo, then a lecturer in exegesis at the Marianum).

The restoration of the Roman Pontifical Academy, with Cardinal Pizzardo as Protector and Piolanti as secretary, also took place under Pius XII in 1956, and shortly afterwards it was endowed with an important review, the tri-annual *Divinitas*.

The integralists' position was thus by now quite strong enough to permit of moving on to the next stage of the conquest. The first objective proved to be the Biblicum itself, which they accused of excessive liberalism because of its use in teaching of the famous *Formengeschichte* (history of forms) method.[2] They found a ready pretext in 1959 in the shape of a 20-page pamphlet entitled *Critica letteraria del Nuovo Testamento nell'esegesi cattolica dei Vangeli*, printed at S. Giorgio Canavese and bearing the signature of the German Jesuit Father M. Zerwick, a lecturer at the Biblicum, which despite its brevity appeared to be 'sufficiently compromising'. However, the 50th anniversary of the Biblicum's foundation fell on 17 Feb-

[1] It was Count Wladimir d'Ormesson who in 1955 communicated to Pius XII the French episcopate's objection to Parente's appointment on the ground that he had been one of those mainly responsible for the condemnation and persecution of representatives of the 'nouvelle théologie'. In 1959, under John XXIII, similar objections were again raised by the new French Ambassador, Baron Guy de la Tournelle. Monsignor Bontempi was by chance in a position to follow step by step the latter's efforts to reach Ottaviani, first with the Pope, then with Tardini, and finally at the Holy Office.

[2] Based on the theory that the historical truth of the Bible depends on the literary form used by each author.

ruary 1960 and was to be celebrated in the Vatican itself in the presence of John XXIII and 22 Cardinals. The Pope's calm and restrained but generous speech on this occasion ('Fifty years of life, growth, and quiet serious work . . .') was such as to prevent them from taking action immediately.

A few months later the integralists' problem of timing their attack seemed to have been effectively solved by the appearance of yet another article by a Biblicum lecturer, Father Alonso-Schokel, published in *Civiltà Cattolica* under the title 'Dove va l'esegesi cattolica?' ('Whither Catholic Exegesis?'). At the end of 1960 *Divinitas* launched the great attack in a turgid and obscure 70-page article by Monsignor Antonino Romeo, a member of the Roman Pontifical Academy but also Cardinal Pizzardo's second-in-command at the Sacred Congregation for Seminaries and Universities of Studies and a member of the editorial board of the *Enciclopedia Cattolica*. With a violence that had at least the merit of casting aside all reticence or subterfuge, Romeo accused the two Jesuit Fathers of acting as rebels against the papal encyclicals and other documents, subverters of tradition, enemies of the Catholic Faith, refuters of the integral truth of the dogma, corruptors of the young clergy, hypocrites, and supporters of a world conspiracy to destroy the Christian religion.

The Biblicum was not mentioned by name but was described as 'a group which agitates indefatigably to open ever wider breaches in the superhuman edifice of the Catholic faith'; but though Romeo termed it 'easily recognizable', he made only a vague reference to that 'propaganda centre' which with its 'lethal orchestration' strove to invade the whole world. As a matter of fact even this fiery Calabrian priest must have found the question quite a difficult one to tackle, as the following piece of imaginative eloquence suggests: 'A continuous network of laborious intrigue, as of ants working away in the background in Rome and all parts of the world, compels us to divine the active existence of a vast plot to outwit and demolish the doctrines on which the Catholic faith is based and nourished. Even more numerous indications from various quarters bear witness to the gradual development of a far-reaching and wide-spread manoeuvre, under skilful and seemingly devout leadership, the aim of which is to do away with Christianity as it has so far been taught and lived for nineteen centuries and replace it by a Christianity of modern times.'

No such example of polemics within the Church had been seen since the days of Pius x and his anti-modernist campaign. The answer was eagerly awaited both in Rome and Italy and in the outer world. An extract from the article, printed by the publishing house of the Lateran University, was sent to all bishops throughout the five continents, and would certainly have produced more reactions had it not been written in Italian.

When the reply came, as it soon did, it proved to be a lesson in moderation and dignity. It took the form of a 17-page article in Latin in the Biblicum's review *Verbum Domini*. It was entitled 'Pontificium Institutum Biblicum et recens libellus R.mi D.ni. Romeo' and signed P.I.B., in other words by the whole teaching staff of the Institute. The article was constructed in scholarly fashion, within a strict framework that did not exclude a certain humour ('incriminationum occasio et fontes', 'Rev.mi A.Romeo metodus "interpretandi" fontes suas', etc.). The third paragraph contained a point-by-point reply to the various 'accusationes gravissimae' listed above. Particularly interesting was the retort to the accusation of love of novelty for its own sake: in Romeo's case, it suggested, the very opposite was true, for any real or apparent novelty was for him an obsessive enemy to be fought at all costs. Yet Pius xii in his encyclical 'Divino afflante Spiritu' had given a clear warning to all who tended to 'believe that everything at all new must therefore be attacked or suspected'. The final comment – obviously inspired by Bea, though some say the whole article was by him – was quite particularly apt, namely that at a time when the Council was in progress 'seemingly authoritative' articles such as that in *Divinitas* did little to further ecumenism or eliminate suspicion in non-Catholic circles.

This article in *Verbum Domini* also went round the world to every bishopric. The counter-reply to it was awaited even more eagerly. Everyone wondered whether Romeo would answer, and even more whether his respective supporting buttresses, the Lateran University and the Urbanian College on the one hand and the Congregations of the Holy Office and of the Seminaries on the other, would reveal themselves. Those prophets proved right who had foreseen, not a prolongation of the dispute or its extension to the various Roman institutes concerned, but a forcible and authoritative intervention in a style consonant with the best tradition of integralism.

The authority to make it could, of course, be none other than the Holy Office; but it did not succeed in doing so in quite the way it would have wished. According to the intentions of Ottaviani, Pizzardo and their colleagues, the Holy Office should have united with the Pontifical Biblical Commission to issue a decree that would, *in die quinta,* receive the sanction of the Pope himself. But John XXIII would not agree, saying that a warning (*monitum*) might have been useful but a decree (*decretum*) might involve implicating in too dangerous and tendentious a way the freedom of Catholic studies, compromising that atmosphere of mutual confidence which Pius XII himself had contributed towards creating by his encyclical *Afflante Spiritu* and had not repudiated in *Humani Generis.*

The *Osservatore Romano* of 22 June 1961 therefore published only a *monitum,* relating to 'opinions and views which, in various regions, endanger the authentic historical and objective truth of Holy Writ, not only of the Old but also of the New Testament, even in relation to the sayings and actions of Christ' and exhorting students of Holy Writ to treat such delicate subjects 'with prudence and reverence' so as not to disturb the conscience of the faithful or harm the truths of the faith.

This did not amount to much and, above all, it did not say precisely what it was aiming at. So the would-be ghost-raisers set about accompanying it with a suitable fanfare. On 28 June the Vatican daily announced that Jean Steinmann's *La vie de Jésus* had been put on the Index and published a long (and as usual anonymous) article in justification. But only two months later the same paper printed an article by Cardinal Ruffini, former professor of exegesis at the Lateran University, which included the following passage: 'The feverish discussion which has raged increasingly during recent years concerning the literary nature of the various Books inspired by God, not excluding the Gospels, is caused in part by comparisons made with the few existing documents of ancient Oriental literatures, but also and more especially by a hypercritical spirit which leaves entirely out of consideration the traditional teaching of the Church and the feelings of believing Catholics which are its faithful echo. The result has been that some critics, including unfortunately some ecclesiastics, have tried more or less explicitly to eliminate from the historical record certain accounts of the greatest importance such as, for example, the first chapters of Genesis and the Gospels.'

Monsignor Spadafora, a follower of Romeo and a fellow-Calabrian, in an article a month later in *Palestra del Clero* asserted that the document of the Holy Office had 'a quite exceptional significance' and 'practically amounted to a sentence', clearly indicating as its objective the 'Teutonic and rationalist . . . method of history of forms' (i.e. *Formengeschichte*). The integralists could not have acknowledged more plainly the failure of their attempt to secure the issue of a *decretum* which would have involved the Pontifical Biblical Institute. But since it is this very article that is now being distributed to the Fathers there can be little doubt that they do not regard the question as closed but are trying instead to secure some success in the Council.

Rome, Saturday, 10 November

The papers mention the lecture given the day before yesterday in the hall of the Council's Press Office by the Chief of Protocol of the Secretariat of State in person, Monsignor Igino Cardinale[1] (*nomen omen*), on 'The Church and Politics' (a last-minute title: the earlier one, 'The Church's Policy', appeared too provocative).

Some of those present must certainly have wondered what such a theme had to do with the Council, and whether its choice and the seemingly impromptu nature of the affair might not conceal an ingenious attempt to get at the Fathers who would soon be debating the draft 'De Ecclesia'. But there was a reason to justify it, if also hardly a fortuitous one, in the appearance in the bookshops during the last few days of a handsome and expensive volume, *Le Saint-Siège et la Diplomatie,* by the lecturer himself.

From the résumé of the lecture given in the *Osservatore Romano* it evidently followed the traditional textbook lines. Probably very few listeners apart from one or two ecclesiastics will have realized the clash between the canonic legalism of its premises and the different conception of the Church according to recent theology. To Monsignor Igino Cardinale, who showed a lack of the necessary up-to-date cultural background in this connection, the Church is still simply and solely 'a visible organized and perfect society which pursues social and concrete aims also in the temporal sphere, in as much as it carries out its mission in this world

[1] Appointed Apostolic Delegate to the U.K. in October 1963.

and its subjects are at one and the same time members of the religious society founded by Christ and citizens of the State . . .'

The kernel of his thesis is naturally much more complex and serious, setting out from the usual theoretical (and in itself irrefutable) relationship between politics (conceived as 'the science or art of directing public affairs'), morals, and religion. But at that point he takes it for granted that the Catholic Church represents not only the sole religion but also the sole organization deputed by God to manifest it and put it into practice, presupposing the primacy of the Pope as the very basis of the Church's stability and infallibility and going on from there to deduce the need to recognize the Pope's right to have a diplomacy of his own.

Put in these abstract and logically coherent terms, the thesis is perfectly correct. On the plane of reality and hence of its application, however, it comes up against the obstacle of the plurality of religions, the ultimate reason for which naturally lies in the belief and uncompromising affirmation of each religion that it and it alone is the one true faith. It thus becomes both absurd and embarrassing to envisage a law concerning diplomatic legation which could be recognized by all the different faiths. In practice, of course, the Catholic Church is the only one to put forward such a claim, because no other religion, not even the Protestant or Orthodox confessions, has ever thought of giving itself an organization at once theocratic and temporal and placing at its head a sovereign of guaranteed infallibility.

Half a century ago, in a work long regarded as authoritative (at least until the learned prelate its author left the Church as the result of a romantic affair), Monsignor Giobbio advanced the theory that the right of legation (i.e. of independent diplomatic representation) derived from the sovereign character of the Pope. Monsignor Cardinale prefers to link that right with the institution of the papacy, giving it a theological basis by the reference to papal primacy. Obviously, however, this variant does not alter the substance of the claim. In any case, the most disturbing thing emerging from the press conference of the day before yesterday is not so much that Monsignor Cardinale should have expounded a thesis of this kind but that an audience of several hundred journalists, i.e. of people who influence public opinion, raised no shadow of doubt about its content.

Lack of expert knowledge in theological and legal matters certainly constitutes some excuse, but is that excuse really valid in the face of such assertions as, for instance, that the Church's diplomatic activity in particular, and its political activity in general, represent 'the free and rightful exercise of a right and duty which the Pope can in no way neglect without committing a very serious fault', or that 'The Church is not, and does not wish to be, a political power purporting to have political aims to be achieved by political means'?

There was, however, some sort of reaction from the lay press, if only of a negative kind, in the omission of any reference to the theoretical part of Cardinale's exposition. Nearly all the papers, in fact, chose to give more space to the speaker's answers to questions during the discussion that followed. Here Monsignor Cardinale, who during the lecture had seemed somewhat pedantic and dry, appeared much more at his ease, besides demonstrating his linguistic ability. (Born at Fondi and now aged 46, before entering a Roman seminary he studied in the United States at St Agnes Academy, College Point, N.Y. After the war he entered the Secretariat of State and was at once sent to represent the Holy See in Cairo, where he remained for seven years until 1953. In addition to English he speaks French, German, Spanish, and Dutch).

His most daring as well as diplomatic reply to the numerous questions fired at him by journalists concerned the possibility of establishing relations between the Holy See and the Soviet Union. Monsignor Cardinale's answer was: 'In conformity with the principles that inspire its action, the Holy See is always ready to negotiate with States requesting diplomatic relations and other kinds of agreements, provided the Church's prerogatives, the freedom of Catholics and, of course, the exercise of the fundamental human rights are respected.' The questions that embarrassed him most, however, were those concerning relations between the Church and régimes which were Catholic but totalitarian, such as those of Spain and Portugal. Asked about the priests arrested by the police in Angola, Cardinale replied laconically that the Holy See had dealt 'through the usual diplomatic channels, as with any other Government'.

For my own part, I cannot rid myself of the suspicion that the real aim of the press conference was precisely to provoke the questions that emerged during the discussion, and these the Chief of Protocol of the Secretariat of State answered with a suppleness in direct contrast to the rigidity of the principles he had just enunciated (I am thinking particularly of his reply about arbitration between countries and the idea of tolerance – though that term deserves to be put in cold storage for a while). But it is probably more realistic to suppose that the idea was to achieve both aims at once. Now, this wish to restate in virtually official form a conception of the Church as a purely worldly and temporal Power, in direct contrast to recent developments in theological thought, is a very serious matter which the more advanced Catholics cannot but view severely and with real alarm. The Curia has evidently decided to resist everything that can constitute a threat to its present organization including, if not especially, its diplomatic corps which is perhaps the greatest source of its prestige, at any rate in the eyes of the general public, and which in any case provides its main possibility of impinging on the temporal sphere, principally in politics, of course, but also in financial, cultural, and other ways.

All this is very obvious, but it is no less certain that the Council cannot and must not ignore this anachronistic aspect of Roman temporalism, and that it is its duty to prepare for, I will not say its suppression or immediate dismantling, but its transformation by means of organs of a less political character. For if it should fail to tackle this problem, the more positive theological results achieved in the realm of Church affairs would also find themselves invalidated or their practical consequences evaded.

Within the framework of a gradual decentralization of Church administration through a broadening of the powers, including the legal powers, of the Episcopal Conferences, there would be nothing to prevent, for instance – as indeed has been the case for some time in the People's Democracies – a bishop being charged by the Conferences with the maintenance of relations with a particular Government in everything relating to ordinary questions: while extraordinary questions could continue, as in the past, to be the province of a papal emissary or legate.

Rome, Sunday, 11 November

I haven't yet discovered why yesterday's attendance at the sixteenth General Congregation suddenly fell by 44 from that of the day before. It was known, however, that it was Ruffini's turn to preside over the assembly, and he was sure to remind his colleagues that their continued withdrawal into the tent of the Secretary of the Holy Office, as a protest against the controversial applause of 30 October, could only redound to their discredit; so I would guess that the 44 absentees must have been progressives.

In any case, Cardinal Ruffini's appeal evoked only mediocre applause. Yet the assembly ought to have been grateful to him for having extricated it from an awkward impasse – from having to find more convincing excuses if Ottaviani had failed to appear in the hall even on the first day of the debate on 'De Fontibus'.

Yesterday evening 32 Cardinals and some 300 bishops were present at the inauguration of the 410th academic year of the Gregorian University, 'Quoddam in Urbe seminarium omnium gentium' (that seminary of all nations within the city), as some Popes have described it. And today the ex-Collegio Romano seemed more than ever to be precisely that, with its 3,021 students (plus another 339 still working on theses for their degrees) coming from 78 nations, 615 dioceses, and 99 religious Orders, and members of 45 national colleges.

From what I hear, the majority of the bishops and prelates present at the ceremony were themselves former students of the Gregoriana. But I wonder if, and in what terms, one can really estimate the effect of the training in institutes of this kind. For if they are formative at all, they are formative only as regards the intellect, and even then only in a distorting sort of way, because their *raison d'être* is not to promote free scientific research, as in any free university, but to submit the student to a definite ideology under the pretext or the illusion that it is identical with the truth.

The Catholic universities in Rome, in other words, resemble an ideological barracks created for an officer-cadre which tomorrow will be responsible for opening other similar institutions in various parts of the world and which is therefore trained according to methods and programmes dictated not by the universities themselves but by the Department of Culture, i.e. the Sacred Congregation of Seminaries. The rising sap of all the new cultural movements, religious as well as secular, never touches them, and should it happen to do so it would be by accident, never officially. The methods used are all tested, decanted, sterilized, and directed above all towards immunization from outside contacts.

Naturally, later on, some of the students have their eyes opened; but such rebels are usually expunged from the episcopate, which is destined to honour only the most docile and those most faithful to the 'spirit of Romanness' (*romanità*). Fortunately, however, life itself is stronger than institutions and systems, and it may sometimes come about that the ex-students of yesterday when they return to Rome, as now for the Council, may indeed be glad to revisit the scenes of their youthful studies, but their main feeling is a longing to rescue them from their inhuman systemization and make them true centres of free research and knowledge. Perhaps, who knows, the silent revolution has already entered unobserved into the great Catholic intellectual citadel.

Rome, Monday, 12 November

The Secretary-General, Monsignor Felici, made an unexpected announcement at the 17th General Congregation today which caused a good deal of surprise among the Fathers: he said the second session of the Council would begin on 12 March 1963 and end on 29 June, the Feast of St Peter and St Paul.

As a matter of fact this is a good thing, for many of the Fathers had feared that the second session might be in the winter, at the end of January or in February 1963. Indeed several episcopates had already said that in that case their presence was not to be counted on. Now, however, the postponement worries a good many of them, not because of the dates fixed but because of the uncertainty about the Council's probable duration, seeing that a month after the opening the discussion of even the first draft is not yet over.

It was even worse at Vatican I, however. Between 8 December 1869 and 18 March 1870, i.e. in over three months (new Rules of Procedure were published on 22 February providing for a ten days' suspension, later prolonged to 25 days), and in two sessions, only 31 General Congregations were held at which only 150 Fathers spoke, with the result that all the drafts discussed were sent back to their respective Commissions. But the time-rhythm was different in those days, and above all there was only one question in everyone's mind, whether as an end to be achieved or averted: the definition of papal infallibility. After seven months it was solved, with, almost incidentally, the launching of another constitution (*De Fide*).

Now, however, no one can say what the aims of the Council are, or rather, the Pope himself defined them but then refrained from arranging in any particular order the 69 drafts drawn up by the Preparatory Commissions. So the only certain prospect, at any rate for the time being, is that this first session will end with little or nothing done.

Some of the ecclesiastics who daily frequent Council circles, bishops' lodgings, and meetings of episcopal conferences think they have detected among the Fathers a certain decline of conciliar zeal, as shown by, for instance, the enthusiasm with which they welcome every opportunity to evade the Council – receptions at Embassies, tourist excursions under the pretext of pilgrimages, lectures or visits to pontifical universities, religious institutions, or exhibitions timed to coincide with the Council.

It is quite true that the Fathers are inundated by invitations of this kind. In the way of receptions, for instance, in addition to those given to the whole episcopal corps by the Quirinal, the Municipality of Rome, and the diplomatic corps accredited to the Holy See, almost daily one of the embassies gives a party for its own bishops. (The Prime Minister gave one for the Italians at Villa Madama on 25 October, the French Ambassador de la Tournelle one for the French, and so on. Surprisingly, even the Iron Curtain countries' embassies seem to intend doing the same, beginning with a Yugoslav party on the 15th followed by the Poles and the Hungarians.) But it is obviously an exaggeration to argue from this that the bishops do nothing but circulate from one embassy to another: indeed usually by no means all of them accept the invitations.

It is more difficult to deny the charge about the pilgrimages (for instance, 70 Brazilian bishops are to go to Assisi on the 15th), but who can say where a pilgrimage ends and tourism begins? Is it fair, moreover, to deny bishops what may be their only opportunity to visit places of historical interest not far from Rome, such as Subiaco, Monte Cassino, Assisi, Siena or Florence? Certainly it would be more questionable for them to go as far as the Gargano to visit that controversial priest with the stigmata, Padre Pio, or to Sicily to contemplate the rather tawdry and no longer weeping picture of the Madonna of Syracuse. But up till now the Fathers do not seem to have wished to indulge in such side-lines.

As far as my own experience goes and that of several of my friends, you have only to enter any of the places where the Fathers are staying to get the definite feeling that at least the great majority of them are taking an eager part in the Council. Centres such as S. Luigi dei Francesi or the Domus Mariae or the headquarters of the White Fathers, for example, are hives of activity where the telephone switchboards are kept almost as busy as those of the Press Office and where in the foyers there is a constant coming and going of prelates, secretaries, expert advisers, visitors and journalists.

The same activity goes on even where only a single Father resides, if he is a person of some consequence. This is notoriously the case in Cardinal Canali's former apartment in the Vatican, placed for the duration of the Council at the disposal of Cardinal Montini by John XXIII (since Montini cannot stay at his usual quarters in the Collegio Lombardo, as it is being rebuilt) and also in Maximos IV Saigh's apartment at the Convent of the Sorores Divini Salvatoris, next door to my own flat. Cardinal Ottaviani's apartment in the palazzo of the Holy Office is another of these nerve centres, and so is that of Cardinal Bea at the Brazilian College in Via Aurelia.

A list of the meetings competing each day for their attendance gives some idea of the number of things the Fathers are called on to do quite apart from the General Congregations, ranging as they do from the Presiding Council and the various Commissions of the Council to meetings of the episcopal conferences at all levels. Then there are the meetings to study some particular subject, addressed only occasionally by one of the Fathers themselves (as for instance when Lercaro gave a lecture on the Liturgy for the Brazilian Fathers) and more usually by some expert; and the inter-episcopal conferences between episcopates of different countries to study common problems.

A good many of these meetings have only a marginal connection with the Council itself and its drafts, but they are none the less important. Indeed in a certain sense, at any rate up till now, the Council has done more in promoting contacts between the Fathers themselves than in its own discussions. For the living Church helps towards a better understanding of the Church in the abstract.

It is doubtless true that the Fathers have little time to study for themselves the problems connected with the different drafts; but group study, a complete novelty for most episcopates, is very possibly more important and fruitful. Many libraries belonging to the ecclesiastical universities or colleges are frequented daily by the Fathers; the work most often consulted by them at the Gregoriana is said to be the *Dictionnaire Théologique Catholique* – not a very recondite work, certainly, but at least a sign of zeal.

Moreover it has to be remembered that the Fathers are not bishops on holiday but are still kept busy, if only by letter or telephone, in the running of their own dioceses. The more fortunate among them who have one or two assistants can hand over some of the work to them; the others receive visits from their Vicars General and daily dictate quantities of letters to their secretaries. But despite all this some of them find the time to report to their dioceses on the work of the Council. Montini makes an excellent weekly report in a 'Letter from the Council' to the Milan paper *Italia,* while others such as Florit of Florence or Gilla-Gremigni of Novara do so at less regular intervals. Some of the bishops, such as for instance Monsignor Borromeo of Pesaro, are keeping a diary of the Council – not a very fruitful enterprise judging by such precedents from the last century as the diaries of Monsignor Tizzani, Arrigoni, and others, all unpublished (Tizzani's is in the Vatican secret archives, Arrigoni's in the archives of the diocese of Lucca).

Certainly this Council is not likely to produce anything like the Council of Constance early in the fifteenth century, when Brother Giovanni Bertoldi da Serravalle, of San Marino, Provincial of the Franciscan minors, Bishop of Fermo, and Secretary of the Council – in fact the equivalent of Monsignor Felici today – translated in the intervals of its labours all three parts of Dante's *Divina Commedia* into Low Latin and added a commentary (that was in classical Latin, however); it must have been quite good, too, for centuries later Leo XIII thought it worth reprinting. True, the somewhat pedestrian method he adopted of translating the original word by word ('ista silva silvestris et aspera et fortis quae in meditatione renovat pavorem' for 'questa selva selvaggia ed aspra e forte che nel pensier rinnova la paura' – *Inferno,* I, 1-2) must have made his work a good deal easier.

It seems the Bishop of Fermo undertook the translation of the

Divina Commedia as the result of requests from several foreign Fathers, especially the Englishmen Nicholas of Bubwyk and Robert d'Alan. Now Monsignor Felici, that massive prelate, placid but strong, courteous but self-assured, simple in manner but capable of inspiring respect for his authority, cordial but on occasion brusque, ceremonious but careful in his choice of words, is also a poet. Up to 8 June 1960 he was a peaceful official in the Congregation of Rites, auditor of the Sacred Rota, and consultant to a couple of departments. Today many consider him the *éminence grise* of the Council, or rather of the Curia at the Council; and in this they may not be far wrong in view of his attitudes on various points as shown in the *Osservatore Romano,* such as the slashing review of Lombardi's book, the praise accorded to a wellnigh anti-ecumenical pastoral by a Spanish bishop, and so on. In addition to all this he is also a poet, and a Latin poet into the bargain, who speaks the language of Cicero as he does the dialect of Segni, the hilltop village of Latium, not far from Rome, where he was born, has written an essay on the ablative absolute, and, according to malicious gossip, never moves without the *Regia Parnassi*[1] – they even say he dislikes going by car because he can make his hexameters and couplets scan better when walking. But in these days of simultaneous translation (even if frowned on across the Tiber) and robots that can chew up and disgorge versions of the most sacred works in the whole of ancient literature, the Bible included, no one has thought of asking Monsignor Felici to translate anything to while away the Fathers' leisure – which is why, still according to the gossips, he is said to have decided to write a poem with the far from recondite title of *Vaticaneides secunda,* once it is all over.

Rome, Tuesday, 13 November

Yesterday afternoon's meeting of the Presiding Council suggested that the debate on 'De Sacra Liturgia' was nearing its close; and today, when after the twenty-second Father – Johann Pholschneider, Bishop of Aix-la-Chapelle – had finished speaking Cardinal Alfrink, the day's chairman, proposed to consider as closed the debate on the last four chapters of the draft, the

[1] A Latin rhyming dictionary.

assembly with a sigh of relief agreed. It had gone on for fifteen General Congregations and over three hundred Fathers had spoken, several of them more than once. Tomorrow the assembly will probably be asked to approve the Liturgical draft in general terms, and the relevant Commission can then begin on revision of the text on the basis of the criticisms and proposals made. The voting might produce some surprises.

There was another surprise in store at St Peter's this morning when the Secretary of State, Cardinal Cicognani, announced the Pope's decision that, 'in response to the wish expressed by numerous Fathers, he had decided to insert the name of St Joseph in the Canon of the Mass immediately after that of the Madonna, so that this may remain as a remembrance of the Council in honour of its patron'. This decision of the Pope's, the Cardinal added, would come into force on 8 December after the Sacred Congregation of Rites had prepared the necessary documents. Naturally, it was approved, but it was all the same disconcerting. Many Fathers turned to take a quick glance at the observer delegates, but they, after a momentary start of surprise and an exchange of looks, reverted to their usual composed and enigmatic demeanour.

I can guess what the Catholic press will say tomorrow, namely that ever since 1815 the Holy See has been receiving similar requests from thousands of the faithful; that 150,000 Italian priests and laymen asked the same thing in 1866; and that in 1870, just before the suspension of Vatican I, 38 out of 42 Cardinals and 218 out of 500 bishops returned to the charge, thereby persuading Pius IX on 8 December to proclaim St Joseph Patron of the Universal Church. All this can be read in the memorandum produced in 1961 by the Centres of St Joseph in Montreal, Valladolid, and Rome, which appeared in five languages (I have the 76-page Italian edition, entitled 'For the insertion of the name of St Joseph in the prayers of the Mass', i.e. in the 'Confiteor', the 'Suscipe, Sancta Trinitas', the 'Communicantes', and the 'Libera nos': as we have seen, Pope John has confined himself to granting it only in the third instance, which is in fact the most important).

This memorandum, which expounds the historical, liturgical, and theological reasons for the request, did not ignore the numerous objections raised against it especially on the ground of its probable effect among Protestants and Orthodox. But the incredible answer given was that the addition of St Joseph's name 'would not, in the eyes of the separated brethren, constitute any more unusual event than that of the proclamation of his patronage or than other dogmatic definitions issued in the last century in favour of the Virgin' (as if to say that now everything is permissible and it only remains to carry on); that similar considerations 'proved no bar to the supreme pontiff's action in previous cases' etc., etc.

Small wonder, then, if even *Civiltà Cattolica* wrote in its review of the memorandum that 'such initiatives meet with an understandable obstacle in the present trend towards simplification rather than expansion, especially of the liturgy, and in the widespread belief that sufficient honour has already been rendered to St Joseph. Not to mention the fact that such initiatives appear hard to understand by the separated brethren for whom it is, in general, wise to try not to multiply needless obstacles.'

Be that as it may, the devotees of St Joseph themselves were until this morning far from cherishing illusions about the success of their requests. Even the Mariologists don't do so about theirs, and their organization is known to be much more powerful, especially since the establishment in Rome in 1946 of the International Marian Academy, later made a Pontifical Academy by John XXIII in 1959. (In parenthesis, the Marian Academy has a dual link with the Roman integralists; Monsignor Piolanti and Monsignor Romeo are in fact the only members of the secular clergy to belong to it, while its President, Balic, a Franciscan minor, is a foundation member of the Council of the Roman Pontifical Theological Academy).

But the Pope himself surpassed all their expectations by forestalling the Council and taking the decision out of its hands, thus compelling it to give an affirmative answer against its will. Undoubtedly he did so in obedience to one of those inspirations in which he believes with such simple faith; but this time the inspiration was of too personal and devotional a character to warrant such zealous fulfilment.

The following is a list of the main questions dealt with in the discussion of 'De Sacra Liturgia'.

(i) *Use of the Vernacular*. The following statements in this connection by Cardinal Gracias and the Patriarch Maximos IV Saigh have been made known:

> The symbols, actions, and prayers that constitute the liturgy should be adapted in such a way as to make them common to every nation. In the earliest expression of Christianity the liturgy adopted different forms in Syria, Greece, and Rome; why should not the new expansion of the Church now produce a Chinese, Indian, or African liturgy? Church unity is not bound to mean uniformity. (Gracias).
>
> It was in a language understood by His contemporaries that Christ offered the first eucharistic sacrifice. The apostles and their disciples did the same. They could not have conceived it possible that in a Christian congregation the celebrant, in reading the passages of Scripture, singing the psalms, preaching, or breaking the bread, should make use of a different language from that of the congregation. St. Paul even said explicitly: 'For if I pray in an unknown tongue, my spirit prayeth, but my understanding is unfruitful . . . How shall he that occupieth the room of the unlearned say Amen at the giving of thanks, seeing he understandeth not what thou sayest?' (1 *Corinthians*, 14, 16). All the reasons invoked in favour of the untouchability of Latin, a liturgical language but a dead one, should yield before this clear and definite argument of the Apostles. (Maximos IV Saigh)

(ii) *The adaptation of the rites*, extended to include music and sacred art, to the different forms of culture and their insertion into the framework of local customs.

(iii) *Communion in two kinds* (already customary in Eastern rites). While this is normally impracticable, it would be desirable on certain special occasions such as the ordination of priests, the taking of religious vows, marriages, Masses following the baptism of adults, etc.

(iv) *Concelebration*, or simultaneous celebration by several priests. This should also be reserved for particular occasions such as congresses of priests, pilgrimages, meetings of priests with their bishop, conventual Masses etc.

(v) *Fixed calendar*, with Easter fixed at the beginning of April.

(vi) *Question of the competent authority* to regulate the local application of all these changes: the Holy See or the episcopate?

As to the number of speeches during the debates, my calculations give a total of 328 speakers. As a matter of fact, however, there were a good many fewer speeches, since 58 Fathers spoke twice, 15 three times, two four times, and one, Cardinal Ruffini, six times.

Excluding the ten Superiors General and a few other Fathers whose place of origin is uncertain, there were 177 interventions from Europe (Italy 60, Spain 33, France 31, Germany 20, Poland 9, etc.); 66 from America (USA 19, Brazil 14, Argentine 10, Chile 6, etc.); 50 from Asia (India 10, China 7); 17 from Africa (incl. Rhodesia 4); and 3 from Australia.

According to the Press Office Bulletin of 17 November there were 625 written interventions.

Rome, Wednesday, 14 November

I didn't mention on 8 November the press conference given that day by Cardinal Bea, because I didn't think there was anything exceptional about it. But the observer delegates thought otherwise. According to them, by answering in the affirmative the question whether he thought the observers were satisfied with what they had so far seen and heard at the Council, the Cardinal had committed 'the imprudence of interpreting the observers' views', thus permitting the press to give the impression of 'indiscriminate agreement' on their part.

It is a fact that one delegation of observers called on the President of the Secretariat for Christian Union to register their disapproval. Cardinal Bea at once expressed his deep regret for his failure to foresee what had happened; and he took two decisions which completely satisfied the protestors, so my Heidelberg friend Müller tells me. He cancelled the press conference announced for today, which Father Gustav Weigl, S.J., a member of the Secretariat, was to have given on 'The enthusiastic attitude of the non-Catholic observers at the Council'; and instead he authorized Professor Oscar Cullmann to hold a press conference giving an observer's point of view and comments on the Council's work.

Dr Müller has told me about another gesture of Bea's which has been appreciated. When the Council first opened the Vatican Radio interviewed Max Lackmann, an ex-pastor of the German Evangelical Church who is now President of the 'League for the Reunification of Catholics and Protestants'. Introducing himself as an Evangelical pastor, although his present position has little to do with his former one, he let it be supposed that he represented the views not only of his League (which is in any case apparently moribund) but also of other important trends among his countrymen. Thus both Catholic and Evangelical listeners unfamiliar with his personal position attached a much wider significance to what he said than it in fact warranted. Consequently there were protests from responsible German Evangelical circles. When the Cardinal came to hear about it he got into touch personally with those in charge of the Vatican radio (two Jesuits, Stefanizzi and Ramírez), who mentioned that a second Lackmann interview had already been recorded. Bea both forbade its transmission and also asked the two Jesuits in future to let his Secretariat know beforehand the names of persons selected to explain on the Vatican Radio the standpoint of the various Christian confessions.

Quite apart from these episodes, the observers certainly seem to be in a highly sensitive state. The chief reason for this is, of course, the delicate position they are in. They are making great efforts to be objective, as the bulletin of the Press and Information Service of the Federal Council of Evangelical Churches in Italy shows. In its second issue (5 November), for instance, it commends in the Message of the Fathers its 'rich Biblical content', a 'Mariological conception closer to the Gospel', and the 'eschatological ecclesiological perspective'; and *à propos* of the Liturgical draft it rightly notes that 'it reflects a spirit of renewal without adopting theological standpoints of a counter-reformationist nature'. In its third issue (11 Nov.), after stressing the draft's pastoral tone, its ecumenical outlook, and its biblicism, it states *à propos* of the basic theological standpoints that 'a) the divine and sacrificial character of the Mass is confirmed; b) the relationship between the act of salvation accomplished by Christ upon the Cross and the sacramental act of the priest remains the same as in Catholic orthodoxy, whereby the priest becomes virtually an "alter Christus"; and c) the relationship between the clergy and the laity does not appear to be altered, for the simple reason that there is no change in the doctrine of the relationship between the Holy Spirit and the Church as the people of God'. Therefore, 'on the basis of these provisional observations, it can be said that while we must rejoice at the practical innovations proposed, which are chiefly evangelical in trend, we cannot but disagree profoundly about the basic questions, namely the doctrinal premisses and the theological framework of the draft.'

An eminently pertinent if severe conclusion, expressed in tones of an exemplary dignity and freedom from controversial spirit.

Rome, Thursday, 15 November

'The Council has split in two,' Monsignor Martinez announced to me this morning in that dramatic way of his; then, calming down a bit, he added, 'or perhaps it has found itself anew. Probably the real Council is only just beginning.'

His account was, as usual, lucid, to the point and wellnigh exhaustive, within the limits, naturally, of what can filter through the net of conciliar secrecy. The first signs of the approaching storm, he said, began to appear late in the afternoon of Tuesday, when Ottaviani, having summoned together at the Holy Office the members of the Commission on Faith and Morals, strongly attacked the alternative draft of the five Central and Western European episcopal conferences. The aim of this intrusion, according to him, was to discredit the drafts worked out by the former Theological Commission, confuse the other episcopates, and generate a heated atmosphere for the debate on 'De Fontibus'. In addition, he said, the proposers of the new draft were trying to overthrow the whole order of the Council's work by disregarding the Pope's approval of the drafts communicated to the episcopate.

Ottaviani's intention was obvious. He knew that the five episcopates had not sent copies of the alternative draft to the Council Secretariat and the Secretariat for Extraordinary Questions, and they therefore presumably intended to make its contents known next day in solemn and official style in the Hall itself by means of a mouthpiece of their own, before he himself could present the Commission's draft of 'De Fontibus'. He therefore thought the best way to prevent them was to get in his own attack first. His adversaries would thus both lose the element of surprise and realize what opposition awaited them.

Ottaviani's tactics proved effective. Warned by the members of the Commission, the Cardinals heading the Central and Western European episcopal conferences hurriedly met together. Forty-eight hours earlier, they had decided on exactly the method that Ottaviani had suspected, and had chosen Cardinal Frings to present the counter-draft so as not to compromise the Dean of the Sacred College, Tisserant (whose turn, incidentally, it was to preside over the assembly) or to make Liénart return to the attack, and also to avoid another encounter between Alfrink and Ottaviani after that of 30 October (they could not well entrust the job to someone outside the Presiding Council – for example Koenig, a strong supporter of Karl Rahner, the author of the counter-draft – because it would have been difficult for him to secure leave to speak before Ottaviani's presentation of the official draft). They therefore suspended their plan. The theses advanced in 'De Fontibus' were in any case so plainly unacceptable that its opponents were sure to get the best of it in a full-scale concerted attack such as they had arranged for in case the presentation of the counter-draft proved impossible.

Yesterday, therefore, everything appeared to go ahead quite smoothly. Before moving on to the presentation of the new draft, the Order of the Day was read concerning the Liturgical draft, on which the Fathers were to vote at 11 o'clock (the results were even more overwhelming than had been expected: 2,162 votes in favour, 46 against, 7 blank). Then Monsignor Felici announced the distribution of the draft 'De Ecclesia', which had not been included among the seven in the volume of drafts already distributed to the Fathers. When finally Tisserant called on Ottaviani to speak, the silence as the Cardinal blindly groped his way to the platform conveyed the assembly's barely concealed feeling of expectancy and anxiety. Many seemed to be watching him as if he were an accused man called to the bar. But Ottaviani, once over his initial emotion, spoke briefly and almost humbly, confining himself to indicating the importance, including the pastoral aspect, of his draft.

The report itself was read by the ever youthful and elegant Monsignor Garofalo instead of by the secretary, Father Tromp. Ottaviani had clearly chosen to put on a biblical scholar rather than a theologian in order to give greater stress to the importance of the draft's statements concerning Holy Writ. Garofalo, however, was without his customary smile; he had seldom had to undertake so thankless a task in defence of a cause he knew to be already lost.

Perhaps because of this, the report proved more controversial in character than its contents called for. Before going on to illustrate its five chapters – (1) the two sources of revelation; 2) the inspiration, infallibility, and literary composition of Holy Writ; 3) the Old Testament; 4) the New Testament; 5) Holy Writ in the Church) – the report stated that 'the primary task of the Council is to defend and promote the Catholic doctrine in its most exact formulation. Not . . . to renovate the doctrine, but to increase study and knowledge of it'. The final peroration was also significant, asserting that 'members and advisers from various countries and numerous universities have contributed to the draft proposed' and that they 'have borne in mind that a dogmatic constitution issued by the Council is not an encyclical or a homily or a pastoral letter but a text of immutable doctrine, even if its presentation is susceptible of improvement'.

At the end Garofalo sketched a wan smile, bowed and left the platform. The curtain rose on the debate.

Many did not catch the name of the first speaker announced by the Chairman. They only guessed from the rustle at the Presiding Council's table that it must be one of the 'Council of Ten'. Soon after a thin, slightly nasal and ironical but decided voice was heard to say: 'Hoc schema mihi non placet'. Everyone recognized it: it was the voice of 13 October, of Achille Liénart, and a murmur ran round the hall.

The speeches for the prosecution had begun. Out of eleven Cardinals who came to the microphone, eight – in addition to Liénart, they were Frings, Léger, Koenig, Alfrink, Suenens, Ritter, and Bea – expressed a drastically negative opinion. But it was not only a case of famous names risen to the purple, for these were the primates of whole preponderantly Catholic countries or countries with a large Catholic population, such as France, Austria, Belgium, Germany, Holland, and Canada, who were speaking also in the names of their respective episcopates. The only advocates for the defence were the Spaniard Quiroga y Palacios and the Italian pair Siri and Ruffini, who however could speak only for themselves.

Liénart had said that the draft was inadequate, even more retrograde than the definitions given at the Council of Trent, cold, scholastic, and arid; Frings added that it was a professional production bearing the traces of the theological schools' disputes and rivalries, and erring in its partiality for some of them; Léger, that it was presumptuous in its attempt to cut short scholarly researches which were still in progress. But the greatest impression of all was made by the calm and detached attack of Cardinal Bea: according to him, the draft (which he, together with Alfrink and others, had strongly contested in the Central Commission) was in open contrast with the pastoral and ecumenical objectives desired by the Pope, both as a whole and in its various parts.

Naturally, no word of all this emerged in the Press Office's communiqué: all the more significant, therefore, was its admission that the Fathers, confronted with the new draft, had divided into two camps about it and that 'all the Fathers who spoke' had maintained that 'the draft as a whole needed to be improved'.

Rome, Friday, 16 November

The most frequent rumours in Council circles yesterday suggested that if the attack on 'De Fontibus' continued with the same violence today as on Wednesday, its fate would be decided by tomorrow.

Today, however, the struggle died down somewhat. The ten Cardinals who spoke were pretty evenly divided. Only two of them, Tisserant and Lefébure, definitely opposed the draft; the others, except for the ingenuous Santos Rufino and Cerejeira, were almost unreservedly in favour and let it be understood that though they were still more pessimistic than optimistic they thought it not impossible that the situation might recover. The most lively part of the debate moved over instead to the bishops, ten of whom spoke, as well as Dom Christopher Butler, Superior General of the Benedictines in England. Bengsch of Berlin and Guerry of Cambrai drove the attack home, equalled if not surpassed in strength by Gargitter of Bressanone and Florit of Florence (who is also a former professor of biblical exegesis at the Lateran University, author of a volume published in 1935 on *Il metodo della storia delle forme e la sua applicazione al racconto della Passione* ('The method of history of forms (*Formengeschichte*) and its application to the story of the Passion').

The proportion of those against the draft seems, in fact, to have gone down from over 80 to more like 65 per cent, while those in favour, with some reservations, have risen from 15-20 to 30-35 per cent. But the atmosphere is nevertheless still tense, as can be gathered from the Press Office's communiqué, which for the first time is unusually circumstantial though it still avoids mentioning names. It says:

> The Fathers who proposed an alternative draft gave as a reason that the present draft is too professional and academic in character, lacks pastoral inspiration, is over-rigid in some of its statements, contains certain points which have not yet been sufficiently established by theological studies, runs the risk of making the truth incomprehensible to the separated brethren, neglects the problem of salvation before the redemption and for the non-baptized, and does little to encourage scientific, theological, and exegetic study.
>
> The Fathers who maintained the usefulness of examining the official draft on the sources of revelation, though admitting the need to modify it in some places, gave the following reasons for their view: the basis of pastoral action lies in the clear exposition of doctrine and it can cause no offence to the separated brethren to affirm the truth, for which they too search; the Council's task is to illustrate and guard the Catholic doctrine in all its integrity; the draft as presented was prepared by bishops and priests eminent for their doctrinal learning and was further approved by the Central Commission, consisting mainly of Cardinals; the seminaries expect from the Council a precise directive on doctrinal and exegetic problems which are today discussed in books and newspapers without sufficient clarity of ideas or depth of analysis.

Rome, Saturday, 17 November

In yesterday's General Congregation, the twenty-first, about an hour was given up to voting on the first four paragraphs of the amended Preface of 'De Sacra Liturgia', which was read out by Monsignor Felici and then illustrated by Cardinal Lercaro and Monsignor Joseph Martin, Bishop of Nicollet, in Canada. The individual paragraphs were approved practically unanimously and so the voting was soon done.

The Fathers' minds were elsewhere, with the duel shortly to be reopened on 'De Fontibus' following its damaging experiences earlier. There were two dramatic moments in the morning when

Ottaviani and Parente spoke. The former had waited in vain for some more pertinent reactions from Cardinals Concha (of Bogotá) and Bacci to Doepfner's attack. The Archbishop of Munich had accused the draft of being the unaided product of a single Roman school, the Lateran University. This was a charge on which many speakers from Frings onwards had touched but which none had dared to express so frankly. But Cardinal Doepfner went further: bringing in the members of the amendments sub-committee as well, he accused those responsible in the Theological Commission of having taken no account of the reservations advanced by other members of the pre-Council Commissions and in particular of the Central Commission.

Ottaviani was bound to react to this, and he rushed in impetuously to the charge, recalling the status and composition of the Theological Commission which under his chairmanship had been responsible for the draft. Its status was familiar to everyone, for it was the most important of the Council's Preparatory Commissions and had, unlike the others, started meeting a fortnight before the work of the Commissions officially began (on 26 October instead of 14 November 1960), being also the first to present its drafts to the Central Committee. It had also produced a record amount of material – 24 booklets, as against 17 from the runner-up, the Commission on the Discipline of the Clergy and People.

Everyone also knew how it had to all appearances recruited its 32 members and 36 advisers with complete impartiality from every theological school, country, and religious Order. It is true that among the theological schools run by the secular clergy the Lateran University headed the list with four members on the Commission, as against three from Louvain, two from the Catholic Institute in Lyons, etc., but this was not an overwhelming or decisive preponderance. Among the Universities belonging to the religious Orders, the Antoniano, belonging to the Franciscan minors, rather unexpectedly took first place with five members against the Gregoriana's (Jesuits') four and the Angelicum's (Dominicans') three.

However, many of those in the hall were by now familiar with the background story of certain of the choices, such as the veto against Père Daniélou's appointment, the banishment of Karl Rahner to the Sacraments Commission, the delay in the acceptance of the Rector of the Biblicum, Father Vogt, as one of the consultants (postponed till 26 February 1961), and so on. Above all, everyone knew that what counts in forming a Commission is the criterion of choice, including the relation between the various tasks allotted to the theologians rather than the universities from which its members are selected. On a Preparatory Commission it is the members who play the decisive part: the consultants' role is subordinate, confined to research and advisory opinions. Now, in the Theological Commission the reactionary members (as opposed to consultants) easily outnumbered the progressives. For instance, among its eleven theologian members coming from the secular clergy, three belonged to the Lateran University, headed by its Rector, Piolanti. Moreover Monsignori Pavan and Agostino Ferrari Toniolo are experts in economy and sociology, clearly outside their own fields in dealing with questions of biblical theology.

Nationality also played a part. Of the eleven theologian members belonging to the secular clergy five were Italians as against one Frenchman and one German, whereas among the consultants the proportions were reversed – one Italian to three Germans and four French. It was the same with the 36 theologian members of the Commission belonging to the religious Orders: four were Dominicans (and all notoriously conservative, from the Master of the Sacred Palaces, Luigi Ciappi, onwards) and two Jesuits, whereas among the consultants there were six Jesuits, four Franciscans, and three Dominicans.

Even more significant was the distribution according to specialist competence: two-thirds of the theologians (whether of the secular or regular clergy) were experts in dogmatic, fundamental, and ascetic theology; the biblical scholars represented barely a tenth, and the moralists and jurists could be counted on the fingers of one hand.

In short, given this arbitrary distribution of office as between members and consultants, allotting the more reactionary to the former category and the less so, even if they were international celebrities, to the latter, and given also the lack of proportion between the representatives of the different theological disciplines, the first of the Preparatory Commissions could hardly avoid producing the unfortunate results now encountering severe criticism from the Council.

But with regard to Doepfner's second and more serious criticism, even admitting the connivance of the amendments subcommittee, is it thinkable that the Central Commission would have let such a draft pass their control without alteration? As a matter of fact that is just what Doepfner denies (as, too, do Bea, Frings, Alfrink, and others). But it could have happened relatively easily seeing that the Central Committee had to deal with the 69 drafts in about 40 days, or nearly two drafts a day. In the case of 'De Fontibus', it was examined and conditionally approved in the single day of 10 November 1961.

Ottaviani answered Doepfner as best he could. But his reply was at once neutralized by Frings. He, like Ottaviani, is half-blind, but whereas the Secretary of the Holy Office gropes and stumbles when he speaks, his dilated and ill-focused eyes protruding like those of a blind man trying to cross a street, his German colleague concentrates in speaking on his own line of thought, adopting an assured and stiff, almost military attitude, calmly and solemnly enunciating his Latin as he stresses the main arguments. Frings coldly and relentlessly contested Ottaviani's statements point by point as if conducting a prosecution, and he carried the assembly with him.

He was the last Cardinal to speak, and it seemed as if a tombstone had already been set up over the draft. But Monsignor Schmit, Bishop of Metz, then took up the attack on behalf of the bishops. He spoke as a theologian, reminding the assembly that the only source of revelation is the person of Christ Himself. But the Fathers, though impressed, were all agog to hear his successor, Monsignor Parente, assessor at the Holy Office. For a moment he seemed to be going to disappoint them when, coming pale and tense to the microphone, he said he had not asked to speak as head of the Supreme Congregation but merely as the titular Archbishop of Ptolemy in Thebes: but he went on to add with tragic emphasis that he had listened in the Council Hall with genuine dismay to statements and opinions from more than one venerable prelate and preceptor of the faith in countries with a long-standing Catholic tradition, which could only be described as 'near heresy'. Some years ago in a speech at the Course for Christian Studies at Assisi he had maintained that 'the preaching of Christ is ordained by

Holy Scripture and *even more* by Tradition, whose organs are the apostles, to whom Jesus entrusts the mandate to preach to all with His own authority . . . Thus God has linked the destiny of man in his search for salvation to that divine Master, who passes on the truth to the apostles – who are succeeded in turn by the Pope and the bishops . . .' This, in substance, was his thesis: a strong defence of tradition and of its essential connection with ecclesiastical and especially pontifical teaching.

After two colourless speeches, the counter-attack resumed with Monsignor Charue, Bishop of Namur, who electrified the atmosphere anew by affirming that no one outside the Presiding Council had the right to impugn the Fathers' freedom of speech by launching absurd attacks on their orthodoxy. After paying homage to the work of contemporary biblical scholars he went on to affirm that the best way of overcoming modernism was not to condemn it but to encourage study and research, as his own country Belgium had always tried to do. Then, raising his voice, he warned the assembly against 'the imprudence of taking too rigid decisions which might one day become no less embarrassing for the Church than the problem of Galileo'.

Monsignor Charue had spoken in the name of the Belgian episcopate. Soon after it was Monsignor Zoa's turn to do so on behalf of the African bishops, illustrating the fascination which the Bible had for the peoples of his continent who, however, are also open to the influence of technical and scientific progress which tomorrow will no longer permit the Africans to view with the same simplicity the contents of the sacred books. After him came Monsignor Hakim, Bishop of Akka of the Melchites, in Israel, who, speaking for the Orthodox Church, proclaimed that 'the doctrinal drafts at present being studied by the Council are foreign to the venerable and ancient tradition of my Church alike in form, structure, aim, and conception . . . In Eastern theology (he went on) in which the liturgy is the effective channel of transmission for the faith, since initiation is carried out within the sacramental mystery and not by means of an abstract conception without symbolical links, the mystery of Christ is put forward directly as an event (*economia*) which develops in the course of history, prepared for in the Old Testament, accomplished in Christ, and realized in the era of the Church. Theoretical explanations, however legitimate and necessary they may be, are never detached in that theology from the structural pattern and the message of the Fathers.'

Rome, Sunday, 18 November

Vatican Radio has just given a report on the debate on 'De Fontibus'. The view put forward was that in the Council hall it was not a question of two conflicting and antithetical doctrinal standpoints but rather of different trends striving to bring out different aspects of the same truth. The Press Office bulletins also continue to insist that the dispute does not concern the theological content but merely the formulation adopted by those who drew up the draft.

As a matter of fact the dispute is certainly quite a substantial one, or at any rate more so than the authorities would have it thought or indeed than the protagonists themselves believe. Moreover, discussion of the draft in general terms favours the progressives' reticence at this moment. They can peacefully content themselves with demolishing it for merely extrinsic reasons: because it has been formulated according to the criteria of a school that has managed arbitrarily to impose itself on others, when it is well known that the Council should not concern itself with *theological doctrines* but should concentrate on the definition of *revealed doctrine*; because it is contrary to the pastoral and unionistic aims laid down by the Pope for the Council, both because of its academic formulation and its indifference to the position of the separated brethren and especially the Protestants; because it is too restrictive with regard to biblical studies; and so on. But it will be difficult for their criticisms to remain so general when they come to deal with the individual chapters. Hence their urgent need to get the draft buried before then.

On the other hand it is significant to observe what efforts the conservatives are making to drag their adversaries into more exposed positions. They are constantly urging that the debate should leave the equivocal plane of general statements and distinguish between substance and form: if agreement could be reached on the substance it would not be so difficult to modify the form whether in the pastoral or the unionistic direction.

Now, if the progressives turn a deaf ear to these exhortations, it means that they have their own good reasons for it: reasons which, to be precise, differ not one wit from a moderate biblical liberalism and a temperate theological liberalism, in other words the ingredients of their neo-modernism.

Theologically speaking, and possibly stimulated (and so at least partially persuaded) by the Protestants, they are by no means opposed to tradition, but they certainly do not favour it to the same extent as the integralists and tend rather to see its sole source as concentrated in the person of Christ. For them, revelation already existed in Jesus of Nazareth and at once materialized first in oral and later in written form. There are therefore not two distinct sources of revelation, but two forms and two manifestations. Are they then equivalent? No, for the scriptural canon is itself established by tradition. But tradition, in turn, cannot be creative (except in an indirect sense, in its explanation of passages in the sacred books that are allusive or unclear): therefore every truth must be explicitly or implicitly contained in the Holy Scriptures and be accepted as such. This statement enrages the integralists. For it places dangerous limitations on teaching, and especially on pontifical teaching. Now it is precisely on this point that the progressives are susceptible or, if you prefer it, highly sensitive.

The primacy of Peter and papal infallibility, besides being the difficult contentions they are, constitute the most insurmountable obstacles to *rapprochement* between Catholics and the Protestant and Orthodox world. The progressives argue that they will need to be adapted, but in order to do that it will first be necessary to reduce the importance of tradition and hence of ecclesiastical teaching. This is certainly not displeasing to the Orthodox, who, if they admit tradition, at least avoid involving it in an idolatrous cult of teaching, since for them the guardian of the truth is the whole Church and not just its ecclesiastical heads; but above all it arouses the sympathies of the Protestants who, nevertheless, show a growing readiness to recognize a certain significance in tradition, at least as a 'sensus Ecclesiae'.

It is at this point in the progressives' theological liberalism that the premiss of biblical liberalism enters in – a liberalism that strives, as the Holy Office's famous *monitum* deplored, to give a less compromising interpretation to many facts in the Old and New Testaments (in the New, particularly those relating to the infancy of Christ) and to the 'logia', or sayings, of Jesus (among them Matthew xvi, which constitutes the basis of the primacy of Peter).

Biblical liberalism is, in any case, only the scholarly aspect of the *rapprochement* effected by the progressives in relation to Holy Writ. But there is also a philosophical, or rather anti-philosophical, aspect, that of a return to the a-logical and existential mentality of the Bible which accords so nearly not only with the mentality of the eastern and coloured peoples but also with that of modern Western man: a return which they put into effect by means of a gradual rejection of scholasticism and its philosophical and theological writings. For while recognizing the merit of those writings in having made it easier at the time to draw up an ordered framework of revealed doctrine, they nevertheless hold them responsible for having irrevocably weakened the evangelical message.

The progressives, aware of all this, are obviously taking good care not to accept the particular battleground their adversaries favour. And if they stick to it they will probably succeed. For besides controlling the Western European episcopates and securing a growing adherence in others more preponderantly conservative, they have the support of the greater part of the Uniate Churches and almost all the Churches in Afro-Asian countries.

There remains the problem of orthodoxy or, rather, whether the progressives can still call themselves Catholics. Now if by Catholicism we understand, as we must, what distinguishes it from other historical denominations of Christianity, namely, papal primacy and infallibility, Curialism, jurisdictionalism, scholasticism, temporal political influence and so on, the answer can be in no doubt. The authentic Catholics are ranged behind Ottaviani with his blind eyes and clumsy convulsive gestures, they are enclosed within the citadel of the Holy Office and drawn up in their serried ranks on the ramparts of the Curia to defend its privileges. The progressives, on the other hand, aspire to a return, both ideologically and structurally, to the Christianity of the first centuries; from the point of view of liturgy, discipline, etc. they are virtually, if in a quite special sense, evangelicals. This is why every initiative of this kind on their part opens a breach in the Roman citadel and tends inevitably towards the de-Catholicization of the Church.

But will the progressives succeed in securing a majority in the Council, and above all will they have the Pope for their leader? This is what we shall see in the coming days and especially, if that point is reached in this session, in the days of the debate on 'De Ecclesia'. In any case, the most paradoxical aspect of the situation lies in the good faith of the majority of them – in their unawareness of whither history (or, if you prefer it, their sense of contemporary needs) is carrying them. They, like John XXIII, cherish the illusion that they are only proposing a modernization of the Church. Whereas the Church's salvation and hope of survival now lie less within itself than with the heretics and schismatics beyond its walls.

Today Antimori brought me the Spadafora pamphlet (*Rationalism, Exegesis,* etc.) and the Biblicum's answer, which I didn't know about, entitled 'Un nuovo attacco contro l'Exegesi cattolica e l'Istituto Biblico' ('A new attack on Catholic exegesis and the Biblical Institute').

The Spadafora pamphlet contains not only the reprint of his article of 15 September 1961 in *Palestra del Clero,* already referred to,[1] and another which appeared just a year later in the same review, but also a third article published in *Settimana del Clero* (edited by Monsignor Vallainc) of 22 and 29 November 1959. As these are all old articles, one doesn't quite see why the pamphlet is described as 'strictly for the Reverend Fathers of the Council alone'. But the justification emerges in the introduction, where the author explains to his chosen readers how 'since the end of 1960 the biblical sector gave clear and public signs of the malaise which had afflicted it for the past fifteen years'. Certain Catholic circles had in fact actually tried 'to introduce into the Church (or to get it to accept) rationalist criticism – Wellhausen's and Grunkel's evolutionism for the Old Testament and *Formengeschichte* for the New'.

The Holy Office had reacted, Spadafora went on, with the *monitum* of 20 June 1961, but the situation remained unchanged. Consequently certain questions arose which he wished to lay before the Fathers:

1. Would it not be opportune, or indeed necessary, to pronounce a direct condemnation or reproof against the method of *Formengeschichte*?
2. Should not precise guarantees be demanded, or more suitable measures taken, to ensure that young priests coming to Rome to study Holy Writ did not lose all they had learnt in theology but

[1] See above p. 246

received a training in accordance with the directives of the Holy See?

This last question, though it does not actually mention it, is aimed at the Biblicum, for there is no other institute in Rome specifically for the teaching of Holy Writ. Hence the immediate reply from the Fathers of Piazza della Pilotta, who maintain that Monsignor Spadafora 'distorts the truth' in attributing to them the use of the method under attack 'as put forward by rationalist authors', while they, who are the first to condemn it in these terms, 'think, in common with all other modern Catholic biblical scholars, that a literary method, although used by Protestant writers, can even be employed with advantage by Catholics in certain conditions and taking as an indisputable basis the inspiration of the sacred texts'. Then, for the first time in the course of this controversy, the reply went on to defend by name Fathers Zerwick and Lyonnet against the accusations made against them.

Antimori learns that Monsignor Spadafora has given some press conferences in the last few days to various groups of Fathers, especially Italians, and that the Jesuit Père Dufour, of the Biblicum, has done so too, particularly to the French.

According to him, certain background reasons account for the defence of their two colleagues by all the Fathers of the Biblicum. In the autumn of 1960, shortly before the opening of the new academic year, the Holy Office asked the General of the Society of Jesus to suspend Fathers Lyonnet and Zerwick from teaching at the Biblicum as they were suspected of supporting ideas contrary to Catholic doctrine. Fr Janssens replied after a time that, having personally investigated the teaching of the two priests and found it free from errors, he awaited a detailed denunciation from the Holy Office. The denunciation failed to appear (nor indeed could it, for the Holy Office never justifies its statements) and the two priests continued to lecture undisturbed. But in June 1962 the two Fathers, apparently as the result of an intervention from the Holy See, were compelled to give up their main teaching duties, though Père Lyonnet remained Dean of the biblical faculty in the Institute. This setback was partly counterbalanced by the appointment a few weeks later of the also suspect Père Dufour as adviser to the Pontifical Biblical Commission.

Antimori also told me that on 8 March 1961 Father Athanasius

Miller, secretary of the Biblical Commission (to which, among others, Monsignor Garofalo belongs), transmitted the following motion to Father Vogt, Rector of the Biblicum: 'The advisers of the Pontifical Biblical Commission, meeting in general session at the Vatican on 5 March 1961, feel it their duty to express to the Reverend Father Rector of the Pontifical Biblical Institute their deep regret for the accusations and attacks launched against the said Institute and its professors by Monsignor A.Romeo in his article 'The Encyclical "Divino afflante Spiritu" and "Opiniones Novae" '. They seize the opportunity to reaffirm publicly their unchanging attachment and solidarity *vis-à-vis* the Biblical Institute.'

Rome, Monday, 19 November

This morning at the 22nd General Congregation the positions in the assembly remained virtually unchanged. Both among the Cardinals and the bishops the uncompromising opponents of the draft (Gracias, Rugambwa, Martín speaking for the Venezuelan episcopate, De Smet, Garrone, D'Avack, etc.) were not in the majority but their interventions were by far the most significant. Gracias, for instance, was strongly polemical, denying that the Pope had (as Ottaviani claimed) approved the draft: having received it from the Central Commission he had confined himself to passing it on to the Council. In Gracias' view the draft required such numerous and extensive amendments that nothing would be left of the original. Like a tumble-down house, it would be better to pull it down and start afresh. Rugambwa associated himself with this view, asking for the draft's replacement by another, to be drawn up by a different team.

Today's Congregation was anyway dominated by the speech of Monsignor De Smet, Bishop of Bruges, who said he was not speaking for himself but on behalf of the Secretariat for Christian Union, of which he is a member. Significantly, for the first time since the beginning of the Council the Press Office communiqué emerged from its usual reserve, both mentioning this speech and giving quite a long summary of it. The whole text was also issued at once by a press agency. According to the Secretariat, the evaluation of the various drafts from the ecumenical point of view presupposes a solution of the following problem: 'What is required in the doctrine and style of a draft so that it may really serve towards achieving a better dialogue between Catholics and non-Catholics?'

'For many centuries,' said Monsignor De Smet, 'we Catholics have thought that a clear exposition of our doctrine sufficed. The non-Catholics thought the same, and so both sides expounded their respective doctrines in their own terminology; but what was said by the Catholics was imperfectly understood by the non-Catholics and vice-versa. In fact no progress was made towards reconciliation by this method of "clearly affirming the truth". On the contrary, prejudices, suspicions, disputes, discussions and polemics became intensified on both sides.

'In recent years a new method, the so-called *ecumenical dialogue,* has been introduced. What does it consist of? Its chief characteristic is that it is concerned not only with the truth but also with the way in which a doctrine should be explained so that others can understand it correctly. Christians of various denominations help each other to arrive at a clearer and more precise understanding of the doctrine to which they do not adhere . . . This new method, in accordance with the desire of the Supreme Pontiff, can also be used in our Council.

'If we want the exposition of our doctrines to be properly understood by non-Catholics, many conditions must be fulfilled:

(i) We must have a clear idea of the present-day teaching of the Orthodox and Protestant Churches.

(ii) We need to know their views about our doctrine, and how far they understand it correctly.

(iii) We need to know what non-Catholics regard as lacking or insufficiently explained in our doctrine.

(iv) We need to examine whether our way of speaking includes forms or ways of speech that are difficult for non-Catholics to understand. Here it must be emphasized that the so-called scholastic language and method represent a serious difficulty for non-Catholics and are often at the basis of their mistakes and prejudices. The same can be said of an abstract and purely intellectual language which is not understood by orientals. On the other hand a biblical and patristic language would in itself avoid and prevent many difficulties, prejudices, and confusions.

(v) The terminology used should be carefully chosen (words,

images, qualifications, etc.), with due regard for the reaction it may produce in the mind and sensibilities of non-Catholics. . . .

(viii) All sterile controversy should be avoided.

(ix) Errors should be clearly rejected but in a way calculated not to offend those who admit them.'

Despite its calmness and objectivity there was a dramatic moment in De Smet's speech when he recalled that the Supreme Pontiff had entrusted to the Secretariat 'the task of helping the other Preparatory Commissions to compile their drafts in a truly ecumenical way'. Yet despite this Cardinal Ottaviani had twice rejected ('*renuit*') the collaboration offered to him. 'I am sorry to say so,' he added, 'but it is the simple truth. And it is for this reason that the draft is perceptibly (*notabiliter*) lacking in ecumenical spirit. In relation to the dialogue with the non-Catholics, it represents not a step forwards but backwards; not a help but a hindrance . . . If this draft is not modified, we shall bear the responsibility for the fact that Vatican II has destroyed a great, an immense hope.'

Rome, Tuesday, 20 November

From one surprise to another. Today, as even the Press Office's communiqué on the 23rd General Congregation recognises, 'the majority of the speeches proved favourable to the draft, stressing the positive reasons adduced in the preceding days'. But notwithstanding this, the Presiding Council 'thought it advisable to ask for a vote of the whole Assembly, so that each Father of the Council may conscientiously express his opinion as to whether or not study of the draft on the Sources of Revelation should be suspended'.

The weight of today's thirteen interventions (five of them from Italian bishops) was not such as to alter, in the opinion of the 'Ten', the position and strength of the two sides. Hence the need for the vote. But why vote on suspending the debate, rather than giving a real judgment on the merits of the draft? For one thing, a vote of suspension is not provided for in the Rules of Procedure, as Cardinal Frings, the chairman for the day, pointed out; but what is more serious is that no real clarification could come out of such a vote, for both adversaries and supporters of 'De Fontibus' could agree on the opportuneness of accepting a truce to the debate.

In any case, it was agreed that the Fathers in favour of suspension should vote 'placet' and those for continuing 'non placet'. As usual, the announcement, given first in Latin by the Secretary-General Felici, was repeated by the five under-secretaries in their respective languages: Spanish, French, English, German, and Arabic. But this did nothing to diminish the confusion. For one thing, Cardinal Ruffini rose three times to remind his colleagues that the voting had nothing to do with a judgment on the merits of the draft. Fortunately, however, the assembly is by now used to his intemperate interventions and no longer takes much notice of them.

The voting went on amid great agitation, which became almost tumultuous when the assembly grasped that the outcome had been reported to the Council of Ten without telling the Fathers themselves. Monsignor Felici then confined himself to announcing that there was not a sufficient majority for suspending the debate and it would therefore go on. There were such strong protests in the hall at this inexplicable reticence that Cardinal Frings recalled the Secretary-General to the platform and asked him to make known the exact results of the vote. There proved to be 1,368 'placets' as against 822 'non placets', and since the required two-thirds majority was 1,460 it fell short by only 92 votes.

As can be imagined, this announcement produced the most lively reactions. Since, however, there could be no doubt that the discussion must go on, despite the absurdity of a minority which thus contrived to condition an overwhelming majority, all listened with great attention to Cardinal Tisserant who introduced the debate on the first chapter, on the two sources of revelation. His attack proved particularly lively, stimulated by the recent success in the voting. But as this was a fresh debate on the details of the draft, it was inevitable according to the by now established tradition of the Council that the Archbishop of Palermo would intervene, supported this time by the biblical scholar Monsignor Vincenzo Jacono, titular Bishop of Patarà. When Cardinal Ruffini's voice began to resound through the microphone the seats in the hall suddenly emptied. And that was a mistake. For the first time Ruffini provided a revelation – he was almost progressive.

Rome, Wednesday, 21 November

Resounding intervention of the Pope in the Council's labours.

In view of the clear majority of Fathers in favour of suspending the debate on the Sources of Revelation, John XXIII has made an exception to the Rules of Procedure (which require a two-thirds majority) and decided that the Council should go on to discuss another draft, that on 'Means of Social Communication' (press, radio, cinema, TV). Not content with that, John XXIII has also announced that a Mixed Commission is to be set up, consisting of some members of the Commission for Faith and Morals and others from the Secretariat for Christian Union, with the task (these are the words of the official communiqué, but they seem also to have used to the letter by Monsignor Felici in making the announcement to the assembly) of 'touching up the draft on the Sources of Revelation, shortening it and bringing out more clearly the general principles of the Catholic doctrine already treated by the Council of Trent and Vatican I'.

This twofold announcement, given by the Secretary-General of the Council 'by mandate of the Cardinal Secretary of State', had exceptional repercussions on the radio and in this evening's newspapers.

No doubt from the point of view of democratic orthodoxy the two pontifical resolutions would be condemned. The fact remains, nevertheless, that they have extricated the Council from an impasse which might seriously have compromised its future. Moreover, the Catholic Church cannot be blamed for acting in accordance with what it is rather than with what it is sometimes useful that it should appear. The Pope, in short, has intervened authoritatively, as an authentic absolute sovereign, but, at any rate in part, in such a way as to respect the requirements of an objective situation (that of a majority paralysed by excessively rigid regulations). He acted with absolute arbitrary power, on the other hand, in establishing the Mixed Commission. It would have sufficed in itself if he had entrusted the task of 'retouching' the draft to the Doctrinal Commission on Faith and Morals, only just set up and consisting in part of new men; but he obviously had serious reasons for not relying on it and moreover on this delicate matter wanted the Secretariat for Union to have a decisive weight.

From today, therefore, the Council has its first Commission suspended (if only as far as the 'De Fontibus' draft is concerned), a new Commission, hitherto unforeseen and possibly only temporary, in process of formation, and a fundamental draft to be recast. The conservative integralists could hardly have sustained a worse defeat, especially considering that the most serious consequences have not yet matured, though they soon will with the discussion of the other theological draft, 'De Ecclesia'.

But above all, from today for the first time Vatican II has become really the Council of John XXIII. Yet not only of the Pope alone, but of the Pope and the majority of the episcopate who have voluntarily ranked themselves with him. As the Pope in question is Papa Roncalli, what might have been a disaster is instead an event rich in good auguries.

Monsignor Martinez told me on the telephone just now that Cardinal Ottaviani was among those down to speak this morning, but as soon as the assembly was told of the Pope's decision he resolved not to do so. It seems certain that in view of the results of yesterday's voting he intended to propose the withdrawal of the draft. The Pope's decision obviously made this unnecessary.

Another result of John XXIII's intervention was that most of the Fathers left the hall, preferring to go into the corridors and bars to discuss what had happened. But sixteen of them spoke, the best being Guano (of Leghorn), Marty (Rheims), Veuillot (Auxiliary in Paris), and Jager (Paderborn).

This evening the *Osservatore Romano* announces two lectures: one for tomorrow, on Means of Social Communication, by Padre Baragli, a Jesuit who works on *Civiltà Cattolica,* and the other for the day after, by Professor Cullmann (who was mentioned to me by Dr Müller). So the flood of press conferences is starting again. Throughout the whole of the biblical debate there was not a single one, a detail which is symptomatic of a good many other things. Yet in the 'cordial invitation' which the Vatican daily of the 14th extended to journalists to tackle 'this difficult subject [i.e. the draft of "De Fontibus"] with the care, prudence, and discretion it demands', 'explanations by experts' were promised 'whenever they appear necessary'. This, as we have seen, did not happen.

To make up for it, there has been a rise in the last few days both in news-exchange values and in the amount of detail provided in the Press Office communiqués. The latter is said by some to arise from the fact that Monsignor Vallainc no longer attends the Council alone but has one or two colleagues there with him; but others attribute it to Monsignor Morcillo, Archbishop of Saragossa, one of the five deputy-Secretaries-General and the 'journalists' bishop', who revises and approves the basic communiqués before their translation into seven languages. As for the news-exchange, this is just the outcome of the journalists' daily meetings when they compare notes on the indiscretions gleaned from various sources of information.

But there are some who have no need to turn to the news mart, and they are usually the best informed among the journalists. It is widely and probably rightly believed, for instance, that the integralists make use of the Rome daily, *Il Tempo,* to spread indiscretions which they consider useful for their own ends. But in any case there is no comparison between the sporadic reports on the Council given by the *Tempo* correspondents and the regular daily ones of the special correspondent of *La Croix,* the main French Catholic daily, who gives both the speakers' names and résumés or whole extracts from the speeches at the Council just as if he had been present himself. Clearly the French bishops have a quite special idea of their own about what the secrecy of the Council signifies. But if they speak readily and with all and sundry (as one journalist who tried to take telecamera shots of them said, 'On aurait dit des midinettes'), this is certainly not out of vainglory.

Rome, Thursday, November 22

I see in a report from a London correspondent that while the biblical debate has been going on in the Council some amused interest has been caused in London by the announcement, made by a well-known botanical scholar, Tatham Whitehead, that Adam could not have eaten the apple in the Garden of Eden for the simple reason that Eve was in no position to offer it to him. Mr Whitehead, who is a lecturer at Bangor University, is about to bring out a book on vegetation in pre-historic times.

'From the indications in Genesis,' he maintains, 'we must presume that the Garden of Eden was in Mesopotamia. Now, apples appeared late in those regions. In biblical and pre-biblical times there were only two fruits in existence there, the apricot and the quince. Quinces have not a pleasant enough taste to lead anyone into temptation. So the fruit in question must have been an apricot.'

The reactions of a number of theologians, including some Catholics, when interviewed by a newspaper about this revelation were varied but unperturbed. The general feeling seems to have been that, irrespective of what may have happened to our two progenitors, the apricot was unlikely to replace the legendary apple now; all agreed, in any case, that 'the bases of faith remain unshaken'.

But what about the problem of scriptural infallibility which has caused such agonizing thoughts to, among many others, the Fathers of Vatican II?

'De Fontibus' had a clamorous aftermath today at the Biblicum when Fr Lohfink, Professor of Holy Writ at the faculty of theology in Frankfurt, defended his thesis on the literary analysis of chapters V to XI of Deuteronomy.

Twelve Cardinals were present: Tisserant, Gerlier, Doepfner, Frings, Bea, Gilroy, Alfrink, Ritter, Léger, Confalonieri, and Testa, in addition to Pizzardo (probably against his will), in his capacity of Grand Chancellor of the Gregoriana, the Biblicum, and the Orientale (Montini and Koenig had sent apologies), and 750 bishops; and there were also the General of the Jesuits, Janssens, and other Superiors of religious Orders, a number of the Council's expert advisers, some observer delegates (including Cullmann, Monsignor Cassien, and Monsignor Sarkissian), the Austrian and German Ambassadors, and over 1,200 others.

The indirect significance of this large turnout lies in the audience's evident wish to pay tribute to the Biblicum as a reaction against the recent attacks.

As I did for the draft of 'De Sacra Liturgia', I give at this point a brief statistical analysis about the speeches made during the debate on 'De Fontibus Revelationis',

In six General Congregations (that is, in a week short of Sunday, a real 'Passion week without Easter'), the 19th to the 24th, 104 speeches were made. Among the 99 Fathers who spoke, there were

33 Cardinals (five from the Curia), one Patriarch, 19 residential and 2 titular archbishops, 31 residential and 11 titular bishops, and two Superiors of religious Orders.

Geographically, the speakers were distributed as follows:

Europe = 62 (Italy 19, Spain 12, France 10, Germany 6, etc.).
America = 20 (USA 4, Canada 3, Mexico, Argentine, Brazil, Ecuador, 2 each, etc.).
Asia = 11 (India 2, Indonesia, Philippines, Vietnam, etc.).
Africa = 4.
Australia = 3.

This evening the *Osservatore Romano* comments ironically on the defence of the Council made by the Communist Senator Ambrogio Donini – a former favourite student of that arch-exponent of modernism in Italy, Ernesto Buonaiuti – in a recent debate on the occasion of the publication in Rome of Mario Gozzini's book *Concilio aperto* ('The Council has opened').

The Communists are undoubtedly in a paradoxical position in relation to the Council, but not exactly in the way that 'F.A.' (Federico Alessandrini) has tried to suggest in his 'Survey of the Scene' ('Ribalta dei fatti'). And the odd thing is that F.A. not only knows it but commits himself to paper about it. Precisely why? To prevent the usual petty critics from believing that the Church is coming to a compromise with the Communists? That may be one of the reasons, indeed no doubt it is. But in that case why indulge in irony rather than explain what the limits are to the *rapprochement* which is in fact coming about between Church and Communism under our very eyes? Moreover, if Donini has agreed to speak in praise of this book by an *avant-garde* Catholic, indeed one might say a La Pirian Gozzini, it is not by pure chance, but rather because the most original part of the book supports the thesis of an opening towards the Communist world and of the Council's need to work for coexistence with the 'Socialist countries' rather than reiterating empty condemnations of them.

During the last few days the Rabbi of New York, Immanuel Jacobovich, has been in Rome, and Cardinal Spellman introduced him to Bea.

There have been a lot of prominent Jewish personalities in Rome during these weeks of the Council. I believe Dr Chaim Wardi, formerly head of the department for Christian affairs in the Israeli Ministry of Religious Affairs, who came to Rome for the opening, has stayed on quite a long time following its work as a private observer, and is still here.

There has for some time been a special section of the Secretariat for Christian Union which is concerned with relations between the Catholic Church and the Jews: its head is Father Leo Rudloff, who was summoned from the Abbey of the Dormition of Mount Sion in Jerusalem. Requests and appeals reach this office from Jewish organizations and individuals all over the world, invoking the abolition of all anti-semitic discrimination in the attitudes and manifestations of Catholic life, whether official or otherwise, in their respective countries.

In practice, at John XXIII's wish and in anticipation of these requests, the Roman liturgy has been purged of all expressions of disrespect for the Jewish people. But some irritating contentions about them are still to be found, especially in certain books and periodicals, such as, for example, the theory of their collective responsibility for the death of Christ. Such is the zeal of the Jewish organizations that they send to Rome whole lists of Catholic works, both scholarly and popular, containing references which are regarded as controversial or slanderous in relation to the Jewish people.

In any case it seems that the Jewish office of the Secretariat has been consulted by the Secretariat of State concerning the problem of diplomatic representation between Israel and the Holy See.

Lastly, I have just received a circular letter dated 17 November which the editors of *Adesso* have sent to their subscribers. The main part of it is as follows:

> We feel it our duty to give our readers an explanation of the decision reached by us on 15 September.
>
> The Holy Office, which had always regularly and carefully followed our publication, had in fact brought to the editor's notice a private warning advising him to 'modify the tone and trend of *Adesso*, which combines numerous professions of Christianity with ideas and attitudes of a censurable nature'.

The Cardinal Archbishop of Milan, in transmitting this directive, added that 'this periodical has maintained its same attitude of uninhibited criticism of the Hierarchy, and its same views about the autonomy of the laity, and he therefore regretfully found himself forced to concur with the reasons for this warning'. At the same time the periodical was told to have no 'collusion' with the French periodicals *Esprit* and *Témoignage Chrétien*, with which, it will be recalled, *Adesso* had established joint subscription arrangements which had proved very successful.

In his reply the editor of *Adesso* illustrated and confirmed the guiding motives of 'this group of adult laymen who have compromised no one but themselves and who strive to discuss world opinion and events by making use of those gifts of God, intelligence and freedom'. As for 'collusion' with the French periodicals, he asked the reason for its prohibition.

From the tone of a second letter and the threats it contained, the editorial board of *Adesso* realized that the only possible answer was silence. The paper could not rebel and so deny its very origins and sense of responsibility, but on the other hand it could not accept unconditional obedience, which would have altered the whole reason for its existence as an organ for comment and discussion, reducing it to one of the many Curial news sheets, whether with or without the imprimatur.

Rome, Friday, 23 November

The Council has run into a period of relaxation; there is an 'intermezzo' sort of atmosphere about. Anyone encountering the Fathers as they met again this morning in Piazza San Pietro after yesterday's usual Thursday pause might have thought they had not the faintest recollection of the past few days, and that for them the Council was not so much continuing as opening for the first time. This capacity to accept and forget both failures and successes is certainly an extraordinary thing to find in an assembly of over 2,000; the only way to account for it is the habit of discipline, especially of submissiveness and obedience, and even more the certainty that no victory or defeat is ever final in an organization that has no time-limit ahead of it.

Consequently nothing could be better suited to the new climate than the discussion of the next draft, which, as was announced the day before yesterday, will be on the press, cinema, radio and television. They are described for this occasion as 'means of social communication' ('De mediis communicationis socialis' is the draft's exact title), and some people seem to be rather pleased with the name. But it is, all the same, both too long and too generic: all sorts of other things – the telephone and telegraph, trains, ships, and aeroplanes – are also 'means of social communication', and soon space cabins will be too.

Anyway, this morning in St Peter's there was an almost romantic feeling of optimism and anticipation. It was, moreover, the first time that the Council had dealt with a theme of this kind (for in 1869-70 morse telegraphy and photography were only just coming into use: the telephone was first generally put into use on an industrial scale in 1877; and the year after Edison invented the gramophone). After a short speech from Cardinal Cento, chairman of the Commission for Lay Apostolate, Press and Entertainment, there was a report from Monsignor Stourm, Archbishop of Sens, in which his reference to the miracle plays with which the mediaeval Church used to amuse, instruct, and elevate people spiritually must have made his listeners even more conscious of living in an age of technical miracles.

This romantic atmosphere which the Fathers evidently enjoyed may have been the more welcome because of their own unpreparedness to confront the mysteries and wonders of modern technique. True, the Church of today has opened its doors, and even those of St Peter's, to the press, radio and television; but was this done of its own free will or only to avoid being forced to do so? In the special stands on the opening day of the Council there were diplomats and politicians, former members of ruling houses and descendants of a centuries-old aristocracy, even knights of equestrian orders; but where were the heads of the big press agencies and newspaper networks or the big cinema and television company directors, in short, the creators of public opinion? Despite its seemingly generous hospitality and fine words, does not the Catholic Church still seem to be looking more towards the past than the present?

Many of the Fathers who spoke in today's debate are regarded as among the most competent in the ecclesiastical world. But competent in what? In sound and visual techniques, or simply in producing scripts for religious broadcasts? And where can you find any reference to such 'means of communication' in the theological students' manuals? All the textbooks on morality in popular use today talk repeatedly 'de spectaculis', but in exactly the same terms in which Sant'Alfonso de'Liguori might have done two centuries ago, or San Bernardino of Siena before him, or, to go back to the beginning, Tertullian. But is there a single one which discusses the various forms of entertainment from the angle of their social usefulness, as instruments of truth or lies, as responsible for diffusing undesirable ideas and practices among the masses? As far as I know, not one. (But I was told afterwards that an exception is Hoering's *La legge del Cristo*.)

Thus there is an atmosphere of adventure but also, inevitably, of improvisation about the Council today. Monsignor Stourm unintentionally emphasized this by quoting a passage from Pierre L'Ermite about the churches in working-class districts that close their doors just when the lights go up and the cinemas open, and mentioning the following statistics about sound and visual communications throughout the world:

Press: 8,000 newspapers with a total circulation of some 300 million, and 22,000 periodicals with a circulation of 200 million;

Cinema: 2,500 films produced annually and shown in 170,000 theatres open for 35,000 million hours;

Radio: 6,000 broadcasting stations and 400 million receiving apparatuses;

Television: 1,000 stations broadcasting for 200,000 million hours a year and 120 million TV apparatuses.

But even he did not seem to me to emerge from the atmosphere of unreality when he explained the main ideas which had inspired the compilers of the draft.

These were the following (as given in the original text issued by the Kipa agency on 27 November):

a) we have wished to affirm that the Church has the right and duty to teach, and that this duty cannot be fulfilled in the present circumstances unless the Church itself makes use of the press and other means of communication (*Ecclesia magistra*).

b) we have wished to affirm that the Church has the right to educate, in other words that with the help of all, believers or otherwise, it has the duty to encourage the press, cinema, etc., and all other things that are good for men and for Christians; and that it has also the duty to remind all those who, in whatever capacity, are concerned with these means of communication of their obligations and their heavy responsibilities should they make bad use of them (*Ecclesia mater*);

c) we have wished to affirm that the Church's work in this sphere must be co-ordinated. Unless this is done the Church cannot fulfil its dual task, which is both doctrinal and formative. The necessary organization should be established at three levels, international, national, and diocesan . . .

This repeated insistence on 'rights' is certainly not likely to please a considerable section of the assembly, and is even less likely to appeal to those outside it. It belongs to a legal conception of the ecclesiastical community which, except in a few countries, is now outmoded; and this makes it not only naïve but also dangerous and provocative, to say nothing of being in direct contradiction to the spirit of the Gospel. The same sort of language, used and abused, but almost always without effect, by Pius XI and more particularly by Pius XII, sounds strange and almost shocking today. But the draft refers back in pedantic detail to the documents of pontifical teaching of the Pacellian era, making no effort to open up new horizons but proposing, for example, the formulation of a universal ethic for the utilization of audio-visual means which will go beyond the somewhat restricted level of the individual particularized ethic to tackle the question on a broader and more generalized scale.

However, the draft, apart from such imperfections as excessive length and repetition, was generally regarded as satisfactory. Spellman was the first to express approval, at the same time giving the assembly a piece of good advice when he urged them to bear especially in mind the need for collaboration from non-Catholics in this particular field. Gossip has it that Spellman is expected to play quite a big part over this draft for at least two reasons: first because of his friendship with Monsignor O'Connor, chairman since its foundation in 1952 of the Pontifical Commission for Cinema, Radio and Television and also chairman of the Secretariat for Press and Entertainment in the preparatory stage of the Council; and secondly to make superfluous any possible intervention from his auxiliary, the magnetic Bishop Fulton Sheen, of whom he is said to be very jealous.

The only other Cardinal to speak apart from him was the inevitable Ruffini, *doctor conciliarius universalis*. Fifteen bishops spoke as well, the best being the first: Monsignori Enríquez y Terrancón, of Solsona in Spain, Beck, of Salford, and Charrière, of Lausanne, Geneva and Fribourg. The bishops of Solsona and Salford both stressed the need for the draft to emphasize more explicitly and illustrate more fully the special role of the Catholic laity in this sphere. They were also among the Fathers who regretted the exclusion of the laity from taking a direct part in the preparation of the draft.

Rome, Saturday, 24 November

A better level of debate today on the means of social communication.

The assembly was expecting the general debate on the draft as a whole to continue. The draft is sub-divided into four parts:

(i) doctrine of the Church on the means of social communication;

(ii) the Church's use of those means in its apostolate;

(iii) the Church's teaching and directives;

(iv) special provisions concerning the different means of social communication: press, cinema, TV, records, tape-recordings, comics, etc.

At the close of the morning session Monsignor Felici rose to say, rather superfluously, that the discussion would be continued on Monday. But the sting, as usual, was in the tail, for he added that it was expected to finish it on that day.

Now they seem to be in an exaggerated hurry to get on. True, the bishops have shown that they had not much to say, but it seems rather excessive to strangle the debate so soon. If there are no more new views from bishops, why not call on some of the specialists or theologians?

The most important speeches today were from Cardinal Suenens and Monsignor Morcillo (who in his references to the relationship between freedom of expression and the rights of the State seems to have had an eye on an audience in Spain rather than on the Council). The African speakers were also appreciated –

Monsignor Perraudin, Archbishop of Kabgay, in the Congo, and Monsignor Nwedo, Bishop of Umuahia, in Nigeria.

The *Osservatore Romano* announced today the composition of the Commission to revise the 'De Fontibus' draft, now to be called 'De Divina Revelatione' (but the new title suggests that the revision has in fact already begun). It includes Cardinals Ottaviani and Bea as co-chairmen and Father Tromp and Monsignor Willebrands as secretaries. Others on it are six Cardinals nominated by the Pope, all the members of the Council's Commission on Faith and Morals, all the bishops who are on the Secretariat for Christian Union, whether as members or advisers, and, lastly, the only Father on that Secretariat who is not a bishop but was co-opted on to it some time ago, Abbot Minisci of Grottaferrata. The Cardinals appointed by the Pope are Liénart (deputy chairman), Frings, Ruffini, Meyer, Lefébure, and Quiroga y Palacios. (The Commission then divided up into five sub-committees, one for each of the five chapters of the draft.)

Rome, Sunday, 25 November

Pope John's 81st birthday, but *in calice amarissimo*.

Yesterday morning the Council assembly approved a telegram of good wishes to him which Monsignor Felici read out. It was terribly banal, talking of 'eyes, minds, and hearts' raised to him but, after all that superfluous anatomy, avoiding the faintest indication of the gratitude the Fathers feel towards him for the impulse he has given to the Council.

This silence, however, was at least honest, and was moreover in tune with the letter which fourteen members of the Sacred College sent to the Pope the same day thanking him for having referred the 'De Fontibus' draft to a Mixed Commission, but at the same time also insisting on the importance of the Tradition and Teaching of the Church. The letter instructed the Pope that there are rules governing Tradition: *sensus Ecclesiae, consensus universalis,* and the analogy of the faith. In addition, it pointed out certain widespread errors among contemporary Catholic theologians and biblical scholars concerning the inspiration of Holy Scripture and the literary forms used therein.

The signatories of the letter were Agagianian, Bacci, Bueno y Monreal, Browne, de Barros Camara, Godfrey, Marella, McIntyre, Pizzardo, Ruffini, Santos, Siri, Traglia, and Urbani[1]. Four others withdrew at the last moment (but John XXIII will have had no difficulty in learning their names). It was moreover obvious that Ottaviani had only refrained from signing for purely personal reasons.

Pope John – according to Martinez who told me all this – was so upset by this document that he abandoned his intention of presiding over the first sitting of the Revision Commission, which met in the Vatican this morning. After this letter he certainly cannot have any illusions about the seeming calm in which the Council appears to have lulled itself.

Rome, Monday, 26 November

The vote on the draft 'De mediis communicationis socialis' was taken at 11.30 this morning (voting being by standing or sitting) and so it emerged to take its place on the very brief list of items completed at the Council.

Before that 13 bishops had spoken, among them Monsignori Hoffner of Munster, Duval of Algiers, and Kempf of Limburg. Hoffner made some interesting references to the opening-up of pluralist societies to Christian thought; and also of interest, especially because of the speaker's authoritative position, was Duval's declaration that the voice of the Church should sound out through the world above all as the voice of human conscience.

The usual malicious gossips are delighted at the trick Fulton Sheen has played on Spellman. The *Osservatore Romano* yesterday came out with an interview with the 'TV bishop' in which that elegant American prelate is photographed in Piazza San Pietro while speaking into the microphone 'in a typical attitude'. The *Osservatore*'s editor describes Sheen as coming towards him waving the pages of his script, 'slim in figure' but 'strong as a horse'. After 'taking a good long look' at him he discovered that he had 'the tortured face of an ascetic'.

A few days ago Adele Cambria, who had run into him in one of

[1] According to later information it was uncertain whether Cardinals Marella, Pizzardo, Bueno y Monreal, and Browne actually signed the letter; but the total number of signatories remained fourteen.

the Via Veneto hotels, gave a rather different description of him in a secular paper: 'the bishop is thin, wearing a short trench coat, his hair shining above the temples and set in tight silver waves slightly tinged with mauve. He has very blue eyes . . . He ordered a table for that evening on the roof-garden: *scampi,* lobster, four guests, and red candles, just like a model's dream of New York.'

These personal descriptions apart, the interview opened brightly. Sheen declared that 'all scientific advances represent a form of revelation of God himself' and proposed that 'the whole Church throughout the world should celebrate a "Science Sunday" to give Our Lord public thanks for our immense scientific, technical, and artistic progress . . .' He went on to compare radio and TV with the Old and New Testament: 'the first may be likened to the ancient law, where the word is heard but not seen; the second has a new dimension and is in some sense comparable to the New Testament, because, besides being heard, the word is also made visible.'

Less scintillating but more interesting was Monsignor Zoa's press conference on modern Africa's widespread need of the 'means of social communication'; he gave a fascinating account of the traditional methods of conveying news, used since the beginning of time by negro societies.

But all that is just local colour. Instead, two questions emerge. First, will the draft just handed over to the relevant Commission for further improvements really help towards the future organization of audio-visual methods at world, national and diocesan levels? And secondly, what sort of spirit will inspire it – a spirit based on rights or on duties, and aiming at overwhelming or at convincing its audience?

Antimori, who has got over his attack of sciatica and has begun running all over the place again among Vatican circles, tells me of a bitter remark of Père Gabel, the former editor of *La Croix*: 'Ecclesiastics today [he obviously had in mind the Fathers of the Council] talk about the press, radio and television in the same sentimental and romantic way in which bishops of seventy years ago under the influence of *Rerum novarum* used to talk of the social question, believing it could soon be solved with a little judicious pressure on the rich and a little suitable improvement in the morals of the poor.'

Debate on 'Ut Unum Sint' Begins

Rome, Tuesday, 27 November

Every time the tree of the Preparatory Commissions is shaken a rain of rotten fruit falls to the ground.

Even the fruit of the Eastern Commission is damaged. Yesterday, when first presented and still wrapped up in shining cellophane, it seemed a fruit from the promised land. The illusion might even have lasted for twenty-four hours if the sharp ironical eyes of the Archbishop of Lille had not been the first to investigate it. Indeed, Ruffini, Browne and Bacci, coming after him, found it sound and appetizing; but by then the worm, indeed a whole colony of worms, had been discovered by Liénart and there was no help for it. (The draft was presented shortly after 11.30 am by the Cardinal Secretary of State, Cicognani, as Chairman of the Commission, and the usual optimistic kind of report on it was given by the secretary, the Brazilian Father Athanasius Welykyj.)

Nobody, however, had anticipated that the first to suggest alterations in the scope of the draft would be the leaders of the drafting Commission itself. True, they chose to speak through the intermediary of the Secretary-General Felici, but the important thing is that they felt it necessary – if late in the day and only after Liénart's criticisms – to explain to the assembly that there would be no difficulty about changing the title of the draft, 'Ut unum sint', to, for instance, 'De Ecclesiae unitate', 'so that it may be clearer that the draft concerns only the separated Eastern Christians and not the Protestants'.

Expectation today was concentrated on the Uniates, who were known to intend speaking *en bloc,* even if not consecutively. Probably not many people are yet aware (I was told it this afternoon by a journalist priest whom I ran into near 'Salvator Mundi', who heard it from Monsignor Edelby, auxiliary of Maximos IV Saigh) that the Patriarch of Antioch of the Melchites has organized a concentric attack on the draft, dividing up the subjects between himself and his four suffragans. As each Father can speak only for ten minutes, he has thus solved the problem of saying everything, or at any rate as much as possible, in a sort of relay-race speech – punctuated as each next speaker takes over – lasting about an hour.

The draft in question is curiously subdivided, not into chapters, but into 52 paragraphs. But three separate sections can be clearly discerned: the first on the theological foundations of unity, in other words the condition of union with Peter (paras. 1-10); the second on the means of facilitating its re-establishment (theological, liturgical, canonical, psychological and practical – paras. 11-47); and the third on legal and practical measures relating to the genuine re-establishment of unity.

The Uniates who spoke this morning were particularly severe about the first section. In this connection the Eastern Commission in the communication read by Monsignor Felici made the excuse that they had wanted to illustrate 'the real situation' arising out of the separation between Catholics and Orthodox, 'without wishing in any way to enter into the arguments that concern the constitution[1] "De Ecclesia".' But in that case why waste ten paragraphs in needlessly going over such delicate ground?

Monsignor Nabaa had already said some days ago, speaking to the French episcopate, that he would reject it *en bloc*. Maximos IV, who was the first to open fire (speaking as usual in French, but this time it was at once translated into Latin by Monsignor Hakim), emphasized that the Eastern Churches, being founded directly by the apostles, are not branch Churches of the Catholic Church. But the draft 'does not show how Peter receives his position as first among the college of bishops. Great emphasis must be given to the collegiate character of the Church and then the Papacy will appear as the basis of this collegiate system.'

Monsignor Zoghby, the Greek-Catholic patriarchal vicar for Egypt, was even more uncompromising. Also speaking in French, he said: 'Though the Eastern Church despite the uncertainty on this point has always recognised the primacy of the Bishop of Rome, it has never formed part of the Latin Church. It is not an emanation of it nor does it owe its existence to it. Its dogmatic and disciplinary development is independent of the Latin Church. The Church of the East is thus a fountainhead-Church, just as is the Latin Church in the West. The dogma is identical in substance, but the theology is different.'

Then came Monsignor Vuccino, an Assumptionist, Greek Archbishop of the Latin rite: 'It is not without lively anxiety that we ask ourselves how far a purely legal description of the unity of the Church can contribute to the dialogue with our Orthodox and Protestant brethren . . . Let us therefore speak to our brethren in that evangelical language that they understand and appreciate.

[1] Used here in its technical sense – see above p. 47 note.

Let us tell them that the primacy of Peter is above all a diaconate, a pastoral office, a service which the leader of the apostles has received from Christ, not in order to exercise power or dominate but rather to pasture the flock of Christ, since, after all, the legal power of Peter is ordained for his pastoral office.'

In the second section of the draft the Uniates criticized chiefly the first two paragraphs recapitulating the story of the attempts at reunion promoted by Rome. Monsignor Edelby said bluntly: 'The Catholic Church has not really done as much for unity as the draft tries to make out.' Other criticisms were of a more marginal kind, concerning terminology (the Preparatory Commission could not agree on such terms as 'separated brethren', 'dissidents', and 'return'), certain harsh wordings which were bound to wound the Orthodox, etc.

To sum up, the focal points of disagreement about the draft, and not from the Uniate side alone, are:

(i) Refraternization between Orthodox and Catholics – to which there is only one fundamental obstacle: pontifical primacy – must set out from a different interpretation of this dogma: and this it is the job of 'De Ecclesia' to produce.

(ii) The draft does not appear to have borne in mind the Eastern federative, or pluralistic, conception of a Church (or of Churches within the Church). It is inspired, instead, by an administrative conception of the centralized and monopolistic kind typical of Western mentality. This angle of vision must also be corrected in the draft 'De Ecclesia'.

(iii) In conclusion, the draft has not sufficient autonomy beyond the limits of a simple pastoral instruction. This draft should deal with the ecclesiological foundations, while the ecumenical foundations in general should be covered in the draft on ecumenicalism prepared by the Secretariat for Christian Union.

In short, the draft has evaporated before the assembly's eyes, and it will be interesting to see what happens next.

This does not mean, of course, that it will be scrapped altogether. There are some useful ideas in the second and third sections which should be retained and developed, such as, for instance, the principle that no more than is strictly necessary should be asked of the Orthodox who wish to unite with the Catholic Church – in particular, those who are Orthodox by birth should not be called on to abjure their faith but merely to make a profession of faith. The draft's conclusion contains the surprising statement that the present situation of the Eastern Churches within the Catholic Church (i.e. the Uniate Churches) should not be regarded as permanent or immutable, for it could be improved in several respects. But in that case, as Monsignor Edelby rightly said, why wait for the Orthodox to reunite with Rome in order to change it? Why not take action instead of merely formulating fresh promises, so that the Orthodox may be certain that they risk nothing by taking the desired step?

The day opened and closed with two important events, one of them now made public, the other still practically secret.

The known event is the announcement, made by Monsignor Felici at the opening of today's sitting, that 'the Pope in order to meet the wishes of many Fathers of the Council, especially those living far from Rome, and also for pastoral reasons, has fixed on 8 September 1963, instead of 12 May, as the starting date for the second period of the Council.'

The Chinese bishops or missionaries expelled from China are especially surprised about this, for they were received by the Pope only yesterday evening. They, like the other episcopates, had said in answer to John XXIII's question about their views on the next session that they would prefer to have a single Council session, no matter how long, in 1963. The Pope then just said that it might be possible; evidently he had already taken the decision announced this morning.

The fact that has so far been kept practically secret was told me by Antimori on the telephone this evening at 11.30 pm. The Pope is said to have had a fresh attack of his old illness accompanied by a general collapse of strength. No doubt we shall get confirmation of this tomorrow.

Rome, Wednesday, 28 November

The Pope is seriously ill. This morning he did not leave his room but stayed in bed. It was, of course, the sudden cancellation of today's audiences that caused the news to leak out; but throughout the morning in the Vatican they merely talked vaguely of an attack of influenza. However, it was not difficult for the journalists to discover that his doctor, Professor Mazzoni, had spent the whole night in the pontifical apartment. The Fathers of the Council pressed insistently for news and finally got the promise of a communiqué tomorrow morning.

By the afternoon the influenza had already become an 'indisposition'. Then all doubts about the seriousness of the illness were removed by the arrival at the Vatican of the pontifical physician, Professor Gasbarrini. As a matter of fact he had just come to Rome (from Bologna, where he lives) for family reasons but Monsignor Dell'Acqua, the Deputy-Secretary of State, hastened to him at once on the pretext of taking him to see his own mother who was ill; once in the Vatican, Gasbarrini of course had to pay his respects to the Pope. He readily fell in with the arrangements made about dealing with the journalists. 'No operation,' he answered tersely when one of them asked him if there was any truth in what the French bishops had already allowed to leak into the French press some days ago. That was all they got, but it was enough.

At the same time there was an absolute whirlwind of rumours. The most sensational and highly romanticized concerned the Cardinals, who were said to have been notified that they should suspend making advance bookings for their journeys home after the Council's closure on 8 December. Spellman, tackled point-blank by a journalist, replied with a laugh, and with the obvious intention of putting the rash inquirer off the track, 'As far as I'm concerned I certainly can't stay. Time is money.' The journalists naturally interpreted this as a confirmation of the rumour.

Nevertheless at St Peter's the 29th General Congregation continued to discuss 'Ut unum sint', under the Easterner Tappouni's chairmanship. No particular novelty emerged. The seventeen speakers included six from the Uniate Church, among them the Patriarch of Antioch of the Syrians, Tappouni himself. Monsignor Cheikho, Patriarch of the Babylon Chaldaeans, spoke only to suggest that the Council should compose a prayer for unity among Christians. The Maronite Archbishop of Tyre, Monsignor Khoury, for a few minutes raised the veil which has hitherto concealed the lively internal rivalry dividing the Uniate Churches with his rather acid remark that the Byzantine Church was neither the sole nor the first Church of the East, and that certain exaggerated statements made in the Council Hall by its exponents were likely to harm rather than help the cause of unity. Unity, he said, was not based on myths but on reality and the fact was that the East needed the West and vice versa. But in any case, quite apart from this outburst, the most advanced Church among the Uniates continues to be the Melchite Church.

Some new developments emerged instead outside the Council Hall during the meeting of the Presiding Council which took place immediately after the General Congregation. It is taken for granted that the debate on 'Ut unum sint' will be brought to an end and the draft sent to another body, yet to be decided, to be fused with the ecumenistical drafts proposed by the Theological Commission and the Secretariat for Christian Union.

The virtual turning-down of the draft, and the reservations raised concerning the questions it has in common with 'De Ecclesia', induced Cardinal Ottaviani to speak at today's sitting in order to propose the postponement of the debate on the ecclesiological draft until the next session. Given its importance, he said, and the short time left in the present session, it could not possibly receive adequate discussion. He suggested that the assembly might instead turn to discuss the draft 'De Maria Virgine'.

Was this a carefully calculated appeal to the Fathers' filial devotion to the Madonna? It is difficult to say, just as it is difficult to verify how much there is in the rumours that some sensational event, naturally of a Marian character, is being planned for 8 December, the Feast of the Immaculate Conception. Even if the real reason for the proposed substitution is Ottaviani's fear that the recent setback to 'De Fontibus' is bound to have a negative influence on the debate on 'De Ecclesia', the reasons given are objective enough in themselves. How will the Presiding Council get out of the difficulty?

Rome, Thursday, 29 November

For today, the last mid-week pause the Fathers will have in this session (since next week the General Congregations are to continue daily without interruption), the Pope has forced a distraction upon the Fathers which many of them would willingly have been spared.

Some time ago a concert was announced for today, to be given by the Italian TV in honour of the Catholic episcopate. It was to have been held in the Basilica of St Paul's Without-the-Walls in the presence of the Pope; but because of his illness people expected that it would be put off. Instead, John XXIII has decided that it should take place. He even wanted to get up and come himself to hear Beethoven's Ninth Symphony.

This last piece of news temporarily cheered up everyone who heard about it in the Vatican. But soon afterwards anxiety returned: the Pope had gone back to bed greatly exhausted, and a consultation had been called between his regular doctor, the pontifical physician Professor Gasbarrini, and Professor Valdoni. But no official bulletin has been issued. Even the Fathers of the Council have been given no privileged treatment in this respect. The Secretary of the Council, in order to keep his promise of yesterday, merely distributed advance copies of the communiqué which the *Osservatore Romano* published this afternoon, drawing their attention to its journalistic nature: which was as much as to say that they could read into it whatever they thought fit.

Antimori is insistent that the return of the Pope's malady is not the most serious thing about the situation – John XXIII has undoubtedly driven himself too hard in these last months. After the journey to Loreto and Assisi, he took part in the penitential procession on 7 October to Santa Maria Maggiore and visited the Church of Sant'Agostino on the 14th; in November he emerged from the Vatican six times: on the 4th to San Carlo in the Corso and to the Chancellery, on the 11th to the 'Gabelli' children's re-education centre, on the 13th to Sant'Andrea by the Quirinale, on the 20th to Santa Maria of Guadeloupe, on the 22nd to the Spanish College, and on the 25th to the Propaganda Fide. During the last weeks, in addition to general and special audiences (including the Prime Minister of Trinidad and Tobago, a group of representatives of the Buddhist Federation of Japan, and the Japanese Prime Minister Ikeda), not a day has gone by without his receiving one or other of the episcopates here for the Council in special audience in the afternoon. After he had given audiences to all the delegations from the Iron Curtain countries he received the nine Archbishops and bishops from Korea and the four prelates from Thailand, 28 Archbishops and bishops from Australia, and four from New Zealand; 45 ordinaries and titular bishops from

Mexico and nine Armenians; the Belgian bishops and those of the Chaldaean rite; the episcopates of Ecuador, Pakistan and Cuba; the Fathers coming from Japan and from Eritrea and Ethiopia; bishops from the Veneto; bishops from the United States, Greece and Vietnam; and the French, Maronite and Burmese bishops.

All this extra physical exertion easily explains the revival of his prostate trouble and of others too (for his alarming pallor of recent times must have some other origin, though, according to Antimori, there is no question of a malignant growth). But it does not account, or at any rate accounts only in part, for the Pope's letting himself go, his seeming readiness to meet death halfway. This, according to Antimori, is really a form of moral collapse. The reasons for it, he says, are obvious: first and foremost, the outburst of serious disagreement within the Council during the debate on the Biblical draft; then, when he had begun to feel reassured by the support he received following his personal intervention, the shock of the letter from the fourteen Cardinals; and now, just when he was recovering from that blow, the failure of the draft on unity with the Eastern Churches.

Antimori, who has an almost blind veneration for Papa Giovanni, does not see in this collapse a yielding of the Pope's will, but simply a great spiritual trial to which God has wished to submit him. In Antimori's eyes this is the 'hour of Gethsemane' from which, like Christ, John XXIII will emerge victorious.

Rome, Friday, 30 November

The anxiety about the Pope's health is reflected in the atmosphere of the Council, which seems to be carrying on with its Congregations more out of necessity than conviction. Clearly the situation is really alarming: Vatican II is like a new-born infant that has only just begun to utter its first cries, and the death of John XXIII would probably be fatal to it. Pope and Council have always lived very close to each other during these first forty days of the initial session, even though since the day of the solemn opening John XXIII has discreetly avoided making any appearance himself in the Hall of St Peter's. Moreover, he needed only to press a button in his private library to set in motion a radio circuit enabling him to hear what was going on in the Council Hall, and this he did very often, indeed every day for a longer or shorter time according to his other engagements, listening with eager enjoyment, as he several times confessed in his weekly talks at the general audiences. And it was enough for the bishops to know that the Pope was listening to feel encouraged even at the most difficult moments. Is the invisible umbilical cord between this great and simple Pope and the child 'senectutis suae' to be severed for good?

It is no more than the truth to say, and for once in a way without fear of exaggeration, that the whole world trembles with the Fathers. Rome, in particular, normally so sceptical, so ostentatiously indifferent about affairs across the Tiber, seems to hold its breath in suspense and anxiety.

Now they talk of a gastric ulcer aggravated by the acute prostate condition, and it seems the most likely diagnosis of the symptoms we have been told: but is it really the right one this time, or will it be superseded by another even more serious? They say that a blood transfusion has given considerable relief: but at once one wonders what may be concealed by the expression that it had 'become suddenly urgent'. Professor Gasbarrini has put off his return to Bologna for a few days . . .

Today's congregation, the 30th, was practically in the hands of those in favour of the draft, which is in itself encouraging – indeed it could be said that its 'tough' exponents prevailed, not excluding the General of the Franciscans Minor, Sepinski, who definitely took the part of the draft, including the dogmatic section. The bishop of Split, Monsignor Franic, notoriously of the Ottaviani trend, reminded his hearers how in certain countries of Europe a far from negligible number of Catholics passed over to the Orthodox, and that it would therefore be a great mistake to favour a policy of 'thaw'.

The Apostolic Exarch for the faithful of Byzantine rite in Pittsburg, Monsignor Elko, showed even greater daring in turning to address the observers. True, there was nothing new in this (a usual beginning on such occasions is: 'Venerabiles patres, dilectissimi observatores'); but the novelty lay in his polemical tone and the obvious discrimination which his words aimed to effect, almost taking pleasure in isolating those of his hearers whom he held 'responsible'. He asked the observers to consider the atmosphere of piety and charity that characterized the Assembly, the discretion of the Pope's interventions, and so on, but especially he wished them to take note of what was happening under their very eyes in the Council, inasmuch as the Fathers could say whatever they wanted 'without risk of being punished or put in prison'.

But though some 'magni passus' might have been taken, they were nevertheless 'extra viam'. Similarly, Monsignor Heenan, Archbishop of Liverpool, rather than showing a real interest in the draft took it as a pretext to express his regret that in this first session the draft on union with the Orthodox had been discussed in preference to that concerning the Protestants. Who had replied most promptly, he asked the assembly, and who had shown themselves the readiest to undertake the inter-church dialogue on the occasion of the Council? The Anglican Church. The Archbishop of Canterbury had given clear proof of this. But instead they had chosen to concern themselves first with the Orthodox, who were undoubtedly closer to themselves in dogma, but were also highly arbitrary on the concrete plane of mutual approaches.

In short, the Council is tired and its heart is elsewhere. The invitation therefore came opportunely to vote by standing or sitting on the suspension of a debate that threatened to go off the rails in all directions, even the most absurd. The result was naturally unanimous.

Rome, Saturday, 1 *December*

Ottaviani's run of bad luck continues inexorably. The Presiding Council has turned down his Mariological proposal and the draft 'De Ecclesia', a tome of 122 quarto pages, including 30 pages of notes, divided into 11 chapters and 55 paragraphs, lies on the Council's table – to be sacrificed, without a doubt.

As for 'Ut unum sint', the Fathers today approved (by 2,068 votes out of 2,116) the following proposal, read out by Monsignor Felici 'The examination of the Decree on the unity of the Church being terminated, the Fathers of the Sacred Council approve it as a document in which are collected together the common truths of the faith . . . This Decree, however, on the basis of the observations and proposals heard in the Council Hall, will form a single document with the Decree on Ecumenicalism, prepared by the

Secretariat for Christian Union, and with Chapter XI, also on ecumenicalism, of the draft on the Dogmatic Constitution of the Church.' In short, if it is not being sent to the cemetery for drafts, its destination is undoubtedly an orthopaedic hospital. This is another bad augury for 'De Ecclesia', while the further voting on the early parts of Chapter I of the draft 'De Sacra Liturgia' (which has been going on in the past few days and today) continues both rapidly and favourably.

The Presiding Council clearly wanted to avoid ending the first session with a Marian celebration, which, among other things, would have had the effect of mortgaging in advance the whole ecclesiological draft, to which 'De Maria Virgine' is for some reason supposed to be the natural appendix (the twelfth chapter). Monsignor Martinez tells me that the Presiding Council met in the Pope's study to tell him the reasons for its communication: only the debate on 'De Ecclesia', confined though it must be to a general discussion, would in fact, given its importance, allow more precise conclusions to be drawn on the work – largely, really, a sort of trial run – of this first session. Martinez thinks next week will see the announcement of important decisions by the Pope concerning the Council.

All this surprises me, seeing that the uncertain state of the Pope's health (even though there was official mention of an improvement today) continues to paralyse Vatican circles. In any case, the Council as such seems to be virtually over. Antimori is right: he smells the odour of decay.

Today, at any rate, was not a day of battles. Perhaps the pulsating current from the Pope's study is keeping the Fathers in order. Even Ottaviani was smiling and almost witty as he presented the 'De Ecclesia' draft from the tribune. True, his wit had a bitter undercurrent, but certainly the Ottaviani of today is very different from the Ottaviani of 14 November. Even Monsignor Franic's report avoided polemics. Most of the Fathers could not believe their ears when, an expectant silence having fallen as Liénart rose to speak, they heard the Cardinal repeat twice over, with a calculated pause between, 'Gaudeo . . . Gaudeo'. But it was true all the same. The Archbishop of Lille said he rejoiced to find that the draft attached suitable importance to the mystical aspect of the Church. True, he went on at once to say that though the effort was appreciable the result was inadequate, but such an opening was enough to disappoint those who had expected the terrible Red Bishop once again to confirm his reputation as a scourge of the conservatives.

The rest of his speech was far from idyllic, especially when he disapproved of the draft's too close equation of the Roman Church with the mystical body and when, in conclusion, he hoped that the draft might be revised in a less legal sense. But by now a certain atmosphere of *détente* had been created, so that many were astounded when they heard Ruffini say, after warmly praising the drafting of the theological Commission, that the logical construction of the draft had nevertheless disappointed him and he would make a detailed proposal of his own about it. Were the two Cardinals by any chance exchanging roles?

Balance, or rather normality, began to be restored with the conservative Bishop of Seville, Bueno y Monreal – although he regretted that the draft devoted too little attention to the priesthood and diaconate – and above all with Koenig, Alfrink, and Ritter. All three indicated some serious lacunae and coincided in some of their criticisms, as for instance on the treatment of relations between Church and State, seen usually from the exclusive angle of the Church's rights, and on the neglect of freedom of conscience. Alfrink deplored in particular the silence or negativeness of the parts about the Episcopal College; Koenig, the fact that the Church was considered almost exclusively as a condition of individual salvation, whereas it had irreplaceable tasks to perform in relation to all humanity; and Ritter pointed out that the defence of the repository of truth was not the exclusive task, even if it was its main one, of ecclesiastical teaching alone but of the Church as a whole. But only Alfrink wanted to see the whole draft revised by a mixed commission.

The strongest attack came, unexpectedly enough, from the Bishop of Bruges, De Smet. Evidently when he made his notable intervention on 19 November he had the honey of Cardinal Bea upon his lips. This time, as only he himself was involved, he spoke 'ex plenitudine cordis', decisively attacking the triad of clericalism, legalism, and 'triumphalism' which, according to him had for too long, except in the most recent years, characterized the Church of Rome. In other words, he criticized that far from evangelical habit of regarding the Church with disproportionate optimism, concentrating only on its more showy and temporal aspects, its success and its claims, citing statistics and indications of support and indulging in an ostentatious style which had nothing to do with an intimate and conscious religious reality – and in this connection he cited as an example the Vatican daily and other Roman documents.

Less polemical but possibly more effective was the suffragan Bishop of Strasbourg, Monsignor Elchinger. He said that a doctrinal document on the Church, inspired by pastoral considerations, should take account of the following prospects for the future: whereas yesterday the Church could be regarded mainly as an institution, today it was seen largely as a community affair; whereas yesterday the main figure in it was thought to be the Pope, today it was the bishop in conjunction with the Pope, and not the bishop alone and in isolation but together with the whole episcopal corps; and, lastly, whereas yesterday theology stressed chiefly the importance of the hierarchy, today it was on the people of God, the 'plebs sancta Dei', that it should insist.

There is not much point in recording the attitudes adopted by the conservatives, which can be taken as said. Symptomatic, on the other hand, as showing the inability of part of the assembly to understand the significance of the problems at stake was the request of Monsignor Lefebvre, Superior General of the Fathers of the Holy Ghost and titular Archbishop of Sinnada in Phrygia. As a means of conciliation and *rapprochement* between opposing standpoints, he actually suggested that the Council should draw up two series of documents, one doctrinal and one pastoral. Thus if this idea, absurd as it may seem, were to be accepted, there would be a series of integralist documents side by side with another, progressive, series. This would be tantamount to saying that the same Council had simultaneously accepted as its own the opposing theses, already found to be irreconcilable, of the two main trends, thus giving rise to a two-headed Council, a synthesis, by juxtaposition, of a Council and an anti-Council, a Church and an anti-Church.

Rome, Sunday, 2 December

Today at mid-day the Pope appeared at his study window. He looked very pale and emaciated, with a strained smile that revealed laborious control of himself, but he did appear. He had been told that the crowd, some tens of thousands, had been standing there in the 'tramontana' wind for two hours, and he would have preferred to appear at once and not wait until the normal hour of the Angelus, mid-day. But he gave in, thinking of all those who would come at the usual mid-day hour and not be able to see him should he appear earlier – for the doctors were inexorable in forbidding him to do so a second time. But so as not to disappoint the people he refused to stand behind the protective glass screen used by Pius XII. And he did not confine himself to blessing them; he spoke to them as well.

The crowd was so astonished at the apparition that for a moment it was struck dumb. Then the applause burst forth. No one felt the cold any more. The Pope was cured. It was like an unexpected Christmas present.

The Pope was cured – up to a point: they had only to look at him to see that (and there were hundreds and hundreds of binoculars there to scrutinize him). But there seemed no doubt that he had won the struggle. It was enough just to hear him speak. His voice, hesitant at first and a little hoarse, quickly became strong, resonant, and sure, with only the slightest occasional wavering. Besides, there were his own words: 'Good health, which for a moment threatened to depart, is about to return, indeed it returns!'

How moving is the tenacity of this indomitable old man whom not even the shadow of death has been able to frighten. He was called a transitional Pope, and instead he has set on foot undertakings that it will take decades to see to the end. A month before the openings of the Council (but the *Acta Apostolicae Sedis* revealed it only around 20 October) he had issued a *motu proprio,* the 'Summi Pontifici Electio', to bring up to date the measures relating to the death of a Pope, the interregnum, and the Conclave. But he did this in order to avoid for himself and his successors any repetition of those macabre and irreverent episodes that had accompanied his predecessor's last hours; not because, like Pius IX, he was afraid that in the event of his death the Council would scorn the privilege of the Sacred College of Cardinals and take unto itself the right to appoint the new Pope. Only superficially did he think about his eventual end before it came.

But during the past days the possibility of death did indeed haunt the apostolic apartment and cast its shadow over the whole world. In the Vatican at certain moments there was even a pre-

Conclave-like atmosphere. Yesterday's *Giornale d'Italia* reported, for example, that according to a Paris paper John XXIII had actually manifested his wish concerning his successor, 'giving the Archbishop of Milan a magnificent ring with an emerald which Pius XII wore only twice during the Holy Year 1950'. 'I am sure,' John XXIII is supposed to have said to Cardinal Montini when giving him this precious ring, 'that you too, at your death, will leave it to the Church.'

I know this episode was being whispered about yesterday evening among the groups of Fathers at the reception which the Diplomatic Corps accredited to the Holy See gave for all the members of the Council at Palazzo Barberini. The story was regarded as an attempt by the conservatives to wreck the chances of their most dangerous opponent.

I believe I was one of the first people to get hold of a large anti-Jewish volume which a clandestine organization is distributing to the Fathers of the Council. Monsignor Bontempi, who since the beginning of the Council has been seeing me less frequently for fear of breaking the reserve imposed by the pledges of secrecy concerning Council affairs, told me about it over the telephone. He said he had read a good deal of it the night before, with extreme distaste, so that he was delighted to get rid of it and hand it over to me.

It is a big book of 618 closely-printed pages called *Complotto contro la Chiesa* (Plot against the Church), with a reproduction below the title on the cover of the upper façade of St Peter's and the Michelangelo cupola, overprinted and blotted out by a triangle in violent red symbolizing the Jewish-Masonic-Communist International.

No publisher is given, and the only indication is the name and address of the Roman firm which printed the volume: a small firm of printers with works near the Vatican, in the Prati district, which is known to work mainly for ecclesiastical organizations. On the title page is the name of the alleged author, Maurice Pinay, but this is probably a pseudonym. Perusal of the text, however, inclines one to think that the author must be a foreigner, faithfully interpreted but literarily badly served by a translation which is often downright vulgar.

The preface bears the date of 31 August 1962: the book must

therefore have been put together in a great hurry and its compilation speeded up after the date of the Council's second session in 1963 was made known, obviously with the intention of getting it out in time to distribute it to all Fathers before they return to their sees.

Nevertheless the work, already massive enough to discourage readers, is not yet complete: a second volume is to follow containing parts V and VI and the reply to the comments and the 'inevitable calumnies' which 'the enemy' will launch against the four parts already published here. The preface also states that the author decided to start on the book in 1961 and that this first volume took him 14 months to write.

A glance at the table of contents suffices to indicate its main ideas: the Jews, the 'synagogue of Satan', are not only 'the secret motive force of Communism' and 'the occult power of Freemasonry' but also even constitute 'the fifth column among the clergy'. This last is undoubtedly a piquant and original idea, and its connection with the Council is obvious. It is already foreshadowed in the Preface, or rather the 'Important appeal to the reader', entitled 'Conspiracy against the Church'. It begins abruptly as follows.

> The most perverse conspiracy is being prepared against the Church. Its enemies are plotting to destroy its most sacred traditions, carrying out reforms as daring and malevolent as those of Calvin, Zwingli, and other great arch-heretics, all on the pretext of *modernizing* the Church and putting it on a par with the times, but nevertheless with the secret purpose of opening the gates to Communism, accelerating the downfall of the free world, and preparing the future destruction of Christianity. Impossible though it may seem, they aim to effect all this in the Second Vatican Council. We have proofs to show that this is what is being plotted in secret by the high powers of Communism and the occult force that controls them.

Despite his zeal the author completely fails to achieve his aim. As far as concerns the first millennium of Christianity his alleged proofs carry no conviction, and proof in relation to modern times is postponed to the second volume.

Rome, Monday, 3 December

The Milan *Italia* today publishes a conspicuous paragraph set in a box on the front page in reply to the *Giornale d'Italia*'s indiscretions of Saturday. Under the heading 'An Imaginary Ring' it comments as follows:

> The quotation is incorrect and completely arbitrary, the information wrong and inexact, and the publicity given to it lacking in respect, in relation to the gift of a pectoral Cross presented, as is not unusual in similar circumstances, by the Pope to Cardinal Montini at the solemn Mass celebrated in St Peter's on 4 November . . . There was no ring, no emerald, no mention of Pius XII, no accompanying words of John XXIII, and above all there is nothing whatever in the flights of imagination with which the newspaper seeks to dramatize the story, completely changed and distorted, of a simple and supreme gesture of the Holy Father's to the Cardinal Archbishop of Milan.

This is a perfectly correct reaction; but if all this enthusiasm in defending the Archbishop had been accompanied by an equal zeal in deploring the irreverent and inaccurate reference to the Pope, might there not perhaps be less malicious gossip about the way in which some people strive to defend their own candidatures?

Today in the Council the lightening of atmosphere produced by the Pope's appearance yesterday persists, if without too great illusions; and the debate on 'De Ecclesia' reflected it by again avoiding anything over-dramatic. Perhaps the main characteristic of this 32nd General Congregation was the Fathers' evident awareness that they had come to the crucial point of the Council's first session. Cardinal Doepfner defined the draft under discussion as 'the centre of the Council's labours', and Monsignor Marty, Archbishop of Rheims, reminded the assembly that it was assuming the responsibility of giving to the world, for the first time in history, a dogmatic constitution for the Church. Monsignor Huyghe, Bishop of Arras, reminded his colleagues that the reply they were preparing to make in the name of the Church to the world's question, 'What have you to say for yourselves?', was the more important because modern means of communication could now make it known in every continent, and 'the Church will be judged, perhaps for centuries, by the documents now being worked out'.

Bishop Huyghe's speech was probably the most thought-provoking in its presentation of the Church's various characteristics.

The picture of the Church that Vatican II must present to the world, he said, should be imbued with the evangelical spirit, *an open-minded and truly Catholic spirit* ('We are no longer living in Christian times. The bishops feel themselves responsible both for believers and for unbelievers ...'), *a missionary spirit* ('the Church is not only a society which defends its own believers from error but also a community open to welcome new members'), and *a spirit of humble dedication and service* ('the Church is not a power which aims to subjugate all nations and peoples to its own rule: there are not two classes in the Church, those who command and those who obey; it is no longer possible to speak of the power of the Church as it was in the Middle Ages').

Naturally, all these bishops have felt how far the draft under discussion is from their own ideas, and they have asked for its re-casting (Doepfner even wants this to be done by means of a mixed Commission resulting from collaboration between the Commission originally responsible and the Commissions for Lay Apostolate and for the Religious, as well as the Secretariat for Christian Union). The Fathers already mentioned were joined in this by Cardinals Gracias and Léger and Bishop Gargitter. But the Press Office's bulletin is quite right in saying that again today the majority (Spellman, Siri, McIntyre, Kominek, Hurley, etc.) defended the draft, while asking for slight alterations or amplifications. Thus it was quite a setback for the latter when, near the end of the Congregation, there burst upon the scene – this is the only way to describe it – *Aquitanensis, Soranus et Pontiscurvi Episcopus*, the Bishop Ordinary of Aquino, Sora, and Pontecorvo, Monsignor Biagio Musto.

This nearly sixty-year-old prelate has ruled over the three dioceses of Lower Latium for ten years, after having already administered them as deputy for another year; before that he was vicar-general of the archdiocese of Benevento. But throughout all that time his name had never been heard outside the region of the Liri river and the surrounding Abruzzese Apennines; and despite his triparte diocese he has care of only some 150,000 souls, divided among a hundred parishes. For these reasons it seemed clear that it was as bishop of the birthplace of St Thomas Aquinas, *theologus princeps Ecclesiae Dei*, that he now rose to speak to convey a somewhat belated greeting to the assembly. So, at least, the foreign bishops thought as they hurriedly turned the pages of the *Annuario*

Pontificio to find out something about their colleague now making his début.

But a few sentences of his speech sufficed to convince them of his remarkably outspoken personality. The speaker, in fact, made up for his lack of theological renown and the small prestige of his three sees by attacking the opponents of the 'De Ecclesia' draft so violently that he managed to rouse even such Fathers as had begun to nod (*tantillum dormitantes*) and precipitated a rush back from the bar by those who had been sipping a soft drink while waiting for the next speaker, the bishop of a diocese in Southern Rhodesia. His theological reasons didn't amount to much; but his strong point was evidently Holy Writ. Against those Fathers who according to him were 'abandoning the truth' he cited the letter of St Paul to Timothy threatening divine vengeance upon all who 'turned their backs on the truth'.

It was at this point that the bishop of a big diocese in the Po Valley turned to his Dutch neighbour with the remark: 'Novissimus ille episcoporum, tamen valde timendus ut jectatorius vir' ('This new bishop seems to be a terrible man of wrath') – a Latin phrase that he probably would not have dared to utter to Cardinal Bacci but which his northern colleague could well appreciate and which enabled him to let off steam.

What, indeed, was the point of being dramatic about something that was merely both pathetic and funny? As the speaker proceeded the smiles and murmurings increased until finally Cardinal Ruffini, chairman for the day, who had for some time been fidgetting and barely disguising his irritation, rang his bell peremptorily and curtly asked the speaker to stick to the point (*ad rem*) and wind up his speech quickly. The daring manipulator of thunderbolts from on high grasped the situation, stammered his excuses, and withdrew.

Rome, Tuesday, 4 December

Monsignor Martinez has told me some more details about yesterday's Congregation. For instance, about Cardinal Léger's speech. This speech at times produced an impressive silence among his listeners, as when the Archbishop of Montreal was heard to say that in order to understand the need for a profound renewal within the Church the Council should not be afraid to live through some dramatic days like those of mid-November, or when he proposed that some organ of the Council should be given the special task of maintaining the attitudes adopted there and stimulating the various Commissions to revise all the drafts in such a way that they would quickly secure the assembly's approval at the second session.

Today Cardinal Suenens returned to the same theme – in which the assembly, now so near the end of its labours, seems to be particularly interested – and asked about the organization and future development of the Council's work. Finally, he said straight out what other speakers so far had ventured to touch on only lightly – that the Council should cease feeling its way forward in obedience to sporadic and short-term impulses, and should instead set its goal clearly before it in order to relate all its means and efforts towards its achievement. Vatican I, Suenens recalled, had as its objective papal primacy; that of Vatican II had been summed up in John XXIII's words, 'Ecclesia lumen gentium'. Hence the need to make 'De Ecclesia' the focal point of all the Council's labours. He then outlined a sort of programme of work, taking the Pope's broadcast message as its basis, and considering the Church first *ad intra*, within itself, and then *ad extra*, in relation to the world and its most urgent problems (respect for the human person and the inviolability of each man's life, social justice, the 'third world', the evangelization of the poor, peace and war, etc.), and finally proposed that to this end a Secretariat for Problems of the Modern World should be set up.

Obviously, after interventions of this kind, speeches, however intelligent and pertinent, which adhered too closely to the draft were bound to be colourless by comparison. Nevertheless those of Frings, Bea, Guerry, and Blanchet (the Rector of the Catholic Institute in Paris – among other things he said the present text put forward a notional rather than realistic theology) had the merit of pointing out the many lacunae of the document, especially in relation to the theology of the episcopate.

Among the supporters of the draft, on the other hand, were Cardinals Godfrey, Bacci, and Browne, and Bishops Seper, Maccari, De Boto, Vairo, and others. Today, however, the communiqué does not say that the majority of the speakers again favoured the draft – though as a matter of fact its defendants probably did outnumber its opponents this morning. But even the Press

Office is obviously beginning to understand that the majority comes not just from the number of speakers in favour of a particular thesis but also from the weightiness of their supporting reasons. Going by a purely quantitative criterion of today's and yesterday's speeches, it could be argued that the conservatives have regained the majority they lost in mid-November. Yet everyone knows the exact opposite is true.

What is beyond doubt and emerges ever more dramatically is that two different and mutually incomprehensible languages are being spoken in the Council. Even more, two mentalities are coming up against each other which are so unlike and so far apart as to prevent any reciprocal penetration or assimilation. It is, in fact, the very idea of the Church itself that divides conservatives and progressives. The conservatives conceive of the Church *per se*, for itself alone, as a supreme reality and ideal to which everything must yield and if necessary be sacrificed, individual and national wellbeing alike, peace no less than war; whereas the progressives conceive of it as *for others*, as an instrument placed by God at the service of humanity, both individuals and peoples.

It is no doubt easy for an outsider to discern something anti-evangelical about the temporalistic and all-pervading conception of the conservatives. Their ideal is in fact realized by adapting the world to the Church rather than by adapting the Church, without of course altering its nature, to the needs of the world; and it is a typically temporalistic and political ideal, whereas that of the progressives is simply evangelical and apostolic. But it must not be forgotten that the first conception is the one more in consonance with the historical development of Christianity, especially from the late Middle Ages onwards, and that, moreover, whether or not with the best intentions, it has been supported and justified by countless theological and spiritual reasons which still retain today an almost magical power of suggestion over many believers and, still more, over many ecclesiastics.

In a word, Padre Serrand was perfectly right when, in an article in *Signes du Temps* of October 1962, speaking of the 'Babel-like difficulty of mutual comprehension in the Church', he said that the most acute point of tension in present-day Catholicism no longer concerned relations between the Church and the world but relations within the Church itself, between believers divided by their different conceptions of it. He described this situation as follows:

> The dramatic division is between those who see the world through the classical forms of theology and devotion, canon law, natural law, and those who see it as it is, in the course of gradual transformation under Providence. Between those who speak the language of encyclicals and pastoral letters, and those who, when they read these documents, no longer clearly recognize the Gospel in them or barely discern the uncertain sound of a trumpet. Between those who believe that the urgent need is to secure possession, by means of indirect power, of some vestige of another power, and those who instead believe that the urgent need lies elsewhere: in revision and re-consolidation before beginning to build anew on the Christian foundations damaged by centuries of slow or violent erosion. The problem for these last is not one that can be answered by the beatification of Pius IX, desired by John XXIII, or of Pius XII, sought by the Spaniards. The real problem for them goes even further back than Boniface VIII, Charlemagne, or Constantine; it is the problem posed in the first question and answer at baptism, in which the Church's rebirth is perpetually fulfilled: 'What do you ask of the Church of God? – Faith'; the problem, in short, posed by the recital of the Lord's Prayer and the Creed.

Rome, Wednesday, 5 December

An example of the complexity of the problems facing the Fathers, to which I referred yesterday, can be seen in a series of questions asked by Cardinal Montini in his 'Letter from the Council' of 18 November, discussing the draft 'De Fontibus':

> Was such a theme necessary? How does it connect up with judgments already delivered by the Council of Trent and Vatican I on this subject? Have we not, in our own times, received authoritative instruction on the subject in the Encyclicals *Pascendi*, of Pius XI, and *Humani Generis*, of Pius XII? And do not all the pontifical documents on biblical studies of recent years, together with those of Leo XIII, suffice to regulate the attitude, whether theoretical or practical, of Catholics in the scriptural field? And are the new trends of study fermenting in the Schools concerned with scriptural matters to be disciplined by dogmatic definitions or by regulations from the Schools themselves? And do the formidable dangers arising out of

certain new methods of scriptural interpretation, and the very curious errors that may lie concealed therein, call for direct and solemn intervention by the Council? Was not all anathema and dogmatic definition excluded? And how can this subject come within the predominantly pastoral programme of the Council recently inaugurated?

This veritable tangle of problems, lucidly perceived and noted here both individually and inter relation to each other, ended by immobilizing the questioner himself and preventing him from taking part, publicly at any rate, in the Council's debates during that historic mid-November week. Today, however, the Archbishop of Milan has for the first time since the beginning of the Council abandoned his reserve. True, the core of his intervention was strictly technical, emphasizing chiefly the personal, indeed intimately vital, relationship existing between Christ and the Church, whence, according to him, the need arises for a less legalistic and more spiritual conception of the Church itself. Even the inadequate treatment of the rôle of the episcopate was apparently regarded by Montini as a failing mainly in the theological sphere. Nevertheless he did reach some practical conclusions which in the end he did not refrain from expressing, though, as may be imagined, he did so with characteristic diplomatic finesse. He said the draft as it stood was inadequate, especially in view of the fact that it was to represent the central theme of Vatican II; and he added that, as Cardinal Suenens had suggested, an overall plan was needed to give a certain, precise, and definite direction to the Council itself.

The adoption of these standpoints by Cardinal Montini was unexpected and caused something of a sensation in the assembly, so that the intervention of the next speaker, Maximos IV Saigh, in itself no less interesting, was rather put in the shade. The Greek-Catholic Patriarch of Antioch also said he regarded the draft under discussion as 'la pièce doctrinale maîtresse du Concile', for Vatican II was called upon to complete the work of Vatican I which had been suspended with the settlement of the question of papal infallibility: Vatican II had to tackle the question of 'l'infallibilité de l'Eglise universelle', especially since the primacy of the Pope was conceivable only within a collegiate episcopal framework. The draft did not contain theological errors but neither did it express the truth in its entirety; and, being incomplete, it falsified the idea of the Church as a whole.

These views, enunciated in the Greek-Melchite Patriarch's brilliant French and animated by a pungent wit, took on a fascination of their own, as for example when he deplored 'l'insistence maladive' in constantly harking back to that truth, pontifical primacy, 'et à l'isoler, comme s'il n'y avait que le Pape', or when he expressed his bitterness about certain 'exagérations flatteuses et intéressées' often used in relation to the Pope, calling him 'God upon earth', 'higher than the prophets' and 'the very angels' and so on.

Among the bishops speaking today notable contributions came from Florit, Archbishop of Florence, and Fiordelli, the bishop made notorious by the episode of the 'concubines of Prato'.[1]

The former, who might be described as the La Pirianized Archbishop, though as a matter of fact his development from conservative to progressive owes less to La Pira than to Cardinal Dalla Costa, to whom he was for a long time assistant, has just sent a very good letter about the Council to his diocese. Today in the Council he called for a better balance in visualizing the Church simultaneously as a mystical reality and a visible society, urging among other things that more regard should be paid to the witness of Eastern Church Fathers on the first point.

The greatest surprise, however, came from Fiordelli, who, since he studied at the Lateran University and has always remained linked with Lateran circles, was thought of as one of the key men of conservative integralism. Ottaviani would have liked him to be a member or at least adviser of one of the Preparatory Commissions, but the answer at the highest level was a definite negative. Fiordelli had given a foretaste of his intentions of bellicose interventionism when he rose to speak, the first of all the Italian bishops to do so, on the occasion of the Fathers' Message to the World. If he has since kept silence, this, so people thought, must be because he was saving himself up for some really spectacular speech at the right moment.

Instead, though adhering to the integralist standpoint, he showed that he wanted above all to be true to himself. The theme he

[1] See above p. 194.

developed this morning was in fact that of the family, its place in the Church, and the importance that should be given to it in the pastoral ministry. According a slightly paradoxical acceptance to his attitude, one might say that as in 1958 he defended the legal position of the family, as formulated in the Code of Canon Law, vis-à-vis the State (the State of course, as it is under the Concordat), so today he went so far as to ask the Church to give greater consideration theologically and pastorally to the institution of the family and, as he insistently repeated, to accord a special place to the family among the other structures defined and distinguished by the Church; the Church should no longer be thought of as divided into three compartments – the universal Church, the diocese, and the parish – but into four, with the addition of the family. Naturally, he added, this should not be done without 'establishing a solid doctrinal foundation to define the relationship between the family and the Church, and the family and the State, and to vindicate certain inalienable rights such as, for example, the Christian education of children'.

Today's General Congregation distinguished itself from all the others by producing fewer interventions – only eight. Nevertheless it was certainly not among the least interesting. Indeed it confirmed the steady improvement in the quality of the Council's debates, which have been at their best this week.

One reason for the small number of speeches today was that a further vote was taken on some amendments proposed to the first chapter of 'De Sacra Liturgia'; another reason was the early closing of the Congregation, to allow the Fathers to join the crowd gathered in Piazza San Pietro to acclaim the Pope, who now seems well on the way to convalescence. I believe the crowd consisted partly of people to whom the Pope was to have granted a general audience had he been completely recovered. It was probably instead of this that John XXIII decided to give a blessing from his window, which gave someone the idea of improvising a special 'tribute of homage' on the part of the Fathers as well. This proved to be a strange tribute which broke all the rules of protocol and ended by mixing up together Cardinals, archbishops and bishops, putting them all at the same remote distance from the 'supreme monarch'. Pope John tried to pass this over with the welcoming words: 'We have a new spectacle today: all the branches of the Church gathered together. Here is the episcopate, here the priesthood, and here the Christian people. The whole family is present here: the family of Christ.' But in point of fact the members of the Sacred College can seldom have felt so ill at ease, conscious of the distance separating them from their head. Obviously this was just a purely physical sensation, but one which expressed in terms that could be felt the measureless distance which the dogma of infallibility has created between each member of the Catholic Church and the Supreme Pontiff.

Rome, Thursday, 6 December

Yesterday evening at the 'Domus Mariae' the 200-odd Brazilian bishops who have been housed there during the Council had a farewell party as if they were already packed up and on the point of departure. The seminarists of the Brazilian College were there too, and even the girls who help in the house. They all sang songs together, bishops, seminarists, *signorine* and all. The solos, however, were reserved for the Père Duval[1] of Brazil, Canon Gerardo Naves, famous in his own country both as a pianist and as a composer of light music, hymns, and even a number of love songs. He must have come to Rome as one of the unofficial experts in the suite of some Bishop, and indeed he is an expert not only in musical matters but also in the cinema, for he has appeared in several films.

The atmosphere of departure, so I hear, is also invading other places where the Fathers have been staying. But the Council, far from packing up, is still showing important signs of activity (it was perhaps just a spirit of perversity that caused today's Press Office communiqué to give a résumé of the whole work of this first session, when they could perfectly well have waited another two days). Today, however, is the last lap, and tomorrow will really see the end. These are among the most exciting moments we have had and, at any rate this morning, expectations were not disappointed.

The debate was dominated by Cardinal Lercaro's speech, the only one from a Cardinal this morning. As many expected, he

[1] Père Aimé Duval, a French Jesuit, became famous after the war as a religious *chansonnier*.

made an impassioned commentary on the definition of the Church given by John XXIII in his broadcast message of 11 September: 'The Church is the Church of all, but today it is more than ever the Church of the poor.' Lercaro showed that this is true in all fields, theological, pastoral, ascetic and disciplinary. The characteristic note of the incarnation, he said, is in fact poverty; but the Church is the projection in time of that mystery, and the poverty of its leader becomes a law for its members. As for the poor, they have been given a new dignity in the Gospel, and today the Church finds itself in a world where two-thirds of the inhabitants are not only poor but starving: its apostolate cannot therefore disregard this tragic fact. Finally, in order to realize its vocation as a Church of the poor, the Church must demonstrate its own poverty in its institutions, manifestations, and individual members. The bishops, many of whom are indeed poor, must be the first to cease shocking the poor by outward display, and the same is true of priests and most of all of monks and nuns who, moreover, are bound by the vow of poverty.

Into a brazier such as this, the interventions that followed fell like straws for the burning – both the controversial speeches of Bishop Compagnone of Anagni and Monsignor Stella of Aquila, who replied point by point to De Smet's triad,[1] and also the calmer if still innately conservative discourses of the Irishman Philbin, of Clonfert, and the Spaniard Hervas, titular Bishop of Ciudad Real.

The chief novelty of the day, however, and a really important one, was Monsignor Felici's communication about the measures decided on by John XXIII to regulate the Council's activity during the interval between the first and second session. During this period the Commissions are to 'provide for the re-examination and re-casting of the drafts, taking into account the work already done'. This was to be foreseen; but how will it be done, and in what spirit? Well, the communiqué expressly refers to and quotes at length the most energetic passages of John XXIII's opening speech in St Peter's on 11 October. It therefore emphazises that a fundamental rule of work for the Commissions should be to concentrate on the solution of general rather than particular problems. Finally, it announces the establishment of a 'Commission to coordinate and direct the work of the Commissions': this super-

[1] See above p. 315.

Commission, which is to be presided over by the Secretary of State – clearly acting as *locum tenens* for the Pope – has the specific task of 'co-ordinating the labours of the Commissions, following their work and discussing with their chairmen not so much on specialist questions but on matters related to ensuring that the drafts are in conformity with the aims of the Council'.

Other details follow concerning the timing of the work. The drafts when recast and approved by the Pope are to be sent to the individual bishops in time for them to be returned to Rome so that they can be further revised on the basis of the bishops' comments by the time the second session opens. But what really matters in this communiqué is that the Council is specifically confronted with the aim assigned to it by John XXIII and has at last taken measures to provide itself with an organ responsible for co-ordinating its labours and preventing them from becoming dispersed or diverted.

Certainly the ideal thing would have been for this to come about as a result of spontaneous agreement in the assembly rather than through an authoritarian intervention by the Pope. During the past days something of this kind has been advocated by many more Fathers than I have mentioned in my notes, and all of undisputed authority. It would have sufficed for their proposals to be adopted by the Presiding Council and submitted for approval to all the Fathers. Unanimity would doubtless not have been reached, but very probably there would have been a two-thirds majority. And after such a vote those contrary to it would no longer have felt obliged to comply from obedience or a simple sense of discipline but would have done so with the conviction that they were acting in the way agreed upon by the majority. But the exercise of authority is clearly an irresistible temptation even for the humblest spirits and those most detached from authoritarianism.

Be that as it may, after this morning's events the running-in period of the Council can be regarded as closed: the Council, which had already found itself again, has now the navigating instruments to enable it to venture on the most perilous seas. One of the Curia exasperatedly remarked to a colleague on 11 October after the Pope's speech, 'But at this rate we shall have to re-do all our drafts!', and that is precisely what is happening. The Council is not beginning all over again from the beginning, but it is setting out afresh with a new sureness, enthusiasm, and conviction.

The Closing Day

Rome, Friday, 7 December

With Achille Liénart, Cardinal Archbishop of Lille, presiding, and with 2,118 Fathers present, Vatican II today closed its first session, which has lasted for 36 General Congregations.

A vote was to be taken on the Preface and the first chapter of the Liturgical draft. Then at midday the Pope in person was expected to be present at the leave-taking. So of the 54 bishops down to speak only ten actually did so; and except for Monsignor de Bazelaire (who stressed the need to revise the complementary concepts of obedience and authority in the Church) and the worker-bishop Monsignor Ancel (who associated himself with Lercaro's intervention, at the same time replying to the conservatives' attacks on that of Monsignor De Smet) the speeches were insignificant. Even the Pope's speech, given after the recital of the Angelus, was rather colourless. But certainly he is saving up the best for the official closing speech he is to make in the Vatican basilica tomorrow.

So, contrary to what might have been expected, there was no spectacular wind-up. Indeed, the close was in a minor key, not to say modest and hurried. On the other hand, after the decisions of yesterday arising out of the Pope's intervention, what more was there to say? Thus the tacit abandonment of the 'De Ecclesia' draft passed almost unobserved. Unlike what happened with all the earlier drafts, no Order of the Day was proposed or voted on about it. Monsignor Felici confined himself to announcing that 'any eventual proposals and amendments which the Fathers may wish to make must reach the Secretariat General of the Council not later than 28 February 1963'. This would seem to mean that the debate is merely suspended. And in a certain sense that is the case. It may be regarded as certain that 'De Ecclesia' will be the draft with which the next session opens – but not, of course, in its present form but as a new draft, revised and co-ordinated with the other drafts which will be discussed at the second session.

I spent the evening at the Bellinis'. Those there were mainly writers, journalists, and artists. At a certain point the conversation drifted towards the Council. Fuschini, of the Communist daily *L'Unità*, began it by firmly and passionately asserting the proletarian aspect of the Council, culminating in Lercaro's speech of yesterday. He also talked about a document which was circulating a week or two ago among the Fathers, called *Jésus, l'Eglise et les Pauvres*, written by Père Gauthier on behalf of some workers of Nazareth. (I saw it a week ago: it amounts to a cautious and indirect but enthusiastic proposal to review the whole question of the worker-priests.)

For Ricci, of the *Tempo*, what Lercaro, Gerlier, Ancel, etc. are advocating is really just a class affair pure and simple: a 'Church of the poor', according to him, is bound to be a class Church, and as such fundamentally anti-Catholic (contrary to the characteristic universality of the Roman Church).

Leaving aside ideological disputes, Monti, a humorous writer who is little known merely because he is so lazy, observed that the Fathers had become increasingly aware of class questions as the Council went on, or rather as their absence from their sees grew longer: their stay in Rome proved more problematical as time went on, not so much from the theological angle, though that produced difficulties, as from the economic point of view as their supplies of currency ran short. He said, and this I know for a fact, that even many American bishops had been forced after some weeks to leave their first-class hotels and put up in religious houses. Shops for the sale of religious mementos and objects of piety, even those in Via della Conciliazione, are known to have been much disappointed latterly about their sales, and so are the vendors of such wares who go round trying to sell to the Fathers in their hotels or lodgings.

The novelist Nobili, who thinks of giving his next book a setting in Rome during the period of the Council and has therefore been investigating in some detail the sort of life the Fathers have been leading, related a whole series of varied episodes he had unearthed: the French bishop who had three suitcases stolen from his car in Florence while on his way to Rome; the madman who rammed several of the best cars belonging to the Fathers as they stood parked by the Bernini colonnade; the amused exasperation of the Irish Fathers because the Council's famous electronic machines regularly took no notice of the apostrophes in their names; the joke played on some bishops particularly addicted to parties, who were decanted by their colleagues on the doorstep of the Soviet Embassy on the evening of 17 October; and many more.

Zolli, an art critic, diverted the conversation from the Council towards his own sphere, talking of Zac's drawings, of the exhibition held in Palazzo Venezia 'in homage to the Council' by some artists living in Rome, and another at the Domus Pacis, in Via di Torre Rossa, of handicrafts to do with liturgical and religious subjects. Risi, a passionate philatelist, was chortling over the incredible number of special issues of stamps brought out in honour of the Council both by the Vatican City State and by other countries, even including Turkey and Ethiopia. Nobili added that numismatics too, both public and private, had also seized on the occasion to produce new series of coins; he thought the best example was of the history of the Church, told in 57 coins minted in the State mint in Vienna. The one-track-minded Fuschini profited by a pause in the conversation to speak of the various religious exhibitions timed to coincide with the Council, including one on the Church, in Via Cristoforo Colombo, and one on the so-called Church of Silence, in Piazza della Pilotta, and this led on to one of his usual outbursts on the distortions perpetrated by anti-Communist propaganda. But at that point everyone arose with one accord – though less to refute his arbitrary insinuations or put an end to an unsatisfactory argument than to propose a move to the buffet.

Rome, Saturday, 8 December

Today's ceremony in St Peter's did nothing to set a solemn seal on yesterday's modest wind-up. Everything was got through quickly in a couple of hours – from the Pontifical Mass at which Cardinal Marella officiated, with Gregorian chants led by the Benedictines of Sant 'Anselmo but sung by all the Fathers together, to the Pope's speech. The Pope himself, whose doctors had allowed him to come to St Peter's only for the very end of the service, arrived almost unnoticed, coming in on foot by a side entrance and appearing on his raised throne without pontifical vestments but wearing simply a red *mozzetta* and stole.

As he finished reading his speech, his voice, till then sure, strong and calm, seemed to break, but by then it was submerged in an outburst of applause. But though impeccable in form there was nothing exceptional about the speech itself. Indeed nothing in particular was expected of it, nor was it needed. The events of the Council's first session speak for themselves.

I will put off till tomorrow any attempt to give a general estimate of the Council's work. Today, instead, I want just to give some practical details and statistics about the main events centring round the drafts.

Looking back over the pages of my diary, I see that I forgot at the time to give the main data concerning the debates on the Means of Social Communication and on Church unity.[1] I will therefore begin with them and also add the data about the debate on 'De Ecclesia'.

Debate on the draft 'De Mediis Communicationis Socialis'

Duration=two and a half Congregations (25th to 27th), from 23 to 26 November.

Number of Speeches=54 (7 Cardinals, 9 Archbishops, 37 Bishops, one Superior of a Religious Order).

Nationality of Fathers who spoke=36 European (10 Spanish, 6 Italian, 4 French, 4 German, 3 Polish, etc.); 8 American (3 USA, 5 Latin American); 5 Asian; 5 African.

Debate on draft 'Ut Unum Sint'

Duration=three and a half Congregations (27th to 30th), from 26 to 30 November.

Number of Speeches=50 (9 Cardinals, 2 Patriarchs, 18 Archbishops, 19 Bishops, 2 Superiors of Religious Orders).

Nationality of Fathers who spoke=24 European and Middle Eastern (5 Italian, 5 Spanish, 5 Syrian, 4 Lebanese, 3 French, etc.); 15 Asian; 7 American (5 USA); 2 African; 2 Australian.

Debate on 'De Ecclesia'

Duration=six Congregations (31st to 36th), from 1 to 7 December.

Number of Speeches=76 (21 Cardinals, of whom three from the Curia), 1 Patriarch, 18 Archbishops, 34 Bishops, and 2 Superiors of Religious Orders.

Nationality of Fathers who spoke=53 European (17 Italian, 11 French, 5 German, 5 Spanish, 4 Polish, 3 United Kingdom, etc.); 8 American (5 USA); 9 Asian; 5 African.

During the whole of the first session, the total number of speeches

[1] For similar data on the Liturgical draft see p. 268 and on 'De Fontibus' see pp. 289-90.

and proposals in writing in the debates on the five drafts discussed was as follows:[1]

Drafts	*Speeches*	*Written Proposals*	*Total*
De Liturgia (Liturgy)	327	360	687
De Fontibus (Sources of Revelation)	103	79	182
De Mediis Communicationis . . . (Means of Social Communication)	54	42	96
Ut Unum Sint (Church Unity)	51	54	105
De Ecclesia (The Church)	76	57	134
	611	592	1,204

The *speakers* as divided by continents were as follows: Europe 222; America 74 (USA 28, Central and South America 46); Asia 59; Africa 26; Oceania 7. Within Europe, division by nationality was as follows: Italy 65, Spain 45, France 34, Germany 15, Poland 14, Yugoslavia 9, Belgium 7, United Kingdom 6, Austria 6, Portugal 6, Holland 4, Ireland 3, etc.

Fathers who spoke only once numbered 244; 78 spoke twice, 39 three times, 15 four times; Ottaviani, Godfrey, Maximos IV, D'Avack, and Garcías Martínez Fidel, five times; Frings, Bacci, and Browne, six times; Spellman, Léger, and Bea, seven times. Ruffini headed the list with 12 speeches.

Attendance varied during the last weeks between 2,200 and 2,100, with a tendency to fall.

The work of the first session occupied 41 days out of a total of 59 covering the entire period from the Council's opening to its close; 36 of these days were occupied by actual General Congregations. During these last, votes taken by ballot numbered 34 (one to elect the members of the Council's Commissions, four to approve the drafts proposed, 29 on amendments to the Preface and first chapter of the Liturgical draft); 7 votes were taken by standing or sitting.

In this first session the Council discussed five drafts, of which one

[1] All the following figures are taken from *Civilità Cattolica*.

('De Fontibus revelationis') was rejected, two were sent back for amendment ('De Mediis . . .' and 'Ut Unum Sint'), one was left in suspense ('De Ecclesia'), and only one, 'De Liturgia', was approved in the amended version, though only as far as the Preface and first chapter were concerned.

At first sight this would seem a disastrous balance-sheet; but the little that has been achieved is not only revolutionary in itself but also contains the seeds of further revolutions.

This is brought out clearly in an article in today's *Osservatore Romano* (the date chosen for publication is significant) on 'General principles of the liturgical reform approved by the Council', by the Benedictine Cipriano Vagaggini, Vice-Rector and Dean of the Faculty of Theology in the Pontifical Academy of Sant' Anselmo and adviser to the Preparatory Commission on the Liturgy. (Another unusual feature about this article is that for the first time in an official publication extracts from the Council's drafts are quoted.) The following are some of the objectives it mentions as having been reached.

(i) *The competent authority to decide on liturgical reforms.* – Henceforth, in addition to the Pope and the Bishop, such reforms can be decided on also by 'a super-diocesan territorial episcopal authority' (an expression used in the new draft, art. 22): in practice, the 'legitimately constituted' competent territorial episcopal assemblies of various kinds (the provincial Council, regional or national episcopal conference, etc.). – According to Vagaggini, this is 'a great novelty because it sanctions the establishment of decentralization in the liturgical field in favour not so much of the individual bishop (which would lead to excessive dividing up) but of a supra-diocesan territorial authority'.

(ii) *Abolition of classes.* – 'In the liturgy, apart from distinction because of liturgical office and from honours due to the civil authorities arising from the liturgical laws, no exception of person or status should be made in ceremonies or outside functions' (art. 32 of the approved draft).

(iii) *Use of the vernacular.* – '1. The use of the Latin language is, except in special circumstances, to be maintained in the Latin rites. 2. But seeing that both in the Mass and in the administration of the Sacraments and other parts of the liturgy the use of the vernacular can be very helpful for people, a greater role is to be conceded to the vernacular, especially in readings, admonitions, and some prayers and canticles, in accordance with the regulations to be described in the following chapters. 3. In relation to the aforesaid regulations, it will be the task of the territorial authorities described in article 22 to establish, if necessary in consultation with the bishops of the neighbouring regions speaking the same language, the method and use of the vernacular, with the reservation that what they decide shall be examined or confirmed by the Apostolic See.' (art. 36.)

(iv) *Adaptation of the liturgy to the legitimate traditions and religious spirit of different nations.* – 'The Church, when no question arises of the faith or of common and general welfare, does not intend to impose rigid uniformity even in the liturgy. On the contrary, it respects and promotes the characteristics and natural gifts of the various races and peoples. It regards with benevolence everything in national customs that is not indissolubly linked with superstition and error, and if it can do so it protects and preserves them; indeed sometimes it permits them in the liturgy itself provided they can be brought into harmony with the true and authentic liturgical spirit' (from the draft; the number of the article is not given). 'This is the first time,' Vagaggini comments, 'that the principle of adaptation, so insistently stressed by the Popes after Benedict xv in the general field of the missions, is explicitly and solemnly extended to the liturgy as well.'

PART III
THE AFTERMATH

Rome, Sunday, 9 December

If I am to try to make some real estimate of the Council's work, I should say that this first session can be considered under two headings: first, the results actually achieved now, and secondly, the pledges advanced as to the arrangement of work in the future.

The results achieved are clearly not confined to those covered by the drafts approved, or in most cases not yet approved, about which I wrote yesterday. The chief success of this first session, as far as the work itself is concerned, is first to have established the focal point of the Council: the ecclesiological draft, and then to have settled upon the general angle from which every particular problem whether theoretical or practical is to be tackled, namely, the angle of pastoral mission combined with effort for union. In particular, the success achieved in polarizing around 'De Ecclesia' the whole disparate encyclopaedia of 69 drafts, prepared without any sense of orientation or inter-connection by the Preparatory Commissions and Secretariats, has furthered both the thinning-out of these drafts themselves and the organic unity of the new synthesis which the parts not discarded will assume.

This is by no means a small result, even though there can be no doubt that this kind of work should have been at least prepared, if not completed, during the pre-Council stage. The foremost concern of the Central Preparatory Commission should have been to fix the aim of the ecumenical assembly and group the various drafts round it; or, better still, it should have worked out a number of different organic plans of work and then let the Fathers, at a preliminary stage of the Council itself, choose whichever seemed most suitable. But since that was not done, it is extremely important that the Council has not allowed itself to be submerged by the shifting sands of the plethoric 69 drafts.

Granted this, it is not too rash to feel a certain optimism about the future of the Council's labours. Much will naturally depend on how much is done in the coming nine-months' interval, especially by the so-called Super-Commission or Co-ordinating Commission. Unfortunately we know by now what the Council's Commissions are like (with mainly reactionary chairmen and several influential members of the Curia in their ranks); but an effectively-functioning Super-Commission can, if it has the will and the means, help to overcome many obstacles. In any case, even if the machinery does not work perfectly, the Council assembly can make up for omissions and imperfections. The Commissions, whether individually or integrated under the Super-Commission, do not by any means constitute that 'miniature' or 'shadow' Council of which the phrase-makers like to speak with such conviction. The sole deliberative body remains the Ecumenical Assembly.

The real question is what the Assembly will look like nine months hence. The time factor might have a good many surprises in store between now and September 1963 – among them, in the international sphere, the possibility that East-West relations might again become more strained; and within the Church, possible alterations among its leading personnel. Many of the outstanding figures at the session just ended – Liénart, Bea, Maximos IV – are men of over eighty: shall we see them again in their places nine months hence? But, above all, nine months hence will it still be Pope John who holds the helm of the Church? And even excluding the idea that any possible successor might abandon the whole undertaking of the Council, with what kind of spirit and method would he approach it?

In a quite long interval such as that agreed on (an interval certainly needed for the work of re-arrangement required in order to make up for the time lost owing to the haste and disorganization of the preparatory period) changes may easily come about in the relations between the present majority and minority. It is obvious, for instance, that if the approaches between the Holy See and the Communist world proceed favourably, the progressive trend will benefit, whereas a setback would be to the advantage of the conservatives.

But whatever may happen in the future, for the time being Vatican II has profoundly changed the whole atmosphere both within the Church and outside it. As Pastor Ronca said to me yesterday, a new type of Catholicism is emerging from the Ecumenical Council, or rather (he was speaking mainly of Italy) a type of Catholicism such as has hitherto been practically unheard-of in Italy, and which, though it may have emerged rather too quickly, seems destined to have the future on its side and to replace sooner or later that authoritarian Catholicism, born of the Counter-Reformation, which after four hundred years of domination seems to be in a spiritual if not numerical minority. This new Catholicism is determined to abandon the arrogant and exclusive attitudes of the past, and to put an end to that centuries-long spiritual conservatism which had gradually relegated the Church to being towed along in the wake of history, even isolating it from the evolution of the other faiths, whether Christian or non-Christian. It is a Catholicism which opposes, if for the time being cautiously, every form of dogmatic rigidity, and is even prepared to re-think, integrate, and reform its own theology in a missionary and ecumenical direction, bringing up to date its subject-matter and conceptual apparatus.

It is true that, as my friend Ronca fears, this substitution of a new Catholicism for the old may be less the result of an internal conversion within the Church than of the needs of the times, needs which the Church must accept if it is to avoid coming to an inevitable end. In his view, this new form is in any case no less Catholic than its predecessor, indeed it is even more so in the sense that in it some typical components of the Catholic phenomenon are brought out more clearly – such as, on the one hand, its prodigious capacity to absorb and integrate within its framework all the religious and historical values of the Christian and non-Christian worlds; and, on the other hand, that universalist ambition which the Catholic Church had to renounce with the advent of the modern era, and which is now very clearly reviving within it. But what counts, for the present, is the fact that this new climate has been created.

And the new climate is not only internal but extends also to the outer world. No Council has ever before been presented in this way as a dialogue between the Church and the world. By comparison with the other Councils, and especially with Vatican I, this is its most typical feature. In all the other Councils there was lacking any such awareness of relationships with a world other than the world of the Church. Even the Councils of the past which undertook intervention in political affairs (such as the first Lateran Council, which was concerned with the question of investiture and the ratification of the Concordat of Worms, or the first Council of Lyons, which deposed Frederick II) were in fact merely taking measures of an internal character, for the civil society with which they were dealing was not a secular society different in nature from their own but a society that was Christian and therefore redeemed and made supernatural; or, at most, there was beyond their borders the barbarian and satanic world of heresy to be anathematized and subjugated.

The present Council is, by contrast, a Council open to outside factors which has abandoned the old traditional historical positions, bound as they were to an absolutist and theocratic conception and practice, and has put in their place a realism which implies, first and foremost, an objective recognition of the autonomy of natural, civil, and religious values, each placed on its own level and in its own sphere. How this has come about is an extremely interesting historical question, but one which need not be answered in order to realize the fact itself. And the fact is incontrovertible. It has, moreover, already been given official consecration in two documents of great importance which have a binding force in relation to the practical conclusions of the Council: the Pope's broadcast Message of 11 September, and the Fathers' Message to the World. Throughout the whole course of the debates, the appeal to the relationship with the world, and the interest in the world's fundamental needs, have been continually present, culminating a few days ago in Cardinal Suenens' proposal for a Secretariat devoted to problems of the modern world.

This is the more impressive when one reflects that the 69 drafts drawn up at the preparatory stage had methodically omitted all such 'profane' material which, according to the Curia representatives, would alter the strictly ecclesiastical character of the Council's debates. A Council is not an assembly of the United Nations, they would say in reply to those bishops who insistently demanded that the outstanding problems of humanity should be dealt with there (from, of course, the specific angle of pastoral theology). For this reason the character of Vatican II, if it remains faithful to the premises established in the first session, will be not introvert but magnificently extrovert.

The most important aspect of the dialogue as so far established concerns union. True, it is not as yet a direct dialogue, and in some instances it is tolerated rather than desired (a good many Fathers did not like the idea of the Church being compelled, so to speak, to wash its dirty linen under the very eyes of the schismatics). It is, therefore, a dialogue *sui generis*, consisting of an awareness of the other side's existence rather than an actual exchange of words and ideas. But, in any case, it is going on. Dom E. Beauduin told Monsignor Martinez of the half-bitter-half-ironical but very acute remark of a Spanish bishop: 'There are only two ways to influence the direction the Council will take: you have to be either a Cardinal or an observer.' The observers' silence, incidentally, has applied only to their presences in the Council Hall. Outside it, not only has the Secretariat for Christian Union maintained regular contact with them, as for instance through the Tuesday meetings at the Hotel Columbus, but the Fathers and theologians were also constantly entertaining them and arranging to meet them.

These two dialogues with the secular world in general – the one with the world of politics, science, and technology, and the other with Christians of different religious denominations – have not so far produced any sensational results, but in spite of this the interest shown in the Council has been impressive: resistance has been confined to a part of the Communist world, for the other part of it has considerably improved its relations with Rome by sending both Catholic delegations and observers from the Moscow Patriarchate. But in any case the important fact is to have made a beginning, and a confidence-inspiring beginning.

Rome, Tuesday, 11 December

The Fathers already began moving off the night before last. Yesterday at the canonization of the three new Saints (Eymard, Pucci, and Francesco da Camporosso) at least two hundred of them were absent from St Peter's. And now the hotels where they have been staying are resuming their normal appearance, and the religious houses are reverting to their usual placid conventual atmosphere.

Not all the Fathers, however, are returning direct to their

countries and dioceses. Several will stay on for a while in Rome or in Italy (where they will visit sanctuaries or religious houses or the seats of dioceses with whose bishops they have become friendly during the Council). Others, like a group of sixteen Latin American prelates who have been invited by the German episcopate, will cross the Alps for a stay in Germany, to visit in particular some of the charitable and social organizations there. Others are going to France for similar reasons.

Lastly, 150 Fathers from thirty countries have accepted the Israeli Government's invitation and left by plane for Israel last night and this morning. Evidently the warnings against the 'Plot against the Church' have had little effect.

This seems the suitable moment now that they are all dispersing to give some estimate of the activities of the most important groups. The data about their participation in the Council's work, which I gave on Saturday, may provide a starting-point.

Those statistics of course confirm that the largest role was played by the episcopates from the old continent of Europe which, besides producing more than twice as many speakers as any of the others, was responsible for three times as many interventions. But they also show that America, Asia, Africa, and Australia, which hardly appeared at all at Vatican I, have given dynamic proof of their presence in this first session, especially in the debates on practical matters (on the drafts on the Liturgy and the Means of Communication).

The *US Episcopate* did not come up to the more optimistic expectations. At Vatican I there were only 45 bishops from the United States, and they represented not only missionary areas dependent on the Propaganda Fide but also a tremendously scattered population (30 of the present States had not yet been admitted to union) which included under six million Catholics. In the words of a contemporary writer, 'the Bishop of Chicago does not represent a Catholic Chicago any more than the Bishop of Babylon represents a Catholic Babylon'. At the present Council there were 250 United States bishops with 43 million Catholics behind them, representing the largest Church in the world and certainly the wealthiest: in fact, it provides almost all (actually nine-tenths) of the finances of the Propaganda Fide, the central Curia, and many other Churches, including those of Latin America. Yet only some thirty United States bishops spoke at the Council. This is significant enough in itself, but much more serious is the fact that no really outstanding personality emerged among them.

In this the Church of the United States was outdone by the *Canadian Church*, which by comparison shone at the Council. The Archbishop of Montreal, Cardinal Léger, abundantly fulfilled the hopes aroused during the Council's preparatory stages, putting up a fight conducted with great enthusiasm and generosity in the ranks of the progressives. On the practical rather than the ideological side he could count on American support from the Archbishop of Boston; but Cardinal Cushing left Rome after the first three weeks, for the reasons I mentioned at the time. However, his colleagues Cardinals Ritter and Mayer, Archbishops respectively of Saint Louis and Chicago, backed him consistently, demonstrating that the trend he represented was stronger than had been thought.

The episcopate of *Latin America* proved a real revelation, and the experience it has gained over the past fifteen years in CELAM has clearly given it a great impetus. All told it sent some 600 Fathers, or more than a quarter of the whole assembly, to the Council, about 200 of them being from Brazil. If, as was originally thought, they had represented a monolithic group of conservatives, they could have blocked any initiative on the part of the progressives merely by joining up with the 400-odd Italian bishops, the 200 Spaniards, and the Curial contingent. That this did not happen arises from the fact that any such bloc was a figment of the imagination. This had indeed already been suspected from statements made before the Council opened by some of the Latin American representatives such as, for example, Cardinal Silva Enríquez, Archbishop of Santiago, the Peruvian Monsignor Dammert Bellido, assistant to the Archbishop of Lima, and the Mexican Monsignor Méndez, Bishop of Cuernavaca. But it was confirmed from the outset of the Liturgical debate: there the Latin American bishops spoke frequently, not only individually but as a collective body, in support of daring or thoroughly revolutionary forms of modernization.

But perhaps the most surprising thing about the Latin American Fathers was their activity outside the Council: they had a positive network of relationships with the other episcopates, as well as holding frequent meetings among themselves on a national or continental basis. The Liturgical Commission appears to have accepted the proposal of an Argentinian bishop, Monsignor Kemerer of Posadas, for a 'Sunday Service', a service instead of the Mass which could be carried out by laymen in the absence of priests. At the penultimate General Congregation everyone was astonished by the daring intervention of Monsignor Méndez of Cuernavaca concerning relations with the Jews and Freemasonry: *à propos* of the former he denounced the unconscious anti-semitism widespread among many Catholics, and of the latter he said that there were many non-Catholic Christians among them who undoubtedly had influence within their Society. It was therefore wrong, he argued, to continue making Freemasons the object of recriminations, especially since it was now well known that the origins of Freemasonry were anything but anti-Christian, and that various Masonic trends were definitely in favour of a reconciliation with the Church.

There is little to add to what I have said during the past weeks about the active and significant presence of the episcopate of Black *Africa*, which has been one of the great new features of Vatican II. I forgot to say at the time that the Pan-African Secretariat set up ten Commissions, as many as those of the Council itself, to examine from the angle of African needs the various problems likely to come up for debate in the Council.

The *Asian* episcopate showed considerable activity (superior at least in quantity of output to that of the Africans, as was to be expected from their long-standing traditions), but it would of course have counted for a good deal more if China and the adjacent countries had not been isolated from Rome by Communism.

Among the *European episcopates* everything went much as had been expected. For that reason a retrospective comparison with Vatican I may be of interest in this respect. Unlike the Latin-Mediterranean bloc (Italy, Spain, and Portugal, though the last of these was at that time much more liberally inclined) and the Churches of Britain and Ireland, which still occupy much the same conservative (and pro-Curial) position which they did then, the trans-

Alpine European episcopates reveal some interesting changes. At Vatican I, for example, the spearhead of opposition undoubtedly came from the Churches under the Austro-Hungarian Empire, naturally supported by the German Church. The Fathers who proved the most intransigent in opposing infallibility were in fact the Archbishop of Vienna (Raucher), the Archbishop of Kalocsa, in Hungary (Haynold), the Archbishop of Prague (Monsignor Schwarzenberg), and, most important of all, the Archbishop of Diakovar, Monsignor Strossmayer. Slightly in the shade behind them came the German Bishops of Rottenburg (Monsignor Hefele, the well-known historian, later Cardinal) and Mainz (Monsignor Ketteler, a sociologist). The most memorable battles of the Council were fought by these prelates who were, moreover, especially the Hungarian Archbishop, great Latinists and brilliant and persuasive orators, since they had every opportunity to gain experience in parliamentary debate in the Diet of the Empire.

Today the situation is greatly changed. For one thing, Hungary and Czechoslovakia are virtually silent and Yugoslavia has produced no outstanding personality (though its episcopate was present in full force and played an active part in the Council). Austria was represented by a young and learned Cardinal (author, among other works, of an Encyclopaedia of Religions), the Archbishop of Vienna, Franz Koenig, known as the patron of progressive theologians such as Karl Rahner and Hans Küng. As Primate of Austria, Cardinal Koenig is also patron of the University of Innsbruck, run by the Jesuits, the cradle before the Second World War of kerygmatic theology (concerned with preaching), forerunner of the 'new theology' – the University which gave the Council such theologians as the Rahner brothers and the liturgist J. A. Jungmann. But despite his personality and the school under his protection, there can be no doubt that the German Church today carries greater weight than the Austrian, both because it is represented by two Cardinals (Frings and Doepfner) and includes in its episcopate such men as Monsignor Spülbeck of Meissen, Monsignor Jäger of Paderborn, and Monsignor Kempf of Limburg, and also because it can summon a body of theologians and experts including such celebrities as Adam, Guardini, Schmauss, Tilmann, Jedin, Hirschmann, and others.

Elsewhere in Western Europe, too, the situation is very different from the days of Vatican I. In France in 1869–70 the anti-infallibility ranks were led by the Archbishop of Paris, Darbois (of whom Pomponio Leto wrote in lapidary style in his *Otto anni a Roma durante il Concilio* – 'Eight years in Rome at the time of the Council' – that 'he only had to hold out his hand for the Cardinal's hat: he preferred the simple satisfaction of doing his duty'), the Bishop of Orléans, Monsignor Dupanloup, and the Bishop of Sura, Monsignor Maret, but they did not represent a majority in the country; and in Belgium, the Primate himself, Cardinal Deschamps, Archbishop of Malines, led the trend in favour of infallibility (even to the point of suggesting the excommunication of those against it in order forcibly to rid the Council of opposition). As for Holland, the same Pomponio Leto marvelled how 'a classic country of Protestantism and positivism could fill – in proportion, naturally, to its small Catholic population – the Roman State with zouaves and the Council with infallibilists'.

The episcopates of Ireland and Britain have remained, as I said, much as they were a hundred years ago. This is the more surprising since in the present century Ireland, with its constant flow of emigrants, has contributed very largely to swell the forces of Catholicism in Britain, the United States, and Australia. Despite this, however, except for the exuberant personal contribution of Cardinal Browne, the voice of Ireland has hardly been heard in the Council, and when heard it was only to support the Curia's proposals.

To Vatican I, the English Catholic community of the day (at that time numbering barely a million, of whom a considerable proportion were Irish) sent no less a figure than the leader of the infallibilist majority in the person of its Primate, the Archbishop of Westminster, Cardinal Manning. Manning had been converted to Catholicism twenty years earlier, when he was Archdeacon of Chichester and a coming man in the Church of England. It was said of him that he 'fell in love with authority as a slave becomes drunk with freedom'. This may be an exaggeration; but there is no doubt that his position, and not on papal infallibility alone, was very far from that of Newman, his future fellow-Cardinal. It will suffice to recall what the English Catholic Church owed to Pius IX – who in 1850 boldly restored the hierarchy, establishing a metropolitan see and twelve suffragan bishoprics where previously there had been merely apostolic vicariates – to explain Manning's realism.

His present successor, Cardinal Godfrey,[1] did not stand out at the Council among the leaders of the conservative trend with which he was associated – consistently following in that alignment the tradition of his predecessors and his own personal close links with Rome especially during the period of his Rectorate of the English College there (he was one of the 14 signatories of the letter of 24 November to John XXIII). But he did nevertheless take a quite active part in the debates. In Italy (where Anglican bishops are often mistaken for Catholic bishops and *vice versa*) his name appeared in the newspapers in 1961 on the occasion of his Lenten Pastoral, when he urged people to spend less on their dogs' titbits and shampoos and give more to the starving ('They would trot along much better on a simpler régime', he wrote). The Archbishop of Liverpool, Monsignor Heenan, is little known in Italy but prominent in the Catholic world for his efforts in favour of union. But the surprise of the English team at the Council was Dom Butler, Abbot General of the Benedictines in England, who not only spoke several times on the various drafts but nearly always adopted a progressive standpoint. To him fell the honour of being the last Father to speak at this first session.

Unfortunately I did not follow in detail the attitude of the *Spanish and Portuguese bishops*. At the beginning they were threatened with isolation, not to say ostracism; then they were given encouragement by the Pope, and afterwards did everything they could to establish good relationships with the other episcopates. In the Council Hall, at any rate, they were among both the most loquacious and, usually, the most retrograde, being second only in both respects to the Italians.

To form an adequate idea of the *Italian episcopate's* loquacity, mere statistical data will not suffice: the numerous bishops who took their stand on the speaker's tribune must also be passed in careful review. For the most part they not only lacked the necessary doctrinal competence but did not even represent a see of any importance. For example, Monsignor Ruotolo, Bishop of Ugento in the province of Lecce, in Apulia, has a diocese of 33 parishes and 90,000 inhabitants, and Monsignor Costantini, Bishop of Sessa

[1] Cardinal Godfrey died in January 1963. His successor, Archbishop Heenan, was appointed in September 1963.

Aurunca, in Campania, has 42 parishes with 60,000 inhabitants; yet they both spoke three times. Several bishops, moreover, had not even had much pastoral experience, having been appointed – like Monsignor Vairo and Monsignor Costantini – within the last few months.

The majority of them were obviously drawn into debate by the leaders of the Curia just in order to make a showing and block interventions from the opposite side. Without special support it is, in fact, quite difficult to intervene in the General Congregations. It is not enough for a would-be speaker to raise his hand and ask the chairman's permission to speak. He must submit his request in writing at least three days before to the Presiding Council, accompanying it with a résumé of what he proposes to say (and he must stick to it, or explain his reasons). But that is not all. The résumé has to be examined by one of the five under-secretaries of the General Secretariat (in practice, by Monsignor Morcillo, Archbishop of Saragossa) who compares it with the other applications he has received; and if he finds similarities he asks supporters of the same proposal to decide among themselves which of them shall speak in the name of them all. But in any case it was taken for granted from the outset that there would be more speeches from Italian bishops than from any others and that their views would conform with those of the Curia. The unexpected miracle was that they ever combined together to form a proper episcopal conference. The miracle, however, like the poet's rose, lasted only for the space of a morning. On 29 October, after the second plenary meeting, a communiqué announced that such meetings would continue to be held weekly on Tuesdays from 6 November. But on 6 November there wasn't one, nor ever after.

The reasons for this were never given, but there can be no doubt that really they boil down to one alone: the progressives' resistance to letting themselves be manoeuvred by the conservative leaders in the assembly. At Vatican I, the anti-infallibility bishops numbered around 20 out of 300. This time the progressives' numbers were certainly larger, but it would be rash to hazard a figure: possibly behind their main exponents, Lercaro, Montini, Florit, D'Avack Guano, Gargitter, etc., there may have been some 70 or 80 bishops.

About the Uniate Fathers I have nothing to add to what I have already said at various stages in this diary. I would like, however, to tell a story about their participation in Vatican I, which was a very different affair from their participation today. At that time the Holy See could count on the absolute loyalty of two particular Uniate Patriarchs: Monsignor Valerga, Latin Patriarch of Jerusalem, who incidentally had formerly belonged to the Curia, and Monsignor Hassoun, the Armenian Patriarch. The Maximos IV Saigh of the day was, instead, the Chaldaean Patriarch, who because of this situation had a very troubled stay in Rome. But Monsignor Hassoun's flirtations with the Curia displeased his far-off subjects at home and they created disturbances and even began to threaten schisms. The Vicar General of the Armenian bishopric of Diarpekir ventured to act as spokesman in Rome for his fellow-countrymen's aspirations, attacking Monsignor Hassoun and the Patriarch Valerga both in writing and by word of mouth and accusing them of having stirred up all the difficulties with which the Chaldaean Patriarchate was contending.

When Pius IX heard about this, he told the daring Vicar General to withdraw for some time to a religious house for spiritual exercises. But the latter, with the approval of his bishop, took no notice of the order, with the result that a decree was issued for his arrest. The Armenian prelate was in the street when he was suddenly surrounded by pontifical *gendarmes*, and as he put up a lively resistance the affair, far from going unobserved, created quite a sensation. The Turkish Minister, who lived in Florence, came at once to Rome to take the unfortunate prelate under his protection as well as any others with him who might be in danger of being treated in the same way, since they were all citizens of the Ottoman Empire. In fact, it came to pass that, in the very midst of the Council, Catholic ecclesiastics threatened by the Vicar of Christ owed their freedom to the Turk.

Rome, Wednesday, 12 December

Yesterday when I made some sort of balance-sheet of the various episcopates' activities during the Council session just ended, I mentioned only a few of their leaders by name. But those who really count most are the four who have emerged as outstanding personalities and leaders at the Council: on the progressive side, Liénart, Bea, and Maximos IV Saigh, and on the conservative side Ottaviani.

Liénart represented and symbolized mainly the pastoral role upheld by the *avant-garde* episcopates (led, in their turn, by such personalities as Frings, Koenig, Alfrink, Suenens, and Lercaro), while Bea and Maximos IV stood for the unionist aims of the assembly (Bea in relation chiefly to the Protestants, the Greek-Melchite to the Orthodox). Lastly, the Secretary of the Holy Office stood out, both personally and because of his official position, as the ever-bellicose but still unbeaten champion of Curial conservatism.

Naturally, only after a lapse of time will history be able to allocate praise and blame in their right proportions and to rectify the inevitable inaccuracies and lacunae of a day-by-day chronicle. But I think it will be difficult to substitute other names in place of the four who have driven (one of them most unwillingly) the chariot of the Council during the first stage of its course. At the most, the name of some *éminence grise* might be added who held all the threads behind the scenes, perhaps influencing in turn those who appeared as the main protagonists.

What can be done now, however, anyway up to a point, is to put in their true light the great unknowns of the Council – the theologians and experts in general, both official and unofficial (it often happened, in fact, that an official theologian was at the same time attached as theologian to some bishop, as for instance Père Congar with the Bishop of Strasbourg). This is not an easy matter to disentangle, but it is important to do so. As a matter of fact many well-known bishops and often even whole episcopates were merely testifying to and defending in public the theses suggested to them by their private mentors, the theologians. Whether one likes it or not, the bishops often played the part of actors and the theologians that of prompters, indeed of authors of texts and prompters at one and the same time.

Till now, however, not even approximate data have been produced about these significant figures, either in general or country by country. The best known teams of experts were the French and German, but even their composition is not certain. The largest group of experts seems to have been that of the United States, but not much is known about their specific qualifications (and possibly for that reason people were sceptical about them). The Spaniards also had quite a solid team of experts, said to number about forty including theologians and experts in canon law, biblical studies and the liturgy, led, it seems, by the Jesuit Father Salaverri, lecturer at the University of Comillas and an adviser to the Theological Preparatory Commission. The French team was about twice as large but had no leader, partly because of the difficulty in singling out any particular one among such men as Congar, Chenu, De Lubac, or Daniélou. There were of course dozens of other teams of experts, but the other outstanding one was that of the Germans, numbering over fifty; here it was easier to point to the leaders, the outstanding 'emeritus' figures being Adam and Guardini, while the leader for all practical purposes was Karl Rahner.

It is not easy to talk about theologians, and this is doubtless the main reason for the press's silence about them. Most of them are monks who in the past have let time go by, living in their monasteries and devoting themselves to study, teaching and writing – monotonous lives shorn of outside interest, for the life-history of most of these men begins and ends with their own works which, for the ordinary reader, are virtually closed books. It happens only rarely that the *Who's Who* particulars about a theologian can be given even in as much detail as, for instance, those of Père Daniélou – son of a Minister of the Third Republic, studied at the Ecole Normale Supérieure in Paris, mother founded a religious cultural society. At most only a few details can be given about some of the others, as for De Lubac, who fought in the First World War and got a head-wound, or Rahner, who was a follower of Heidegger and lost his teaching post under the Nazis, or Père Chanu, one of whose books has been put on the Index.

Yet these are men, almost featureless as far as their personal lives are concerned, whom the Council has of a sudden transformed from university professors to be the mentors of the episcopate. Almost every evening, for example, anyone entering the Cultural Centre of San Luigi dei Francesi would have found one of them speaking to dozens of bishops, all absorbed in taking notes and demanding explanations perfectly regardless of their own prestige. The same scene was repeated, perhaps a little less informally, in practically all the main centres where the Fathers were staying. When not occupied in giving lectures of this kind the experts sat at the same table as the bishops discussing with them the most difficult points in the drafts and suggesting suitable criticisms. At the most intensive periods of work they were even more inaccessible than the Fathers. During the General Congregations they usually stayed outside the hall; but the words that resounded in

St Peter's, though not pronounced by them, were precisely the same words that they had suggested in conversation or even provided in draft.

The great majority of the theologians were either Jesuits or Dominicans, and it was interesting to observe how the stamp of their Order predominated over everything else, their country of origin included. A Jesuit or a Dominican is first and foremost a Jesuit or Dominican and only afterwards an Italian, Frenchman, or German. And a Jesuit is always self-possessed, aristocratic, measured, controlled, a Dominican relaxed, impulsive, close to the people.

One evening last week I went to the Agostiniana, in Piazza del Popolo, to hear Henri De Lubac talk about 'The scientific and religious interest of Theilard de Chardin'. Last June the Holy Office had criticized his book about his famous *confrère*. Now (he said) in obedience to his superiors he had come back to talk about it and defend it. In front of him, isolated from the public, there sat taking notes with the air of a kindly judge the Pope's Sacristan, Monsignor Van Lierde, titular bishop of Porfireone. At the end of the lecture (which was actually rather thin, but the poet Padre Turaldo, who was sitting near me, told his friends that De Lubac was absolutely worn out with his work at the Council) the papal Sacristan raised some polite objections, remarked extremely courteously that he was not wholly convinced by the replies, and departed beaming with his precious notes in his pocket.

The theologians most neglected by the press were, I think, the Italians, whether official or otherwise. Indeed no one took any interest whatever in the private ones. But, Siri and Ruffini apart, who are both walking encyclopaedias and probably had no recourse to anyone else, it is impossible to think of Montini or Lercaro without seeing them surrounded by a little court of experts. Montini in fact had with him Carlo Colombo, the greatest living Italian theologian even if he does not produce much, and Monsignor Grazioso Ceriani, formerly a neo-Scholastic philosopher, then a theologian concerned with the doctrine of the mystical body, and now firmly anchored, for good, it would seem, in pastoral theology; and he also had, of course, his auxiliary bishops – Oldani for canon law and Giovanni Colombo for the department of studies and seminaries – and his liturgists Moneta-Caglio and Cattaneo, and others. As for Lercaro, I heard only yesterday that he was regularly assisted throughout the whole session by Don Dossetti, though also of course by others from the Bologna Documentation Centre as well, by Padre Toldo, director of the Sociological Statistical Centre in his diocese, and so on.

Rome, Thursday, 13 December

Yesterday I described the experts as prompters and behind-the-scenes personalities at the Council. But there is another aspect of the Council that I have not seen analysed anywhere or even touched on by the hundreds of reporters who flocked to Rome for it. This is the fact that it has served as a meeting-ground and cross-roads for people of all kinds of different trends who have converged on Rome, some to find out what goes on at the Council, others to try to influence it; some whose aims are highly irregular, others purely religious; some to propose reforms, others to ward them off; some (under the pretext of ecclesiastical interests) as shadow men and informers of the most diverse organizations, other for political ends.

In October, for example, Abbé Boulier, a 'red priest' or nearly so, like Canon Kir, spent two weeks in Rome. An ex-Jesuit before the Second World War, then *curé* in the principality of Monaco during the war, and finally in Paris after the peace, he was for a long time a lecturer in international law at the Catholic Institute there. This did not prevent his being simultaneously drawn into the 'Peace Movement', which he supported, eventually becoming one of its most influential leaders in France. Rome naturally intervened, first to admonish him, then to request his resignation under pain of sanction; he yielded, but probably continued to support the movement secretly. In any case in 1961 it was rumoured that he had given a lecture in Hungary and, immediately afterwards, that Ottaviani had struck at him and reduced him to lay status.

Boulier is a most upright priest of very wide culture and a formidable orator. But during the fortnight he was in Rome what he said was strictly of a private nature. The same was true of Wyszynski's 'Satan', Piasecki, founder and president of the 'Pax' movement in Poland, in Rome in the last days of November and December. It was, of course, Dr Silvani who told me of his visit, unfortunately only after he had left. He could not tell me exactly what was the object of Piasecki's journey and his stay in Rome; but probably there is no great mystery about it. Given the pre-Concordat atmosphere prevailing in his country, it is obvious that his Catholic progressive association once again runs the risk of becoming a bargaining-counter for the government. For this reason he may have come to Rome to try to persuade the Vatican leaders that the suppression of 'Pax', which Wyszynski ardently desires, in the event of an inevitable turn of the screw from the régime would mean quite simply the end of any possible alternative of survival or reconstitution for the Polish Church.

Silvani, who has no sympathy for the Polish Mephistopheles-theologian, as he calls him, is sure that Piasecki has secured nothing from the Secretariat of State and that all his efforts have therefore been directed towards sabotaging an eventual Concordat. Piasecki's meetings with various personalities from the Secretariat of State, Dell' Acqua among them, are said to have taken place in a villa at Fregene belonging to Count Gabrinski's family, who are great friends of his.

Rome, Sunday, 16 December

Lunch with Monsignor Martinez at a village in the Agro Romano where the prelate goes to 'carry on the apostolate' every Sunday morning. From today he has as assistant a priest who during the Council was one of the 42 official stenographers of the assembly. I took them both to a quiet and little-known *trattoria* not far from their chapel.

Don José Galvez, the stenographer in question, is a thin 25-year-old Argentinian with coal-black eyes and hair and a dark complexion. Main characteristics – physiological: long hair, and hair in improbable places on his body; psychological: sudden unexpected nervous jerks alternating with long periods of a most attractive gentle and calm serenity. Perhaps these are the two transitory sides of a man – or rather a diplomat – in the process of formation, for next October Don José is to enter the Academy of Ecclesiastics in Piazza della Minerva, where would-be diplomats go to be trained.

In conversation, too, he was sometimes impetuous and inclined to confidences, sometimes reticent and almost taciturn. The truth is I didn't get much out of him, except for a list of the regulation phrases in daily use in the Council Hall ('Audiant omnes', 'loquatur dominus . . .', 'Accedat ad microphonium . . .') and of some of the most notorious slips of the tongue made in the course of its labours and unkindly noted down by him.

From the enthusiastic way in which he spoke of Cardinal Bacci, I gathered that he must have won favour with him. He showed me a little handwritten dictionary compiled by himself which he takes everywhere with him, and told me that he had extracted it (since he is making a collection of the most recent words in use) from the proofs of the fourth edition, due out in a few weeks, of the *Vocabolario italiano-latino delle parole moderne e difficili da tradurre* (Italian-Latin Dictionary of modern words and words difficult to translate) by that famous Latinist. He there and then translated for me the names of all the different kinds of food (*escarum ordo*) which we had on the table, showing no hesitation at the strangest words, and finishing up with the coffee, described in Tacitean terms as *potio arabica coram expressa*.

He was very much touched and pleased, though of course he tried not to show it, when I told him as we said goodbye that he plainly had no need of special good wishes for his career seeing what success the stenographers of Vatican I had in after life. He answered with a laugh that he, like the former President of the Accademia dei Nobili, Monsignor Giovanni Maria Zonghi, had made a will in shorthand and, of course, in Latin, using the Kennerknecht method.

Later, on the way back to Rome, Monsignor Martinez told me the story of what happened in Parliament last Thursday during the debate on the law on compulsory secondary schools, which I had missed when reading the papers, and he gave me the relevant texts. A Neapolitan Christian Democrat deputy, Stefano Riccio, on 13 December astonished everyone by beginning his violent speech against the abolition of Latin with the words:

> Licet mihi hodie latino sermone vos alloqui. Attamen latinam linguam summopere accommodatam esse ad res clara breviterque dicendas nemo negabit, quin etiam probat usus praesentis Concilii Oecumenici, cuius patres omnibus ex nationibus convenientes latino sermone argumenta tractant momenti aliquando maioris atque universalioris quam nostra.
>
> (Allow me today to address you in Latin. No one will deny that the

Latin language is eminently suited for clear and concise exposition, and for this reason it is also used in the Ecumenical Council, where the Fathers from all countries readily discuss in Latin subjects of considerably greater and more universal moment than ours here.)

Naturally, this was not an improvised speech; Riccio was reading it, though quite quickly. At a certain point, having finished his translation of the usual arguments in favour of Cicero's language, he even went on to cite the example of present-day Russian humanists:

> Audiatur vox russici cuiusdam doctoris, cui nomen est Borowskij, qui in studiorum Universitate Leninipolitana anno transacto elegantem scholam, sermone latino usus, habuit qua ipsam linguam litterarum et artium optimam magistram praedicavit atque utillimam dixit ad 'gravissimam illam causam liberalioris institutionis publicae' quae nostros rectores angere nullo modo videtur.
>
> (Let us heed the words of the Russian, Dr Borowski, who last year at the University of Leningrad made a fine speech in Latin in which he maintained that this language was an excellent teacher of literature and the arts and declared it most useful for 'that most serious purpose, more liberal public instruction', which in no way seems to concern our Rectors.)

According to Monsignor Martinez, the text of Riccio's intervention undoubtedly came from the Vatican Secretariat for Briefs. Undeterred by this, another deputy, Vittorino Colombo, also a Christian Democrat but evidently with different ideas, is said to have threatened to prepare a speech in Hebrew, declaring that 'the main thing is to get someone to write it and then to be able to read it'.

The most piquant aspect of this episode, however, lies in its background. At a sitting of the Parliamentary Commission appointed to discuss the law in question, various Christian Democrat deputies had reiterated that the chief opponents of Latin were technologists or unsuccessful humanists, that the characteristics of Italian national culture must be preserved, etc. Amused and stimulated by these arguments *ad hominem,* the Communist Senator Ambrogio Donini, former student of Ernesto Buonaiuti and Professor of the History of Christianity at Bari University, proposed that in order to be more closely in tune with the subject and enter into it more deeply the sitting should be continued in Latin; and without more ado he began to expound his own view with ready ease in elegant Latin. How many of his hearers understood his arguments is not known; but in any case no one dared to follow his example and the sitting terminated.

Rome, Monday, 17 December

This evening the *Osservatore Romano* published the names of the six Cardinals chosen by John XXIII as members of the Super-Commission (the Commission for the co-ordination of the Council's work) under the chairmanship of the Secretary of State, Cicognani. They are Liénart, Spellman, Urbani, Confalonieri, Doepfner, and Suenens.

Here at last is a Commission that is supple, homogeneous (all its members, in fact, are progressives except for Spellman, who in any case always remains silent on theological questions), and young (the only eighty-year-old, not including Cicognani, its chairman, is Liénart, one of the youngest Fathers in spirit of the whole Council). But, above all a Commission that will leave no one in doubt about what its choices will be.

It is now clear that John XXIII is the sole pilot who decisively holds the helm of the Council in his hands.

Rome, Christmas Day, 1962

On the morning of Christmas Day 1934, in the Church of the Capuchins in Sofia, thronged with people, the then Apostolic Delegate after reading of the Gospel turned to the congregation and said:

> This Christmas Day is the tenth I have been happy to spend among you. But it is also the last . . .
>
> If I could be sure of not being misunderstood I would like to address a word also to all our separated brethren. The divergence in the conditions of faith concerning one of the fundamental points of the doctrine of Christ related in the Gospel, namely the union of all the faithful of the Church of Christ with the successor of the chief of the Apostles, counselled me to impose certain restrictions in my relations and personal behaviour towards them. This was quite natural

and I think was fully understood by them. The respect which I have always striven to entertain, whether in public or in private, for each and every man; my inviolate and unoffending silence; the fact that I have never stooped to pick up the stone thrown at me from one side or other of the street – all this gives me the simple certainty that I have shown to all that I love them too in the Lord, with that brotherly, heartfelt and sincere equality that the Gospel teaches us . . . The day must finally come when there will be only one flock and one pastor, for Jesus Christ has so willed it.

These were words of great discretion, clearly imbued with a deeply sincere open-mindedness but all the same slightly commonplace. But the words that followed tore away the veil concealing a deep inner anxiety and in their lyrical quality attained the truly poetic:

[In Ireland, according to a happy tradition], on Christmas Eve a light is put in the window of every house, so that Joseph and Mary, passing by on that night in search of refuge, may know that within it there is a family awaiting them round the fire and at the table spread with the good things given by God. Wherever I may go in the world, if anyone from Bulgaria passes by my house at night in distress, he will find a light in my window. Knock, knock! I shall not ask you whether or not you are a Catholic, my Bulgarian brother. Enter! Two fraternal arms will welcome you, the warm heart of a friend will rejoice at your coming.

No one knows the paths of the future. Twenty-four years later – the prelate who spoke in Sofia was then fifty-three – that light was to be lit in the cupola of the Vatican. I have no need to get up and look from my balcony on the Gianiculum towards the Vatican. I know that that light burns there every night in a perennial Christmastide and that it calls not only Bulgarians or Greeks or Turks but all peoples. That light was lit by a humble apostolic delegate of those days, but it no longer belongs to him, nor will it belong to his successors: that light is the eternal patrimony of all humanity.

Appendices

I THE ROMAN CURIA

THE Curia is the whole complex of departments of which the Pope makes use in the general government of the Catholic Church. It consists of 12 Sacred Congregations (so called because at their apex stands an assembly or *congregation* of Cardinals, of whom the 'prefect', the one put in charge over them all, is the Pope or a Cardinal appointed by him), three Tribunals, and six Offices. (The names of the Prefects of each Congregation at the time of the Council are given in brackets. All are Cardinals except where otherwise stated.)

POPE

SACRED CONGREGATIONS

Supreme Congregation of the Holy Office (Ottaviani)
Consistorial Congregation (Confalonieri)
Congregation for the Eastern Church (Cicognani)
Congregation of the Sacraments (Aloisi-Masella)
Congregation of the Council (Ciriaci)
Congregation of the Religious (Valeri)
Congregation of the Propaganda Fide (or Propagation of the Faith) (Agagianian)
Congregation of Rites (Larraona)
Congregation of Ceremonial (Tisserant)
Congregation of Extraordinary Ecclesiastical Affairs (Cicognani)
Congregation of Seminaries and Universities of Studies (Pizzardo)
Congregation of the Fabric of St Peter's (Marella)

TRIBUNALS

Apostolic Penitentiary (Larraona)
Supreme Tribunal of the Apostolic Signature (Roberti)
Holy Roman Rota (Mons. Brennan)

OFFICES

Apostolic Chancellery (Copello)
Apostolic Datary (Giobbe)
Reverend Apostolic Chamber (Aloisi-Masella)
Secretariat of State (Cicognani)
Secretariat of Briefs to Princes (Mons. Tondini)
Secretariat of Latin Letters (Mons. Del Ton)

II THE PREPARATORY ORGANS OF THE COUNCIL

The Second Vatican Council was first announced by Pope John XXIII on 25 January 1959.

On 17 May 1960 John XXIII established a *Pre-Preparatory Commission*, presided over by the then Cardinal Secretary of State, Tardini, which virtually confined itself to sending a questionnaire to the world episcopate and cataloguing the replies received.

On 5 June 1960 the constitution was announced on behalf of the Pope of ten *Preparatory Commissions* and one Central Preparatory Commission, also of two Secretariats (one for Methods of Popularization and one for Christian Union). In November 1960 an eleventh Preparatory Commission was appointed, for Ceremonial.

At the end of 1961, the whole complex of preparatory organs of the Council was as follows:

JOHN XXIII

PRESIDENT OF THE CENTRAL COMMISSION

PREPARATORY COMMISSIONS

(*Chairmen in brackets*)

Theological Commission (Ottaviani)
Commission on Bishops and Diocesan Government (Marella)
Commission on the Discipline of the Clergy and the Christian People (Ciriaci)
Commission on the Religious Orders (Valeri)
Commission on Discipline and the Sacraments (Aloisi-Masella)
Commission on the Liturgy (G. Cicognani, later Larraona)
Commission on Studies and Seminaries (Pizzardo)
Commission on the Eastern Churches (Cicognani)
Commissionon Missions (Agagianian)
Commission on the Lay Apostolate (Cento)
Commission on Ceremonial (Tisserant)

SECRETARIATS

Press and Entertainment (Mons. O'Connor)
Christian Union (Bea)
Administration (Di Jorio)

ALSO DEPENDENT ON THE CENTRAL COMMISSION

The Secretariat General (Mons. Felici)
The Technical and Organizing Committee (Testa)
The Sub-Commission on Rules of Procedure (Roberti)
The Sub-Commission on *Materie Miste*[1] (Tisserant)
The Sub-Commission on Amendments (Confalonieri)

[1] i.e. overlapping subjects.

III ORGANS OF THE COUNCIL DURING THE FIRST SESSION

On the basis of the Council's Rules of Procedure promulgated at the beginning of September 1962, the Organs of the Council during the first session (11 October to 8 December 1962) were as follows:

JOHN XXIII

PRESIDENT

PRESIDING COUNCIL
(*10 Cardinals*[1])

SECRETARIAT FOR EXTRAORDINARY QUESTIONS
(*7 Cardinals*[2])

Commissions of the Council

1 Doctrinal Commission on Faith and Morals (Ottaviani)
2 Commission on the Bishops and Diocesan Government (Marella)
3 Commission on the Discipline of the Clergy and People (Ciriaci)
4 Commission on the Religious Orders (Valeri)
5 Commission on Discipline and the Sacraments (Masella)
6 Commission on Seminaries, Studies, and Universities (Pizzardo)
7 Commission on Missions (Agagianian)
8 Commission on the Liturgy (Larraona)
9 Commission on Lay Apostolate, Press and Entertainment (Cento)
10 Commission on the Eastern Churches (Cicognani)

[1] Tisserant, Liénart, Tappouni, Gilroy, Frings, Pla y Daniel, Spellman, Ruffini, Caggiano, and Alfrink (presiding in turn).

[2] Cicognani (Chairman), Siri, Montini, Confalonieri, Meyer, Doepfner, Suenens.

All ten Commissions of the Council were to be assisted in their work by the *Secretariat for Christian Union*, with the status of a Commission.

The Presiding Council was assisted in the conduct of affairs by the *Secretariat General*, consisting of the Secretary (Mons. Felici) and five under-secretaries.

In addition there were also the *Administrative Secretariat*, the Press Office, etc.

In November 1962 John XXIII established a special *Mixed Commission* for the recasting of the draft 'De Fontibus Revelationis'.

On 6 December 1962 he caused an announcement to be made declaring the formation of a *Commission for the Co-ordination of the Work of the Council*, which was at once christened the 'Super-Commission', with the duty of controlling and directing the work (other than that of a specialized nature) of the individual Commissions. Its members, as announced on 14 December 1962, were: Cicognani (Chairman), Liénart, Spellman, Urbani, Confalonieri, Doepfner and Suenens.

IV THE POPES, VATICAN I TO VATICAN II

PIUS IX (Giovanni Maria Mastai Ferretti), 1846-78
LEO XIII (Gioacchino Pecci), 1878-1903
PIUS X (Giuseppe Sarto), 1903-14
BENEDICT XV (Giacomo Della Chiesa), 1914-22
PIUS XI (Achille Ratti), 1922-39
PIUS XII (Eugenio Pacelli), 1939-58
JOHN XXIII (Angelo Giuseppe Roncalli), 1958-63
PAUL VI (Giovanni Battista Montini), 1963-

Index

(*Figures in italics refer to the Appendices*)

Acta Apostolicae Sedis, 190, 192, 313
Acta et Documenta Vaticano II apparanda, 88
Adesso, 94–7, 99, 291–2
Ad Petri cathedram, encyclical, 24
Aeterna Dei sapientia, encyclical, 191–2
Aeterni Patris, encyclical, 226
Africa, Church in, 97, 172–3, 185–9, 233, 234–5
African episcopate at Council, 245, 276, 296–7, 344
African episcopal conferences, 185
Alessandrini, Federico, 58–9, 290
Alfrink, Cardinal, 53, 156, 228, 262, 289, 350; and 'De Fontibus' debate, 269, 270–1, 275; and 'De Ecclesia' debate, 311, *363*
American episcopate at Council, 91; 94, 134–5, 173–4, 329, 342–3
Angolans, attitude of, 203
Annuario Pontificio, 44, 101, 105, 175, 234, 317–18
Antimori, Signor, 38, 97, 119–20, 128, 132, 134, 136, 137, 153–4, 192, 203, 211, 237, 299, 303, 306, 307, 310
Asian episcopate at Council, 344
Asmussen, Dr D. H., 59
Athenagoras, Patriarch of Constantinople, 59, 60, 182, 184

Bacci, Cardinal, 193, 240, 273, 298, 319, 355
Baltic States, delegation at Council, 100, 131, 180
Bea, Cardinal, 59, 181, 182, 205–8, 225, 240, 247, 260, 266–7, 289, 319, 349, 350; and 'De Fontibus' debate, 270, 271, 275; on Mixed Commission, 297, *362*
Benedict xv, Pope, 43, 54, 55, 56, 58, 61, 213, *364*
Benedictines, part played by in Council, 240; *see also* Butler, Dom Christopher
Betancourt, Cardinal, 219
'Biblicum' dispute, 280–2
Blomjous, Monsignor, 233, 235
Bogomolov, Russian Ambassador to Paris, 15, 118
Bologna, Archbishop of, *see* Lercaro, Cardinal
Bologna Historical Conference, 54

Bombay, Archbishop of, *see* Gracias, Cardinal, and Roberts, Monsignor
Bontempi, Monsignor Alfredo, 111–13, 132, 178, 181, 229, 245, 314
Borovoi, Archpriest Vitali, 183, 184
Boston, Archbishop of, *see* Cushing, Cardinal
Boulier, Abbé, 353
Brezonoczy, Monsignor Pal, 100, 181
Browne, Cardinal, 224, 298, 319, 346
Bueno y Monreal, Bishop of Seville, 298, 311
Bugnini, Padre, 223–4, 244
Bukavu, Monsignor, 185–6, 233, 234
Bulgarian episcopate at Council, 131
Butler, Dom Christopher, 271, 347

Caggiano, Cardinal, 53, *363*
Camara, Cardinal de Barros, 50, 298
Canadian episcopate at Council, 343
Canali, Cardinal, 90, 163
Capovilla, Monsignor Loris, 38, 62
Cardinal, office of, 73–4, 108–10. *See also* Curia
Cardinale, Monsignor Igino, 253–6
Cardinals' letter to the Pope, 297–8, 307
Carretto, Brother Carlo, 76, 83
Castaldo, Cardinal, 178
Catholic Action, 44–5, 74, 75, 76, 123, 153
Catholic universities in Rome, 245–53, 257–8, 280–2
Cavagna, Monsignor Alfredo, 27, 38
CELAM, 164, 343
Cerejeira, Cardinal, 136–7, 225, 271
Charue, Bishop of Namur, 276
Chenu, Père, 188, 193, 351
Chiesa al bivio, La, 83
Christian Democracy, 75, 77, 78, 79
Ciappi, Padre, 38, 274
Cicognani, Cardinal, Secretary of State, 54, 121–2, 182, 183–4, 193, 203, 223, 357, *361*, *362*, *363*
Civardi, Monsignor Luigi, 112
Code of Canon Law, 16, 43, 46, 165, 176
Cologne, Archbishop of, *see* Frings, Cardinal
Colombo, Monsignor Carlo, 59, 352
Colonna, Don Aspreno, 101, 105
Commissions, 50–4, 159–60, 164, *362–4*; Preparatory, 18, 47–8, 88, 100–1, 122, 164, 337, 362; voting for membership of, 156, 174–5, 195–6, 199; national representation on, 199–200; Pope's nominations to, 224; Theological, 273–4; Mixed, 286, 297, 364; 'Super-Commission', 326–7, 338, 357, 364
Communists and the Council, 119, 173, 290
Complotto contro la Chiesa, *see under* Jews
Conciliorum Oecumenicorum Decreta, 115
Confalonieri, Cardinal, 53, 54, 289, 357, *361*, *362*, *363*, *364*

Congar, Père, 100, 193, 222
Cronache Sociali, 78, 79, 117
Cuba, 29, 202–3, 218–19
Curia, the 48, 49, 51, 72–3, 100, 111–12, 160, 240, 247, 361; versus Episcopate, 161–6, 168–9; at third general congregation, 192–5; and Commissions, 224–5. *See also* 'Pentagon, the'
Cushing, Cardinal, 134–6, 237, 343
Custodians of the Council, 101–2, 236; *see also* Colonna, Torlonia
Czechoslovakia, Church in, 111, 113, 131, 181, 345

Daniélou, Père Jean, 100–1, 273, 351
Dante, Monsignor, 201, 224, 240
De Castro Mayer, Monsignor, Bishop of Campos, 241–2, 243
'De Divina Revelatione' draft, *see under* 'De Fontibus'
'De Ecclesia' draft, debate on, 164, 269, 309–12, 316–20; statistics on, 331, 332; suspended, 328, 333, 337
De Fide, 259
'De Fontibus Revelationis' draft, counter-draft, 245–6; manoeuvring before debate, 268–9; draft introduced, 269–70; debate, 270–80, 282–87, 289; Pope's intervention, 285–7; analysis of speeches on, 289–90; name changed, 297; Mixed Commission for, 286, 297, 364; statistics on, 332; rejected, 333
Dell'Acqua, Monsignor, 121, 132, 178–9, 224
De Lubac, Père, 101, 351, 352
'De Maria Virgine' draft, 305, 310
'De mediis communicationis socialis' draft, debate on, 292–7; voting, 298–9; amended, 333; statistics on, 332
'De Sacra Liturgia' draft, debate on, 197, 200–2, 221–4, 239, 242, 244, 262–3, 264–6, 267–8; voting, 272, 310, 324, 328; statistics on, 266, 332; approved, 333
De Smet, Monsignor, Bishop of Bruges, 282–4, 311–12
Dibelius, Bishop Otto, 157, 207
Di Jorio, Cardinal, 88, 90, *362*
Divino Afflante Spiritu, encyclical, 53, 247
Documentation Centre, Bologna, 77, 79, 83, 115
Doepfner, Cardinal, Archbishop of Munich, 53–4, 94, 160, 201, 273, 275, 289, 316, 317, 357, *363*, *364*
Dossetti, Don Giuseppe, 77–82, 83, 84, 115–16, 353
Duschak, Monsignor, 240, 241
D'Zouza, Monsignor, 240, 241

Eastern Churches, 52; and Rome, 212–18, 225. *See also* Uniate Church, 'Ut Unum Sint'
Eastern Law, New Code of, 213–6
Edelby, Monsignor, 300, 302
Egidi, Renzo, 179–81
L'église a-t-elle encore sa chance?, 40
Elchinger, Monsignor, Bishop of Strasbourg, 312
Encyclicals, *see under* respective titles

Episcopates, 161–6, 169–74, 342–8; episcopal conferences, 175–8
Evangelical Churches in Italy, 203–4

Fanfani, Amintore, 78, 79; government, 32
Fathers' Message to the World, 192–5, 235, 267, 340
Felici, Monsignor, 93, 174, 193, 224, 239, 258, 262, 300, 301, 326–7, *362*, *363*
Ferrari Toniolo, Monsignor Agostino, 112, 274
Fiordelli, Monsignor, 194, 323–4
First Vatican Council, *see* Vatican I
Florence, 116–19; congresses, 116–17; *see also* La Pira, Giorgio
Florit, Archbishop of Florence, 158, 261, 271, 323
Formengeschichte, 249–53, 280–1
Forni, Efrem, Cardinal, 71
Freemasonry, 315, 344
French episcopate, 162, 172
Frings, Cardinal, 156, 159, 160, 161, 166–8, 201, 289, 297, 319, 350, *363*; and 'De Fontibus' debate, 269, 270–1, 275
Fulton Sheen, Bishop, 295, 298–9

Galvez, Don José, 354–5
Garofalo, Monsignor, 248, 269–70
Gasbarrini, Professor, 304, 306
Gargitter, Bishop, 196, 271, 317
Gemelli, Padre Agostino, 136–7
Genoa, Archbishop of, *see* Siri, Cardinal
German Church, 345; episcopate, 172; German-Polish relations, 178–9
Gilroy, Cardinal, 53, 199, 239, 289, *363*
Giovinetti, Monsignor Alberto, 58
Godfrey, Cardinal, 240, 293, 319, 347
Gracias, Cardinal, 39, 94, 237, 240, 265, 282, 317
Gregoriana, the, 246–7, 257
Gronchi, President Giovanni, 119, 232
Guitton, Jean, 25

Hakim, Monsignor, Bishop of Akka, 276–7, 301
Hamvas, Monsignor, 181, 194
Heard, Cardinal, 50
Heenan, Cardinal, 207, 309, 347
Heinzelmann, Frau Gertrud, 226
Hogan, Monsignor, Bishop of Bellary, 91
Humani Generis, encyclical, 100, 247, 248
Hungarian episcopate at Council, 100, 131, 132, 181, 345
Huyghe, Monsignor, Bishop of Arras, 316–17

India, frontier crisis, 203
Indian episcopate at Council, 244
Israel, 291, 342
Italian episcopal conference, 176–7, 178
Italian Episcopate at Council, 347–8

Jacobovich, Immanuel, Rabbi of New York, 290–1

Janssens, Father, 225, 281, 289
Japanese episcopate at Council, 245
Jesuits, 225–6, 246–7
Jews and Catholicism, 291, 344; and the Council, 290–91; anti-Jewish propaganda volume, 314–15
John XXIII, Pope: in France (as Nuncio), 15, 25, 26, 28; in Balkans, 25, 31, 357–8; election, 14–16; '*fioretti*', 15, 46; aims, 16–17, 111–12; concept of the Church, 19; international policy, 20, 21, 23; Council policy, 19; ecumenism, 23; announces Council, 45–6; character, 24–33, 65; broadcast, 66–9, 340; 'fundamental' encyclical, 111, 112–13; journey to Loreto and Assisi, 114–15, 120; receives Polish bishops, 133, 178–9; at opening, 147–8; speech at opening, 149–53; greets Catholic Action at opening of Council, 153; greets diplomatic missions, 154–5; gives audience to journalists, 156–7; gives audience to observers, 157–8; recognition of episcopal conferences, 163–4; and Curia, 16–18, 165–6; textual differences in opening speech, 189–92; nominations to Commissions, 224–5; and Jesuits, 225–6; re-affirmation of Council's aims, 244; and dispute between theological colleges, 252; his insertion of name of St Joseph in the Mass 263–4; intervention in 'De Fontibus' debate, 285–7; establishes Mixed Commission, 286; and conservative Cardinals' letter, 297–8; illness, 303–4, 305–8, 310, 312–14, 324–5; his 'Summi Pontifici Electio', 313; the ring for Cardinal Montini, 314, 315–16; decisions on activity between sessions, 326–7; speech on closing day, 328; appearance at closing ceremony, 330; retreats, 13, 20, 37–8; death, 13–14
Jullien, Cardinal André, 50, 224

Kemerer, Monsignor, 240, 344
Koenig, Cardinal, 156, 160, 209, 269, 289, 345, 350; and 'De Fontibus' draft, 269, 270; and 'De Ecclesia' draft, 311
Kotliarov, Archimandrite, 183, 184

La Pira, Giorgio, Mayor of Florence, 78, 79, 100, 116–19
Larraona, Cardinal, 50, 200, 223, *361*, *362*, *363*
Lateran Biblical School, 246–53, 281–2
Latin American episcopal conference, *see* CELAM.
Latin American episcopate at Council, 172, 343–4
Lee, Belinda, 103–6
Léger, Cardinal, 193, 270–1, 289, 317–19, 343
Leo XIII, Pope, 54, 173, *364*
Lercaro, Cardinal, 80, 115, 178, 196, 201, 240, 325–6, 350, 352–3
Liénart, Cardinal, 53, 156, 159–60, 161, 166–8, 176, 228, 238–9, 269, 297, 349–50, 357; and

Liénart, Cardinal—continued 'De Fontibus' draft, 270–1; and 'Ut Unum Sint' draft, 300; and 'De Ecclesia' draft, 310–11, *363*, *364*
Lille, Archbishop of, *see* Liénart, Cardinal
Lisbon, Patriarch of, *see* Cerejeira, Cardinal
Liturgy, reform of, 333–4; *see also* 'De Sacra Liturgia'
Liverpool, Archbishop of, *see* Heenan, Cardinal
Lombardi, Padre, 226, 262

Malines and Brussels, Archbishop of, *see* Suenens, Cardinal
Manzini, Raimondo, 118
Marella, Cardinal, 129, 298, *361*, *362*, *363*
Mariology, 264
Marsili, Dom Salvatore, 242–3
Martinez, Monsignor, 91, 222, 223, 224, 238, 245, 268, 287, 310, 318, 341, 354–6
Mater et Magistra, encyclical, 23, 112, 154, 191
Maximos IV Saigh, Patriarch of Antioch, 193, 209, 211, 212, 214, 216, 217, 218, 260, 265, 349, 350; and 'Ut Unum Sint', draft, 300–1, 322–3
Mazzolari, Don, *see Adesso*
Mazzoni, Professor, 304
'Means of Communication' draft, *see* 'De mediis communicationis'
Melchites, Bishop of Akka of the, *see* Hakim, Monsignor
Méndez, Bishop of Cuernavaca, 343, 344
Meyer, Cardinal, 53, 54, 297, 343, *363*
Milan, Archbishop of, *see* Montini, Cardinal
Minisci, Abbot, 196, 297
Missionary work, 169–71
Montini, Cardinal, 49, 53, 54, 75, 76, 82–3, 94, 178, 201, 230, 260, 261, 289, 352, *363*; enigma of, 96–9; journey to Africa, 97, 186; and *Adesso*, 96, 292; and John XXIII's ring, 314, 315–16; and 'De Fontibus' draft, 321–2; and 'Ut Unum Sint' draft, 322; Pope Paul VI, *364*
Montreal, Archbishop of, *see* Léger, Cardinal
Morcillo, Cardinal, 288, 296
Moscow Patriarchate delegation to Council, 141, 203; negotiations about, 181–5; arrival, 183
Munich, Archbishop of, *see* Doepfner, Cardinal
Musto, Bishop Biagio, 317–18

Nabaa, Monsignor, 301
Namur, Bishop of, *see* Charue
New York, Archbishop of, *see* Spellman, Cardinal
Nicodemus, Monsignor, 181–4

Observer-delegates, 138–41, 157–8, 203–5, 266–8
Orsini, Prince Filippo, 102–6
Osservatore Romano, 27, 47, 66, 99, 106, 114, 123, 132, 137, 149, 153, 189, 190, 244, 252, 253, 262, 287, 290, 297, 298, 306, 333–4, 357
Ottaviani, Cardinal, 30, 51, 100–1, 127, 128, 163, 174, 228–33, 247, 248, 249, 252, 257, 260, 284, 287, *361*, *362*, *363*; encounter with Alfrink, 228,

Ottaviani, Cardinal—continued 238–9; and 'De Fontibus' debate, 268–9, 273, 275, 279; on Mixed Commission, 297; and 'Ut Unum Sint' debate, 305; Mariological proposal, 305, 309; presents 'De Ecclesia' draft, 310; outstanding figure at Council, 349–50

Pacelli, Eugenio, *see* Pius XII, Pope
Pacem in terris, encyclical, 21, 22, 23, 112–13
Pan-African Secretariat, 185, 189, 233, 235, 344
Parente, Monsignor, 193, 240, 248; and 'De Fontibus' draft, 273, 275–6
Patriarch, office of, 52, 108–10
Pavan, Monsignor, 112, 274
Pellicani, Signor, 62–6
'Pentagon, the', 127, 128, 163
Piasecki, Monsignor, 353–4
Piazza, Cardinal, 75, 119, 163
Pignedoli, Monsignor, 77, 97, 186
Piolanti, Monsignor, 248, 249, 264, 274
Pius IX, Pope, 72, 101, 213, 236, *364*
Pius X, Pope, 43, 197, *364*
Pius XI, Pope, 22, 43, 44, 45, 56, 58, 64–5, 98, 137, 163, 166, 213, 230, 295, *364*
Pius XII, Pope, 15, 16, 22, 26, 38, 43, 56, 65, 95, 119, 127, 129–30, 163, 247, 295, *364*
Pizzardo, Cardinal, 51, 126–7, 163, 230, 247, 249, 252, 289, *361*, *362*, *363*
'plain-clothes saints', 118, 120
Pla y Daniel, Cardinal, 53, *363*
Plenary Sessions of Council, *see* under Vatican II, General Congregations
Polish episcopate at Council, 131–3; attitude of Poles, 203
Pontifical Biblical Institute, 246–53
Portugal, Primate of, *see* Cerejeira, Cardinal
Prato, Bishop of, *see* Fiordelli, Monsignor
Press Conferences, 240–3, 266, 287, 299
Press Office, 121–4, 134, 237, 287–8; communiqué on first session, 158–9
Princeps Pastorum, encyclical, 21–2

Rahner, Karl, 40–2, 167, 245, 269, 273, 345, 351
Ramsey, Dr, Archbishop of Canterbury, 18, 181, 207
Rationalism, *Catholic Exegesis*, *and Teaching*, 245–6, 280–1
Ratti, Achille, *see* Pius XI, Pope
Recoaro Conference, 70–2
Religious Orders at Council, 99, 171, 225, 240, 352
Ritter, Cardinal, 270, 289, 311
Roberti, Cardinal, 49–50, 174, *361*, *362*
Roberts, Monsignor, 38–40
Rome diocesan synod, revival of, 16, 18, 46, 60–2
Roman Theological Colleges, dispute between, 245–53, 280–2
romanità, 135, 258
Romeo, Monsignor, 250, 251, 264
Roncalli, Angelo Giuseppe, *se* John XXIII, Pope

Ruffini, Cardinal, 53, 174, 178, 201, 240, 252, 256–7, 266, 297, 298, 352, *363*; and 'De Fontibus' draft, 270, 285; and 'De mediis communicationis' draft, 296; and 'De Ecclesia' draft, 311

Rugambwa, Cardinal, 94, 185, 189, 233–34, 282

SS Cyril and Methodius, 111, 113

St Peter's, bomb in, 84–8; preparation of for Council, 88–9

Santis Rufino, Cardinal, 271

Scapinelli, Monsignor, 201, 240

Scharf, Dr Kurt, 207

Scherpenberg, Dr, 178–9

Second Vatican Council, *see* Vatican II

Secretariat for Extraordinary Questions, 51–2, 53–4

Secretariat for Christian Union, 18, 52, 138, 181, 182, 203–5, 208–9, 286, 291

Sidney, Archbishop of, *see* Gilroy, Cardinal

Silva Enriquez, Cardinal, 201, 343

Siri, Cardinal, 53, 54, 76, 124–8, 178, 270, 298, 317, 352, *363*

Sonnino, Signor, 38–40

Spada, Monsignor, 180

Spadafora, Monsignor, 253, 280–1

Spellman, Cardinal, 53, 94, 134, 135, 136, 201, 240, 295, 298–9, 317, 357, *363*, *364*

Spoleto Historical Conference, 54–9

Stankevicius, Canon Josef, 100, 180

statistics on population and religion, 41–2

Stefanovicius, Bishop, 180

Stourm, Monsignor, 293, 294

Sturzo, Don Luigi, 75

Suenens, Cardinal, 53, 54, 270, 296, 319, 340, 350, 357, *363*, *364*

Tappouni, Cardinal, 53, 211, 239, 304, *363*

Tardini, Cardinal, 18, 47, 88

Tatsuo Doi, Cardinal, 128–9, 201

Testa, Cardinal, 93, 94, 289, *362*

Tien-Ken-Sin, Cardinal, 128, 129–30

Tisserant, Cardinal, 53, 174, 177, 182–83, 289, *361*, *362*, *363*; and 'De Fontibus' draft, 269, 271, 285

Torlonia, Don Alessandro, 101, 105

Traglia, Cardinal, pro-Vicar of Rome, 94, 298

Tromp, Father, 269, 297

Ukranians, 193, 194, 195, 203

Uniate bishops, 109–10, 171–2, 177, 225, 348–9; Church, 211–13, 216–18; and 'Ut Unum Sint' draft, 300–03

Urbani, Cardinal, 70–2, 74–6, 178, 298, 357, *364*

'Ut Unum Sint' draft, debate on, 300–3, 304–5; voting, 308–9; statistics, 331, 332; amended, 333

Utrecht, Archbishop of, *see* Alfrink, Cardinal

Vagaggini, Dom Cipriano, article on liturgy, 333–4

Vagnozzi, Monsignor, 201, 240
Vallainc, Monsignor, 121, 123–4, 288
Van Bekkum, Monsignor, 240, 241
Van Lierde, Monsignor, 240, 352
Vatican I, 19–20, 72, 107, 138, 164, 179, 213, 236, 258–9; compared with Vatican II, 344–8, 349
Vatican II, 16, 17, 18; reasons for, 43–5; announcement of, 45–6; reaction of Cardinals, 45–7; rules of procedure, 45, 49, 50–2, 110, 159, 160, 174–5; Presiding Council, 53, 239; television on, 59–60; practical preparations for, 87–91; arrival of Fathers, 91–4; Technical and Organizing Committee, 93, 94; experts, 99–100, 350–1; Council Hall, 106–8, 110; arrivals from East, 128–30; opening day, 145–9; first general congregation, 158–60; second general congregation, 174–5; Fathers' Message to the World, 192–5, 235, 267, 340; accommodation, 209–10; City of Rome's reception for the Fathers, 235–6; attendance, 237–8, 256–7; deaths at, 238; speeding up discussion, 239; character of debates, 239–40; announcements of second session, 258, 303; extra-conciliar activities of Fathers, 259–62; effect of Pope's illness upon, 307–8; fundamental difference of opinion in, 277–80, 320–1; departures, 325, 341–2; activity between sessions, 326–7; loss of interest in, 309, 310; closing day, 328; closing ceremony, 330; speeches, statistics on, 331–2; drafts, results of, 332–3; survey of first session, 337–41. *For* drafts, and debates on, *see under* separate titles. *For* Commissions, *see* Commissions.
Vaussard, Maurice, 57
Venice, Patriarch of, *see* Urbani, Cardinal
Vienna, Archbishop of, *see* Koenig, Cardinal
Visser 't Hooft, Dr, 59
Vogt, Father, 274, 282
Vuccino, Monsignor, 301–2

Warsaw, Archbishop of, *see* Wyszynski, Cardinal
Welykyj, Father Athanasius, 300
Willebrands, Monsignor, 182–3, 184, 297
Women in Church offices, 226–8
World Council of Churches, 45, 123, 181, 184, 207, 209
Wyszynski, Cardinal, 17, 132, 133, 193

Yugoslav episcopate at Council, 131, 345

Zoa, Monsignor, 233, 234, 276, 299
Zoghby, Monsignor, 301